Child Rearing in Rural China

Modern China Series

Child Rearing in Rural China

Jiang Youchun

Yang Yunyi

North American Business Press

Child Rearing in Rural China

ISBN: 9781948915151

NORTH
AMERICAN BUSINESS
P R E S S

North American Business Press
Atlanta, Georgia
Miami, Florida
New York, New York,
Toronto, Canada

FIRST PRINTING, 2020

About Modern China Series

China, as one of the oldest civilized regions in the world, has emerged as something of a "new world" because it is working to embrace its essence and heritage and link them to viable economic strategies. In the last 25 years, China has made tremendous strides by doing so. The country and her people have every right to take pride in these accomplishments. With these successes under their belt, many Chinese leaders and intellectuals anticipate continuing growth. China's plans and strategies, furthermore, are often based upon this premise.

There is tremendous interest in the US on the Chinese economy and business environment. China has emerged as a global superpower, and scholars and people in business in the US are keenly interested in learning how this is going to continue to affect them and how they can do business with China. In response to growing interest from international and Asian scholars, North American Business Press is pleased to announce our Modern China Series (MCS) books, which is first of such series in the US and has garnered tremendous interest both in the US and around the world. With our first book reaching stores in September 2011, this initiative is aimed at developing relationships between NABP and Chinese scholars who desire to promote their academic and applied business writings to the rest of the world.

We have had an overwhelming demand for the Modern China Series from both authors who would like to publish in the series and people who would like to read the books. Currently, there are ten books published in the series, and, additionally, we have a couple of dozen books that we are considering for the series. The books have been viewed by tens of thousands of people from the U.S. and the rest of the world.

We have published books relating to several areas revolving around the Chinese business environment. We have some books that focus on the best practices in marketing in China; some are related to "best practices" in doing business in China, and some of the outlook of the Chinese economy. The market for the Modern China Series is enormous. There are tens of thousands of scholars that are keenly interested in the continued growth of the Chinese economy and the implications that will have on the business world. Even more significant are the millions of people in the business that are interested in the impact that China will continue to have on the global economy. It is difficult to pin down the exact demand for the series, but it is tremendous.

We have big plans for growing the Modern China Series. It has the potential to one of the most significant economic/business series ever produced. We are very selective with the books that we will add to the collection, but we encourage any scholars who think they have unique and interesting perspectives on China to submit their books to us. From the readers' perspective, we are committed to producing high-quality books on a regular basis so that readers should expect a steady stream of insightful books to be coming out for many years to come.

This initiative is headed by Dr. Robert Tian, a renowned researcher and academic, who spearheads our efforts in partnering with foreign authors and administering day-to-day operations of this series. Dr. Tian, a Vice-President with North American Business Press and Editor of this series, spends much of his time in Beijing, Shanghai, and other Chinese cities, focusing on developing and managing our interests with authors and universities. Below is the list of the books we have published:

Enterprise Strategy: New Horizon authored by Zhang Xiuyu
Governance of Private Enterprises in Modern China authored by Zhong Qin
The Art of War and Enterprise Strategy Management authored by Fu Shouzhi
Marketing Issues in Modern China edited by Robert Guang Tian et al.

The Footprints of the Academician authored by Fu Zhouzhi
Marketing and Economics in Modern China (I) edited by Xiaoguang Qi et al.
Marketing and Economics in Modern China (II) edited by Wang Tianjin et al.
An Islamic Heritage in China authored by Ma Zhanming
China Environmental Anthropology authored by Wang Tianjin, Tian Guang, and Ma Jianfu
Can China Rule the New World? Authored by Tian Guang and Chen Gang
Critiques on Pan-marketization authored by Li Cunlin, Liu Hongfei, and Tian Guang
Economic and Economic Economical and Business Anthropology in China edited by Xiaoguang Qi and Tian Guang
China-Mongolia Economic Corridor authored by Eerdun Taoketao, Zhang Zhe, Wang Gang, and Wei Lisi
Anthropology of Chinese Foodways authored by Tian Guang and Chen Gang
Urbanization of Rural China authored by Li Taohong
Political Connection and Financial Fraud in China by Peng Jinqian
The Science of Success in China by Zhang Xiuyu
Child Rearing in Rural China by Jiang Youchun and Yang Yunyi

Preface

In the contemporary era, the academic circles are inundated with the post-modern discourse, and the studies of globalization, culture, and power, signs and symbols, ethnic groups, and identity seem to become the most popular topics. Anthropology, however, is a discipline concerned with the way humans live and the complex cultural phenomena they create. The most exceptional charm of anthropology lies in applying the method of field investigation and adopting a relativistic attitude to get close to the object of study, observing the lifestyle of a specific community or group, understanding their culture, and interpreting the mechanisms of their cultural changes and inheritance. Of all the constituent elements of culture, the mechanism of human reproduction plays an essential role. Since the birth of anthropology, the various schools of contemporary anthropology have been focusing on the topic of child rearing. In this sense, it is a proposition that will never go out of date to study the child rearing system of population reproduction for human beings. As declared by Haviland, W. A., an American anthropologist, in Chapter 5, "Human Growth" in Cultural Anthropology, The Human Challenge, ethnographic research shows a wide range of research on child rearing, and anthropologists have always been highly interested in the issues concerning the differences in child rearing and their potential impact on the adult personality.

Anthropological analysis of the concepts and behaviors of childbearing has the most considerable advantage in applying the conceptual tool of culture and laying stress on the study of the impact of livelihoods, family, clan, folk customs, rituals, symbols and other cultural systems on people's way of life and survival value, and the mechanism of these systems affecting the concepts and behaviors of childbearing. Child rearing is a crucial means to guarantee the continuity of human beings, sustain the cultures, and complete the production and reproduction of society. Human beings are social beings because they can adopt a set of cultural mechanisms to ensure that they can be passed down from generation to generation without interruption. Moreover, these cultural mechanisms not only provide the linkage of family, affiliation, and kinship but also guarantee the continuation of human genes and races.

To achieve such continuation, human beings, first of all, need a cultural system to obtain food, and then a reproductive system to guarantee the reproduction of human lives from generation to generation. The human reproductive system is never purely biological, but its primary feature is social, so it is full of human emotions, value preferences, and rational choices. As a result, human reproduction is, first and foremost, a cultural act. However, culture has been eternally changing, and the cultures of different groups in different stages display different patterns, which require researchers to explain these patterns from an academic point of view. The fundamental starting point to describe a culture is on how people create and pass on a set of traditional rules and systems centered on child rearing, including the standardization of courtship, marriage, parenthood, and social organization. It is why anthropologists have been taking great pains to study child rearing.

One of the classic works on the childbearing culture in China is the System of Reproduction written by Fei Xiaotong, which laid the research framework of social anthropology on child rearing. Although many scholars explored the child rearing practices of all nationalities in China, researchers are most concerned about the traditional customs, aiming to build the conventional cultural schemata of child rearing for all nationalities and to demonstrate the diversity of culture by comparing the differences of their cultures. Some works focus on the connection between the traditional culture and the concepts and behaviors of childbearing in rural China, such as Li Yinhe's Fertility and Village Culture, but there have not yet been many studies on the thick description of ethnography based on the system of reproduction in a rural community. This book is written against this background.

Since it is an ethnographic field study of a rural community, we can not explore the function of the holistic social structure in general terms, but need to understand the community culture through in-depth observations and interviews truly, and analyze how its cultural values infiltrate into people's actions and how it determines the mode of child rearing. That is to say, when investigating the child rearing system in a region, we must give a comprehensive description of the local cultural phenomena, including customs, beliefs, taboos, family education, marriage practices, and values, as well as all kinds of new cultural matters arising from the social changes, to understand childbearing from the general sense of cultural symbols.

The analysis of any behavior cannot be separated from the cultural context of the practice, and it is necessary to observe facts and find historical traces in a specific space-time field. With a rural community in Hunan Province as a field survey site, this book conducts a holistic thick description on the child rearing system of the community in the form of ethnography, elaborates the history and current situation of the local people on their reproduction, and gives a preliminary cultural interpretation of the child rearing system in the community by applying the theoretical paradigm of interpretive anthropology. First of all, starting from the cultural ecology of the community, it gives an introduction into the ecological and cultural background of the community; second, it conducts thick description of the child rearing system from four aspects of childbearing, child rearing, child education and the problems in the breeding of left-behind children due to modernization; finally, from the perspective of the values of procreation as an in-depth element of culture, the changes in the rearing behavior are narrated from an objective angle. The narrative and analysis not only pay attention to the horizontal connections of the cultural elements that constitute the child rearing system but also take the changes of the child rearing system on the vertical degree of time into account.

The author obtained the ethnographic materials in the book through field research at Tancun Village, during which they were carefully screened and sorted out. Following the etic position and requirements of field investigation and ethnographic research, the author tries to follow the authenticity of the materials and present the narration of the respondents in the book objectively and authentically. The people involved in the investigation were all natives at Tancun Village, and their real names had been withheld under common academic practice, replaced by the initials of their names.

The book consists of eight chapters. Chapter 1 and Chapter 2 sort out the relevant literature, expound the primary research methods and give a brief introduction into the population, economic, and cultural situations and ecosystem of Tancun Village. Chapter 3 mainly describes the cultural mechanisms in the preparatory stage of childbearing, including marriage, the customs of praying for children, birth taboos, related rituals, and the daily lifestyle of pregnant women. Chapter 4 discusses the economic and cultural problems arising in the course of child rearing at Tancun Village, including the daily fiscal spending of child rearing, new feeding methods of children, children's games and their social metaphors, changes in the medical system, and child adoption system and continuity system of childless families. Chapter 5 mainly elaborates on the power structure and all kinds of cultural disciplines in children's education of Tancun Village. Chapter 6 depicts the primary causes for the production of left-behind children at Tancun Village and the family network resources fully mobilized by the local people to solve the problem of left-behind children by the children's families. Chapter 7 discusses the values of childbearing through the description of the childbearing behavior and the change process of childbearing control of the villagers of Tancun Village. Chapter 8 gives a conclusion.

The eight chapters of this book are roughly described as above. Since the book is revised based on the author's thesis, and it is the first book published by the author, the research is relatively superficial. Many of the ideas are not mature, and the writing specifications are not perfect. There should be no such mistakes and shortcomings, but I am looking forward to receiving your criticism.

Jiang Youchun

Jinhai Garden, Huaihua City, 2012

Table of Contents

Chapter 1 Introduction

Since the implementation of the reform and opening up more than twenty years ago, China has witnessed rapid social and economic development, and rapid social changes, accomplished by various prominent problems. With the shift in economic structure, China's population structure and situation are changing accordingly. At present, China is one of the developing countries with the largest number of older people. By 2000, the fifth national census showed that the population aged 65 and over accounted for 7.09 % and 10.45 % of the total population respectively (the Population Census Office of the State Council of the People' s Republic of China, Department of Population, Social, Science, and Technology Statistics, National Bureau of Statistics of the People's Republic of China, 2002). According to the United Nations, a country steps into the aging society if the people aged over 65 years old account for 7 % of the total population, or the people aged over 60 years old account for 10 % of the total population. Based on this standard, China has stepped into the ranks of aging countries.

According to the estimation of the National Population and Family Planning Commission of the People's Republic of China, there are more than 30 million one-child households and more than 10 million two-daughter households in rural areas of China, and there will be more than 3.5 million new one-child households and about one million new two-daughter households every year (Zheng, 2004). Such a dramatic change in the population and family structure has made it of great academic significance and social value to carry out in-depth and comprehensive research in this respect. The exploration into the rearing system, an essential component of the population and family structure, also shows a more significant theoretical value. Moreover, it is also of great practical significance to maintain the stability of rural society, the prosperity of the rural economy, guarantee the implementation of pension policies, and coordinate the relationship between population, economy, and society in China.

With the development of the rural social economy, we have to face many practical problems. As the economy develops rapidly, and the family planning policy is implemented, the most crucial support for the elderly comes from the family. While the family's core trend is strengthened, the pension function is gradually weakening. As the inter-generational relationship in the family is on the decline, the behavior mode and the idea of the younger family members on providing for the aged have also been reversed, while the concept and action of filial piety in traditional culture are becoming less and less critical. The changes in occupation structure are caused by industrialization and urbanization. In rural areas, the young and middle-aged people are out for work for many years, so they can not take good care of their children, even including the infants. The traditional happy family relationship is on the verge of breaking down. The phenomena of grandparents raising grandchildren and education for left-behind children in rural areas have become hot issues in academic circles. From this point of view, the research on the changing system of a rural community and its changes not only reveals the urgency to solve the social problems in rural areas but also shows its essential practical significance.

The author selects Tancun Village, a remote rural community in the southwestern region of Hunan Province, as the object of study to investigate the current situation and the changes of child rearing in the community. Fertility has always been one of the core issues of human concern. It not only regenerates the human beings themselves to realize the reproduction of human beings from generation to generation without interruption, but the production of each new generation of life also means a reproduction of culture. It not only inherits the cultural wealth that people have accumulated in history but also realizes the historical continuity of culture through the new memories and recognition. Therefore, the child rearing system is also a process of reproduction of cultural symbols. The study of child rearing provides a perspective to have a thorough understanding of the tiniest aspect of culture. In this aspect, all kinds of folk traditions, habits, values, economic life, religious beliefs, and modern technology are involved in the process of child rearing as a type of cultural force. Here, the tradition and modernity of community culture are interwoven together, so that we can perceive the whole look of social change through the child rearing system.

This book will describe the changes and current situation of the child rearing system in Tancun Village since the 1950s in detail. It not only intercepts the cross-section of culture to conduct horizontal observation but also analyzes its changes from the vertical aspect of history. As we all know, there are two primary forms of cultural change: gradual change and sudden change. However, as for the changes of such culture as the child rearing system, it is dominated by progressive change. That is to say, the child rearing system can not be changed by divorcing itself from the historical situation and cultural characteristics of the original culture itself but should be bound with the adaptive response of the local people, accompanied by conscious selectivity of the cultural perceivers. Researchers should be aware of the process of gradual change and its specific cultural environment, and should not be indifferent to the progressive change that the local people do not think will occur for decades but takes place at all times. As Marshall Sahlins said, "The more immutable the thing is, the greater changes it will undergo since every reproduction of the sort in the category varies from one another. As far as behavior is concerned, every reproduction of culture is a kind of change, which allows those categories that exist in harmony have some new experience content at the time of every change (Sahlins, 2003)." On this basis, the author tries to return to the topic of human reproduction, so explore into the issue of how human beings reproduce cultural symbols passed down from generation to generation while realizing human reproduction.

Section 1 Definition of Research Object

In a narrow sense, rearing refers to childbirth and nurturing, which refers to the process that a new life comes into being and grows to an adult that meets the social and cultural standards expected by the society via the care of its parents and society. It has been proved in anthropological research that human society can be continued from generation to generation, mainly due to two primary motivations. One is the genetic genes of biology, which are the common features that all advanced primate animals are born with and share, while the other is the culture created by human activities, which is acquired by the ethnic groups or groups within a specific range via the postnatal and socialized learning of generations of the people by various means, such as customs, conventions, education, taboos, religions and so forth.

Therefore, it can be said that rearing culture is a functional system for an individual infant to grow from a pure organism to an adult that conforms to the social norms. There is no doubt that human beings can produce Pavlovian conditional reflex towards the outside world when they are still in infancy. Such a fundamental biological reflex is essential for children's growth, which marks the beginning of the development of the sensory system, perceptual system, and cognitive ability of human beings.

However, when the children grow old, they will never content themselves with the stimulation brought by vision or sound, since such stimulation has no longer made them aware of the strange outside world and the self. These impulses are the fundamental difference between human beings and other common primate animals. In other words, the unique character of human beings is intelligence, and the product of intellectual activities is culture. Among the cultures, the rearing culture is a complex of customs, beliefs, food, social organizations, and social structures related to the growth of a life. Furthermore, the rearing culture is the basis for the combination of human groups and the construction of the cultural edifice and has always been the starting point of anthropological, cultural research.

In a broad sense, the concept of rearing in this book includes not only childbirth and nurturing, but also the socialization process before delivery, involving mate selection, marriage, mating and pregnancy, as well as the nurturing and education after the childbirth, and a variety of technologies, production, values, and beliefs throughout the process. In short, it is all the material, spiritual, and cultural means that human beings take to ensure the successful completion of the rearing. Therefore, this book is called the rearing system. It can be divided into marriage, reproduction, nurturing, education, and other stages. As Mr. Fei Xiaotong argues, to study the human fertility system, we need to consider the division of labor between men and women, bi-parental raising, the marriage system, the family structure and function, the relationship between husband and wife, the descent system and the kinship, and even the sexual ethics, which is to understand the fertility system from the perspective of the whole social culture (Fei, 1998).

The term "institution" has been widely used in politics, economics, law, life-extension, and administration under the modern national state system, and it is generally understood as a normative system established by the authority of state power or organization, such as legal institution, political institution, economic institution, and administrative institution and so forth. These views are more or less violent and submissive, as they are all made or concluded. However, in the traditional fields of social sciences, such as anthropology, folklore, sociology, etc., institution is understood as a term indicating an action or process, mainly referring to practices established in a certain way, using the same language, using the same etiquette, institution, and law, with the implications of custom and convention (Williams, 2005).

Generally speaking, there are several statements as follows: first of all, social institution is a complex of behavior patterns with the dominant central interests as the core; second, it is evident that there is a set of permanent social conventions, which is a reasonable and lasting, complex and integrated behavior mode. Only with it can a society be maintained, and it is an essential factor for humankind to obtain the basic social aspirations or needs; third, all cultures are made up of institutions that are generally accepted to fulfill the needs of life; fourth, the concept of institution has some serious natures, which make it different from customs and practices in general. It is adopted as a permanent part of the social organization of a group. Moreover, it is because of this that the institution has become the most dominant social role (Rui, 1980). The concept of the institution has been widely applied in varied disciplines, but it is not a term that is easily defined and consistently used. Among the above four statements, the analysis method of anthropological functionalism plays a dominant role. The functionalists, represented by Bronislaw Kaspar Malinowski, lay stress on two cultural analysis methods, function and institution, believing that all knowledge, technology, belief or material equipment exist to meet the specific needs of human beings. Expect for this, and there is no way to comprehend the culture. In other words, the function of culture is nothing more than to meet the needs of the following three aspects, basic physiological desires, institutional requirements, and demand for integration.

The primary psychological desires are divided into seven desires, nutrition, reproduction, bodily comforts, safety, relaxation, movement, and growth (Marwin, 1968). The demand for integration refers to the interdependence of various parts in a larger whole. The best way to understand the trait of a culture is to put it into the entire cultural context since culture is an integration of a part of autonomous institutions and a part of coordinated institutions. Bronislaw Kaspar Malinowski defined the institution as a system of organized and purposeful activities. Each institution can be divided into six aspects, namely, charter that is a set of values, myths or beliefs that legitimize the event, person that is the people involved in the pursuit of such values, myths or beliefs, norms that the group should abide by, material apparatus that is adopted, the activities themselves, and the function of the institution (Elvin, 1973). The institution is to organize the human groups and integrate them into a complete system to ensure that human needs can be critical.

Therefore, functionalists argue that the institution refers to the recognition of traditional values. In the institution, people are integrated into a whole. It also means that there is a specific relationship between people, as well as between people and specific physical parts of the natural or artificial environment. People follow the particular norms of their groups under the constitutional framework of their purposes or the traditional standards (Malinowski, 1999). Thus, we can see that our understanding of the institution can not be confined to the categories of political science and legal science and that when we jump out of the types of the national system and political system discourse, we can understand and grasp the cultural meaning of the institution. From the perspective of anthropological functionalism, institution firstly refers to the tradition, custom, convention, belief and material technology, etc.; secondly, it refers to a set of normative behavior patterns arising by combining he institution with human needs. Through the institution, social groups not only meet the needs of survival but are also integrated and become a community.

The rearing system is the fundamental analysis unit to study the community formation of human groups. Moreover, when social groups need to integrate and realize their reproduction, they must carry out cultural activities such as lactation, language training, physical training, labor training, behavioral norms, psychological cues, etc. around their offspring, the life-extension of the mother, while these cultural activities are known as the rearing system. In the fields of anthropology, folklore, and sociology, it has been made clear that in any society of any structure, including tribal society and industrial society, barbaric society and civilized society, people in all cultures have formed a variety of consanguineous communities around the rearing system.

Under this premise, we can see the human relationship between husband and wife and between parents and children, blood relationship, and marriage relationship, which leads to the formation of the rules of the marriage contract, inheritance rules and family structure. These are all the intrinsic meanings of the research on the rearing system. Anthropologists and folklorists tend to be interested in all kinds of consanguineous communities in their field survey, such as clans, kinship, patriarchy and matriarchy, patrilocal residence, matrilocal residence, principles of inheritance and marriage patterns. The above are the main dimensions to judge the nature of the rearing system of a group, as Bronislaw Kaspar Malinowski explained in the book titled The Scientific Theory of Culture, "As in the discussion of nutrition, it can be seen that reproduction has become a cultural system in human society. The continuation of race is not satisfied by simple physiological impulse or physiological function, but the outcome of a set of traditional rules and a set of related material and cultural equipment and activities. Such a cultural system of reproduction is composed of various institutions, such as standardized courtship, marriage, parent-child relationship, kinship and clan organization. In the same way, we can divide the nutrition system into consumption institutions, such as the families and clubs where people have dinner on the same table, production institutions, such as cultivation, hunting and fishing, as well as transaction institutions, such as markets and stores (Malinowski, 2002). "

The term "childhood" is a well-known concept in the terminology system of psychology. According to Sigmund Freud, childhood refers to the whole stage of a person from infancy to adolescence (Freud, 1999).In other words, childhood refers to the period from birth (newborn) to maturity (early youth). This stage is the occurrence and formation of a person's psychology, so psychologists highly value the study of children's psychology. According to the development process of children's intelligence and psychological operation, Jean Piaget, a famous psychologist in Switzerland, divides the childhood into four stages, among which a child in the last step is aged between eleven and sixteen years old (Piaget, 1982).In 1690, John Locke proposed the Theory of Tabula Rasa in the book An Essay Concerning Human Understanding. According to this theory, a newborn is like a whiteboard, and its life experience can write it clearly on the whiteboard. That is to say, everyone is born with a unique genetic disposition, but this is only one side of personality formation. The most important aspect of personality formation is life experience, namely, the way of child rearing, life experience, and cultural environment, which is the core of psychological anthropology research. Psychological anthropologists begin with the observation of children and carry out a cross-cultural comparative study based on the review of national disposition or national character and then construct the cultural morphology of an ethnic group. In this regard, the group of children has become a traditional but lasting research topic in the fields of anthropology and folklore sciences.

Based on the existing definition of children in the field of psychology, this book defines children at the stage from infants to the age of fourteen or fifteen combined with the actual situation of field investigation and the convenience of writing ethnography, while the children at this age group are roughly equivalent to the children who have not graduated from junior high school, which is also within the range of the children expounded in this book. According to the local situation, the children graduating from junior high school mainly develop themselves in three ways: first of all, they may go to high school and some vocational secondary schools; second, they may learn some practical technologies, such as computer, driving, mold technology, repair technology, etc.; third, they may choose to work in Shenzhen or Zhejiang and other coastal areas. In the eyes of the parents in Tancun Village, their children have not yet grown up before they graduate from junior high school, but they become grown-ups who can support and take care of themselves after graduating from junior high school. Therefore, the author limits children to 14 or 15 years old, which not only conforms to the existing conceptual principles of psychology but also conforms to the radical views of the local people.

Section 2 Research Review on the Child Rearing System

The study of children has a long history in the fields of psychology, sociology, and anthropology. Although different theoretical achievements have been made in the research of different disciplines, a frequent topic of concern for children's research is the research on children's socialization. According to Ember, C. R., and Ember, M., a couple of anthropologists in the United States, socialization is the process of adapting children to the expected behavior patterns of culture. Socialization can be either direct or indirect. Moreover, parents and other people tend to reward their children for some behaviors and ignore or punish them for other practices to socialize their children (The Embers, 1983) directly.

Other anthropologists in the United States hold that "socialization is a process in which a person needs his / her skills in society, knowledge of behaviors that can be understood and accepted in society, attitude and values that are consistent with the social rules and his / her meaning, or even that he/she feels satisfied (Plog and Bates, 1988)." When a person is born, he/she is merely a biological person, a natural person, but not a social person. The socialization of the individual is to enable his / her fundamental needs and physiological abilities to develop a fixed conditioned reflection according to certain norms, which means that his / her behavior should comply with the current codes of conduct and ethics in society and he/she should internalize them into his / her needs.

Haviland, W. A., in his famous book Cultural Anthropology: The Human Challenge, explores that human socialization begins with the method of acculturation by taking the item acculturation as the keyword, and then exerts an effect on the personality of an adult via the acculturation. Acculturation refers to a process in which culture is passed down from one generation to the next, through which an individual will become a member of its society (Haviland, 2006).

A person starts to develop its self-awareness shortly after birth, which means that when a person is in his / her infancy, he/she can feel that he/she is an existence in time and space, and learns to know about the world under the nurturing of adults, especially his / her parents. Acculturation starts with the development of children's self-awareness. Anthropological research is to observe and analyze the differences between the ways people adopt in different cultural patterns in the course of child rearing and education, and the mode that they affect the formation of their personality. By comparing the traditional way of breastfeeding of the people in North America and the Juvasi in the Kalahari Desert of South Africa, Haviland, W. A. found that due to different ways of breastfeeding, children develop their self-awareness in varying degrees and different ways. As for the Juvasi in the Kalahari Desert of South Africa, babies are breastfed about four times an hour, one or two minutes at a time. In 15 weeks, a Juvasi infant will spend about 70 % of its time in close contact with its mother, while the infant that is bred in an American family spends only 20 % of its time in close contact with its mother. As a result, the infants in North America could not be able to precisely distinguish those that are theirs from those that are not theirs until they are about two years old, which is later than that of the Juvasi. This kind of comparative study is the most typical research path in the field of anthropology.

Psychological and Sociological Research on Children's Socialization

As early as Sigmund Freud's time, his psychoanalytic theory focuses on the practice of family relationships in raising children, which provides the most direct theoretical contribution to the study of children's socialization. Sigmund Freud believes that children who grow up in family relationships perform in different ways in different stages as libido changes. These stages represent the development direction of children's psychological ability, while children's growth and various parts of the body become the parts that libido needs to focus on (Zigler, Child, and Lamb, 1988).

According to this hypothesis, Sigmund Freud divides the development process of children into five stages:

(1) Oral stage: It is mainly about the experience of eating, which means that the emotion of an infant's initial social relationship is to those who feed him to make them delighted;

(2) Anal stage: Micturition and excretion will bring the greatest happiness to children, and the parents care about how to dress their children better;

(3) Phallic stage (About four or five to seven years old): At this stage, children have the illusion of a sexual relationship with others, which is commonly known as Oedipus complex, to establish the psychological basis of superself;

(4) Latency stage (Seven to eleven or twelve years old): At this stage, children's sexual desire is suppressed, and libido's energy is transferred to the creative game and learning activities that can be accepted by the society;

(5) Genital stage (Over twelve or thirteen years old): Because of the increase of libido, children will have all kinds of psychological depression, excitement, and emotional conflicts and contradictions (Freud, 1999).

Sigmund Freud has formed a basic understanding of the research on children's psychological anthropology that the experience in early childhood has a profound impact on the formation of an adult's personality. We have been clear that, to some extent, all people have the same experience, so we are all combined in the common humanity. Moreover, we are well aware that each person has a unique history and that the personalities vary from one to another in some way. There is another dimension to the formation of childhood personality, which comes from different styles of raising children among various societies. As a result of these social customs with distinct cultural characteristics, social members in each culture have formed some unique personality characteristics (Murphy, 2004).

Based on Sigmund Freud's theory of the stages of children's social development, Erik Erikson divided the development stages of an individual into eight stages from the infancy stage to the late adulthood stage, namely, infancy stage, toddler-hood stage, preschool years, earl school years, adolescence stage, young adulthood, middle adulthood, and late adulthood. Erik Erikson explores the fundamental contradictions and inner conflicts that social individuals may have to deal with in different periods of socialization from the perspective of personality development (Erikson, 1998). Like Sigmund Freud, Erik Erikson also pays attention to the feeding experience in the first few years after an infant is born, but his main concern is the establishment of trust between the infant and the caregiver rather than the absolute power of libido.

According to Jean Piaget, a Swiss psychologist, the process in which a child is socialized can be measured by the change and improvement of the moral judgment ability of the child. In the book The Moral Judgment of the Child, Jean Piaget pointed out that the moral development of children can be divided into two stages, namely, before and after the age of seven or eight. From the previous stage to the later stage, a series of changes have taken place in the moral judgment ability of the child. He started his research from the children's pinball game. Here, children's participation in the game represents the process of socialization. He believes that, first of all, adults teach the children the moral rules, which is heteronymous. In the process of children's nurturing, they are socialized continuously, so the moral rules of heteronomy gradually develop into the laws of autonomy, that is, the nature of self-discipline. Second, the child makes a righteous judgment according to the scale of responsibility from the consequences of his behavior rather than his intention. It is bound by the moral rules formulated by adults. In the process of children's socialization, there are two kinds of morals, the moral of restraint or heteronomy and the moral of cooperation or self-discipline. Third, children's acceptance of punishment for wrongdoing changes from general punishment to targeted punishment in different ways (Piaget, 1984).

Psychologists have put forward a variety of theoretical analysis models for the study of children's socialization, some of which are even contradictory, some of which have been revised by anthropologists and sociologists, but almost all psychologists have been concerned about the significance of children's early parenting model for the formation of children's personality. In a word, children's parenting model or institution has always been an essential topic in the psychological research of children's socialization.

In the field of sociology, sociologists mainly expounded children's socialization from the perspectives of personality and self at the initial stage. George Herbert Mead's symbolic interactionism is one of the representative theories in this aspect.

Coodley C. N., one of the pioneers of symbolic interactionism and sociologist in the United States, proposed a view on personality and self, which had a significant impact on later theories of children's socialization. Coodley C. N. believes that the self or character is the product of social interaction. He expresses how the self is perceived in social interaction with the famous viewpoints of the reflective self or the looking-glass self. In his research, he mainly explored how the concept of "self" came into being in the process of children's socialization. In their interactions with their parents and with other children, children gradually discover "self" and cultivate the experience of "self" in the mirror, and progressively learn to express their feelings to other people from their infancy. For example, they will attract others' attention to my desire to utilize crying and screaming or raging (Coodley, 1999).

George Herbert Mead, the founder of symbolic interactionism, studies the "self" from the perspective of social interaction and divides the "self" into two parts: I and me. The term "I" is the self of action, while the power and characteristics of personality come from the power of I. The word "me" is the self of society, reflecting the experience in society. The term "me" has to come into being and develop with the aid of social interaction, which represents the attitude of other people in the community. It is the social definition of the individual self by other people in social organizations and social institutions. It is evident that Mead's two distinctions of self provide a crucial psychological basis for the theory of social interaction and discuss the formation process of children's self-concept by using the theory of interaction. In the process of interaction, children's self experiences the stages of preparation, the forms of play and the forms of the game. They first communicate with their elders through facial expression, which is called simulated posture, and then communicate with them through oral posture, while their elders respond to the symbols expressed by children accordingly. As a result of the interaction, children will evoke themselves to assume the social roles required by other people at the bottom of their hearts, and ultimately obtain the self-awareness with a distinct personality (Mead, 1999).

Anthropological Study of the Rearing System

Scholars in the field of anthropology first paid attention to the child rearing system in the 1920s. At that time, under the influence of Sigmund Freud and John Dowy, the educational theorist, a group of anthropologists began to shift their focus to the relationship between the formation of typical personalities of adults and the culture, so that they showed high interest in the environment where the infants grow. Since then, anthropologists have paid more attention to culture and personality and the child rearing system, which has always been an important topic. As declared by Haviland, W. A. in the introduction of Chapter 5, "Human Growth" in Cultural Anthropology: The Human Challenge, ethnographic research shows a wide range of research on child rearing. Anthropologists have been concerned about the differences in child rearing and their potential impact on adult personality. In different cultures, children's nurturing and education are arranged in different ways. Thus, these customs and their influence on personality are essential topics in the field of anthropological research (Haviland, 2006).

Franz Boas and Bronislaw Kaspar Malinowski were the first to pay attention to the influence of culture on personality and social behavior, while Margaret Mead and Ruth Benedict confirmed the role of culture in shaping the character through a large number of ethnographic surveys. However, the interpretation of the theory of the interaction between culture and personality is mainly completed by Ralph Linton and Abram Kardinar.

Franz Boas, the founder of the relativistic, culture-centered school of American anthropology who was rated as the father of modern anthropology of the United States, paid particular attention to the influence of the child rearing system on cultural traits. He wrote many books, including The Mind of Primitive Man, The Growth of Children, Anthropology and Modern Life and Race, Language and Culture, and so on. In the works, Franz Boas adopted various comparative research methods, such as physical anthropology, anatomy, genetics, archaeology, and eugenics, to demonstrate that different nations and races in the world vary from each other in terms of physical appearance or structure, but these nations and races are neither superior nor inferior to each other in terms of physiologic function or talent. Thus, he put forward the view of cultural relativism and severely criticized the theory of Nordic superiority of the euro centrists at that time. He solemnly pointed out that if they take into account the great achievements made by the ancient Greek and Roman cultures, especially those by ancient Egypt and China, and the numerous outstanding talents that have arisen in history, the Nordic people at that time belong to the typical inferior nationalities (Boas, 1940).

Although it is undeniable that the selection of heredity and environment may result in cultural traits, especially the adaptability of physical characteristics, eugenicists have tried their best to emphasize that rational and wise methods can improve the physiological and psychological standards of human beings. They hypothesized that by preventing the reproduction of inferior psychological and physiological lineages, the overall average standard of a nation could be improved. However, we can not conclude that the decisive factor for human evolution and reproduction is nature, rather than nurturing. For a reason, the eugenicists usually come to a conclusion through some experience, but it tends to involve lingering prejudice. It means that it is difficult to avoid the subjective cultural standpoint of self-superiority, aiming at what characteristics are inherited and what features are not.

However, anthropologists believe that the same social function creates many different anatomical forms, and they are convinced that, in most cases, the difference of real figure may depend on the adaptation of different functions. Furthermore, they believe that all human beings of various forms can achieve the same civilization and that it can guarantee the excellent physical condition of the human beings of different types from the availability of favorable conditions for child rearing (Baos, 1999). There are different nurturing systems in different ethnic groups. These systems are determined by their environment, history, politics, economy, and other conditions. And they come into being to satisfy the needs of different cultures. However, the nurturing systems are neither superior nor inferior to each other, as they are all the products of human beings in the course of the transformation of nature and human beings themselves. Therefore, Franz Boas criticizes the prejudice and fallacy of nationalism and racism from the scientific theory of culture of the child rearing system.

In the 1930s and 1940s, at an expert seminar at Columbia University, the anthropologist Ralph Linton and the psychoanalyst Abram Kardinar explained some extraordinary anthropological views on the study of culture and personality. Abram Kardinar proposed that there is a fundamental personality in every culture that arises from some shared cultural experience. In other words, just as a child's later personality may be shaped by his or her early experience, the character of adults in society should also be formed by some shared cultural experience. "This sharing custom stems from the primary institutions of society, while the basic institutions have something to do with the traditional way of making a living, the conventional family composition and the habit of parenting (The Embers, 1988).

In the book The Individual and His Society: The Psychodynamics of Primitive Social Organization, Ralph Linton and Abram Kardinar proposed the concept of basic personality structure, which is an integrated type of personality characteristics that describes some early experiences and possible experiences shared by social members in a culture (Kardinar, 1939). This kind of overall primary personality type, in turn, creates and maintains the traditional contents of a culture so that the culture can be integrated. Therefore, they divide culture into two parts, the primary institution that leads to common characteristics and the secondary institution that is caused by the basic personality structure. They design their research idea according to these concepts: from the environment to the primary institution (including the way of livelihood, family form, and parenting system), to basic personality types (including shared anxiety, preparedness, and neural touch), and finally to the secondary institution (religion, myth and folk custom). Besides, they pay special attention to the ways of parenting, including the methods of infant feeding and weaning, the ways how the primary institutions, such as excretion and sex education, family structure and scale, transmit the elements of culture to social members to form the primary personality type. Therefore, the rearing system is regarded as the leading cause of cultural differences among different ethnic groups, while family, mode of production, interpersonal relationship, and various social forces that are associated with the family are regarded as the significant cultural context that affects the formation of the primary personality types.

It is a traditional anthropological research topic of "culture and personality" to analyze the personality differences between men and women by observing the child rearing system of the people living in different cultural environments. Margaret Mead is undoubtedly one of the best anthropologists in this respect. In the book Coming of Age In Samoa: A Study Of Adolescence And Sex In Primitive Societies, Margaret Mead made a cross-cultural comparative study of the adolescent girls in Samoa and those in the United States and found that the teenage girls in Samoa do not suffer from depression, mood fluctuation and other troubles as the girls in the United States. It is caused by the cultural environment of Samoa society, in which it does not mystify the whole process of life, nor involve too many taboos and competitions, while the children can get in casual contact with the adults, and premarital sex is so free that both parties do not need to input intense affections to each other. It is an entirely different cultural view from that of American society. Through a cross-cultural comparative study, Margaret Mead elaborated on how a colorful cultural environment shapes the personality.

In the book Growing up in New Guinea: A Comparative Study of Primitive Education, Margaret Mead studies the education of the Manus people in New Guinea in their childhood, and compares it with various kinds of school education of children in a civilized society, demonstrating that the method of children's education in different cultural environments has a considerable impact on children's personality. Mead's research on sex and temperament in three primitive societies of New Guinea can be rated as one of the most famous cases of the study on culture and personality (Mead, 1988). Moreover, she believes that there is no universal or nearly universal personality difference between men and women, which means that there is no global standard for the formation of gender differences between men and women in terms of personality.

As described in her works, the Arapesh men are mostly similar to the Arapesh women, as they all tend to be feminine. They all have some maternal characteristics of mild action, gentle temperament, responsibility, and cooperation. The men and women of the Mundugumor people are similar, but contrary to the Arapesh, they tend to be masculine. All of them are accustomed to resorting to force and competing with each other, advocate male ferocity and polygamy, and they are always regressive, while women show some masculine characteristics, such as craziness, parochialism, and selfishness. There are significant differences in temperament between men and women of the Tchambuli. Women tend to be in charge of both inside and outside affairs, and they are masterful and practical and are never swayed by personal considerations, showing a robust masculine tendency. However, men are sensitive, weak, somewhat neurotic, and have a strong feminine tendency. They are not engaged in production but focus on dressing themselves up and striving to make some religious and artistic achievements.

Despite the fame of Margaret Mead's studies, her conclusion that there was no consistent gender difference between men and women was not accepted by later anthropologists. Many cultural anthropologists have studied the influence of different cultures and parenting methods on children's socialization or acculturation through a wide range of comparisons and put forward some different views. For example, Beatrice Whiting and John Whiting, in the large-scale cross-cultural comparative research program Six Cultures: Studies of Child Rearing (hereinafter referred to as the Six Culture Project) (The Embers, 1988), pointed out that children had shown the differences in gender as early as they were three to six years old in some observable experimental studies. Moreover, it was found that boys were generally more aggressive than girls.

Generally speaking, in those societies where children are required to complete a lot of tasks, children are more responsible and happier to help others. Because adults almost always ask girls to do more work than boys, girls tend to be more accountable for what they are doing, including providing patient nurturing services and aids for others. However, boys tend to control and instruct others for their personal affairs. Anthropologists generally explain the consistency of these gender differences in the cultural environment of different parenting systems from two aspects of biological heritage and social acquisition, among which the former holds that gender differences are so consistent because they are likely to exist in the genetic quality of both sexes, while the latter attributes the reason to the fact that adult men and women are required to play different types of roles in almost every society. Because of the social expectation of the gender role, people have adopted different ways to cultivate boys and girls since they were born.

The Sixth Culture Project, hosted by Beatrice Whiting and John Whiting et al., began in the 1950s and covered six countries or regions including India, England, Mexico, Kenya, Japan, and the Philippines, most of which are the settlements of primitive peoples. Their research explored the relationship between parenting style and children's behavior from nine aspects, including help-seeking, achievement, sense of responsibility, obedience, domination, sociality, aggression, nurturing, and independence. Beatrice Whiting and John Whiting found from the research that different cultures have different effects on children's socialization and behavior modeling. Whiting divides these six cultures into A-type cultures and B-type cultures, while there are distinct differences in children's behaviors between these two types of cultures.

It can be seen from the previous discussion that cultural anthropologists are very concerned about the impact of different ways of parenting on children's acculturation. In other words, the way mothers raise their children shows a theory of how the methods of training children relate to other aspects of personality and culture. The basic training methods on children reflect that they are influenced by the nature of cultural family, social, political, and economic institutions, which, in turn, are affected by the ecosystem. The methods of child rearing are also constrained by the needs, drivers, and receptions. They are common to all infants that are determined biologically, such as the impulses of the mouth, anus, and genitals. In terms of the methods and above needs of child rearing, the interaction between driving forces and receptivity creates personality. Subsequently, the character expresses itself in the second level of establishment, which is collectively referred to as the superstructure (Harris, 1989). That is to say, anthropologists believe that early childhood rearing methods have an undeniable connection with the development of children's personality, but this connection is not single, because it is also constrained by the social and cultural environment where the children grow and their biological needs. As a result, it is necessary to have a holistic point of view for the exploration into the child rearing system, which needs to be analyzed and investigated from the perspective of comprehensive and overall factors. From this point of view, the study of functionalism provides us with a model to study the child rearing system.

In the study of children's fertility institution, it has made a precious explanation by the theory of functionalism. Fei Xiaotong is the one who uses functionalism to give systematic interpretations to the fertility institution. He believes that the survival of individuals should be based on the premise of maintaining the integrity of social structure and that the fertility institution is to use social sanctions to continually give birth to babies so that they will have the opportunity to grow up, to ensure the continuity of human race and the integrity of social structure. In this regard, fertility is not only a vital skill but also a social and cultural means as well as a cultural institution. The fertility institution is an artificial guarantee for the continuity of the human race (Fei, 1998).

Bronislaw Kaspar Malinowski classifies human needs into three categories. First of all, it is the basic needs of biology, such as nutrition, reproduction, safety, etc.; second, it is the needs of means, such as production technology, social organizations, etc.; third, it is the comprehensive needs. The function of the fertility institution, including courtship, marriage, and nurturing, is not to meet the first level of sexual needs, but to achieve the continuity of human race through a series of cultural settings to restrict the sexual needs. "Reproduction has become a cultural system in human society. And the need for the continuity of human race is not satisfied by simple physiological actions and physiological functions, but the outcome of a set of traditional rules and a set of related material and cultural equipment and activities. Such a cultural system of reproduction is composed of a variety of institutions, such as standardized courtship, marriage, parent-child relationship, and clan organization (Malinowski, 2002)."Therefore, Fei Xiaotong believes that to study the fertility institutions of human beings, we need to consider the division of labor between men and women, biparental raising, marriage institution, family structure and function, conjugal relationship, heir institution and kinship, and even sexual ethics (Fei, 1998).In other words, we need to understand the fertility institution from the perspective of social culture as a whole.

In the book, The Sexual Life of Savages in North-Western Melanesia: An Ethnographic Account of Courtship, Marriage and

Family Life among the Natives of the Trobriand Islands, British New Guinea, Bronislaw Kaspar Malinowski, the founder of functionalism, focuses on the significance of the rearing system in maintaining the cultural integration of a national community. According to the functional school, fertility and nutrition are the most important among all the fundamental biological needs of human beings. Human beings must take advantage of some tools or implements to meet their basic needs for survival. Hunger and sexuality, two primitive impulses, constitute the core of the most traditional institutions of human beings. In the book, Bronislaw Kaspar Malinowski proves that if a social group wants to survive, the individual's animal impulse, like other basic human needs, must be molded by the power of education to make it give in. Through the extensive and detailed ethnographic study of the natives of the Trobriand Islands, Bronislaw Kaspar Malinowski found that the traditional norms constrained the sexual desire of the indigenous people from their childhood, and they must conform to specific institutions in the course of courtship and spouse selection (Huang and Gong, 2004). It means that their sexual relations must be subject to the principles of succession, residence, the style of family life, marriage custom, family form, ethics, age organization, religion, witchcraft, and belief.

The cultural institution of pregnancy of the natives of the Trobriand Islands reflects the concept of their soul, the relationship between men and women, and the fundamental institution of matrilineal society (Malinowski, 2000). They do not think that women get pregnant for no reason, as the fact of pregnancy comes from the reincarnation of the soul or the regeneration of life. Whether it is the rejuvenated souls or the unformed babies or soul babies, they are the only source of human beings to supplement the new population. Moreover, in most cases, these reincarnated souls are the deceased grandmother, mother of a pregnant woman, or the brother of her mother. In other words, the lineage of matrilineal society is maintained by way of soul parasitism. In aboriginal beliefs about pregnancy, the biological relationship between father and son is wholly ignored. They believe that "The soul infant was born from Tuma (the place where the soul of the dead goes, i.e., the island of death, which is also the paradise of the natives of the Trobriand Islands), traveled to the tropical islands, and then conducted a series of activities in the mother's interior. Blood flows from the abdomen to the head and from the head down into the uterus. The correlation between the confounding factors and physiological factors in the belief provides a theory about the origin of human life." It is this theory of origin that has laid an excellent theoretical foundation for the matrilineal institution, because the birth of new life in a community connects the relationship between the reproductive organs of maternal ancestors and those of the living women, while there is no paternity in a biological sense. As a result, people can inherit the principle of matrilineal succession and value the relationship between mother and child from a sociological viewpoint.

After World War II, with the rise of postmodern thoughts, anthropologists shifted their focus on the research of the child rearing system. They began to pay attention to the changes in children's discrimination, inequality, and power, as well as children's nutrition, disease (such as AIDS), mortality, and the child adoption institution and the relative institution in the process of urbanization (Esterik, 2002; John and Judith, 1994). Some anthropologists have studied China's family planning policy, the one-child families in cities, and the change of the family relationships. They conclude that the girls in China's cities benefit from the demographic model of the one-child policy. Under the patriarchal system, Chinese people have been reluctant to spend money on training their daughters for a long time. However, after the implementation of the one-child policy, the parents do not need to take care of any other children. Then, the only daughter in a family can be fostered by her parents to their best. Low fertility allows mothers to have stable jobs so that they can also prove their filial piety to their aged parents. Compared with the gender standards that discriminated against women in the past, girls also showed more exceptional abilities and advantages (Fong, 2002; Deborah and Harrell, 1993).

Folklore Research on Birth Culture

The traditional Chinese culture attaches great importance to fertility-related issues. There are a great many documents about the folk customs of childbearing, such as ancient books, historical books, local records, family instructions, and various biographies, which need to be clarified by designated researchers. The book An Introduction to Birth Culture in China (Volume I and Volume II), edited by Pan Guiyu, sort out all kinds of fertility cultural phenomena since the primitive society in China. The book covers a wide range of contents, including the ancient birth customs, beliefs, religions, official population policies, population thoughts and concepts of past dynasties, marriage institution, birth technology, and parenting mode, as well as the Marxist new birth culture and family planning institution since the founding of new China. Moreover, it makes a scientific investigation on the interaction between the family planning institution and family tradition, women's and minors' issues, and shows the development of Chinese birth culture in a diachronic way (Pan, 2001).

It can be said that Fei Xiaotong is the first humanist in China to explain the childbearing behavior of human beings, according to functionalism. Childbirth Institution, which he wrote in the 1940s, has always been a classic work on the issue of human fertility. In his view, the childbirth institution is a set of activities that a man gets married to a woman, that they give birth to a child and bring him or her up. Childbearing is not only a biological behavior, but also a social act, so it is known as social nurturing. Only through social nurturing can every living individual grow into a cultural person, and realize the continuity of social norms from generation to generation. The set of the social upbringing system involves the biological basis of childbearing, social foundation, marriage and family, kinship institution, heir institution, etc. "The transmission of social knowledge is of great importance to a person's life, since he or she can not strive for existence from nature alone, but must make a living in the crowd. A person who fails to acquire a way of action, just like a person who is physically deficient, is unable to live a healthy life. As a result, he has no chance to do his best in the continuity of the human race. The work of imparting this way of act to children can be called social nurturing. Social nurturing is just as important as physiological nurturing for the growth of children, the cultivation of new social elements, and the continuation of the race (Fei, 1981)."

After Fei's studies, especially since the 1990s, scholars have been involved in the research of child rearing, which can be found in a large number of ethnological, sociological, and anthropological investigations or studies. These related works include Li Yinhe's Fertility and Village Culture (1994), Zhang Yibing's The Culture of Birth (1991), Peng Xizhe and Dai Xingyi's The Culture of Birth in China's Rural Society (1996), The Childbearing Health Centered on Women (1995) and The Childbearing Health Based on Communities compiled by Yunnan Health and Development Research Association, and Wu Geyan's Customs of Praying for Children in Ancient China (1994), Customs of Child Rearing from Ancient Times to Present (1988) by Zhang Jingsong et al. , Song Deyin's The Interest of Pregnancy: A Probe into The Customs of Child Rearing (1992), Zhao Guohua's On the Culture of Fertility Worship (1996), Fu Daobin's On the Culture of Fertility Worship in China (1990), Zhang Shiya's Altar and platform: a comparative study of national religious education in Southwest China (1992), Du Fangqin's Historical Investigation into Birth Culture (1998), Song Zhaolin's Beliefs in Birth in Ching (1999) and Research on the God of Childbirth and the Sexual Sorcery (1990), Zhang Shiwen's The Society and the Childbirth (1991), and Xu Guilan's Cultural Overlapping of Chinese Reproduction Custom (2002), etc. These research results either make use of historical documents to carry out a diachronic exploration into a variety of customs of childbearing in Chinese history and even the present combined with ethnological and anthropological field research methods or make use of multi-disciplinary comparison and community survey to explain the birth phenomena related to women and children from multiple perspectives. All these studies provide us with an abundance of knowledge resources to understand the birth customs and the corresponding cultural systems of all the nationalities in China.

Although the research results, since the 1990s, have focused on the birth culture and the customs of childbirth, it can be seen from their analysis that they can yet be regarded as the traditional research on the rearing system in the field of anthropology. In the book Culturology of Childbirth edited by Zhang Chunyuan and Chen Shengli, birth culture is defined as a variety of social and cultural phenomena related to people's childbearing activities, which means the sum of the ideological theories, values, knowledge and ability, customs and habits, ethics and corresponding laws and regulations, and institutions that come into being in the course of people's marriage, family, childbearing, birth control and other activities (Zhang and Chen, 2004). In the book A Study of Reproduction Culture of Ethnic Groups in Southwest China, Yang Zhuhui holds that "Birth culture refers to a set of concepts, beliefs, customs and habits, value standards, norms, and behavior patterns that have been gradually formed in the long-term practice of human reproduction (Yang, 2006)." Besides, she conducted in-depth research on the vibrant and colorful birth culture of ethnic minorities in Southwest China, focusing on the main contents of fertility worship, birth concept, marriage, birth custom, family planning, and so on (Yang, 2006). These definitions of birth culture can still be understood as the parenting system in the discourse of functionalist anthropology, which refers to all kinds of cultural equipment, customs, norms, values, social organizations and marriage institutions that come into being based on the idea of child rearing, as well as the laws, policies and related institutions that come into being in the process of the state's intervention in population control.

Section 3 Research Paradigm and Methodology

The research on the child rearing system has been explored from many levels and angles in many disciplines, but from the perspective of the existing achievements, there are no more than the following orientations: first, it is the tradition of cultural anthropology, which discusses the research on acculturation, culture, and personality, the relationship between child rearing model and education, such as the studies by Margaret Mead in 1986 and 1988; second, it is the tradition of culturology and folklore to sort out the folk patterns of the child rearing system, starting with historical documents, supplemented by ethnographic materials, such as the study by Pan Guiyu in 2001; third, it is a tradition of demography, which mainly focuses on the relationship between child rearing and fertility concept, population quantity and quality, and population control, such as the study by Peng Xizhe and Dai Xingyi in 1996. Some scholars, such as Li Yinhe, study the influence of cultural traditions and changes of a place on child rearing, but few scholars follow the rules of the field survey to carry out the overall thick descriptions of the child rearing system in the way of ethnography. This book tries to make a superficial attempt from this angle.

Theoretical Paradigm and Methodology of Research

Thamas Kuhn first proposed the term paradigm. It refers to the theoretical basis and practical norms on which conventional sciences operate. Moreover, it is the world outlook and way of conduct that the scientists engaged in a specific science domain abide by together. The scientific paradigm determines the shared belief and essential viewpoints of a scientific community in a particular field, providing them with a common theoretical framework and a framework for solving problems, thus forming the common tradition of the discipline and determining the direction for the development of the subject. Since anthropology was introduced into China, a variety of research paradigms have been formed in the process of sinicization, such as community research, clan research, theoretical research of regional market system, historical anthropology research and anthropology re-study (Zhao, 2009). However, it is the most basic way of anthropological research to carry out a field survey and explain its culture with the community as the domain.

Therefore, the theoretical paradigm of interpretive anthropology becomes the most direct methodology basis of this book. In the book Anthropology as Cultural Critique: An Experimental Moment in the Human Sciences, George E. Marcus and Michael M.J. Fischer explained the interpretive anthropology as a general term for the reflections on various ethnographic practices and cultural concepts. It came into being in the 1960s and 1970s under the joint influence of the then-dominant Parsons School, the classic Max Weber sociology, phenomenology, structuralism, structural and transformational linguistics, semiotics, the critical theory of the Frankfurt school and hermeneutics (Marcus and Fischer, 1998).

In the book The Interpretation of Cultures, Clifford Geertz, a representative of interpretive anthropology, pointed out that "man is an animal that is hung on the web of meaning woven by himself. Cultural analysis is not an experimental science to explore the law, but an interpretative science to explore the meaning (Geertz, 1999). "The description of ethnography by interpretive ethnology has three characteristics that go far beyond the traditional ethnography. First, it is interpretive. Second, it interprets the social discourse flow. Third, such interpretation lies in trying to rescue the speech of the discourse from the situation that is gone never to return and fix it in the reading form. And it embodies the fourth feature in the concrete work, as it is a micro description (Geertz, 1999)." Clifford Geertz came to the conclusion that the work of an anthropologist is to choose a cultural event that attracts his attention, and then enrich it with detailed description and make it explanatory, to tell his readers to understand the meaning of the culture he describes (Marcus and Fischer, 1998).

According to such a research idea, dialogue becomes the core concept of ethnography writing. On the one hand, the researcher is required to have a conversation with the culture he is studying. On the other hand, their readers are required to have a dialogue with the foreign cultures that they describe, so as to achieve a real understanding of the local concepts. The writers of ethnography are always in the intermediary position of culture, and the different cultures and ideas they observe and describe are in constant interaction with one another in the course of ethnography writing. It requires the ethnographic workers to have a dialogue with the local culture from the perspective of objectivism when conducting ethnographic investigation and writing and to have insight into each cultural detail and the situation of each cultural performance during their dialogue and interaction with the local culture.

Under the guidance of the theoretical paradigm of interpretive anthropology, the author tries to take part in the daily life of local people as much as possible, takes the initiative to approach them, and carefully observe their routine behaviors, and tries not to interfere with their production activities while having interviews with them casually. Through a great deal of careful observation, the author obtains the real text as much as possible, establishes the cultural facts that have to do with the child rearing system, and repeatedly tells about the world he has observed in detail as much as possible. However, some facts merely represent the interpretation of local people towards their cultures. In practical terms, these interpretations are just a kind of conscious, friendly, and passionate cooperation of local people or even shallow debates out of good intentions. Therefore, when writing ethnography, the author needs to reinterpret these interpretations made by the local people, so that they can expound the cultural understandings of the local people.

Based on such thinking, according to the anthropological concept of holistic, this book does not regard the rearing system as an isolated aspect of society and culture but puts it into the whole context of community culture. First of all, starting from the cultural environment of Tancun Village, the author explains all the necessary natural and cultural backgrounds of Tancun Village. Second, the author carries out a full description of the child rearing system in Tancun Village from the four aspects of childbirth, child rearing, child education, and the rearing of the left-behind children, which is caused by the rural labor force going out to work. Finally, starting with the values of reproduction, which is a deep meaning of culture, the author makes a more objective cultural explanation on the change of rearing behavior. The whole narration and analysis of this book not only pays attention to the horizontal connection of the cultural factors that make up the child rearing system but also takes into account the vertical change of the child rearing system.

In this way, on the one hand, it allows the people to have a distinct understanding of the cultural integrity of the rearing system. On the other hand, it enables people to become aware of the basic situation of the change of various related cultural factors of the rearing system in an organized way. As George E. Marcus and others pointed out after reflecting on the discourse hegemony of anthropology since the 20th century, one of the most dramatic changes in the methodological innovation of ethnography in the 20th century is that anthropologists focus on a holistic view different from the past and that they no longer put forward any macro theory that is valid everywhere, but shifts their focus to the full expression of a specific way of life. The new holistic view aims to provide a panoramic view of a way of life through the most detailed observation. Now the critical point is that the responsibility of ethnographic researchers is to describe the society they see as comprehensively as possible and to enable the readers to understand the culture they represent in an all-round way. The holistic expression of modern ethnography is to contextualize cultural elements and to establish systematic relations among cultural elements (Marcus and Fischer, 1998).

Major Research Strategies and Methods

The author is a native of Tancun Village, where the field survey was carried out. As a native, the author is very familiar with society and life there, which also facilitates the author to carry out the study and integrate into the life of the local people. But also because the author is a native, he may not feel such culture shock as in a foreign culture for the local culture that he has been exposed to since childhood. Moreover, the author is full of passion for the people there, all of whom are his relatives, friends, and acquaintances. The author belongs to one of them, but he has been away from his hometown for many years, so in the eyes of local people, the author is a stranger who comes back from a distant city to visit his relatives and friends.

The personal emotional bias and identity duality have made it necessary for the author to remind himself to pay attention to the identity transformation between emic and etic. If we want to make the cultural understanding and analysis of etic from the standpoint of emic, we must defamiliarize ourselves with the local culture and then have a new understanding of it. The customs, beliefs, institutions, and technologies in the local culture are not only the knowledge crystallization passed down by our common ancestors from generation to generation but also our things and the research object of the author. Therefore, a researcher should consciously cultivate the qualification of a marginal man, as Francis L. K. Hsu stated in his work (Hsu, 1989). Only in this way can we feel our research objects and have an objective and fair understanding and analysis of the materials we have investigated. Only in this way can we make a scientific explanation of their culture from the context of the local people.

Just as Bronislaw Kaspar Malinowski studied the marriage activities of the natives of the Trobriand Islands, especially the economic behaviors in the marriage customs, only when he is involved in the cultural system of the Trobriand Islands can the marriage activities be investigated, described and understood in a reasonable way. If we were divorced from the local cultural context in the study, we would be unable to know the meaning of the presents in the marriage activities of these islanders. As a native, the author can easily understand his own culture from the perspective of insight by understanding the local context and have interviews with the local people on their production and lives. However, as a researcher, the author has to work as an outsider to make a reasonable explanation of the materials he has obtained by using the anthropological theory and methods. Only when we have a sober understanding of ourselves can we make practical choices on the corresponding research methods. These methods include participant observation method, interview method, qualitative and quantitative research methods, questionnaire method, literature method, etc.

As a native, the author has no barriers with the local people in language and emotional communication during the investigation. Since the local people are all the fellow townsmen, friends or acquaintances of the author, he can get quickly involved in the production activities and lives of the local people, and observe the rules of action and inner world displayed in their daily life, various rituals, festival activities and acts of faith. At the same time, although the author is a native, he left his hometown after graduating from junior high school and spent most of his time on campus. He returned to Tancun Village occasionally before, but he had not developed an academic consciousness to pay attention to the countryside culture around him that he had been accustomed to until he began to learn the professional knowledge related to anthropology and folklore. Therefore, the author is unfamiliar with the local culture. Therefore, a large number of interviews were conducted at the same time as a participatory observation. In the course of the conversation, he had not only separate interviews with individual respondents but also called several respondents to attend the symposiums. He not only paid attention to conversations with farmers who worked in the fields but also conducted in-depth interviews with their families. Moreover, he attached great importance to the varied forms of the interviews with the male and female villagers who were at different age groups, of various educational levels, and organically combined formal interviews with informal discussions, in-depth interviews, as well as chatting-based interviews.

Participation observation and interview enable the author to obtain a large number of writing materials, thus providing sufficient cultural facts for the useful study of local culture. However, there is no criterion for the quantity of the materials obtained from participant observation and interviews. Therefore, field observers must combine qualitative and quantitative research methods to have a more comprehensive understanding of the local culture. In the process of investigation, the author must also design some questionnaire schemes according to the actual situation of the study and know about the economic situation, values and rules of actions of the local people using the questionnaire survey.

Each community exists in a specific time and space, and the community members from generation to generation have created the history of their communities with their experience of life. Therefore, when we study the culture of a community, we can not ignore the history of the community. Otherwise, our research will be merely an interpretation of the local culture out of context. Through contact with local officials, folk intellectuals, older people who are familiar with local traditions, the author collected the annals of local history, local records, pedigrees of local clans, written documents, sacrifice, and sorcery texts, archives, inscriptions, legends and stories from the Qing Dynasty. Therefore, the author can have a comprehensive understanding of the historical form and change process of local culture.

Folklore Research and Field Survey of Ethnography

Since the restoration and reconstruction of folklore in the late 1970s, on the one hand, Chinese folklore research has inherited the research tradition since the 1930s and 1940s. On the other hand, it takes the initiative to learn and introduce new theories and methods of foreign folklore. Generally speaking, there are two viewpoints. One view is that Chinese folklore is an independent discipline with its unique discipline theory, concept system, and discourse system. In modern China, folklore research should follow its path and have the independence of different disciplines from anthropology, ethnology, and sociology (Zhong, 1999). Another point of view is that folklore has never been fundamentally separated from other social sciences, especially anthropology, no matter in western academic tradition or Chinese academic tradition, emphasizing the anthropological trend of folklore or the folklore origin of anthropology (Gao, 1996; Huang, 2001).

From the perspective of the academic history of Chinese folklore, folklore has been developed under the promotion of anthropology, ethnology, sociology, and other disciplines. For example, in the earlier days, Yang Chengzhi, Lin Huixiang, and Yang Kun and other scholars advocated the anthropological folklore and adopted an inclusive attitude towards anthropology and folklore (Yang, 1989; Lin, 1991; Yang, 1997). Professor Gao Bingzhong also believes that "there is an indissoluble bond between the development of Chinese folklore and anthropology. The academic norms of the Chinese folklore, which have been accumulated in the whole process from its beginning to its initial finalization, mainly involve two sources. One is the study of the humanities of myths, legends, and stories, and the other is the early anthropology, which studies folklore as a remnant of ancient times. The theory and method of contemporary anthropology may become the most important academic orientation of Chinese folklore research and the most effective growing point of Chinese folklore (Gao, 1996)."

Based on the analysis and conclusion that Chinese anthropology and folklore develop independently from each other and permeate each other, and overlap to some extent in the academic orientation of different cultures and books, Professor Huang Ze further put forward the folklore origin and academic orientation of Chinese anthropology (Huang, 2001). When speaking of the concept, nature, structure, and function of folklore fieldwork, Professor Dong Xiaoping of Beijing Normal University also keenly saw the trend of ethnography research in anthropology, ethnology, folklore, sociology and other disciplines at home and abroad, as the scholars have put continuously forward new ideas, theories and methods of field survey through the revolution of ethnography writing. She pointed out: "folklore, anthropology, sociology, and other disciplines have a broad overlapping domain, shared resources and a field platform in the research object of folklore. In this new international academic trend, ethnography plays a leading role (Dong, 2003)."

The author has also combed and discussed the subject reactions between folklore and anthropology from the context of the academic history of Western lore and anthropology, revealed the theoretical influence of anthropology on folklore research in different development stages of crucial theories, and believed that folklore and anthropology are developed in the long-term process of subject interactions (Jiang, 2006). Folklore is not self-satisfied with being a stick-in-the-mud. As a young and vigorous discipline, it should break the barriers of discipline, absorb nutrients from other disciplines, especially anthropology, and continually enrich and develop its theoretical vision and research methods. As a result, from the perspective of discipline interaction, it is conducive to the development of the folklore discipline to draw on and introduce anthropological research methods to carry out folklore research.

As we all know, the rapid development of anthropology is attributed to its most basic and characteristic research methods, ethnography, and fieldwork. Both folklorists and anthropologists take "culture" as their research object. Therefore, folklorists can borrow ethnographic research methods of anthropology to study folklore-related issues and interpret the colorful life of folklore culture. It requires the folklore researchers to go deep into the field, carry out substantial fieldwork, and participate in and observe the various cultural phenomena that they are exposed to. Substantial fieldwork is an essential means for anthropologists and folklorists to obtain information. Only through fieldwork can folklorists possess plenty of cultural facts, and then write ethnography to explain the culture they study and carry out a theoretical dialogue with various disciplines. Because fieldwork is of considerable significance to anthropology and folklore research, some scholars even call fieldwork writing culture (Clifford and Marcus, 1986), or writing ethnographic fieldnotes (Emerson, Fretz and Shaw, 1995). According to such research ideas, this book has carried out long-term and in-depth fieldwork on the child rearing system, obtained rich field data, and described and processed the investigated materials with the folk research orientation of ethnography.

The precondition of ethnographic folklore research is to carry out long-term fieldwork on the research object, to go deep into the local culture, and to understand and grasp the local people and their cultural concepts from the dual perspectives of emic and etic. The author is a native and lived in Tancun Village until he graduated from junior high school, so he is very familiar with everything there. But before the author decided to take Tancun village as the location of field investigation, he was insensitive to the local culture and used to the people and environment that he had been familiar with just like breathing air. For this reason, the author worried about whether he could exceed his limitations, and view the culture of his hometown out of the circle of his self-culture, as well as get insight into the local cultural phenomenon that he has seen since he was a child but that he had never kept in mind. Moreover, it can be even said that the introspection and vigilance had always accompanied the author to self in the whole process of field investigation. Such vigilance has reminded him that, in the course of observing the local culture, he should pay attention to not only the consciousness mode of the culture but also the essence beyond the surface to understand and grasp the unconscious mode of the local culture. Only in this way, the author can not only give full play to the advantages of the identity as a native during the investigation but also return to the status of the investigator.

From August to September 2005, the author took advantage of the summer vacation to visit his relatives in his hometown and tried to enter the community as an investigator for the first time. This survey is only to know about the necessary information, such as population, history, economy, agricultural production cycle, major festivals, etc. This time, the author got to know Mr. Deng Xuqing, a folk intellectual in Tancun Village. At that time, the older man was writing the Local Records of Huangtingshi Town, while collecting a wide range of folk materials. Many local allusions that the author knew were learned from the older man. During this investigation, the author, together with Mr. Deng, went deep into the local people for many times to know about the religious sites that had existed in the local history, such as temples, ancestral halls, land halls, etc., and directly participated in the reconstruction of the Wutongling Temple, the ancestral temple of the Deng family. In order to learn about the history of local families in detail, the author paid frequent visits to the homes of the elders of various families and some local sages, and he received their enthusiastic assistance. At that time, the elderly would keep on talking about their families' history in the local area. Sometimes they would suddenly think of the old stories that had been forgotten for a long time, and then tell them to the author, the most loyal listener, with great honor.

Generally speaking, this survey is an exploratory attempt, just for a preliminary understanding of the local culture, and the investigation is mainly targeted at those with prestige, focusing on the history of local clans and folk religions. Of course, it is also an issue of interest to the elderly, so the investigation went well.

From November to late December 2005 and from late April to early October 2006, the author had been living in Tancun Village for nearly seven months, where he got along with the local people day and night, thus making it convenient to carry out fieldwork. Before the investigation, the author was worried that it would be difficult for him to realize the identity transformation of emic and etic successfully. So, in the inquiry, he always reminded himself to keep sensitive to culture, but to his surprise, this time, the local people could not understand the investigation at all, and they always asked the author about why he investigated these useless kinds of stuff. So for a long time, the study didn't go as well as he thought. Some respondents tended to answer his questions, and they would send away the troublesome harasser around them in a few words, because, in their views, what the author investigated was the life that they had been so accustomed to that it was not worth mentioning, resulting in the silence between the author and the respondents. Moreover, they think that a doctor should stay in the laboratory of the research institute to engage in inventions and creations, that what happens in the folk is not worthy of being written in the book.

Therefore, every time the author investigated, he would be interviewed by his respondents in the investigation instead. They used to consult with the author about the education and life of the university, hoping to listen to the author talking about how the excellent intellectual came back from university evaluated the current policies for rural areas. Some people regard the author as a psychologist to whom they could talk about what made them feel depressed. This situation made the author hesitate about which way to go on the investigation, and it was not until the investigation strategy was adjusted that it gradually improved.

The author analyzed that his research was targeted at the daily life and culture of local people, so he must adopt a conventional means to obtain the materials that he needed in the study. After that, the author changed the stereotyped image of investigators in the past, who would carry a bag with a notebook and a camera in the bag every day, just like a well-known journalist. Instead, he did not investigate for the sake of investigation at first and then attempted to get involved in the activities of the local people as an ordinary person. For instance, the author would learn to play mahjong and cards with the local people, and chat, drink, and work with them at will to make them feel that he is interested in their daily life.

But an action that plays a crucial role in the whole investigation process is that the author takes photos for the local elderly free of charge. At that time, the author would first tell some respondents the idea of taking pictures of the old free of charge, which was quickly spread among the elderly via these respondents. The idea was so useful that many older people took the initiative to come to the author for help. Therefore, the author took the opportunity to explain to them the purpose of the investigation and the great significance of the general knowledge in life that they had known to him. In this way, he could establish an interactive relationship with the elderly in a practical approach to obtain an understanding of the local people towards what the author did.

Then, both the elderly and the young cooperated with the author's work in the following procedures for investigation, such as interviews, household surveys, symposiums, questionnaire distribution, and so forth.

Some people even take the initiative to help the author pay attention to some activities in the village, to capture the information needed for the author in an investigation in time. Every time a family conducts a superstitious event (a local saying about folk religious activities), or a child of a family is engaged, or a family is prepared for a happy occasion (which means holding a banquet to celebrate some essential occasions in life, such as giving bath to the infant on its third day, grabbing test on the event of an infant's first birthday, and the older man's birthday), some people would come over to tell the author. In the later stage of the author's investigation, he lived a relatively happy and relaxed life, because the enthusiasm and generosity of the local people made the author establish a very friendly interpersonal relationship with them. Trying to make the local people understand the significance of the investigation is of great importance to carry out the field investigation, which allows them to dispel their misgivings and get so close with the author that they can keep no secrets from each other.

Chapter 2 Overview of Tancun Village

Holistic is a research tradition of anthropology. Especially for functionalists and structuralists, any culture is an integrated system. In the system, each cultural element is associated with the culture as a whole. As a result, when we intend to study and explain the culture of an ethnic group or a community, we must investigate the culture by placing it in a specific cultural entity, such as nature, history, custom, institution, and belief. Only in this way can we scientifically understand the culture and find the hidden meaning behind the ethnographic materials. Thus, it is the central position of field workers to put cultural research in a specific cultural situation. Generally speaking, the cultural context that constitutes a culture consists of geography, history, nature, environment, livelihood mode, lifestyle, as well as the cultural ecosystem that integrates a series of folk customs, religions, marriages, funerals, festivals, and recreational activities.

Section 1 Geography and History of Tancun Village

Tancun Village, a small village in the west of Shaoyang County, Hunan Province, is Tancun village is located in the transition zone from the Hengyang-Shaoyang Hilly Bathtub to the southwest edge. The east and west sides of the village are rolling hills, while the north-south range is a long and narrow bathtub. The village houses and main paddy fields are distributed in this bathtub. The northernmost end of the bathtub is the lower reaches of the Nanshui River. From the west to the east, the river flows into Shuangjiangkou, about 15km away, and merges with the Fuyi River, another river in the county, thus forming the Zijiang River, one of the four rivers in Hunan Province (generally speaking, the four rivers refer to Xiangjiang River, Zijiang River, Yuanjiang River, and Lishui River). Tancun Village is a typical rural area in the southwest part of Hunan Province. When people stand on the mountains, they can look far into the distance, where the hills are green, and the waters are beautiful, the fields are fertile, there are crisscross footpaths between fields, and the peaks are ready to dance, showing their unique and majestic appearance. Along the Nanshui River in the upper riches, the terrifying waves are about to break the banks on the dangerous shoal. Along the Zishui River in the lower reaches, the river is clear and continually flows down.

Nanshui River, known as Zishui River and Duliang River in the old records, originates from the west foot of Huangmajia, the highest peak of Qingjie Mountain, Ziyuan Township, Chengbu Miao Autonomous County. According to the Records of Mountains and Rivers of the Local Gazetteers of Baoqing Prefecture in the Daoguang Regime, Zishui River, also known as the Shijing River, Duliang River or Jishui River, originates from Maoping'ao. Besides, according to the Annals of Mountains and Rivers of the Local Gazetteers of Hubei and Hunan Provinces, it was recorded in the Geographic Atlas of Duliang River that the river originates from the southwest of the Wugang prefecture, merges with the Fuyi River, and then flows into the Dongting Lake via the border between Xinhua and Yiyang. Zijiang River is known as Haoshui River in Cihai (an encyclopedic dictionary first published in 1915, and frequently revised). According to the Cihai published in 1979, Haoshui River, the west origin of the Zishui River, is located in the southwest of Hunan Province. It originates from the north of Chengbu Miao Autonomous County, flows along the northeastern direction to Shaoyang County, and merges with the Fuyi River as the Zishui River.

As the map published in the 36th year of the Republic of China marked the west origin of Zishui River as Haoshui River, the west origin of Zishui River is defined as Haoshui River in Cihai. Now it is called Nanshui River, which was first seen in the data of water conservancy and transportation departments in the 1950s and 1960s. In 1982, the general survey of geographic names was carried out, and it was named as Nanshui River according to the statement of the water conservancy department, and it was recorded in the Encyclopaedic Dictionary of Geographical Names in the People's Republic of China.

The village belongs to Huangtingshi Town (formerly known as Wangting city) in terms of administrative division. Huangtingshi belonged to Wangtingtuan of Wugang prefecture in the Qing Dynasty and belonged to Weiyi Township of Wugang County during the Republic of China. After the founding of new China, it belonged to the 17th district of Shaoyang County. In 1952, it was established as Huangtingshi Town, under the jurisdiction of the 9th district of Shaoyang County. After the movement to form rural people's communes in 1958, it was divided into Shengli People's Commune, Huangtingshi People's Commune, and Jinfeng People's Commune. In 1965, the three people's communes were integrated into the Huangtingshi People's Commune. After the reform of the rural structure, it was changed into a township in 1984 and restored to Huangtingshi Town in 1985. At that time, it had jurisdiction over 13 villages and one neighborhood committee, including Huangtingshi (neighborhood committee), Chapu, Butian, Pingtang, Hongmiao Chong, Zanyang Bay, Shichong Yangjia, Zangtang Yangjia, Tancun Village, Matou, Zixi, Yousitang, Xintian and Zhushan Luojia.

In 1995, with the reform of township organizations, sub-county administrative offices were removed, and the townships were merged into a town. The current Huangtingshi Town merges the surrounding Yongxing Township and Shuangqing Township, with a total area of 134.82 square kilometers. It has jurisdiction over 40 villages and one neighborhood committee, with 544 village groups, a total of 16,089 households, 58,634 residents, and 3.64 persons per household on an average basis.

As the seat of town government to the south of Tancun Village, Huangtingshi is the largest traditional market town in the area. Huangtingshi was formally known as Wangting, Wangjia Tingzi, or Huangtingsi, while all of its names were labeled as the word "Ting" (kiosk in Chinese). In the old street of the market town, there was a kiosk completed in 1859, the ninth year of the Xiafeng Regime. The south gate of the kiosk faced the market, so the kiosk was named Huangtingshi (meaning a market in Huangting in Chinese).

Thus, it can be seen that the market town is indeed the place of the ancient post kiosk. In October 1423, the eleventh year of the Yongle Regime of the Ming Dynasty, Zhu Pian, the eighteenth son of Zhu Yuanzhang enfeoffed as the Prince of Min, moved from Yunnan Province to the Wugang Prefecture. The next year, he asked the servants to establish the palace, which was inherited for 14 generations, a total of 272 years. The Prince of Min in the past generations governed the Wugang Prefecture and organized the personnel to renovate and expand the postal kiosks in the towns on his feud for many times so as to welcome visitors and see them off. At that time, the postal kiosks in the towns had become the domestic kiosk of the Prince of Min. Therefore, it was known as Wangting (meaning the booth of the prince in Chinese) or Wangjia Tingzi (meaning the kiosk of the royal family in Chinese). After the collapse of the Ming Dynasty, Zhu Youlang, the descendant of the imperial family of the Ming Dynasty, proclaimed himself emperor with the reign title of Yongli, also known as the Regime of Southern Ming Dynasty.

In April 1671, the fourth year of the Shunzhi Regime of the Qing Dynasty and the first year of the Yongli Regime of the Southern Ming Dynasty, Zhu Youlang moved to Wugang and lived in the Palace of Prince of Min as the imperial palace. He renamed the Wugang Prefecture to Fengtian Prefecture. In the subsequent seesaw battles between the Regime of the Southern Ming Dynasty and the troops of the Qing Dynasty, Emperor Yongli repeatedly sought shelter in Wangting. Since the emperor lived there, there is no doubt that it is named as Huangting instead of the postal house. Later, with the rapid development of folk commerce and trade, the town became a market in the surroundings, and the market was named after the postal house, which was more familiar to people. Therefore, Huangtingshi, as the place name of the market town has been passed down among the people since then.

There is no clear historical record about the creation of the market town. According to legend, it was founded 500 years ago by a woman surnamed Xiao. The woman followed her husband, who was sent to the local official, and thus, she was far-sighted. However, unfortunately, her husband died early, so she had to go to her parents' home and live in widowhood. During her widowhood, she bought the barren land where the town is now located with all her savings, and then set up shops to revitalize the market there. It is said that she presided over the construction and donation of more than 360 shops in the town, and only received a little bit of land rent every year. When she died in her old age, in order to thank her for her kindness, the town people still sent some money and rice to the Xiao clan, where her parents' descendants lived at the end of each year according to the needs of the local middle-class family for one day. The custom lasted until the early years of the liberation of new China.

For this custom, the author was lucky to get the book Notes on Geomancy from Deng Xuqing, an intellectual in the town, as a textual evidence. The Notes on Geomancy was edited and copied by a Xiucai (one who passed the imperial examination at the county level) named

Deng Zanchi in Hongmiao Chong during the Guangxu Regime of the Qing Dynasty and passed down to the later generations.

According to the handwritten records of folk geomancy, it provides valuable historical materials that can prove the widow surnamed Xiao made painstaking efforts to choose a proper site for the town seat, revealing some clues about the difficulties of the town for about 500 years. Today, the dense wooden houses on both sides of the old block in the city and the narrow and long flagstone pavement in the middle seem to tell us how the town was prosperous at that time. In the classification of local people, the market is on the street of Huangtingshi Town, and the rural areas with a circumference of 15 kilometers are called the countryside. The road becomes the most important trading place in the area. The villagers trade their products of labor on the street in exchange for the means of life and production they need. The market opens every day on the street, but it is more crowded during the traditional festivals, attracting the surrounding villagers to go into the street to play, buy products, sell their products and meet their friends in groups.

Tancun Village is located half a kilometer north of the market. As shown in Figure 2.1, Tancun Village is an administrative village, which governs five natural villages, including Huangjia, Xiangche, Tanshan, Wanli, and Tiantang from the south to the north. The total population of the village is 2,234, including 1167 males and 1067 females, with a ratio of males to females of 109.3:100. There are 602 households with an average number of 3.7 persons per household. Except for only a few villagers who graduate from technical secondary schools and junior colleges and those army persons transferred to civilian work to obtain relatively formal jobs, the villagers in Tancun Village have been engaged in agriculture from generation to generation, while Tancun Village is a typical farming society in the southwest mountainous area of Hunan Province. The people tend to be attached to their native land and unwilling to leave it, so they rarely move to other places, thus developing into a relatively stable pattern of groups with specific consanguinity and geographical relationship.

However, since the implementation of reform and opening up, the movement of the population began to accelerate. Nowadays, the young adults and part of the middle-aged workers in the village are away from their hometown all the year round to earn money, which is changing the inherent livelihood mode of the people in Tancun Village, while their careers have been gradually diverging. Some young mothers even leave their babies to their parents and work in Guangdong, Jiangsu, and Zhejiang. The traditional parenting model is also quietly changing.

Tancun Village is mainly inhabited by the Deng clan and the Jiang clan, and the settlements of the two clans have relatively clear boundaries, either a field ridge or a stream, which is commonly known as Tanshan Baxi, formerly known as Wangting River. The Deng family is distributed in Huangjia and Tanshan, with a total population of 930, while the Jiang family is distributed in Xiangche, Wanli, and Tiantang, with a total population of 1,274. In addition,, there are some small families, including two households surnamed Yang with nine persons in total, one household surnamed Yi with five persons in total, three households surnamed Luo with 12 persons in total, and one household surnamed Wang with four persons in total, amounting to 30 persons in total. The Deng family and the Jiang family have been related to each other by marriage for generations, so they have been on good terms with each other. Moreover, there has been no fierce conflict among families in history. However, in the drought years, there would inevitably be some disputes among the families for the distribution of water resources. But these disputes are not so much because of consanguinity, but rather because of geographical relationship since the disputes mainly arise between natural villages. So even the people of the same clan living in different natural villages may encounter similar irrigation disputes.

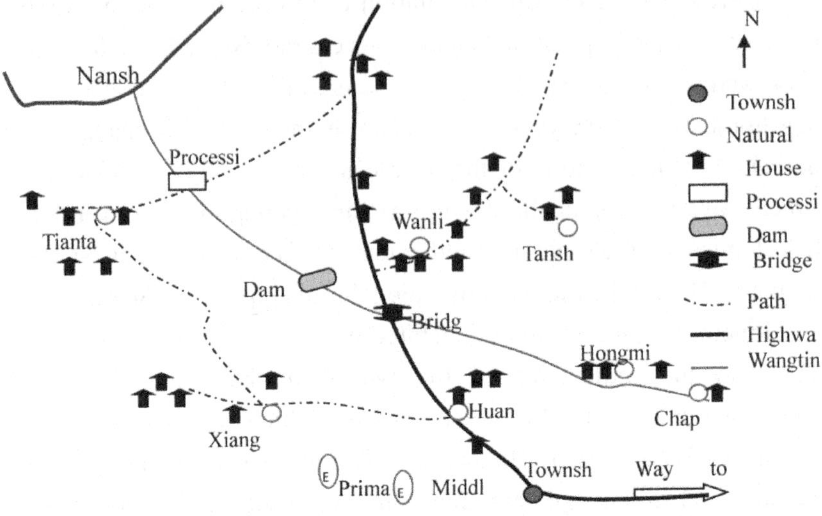

Figure 2.1 A sketch of the distribution of villages in Tancun Village

Like many villages in the south, Tancun Village is also inhabited by the clans in groups. As far as the whole administrative village is concerned, it is one of the villages inhabited by the families of different surnames, but each natural village has a single clan, while the small number of families with different surnames have moved here since the founding of new China in 1949. Tancun Village has a long history. According to the local historical documents and pedigrees of the clans, the Deng family and the Jiang family were both migrated from Jiangxi in the Ming Dynasty. According to the newly revised Pedigree of the Clan of Jiang, Wan Er Gong, and Wan San Gong, two ancestors of our clan, moved from the village in Zaohe Township, Taihe County, Ji'an Prefecture, Jiangxi Province to Shaoyang County in the east of Baoqing Prefecture, Hunan Province in 1369 (now in Shaoyang City and Shaodong County), the second year of the Hongwu Regime of the Ming Dynasty. After Wan Er Gong, Wan San Gong and Da Quan Gong became the first generation of ancestors, all the members of the Jiang clan in Shaoyang have integrated their pedigrees into one pedigree and returned to their original clan.

It has been 637 years since the ancestors first moved here. However, some of the descendants of the two ancestors of the Jiang clan who first came here to lay the foundation for later generations moved to Wugang (formerly known as Duliang), Guizhou, and Sichuan. In addition to some descendants of Wan Er Gong and Wan San Gong of the people of the Jiang clan who have been living in Shaoyang up to now, some descendants of Da Quan Gong, who immigrated in 1371, the fourth year of the Hongwu Regime of the Ming Dynasty, have lived here since then.

The branch of the Jiang clan who have moved to the current Tancun Village has a history of at least six hundred years since Ting Han Gong, the eighth son of Da Quan Gong, moved to Nipi Chong in the north of the stream of Wuyoudong Township (now Tancun Village) from Baoqing Prefecture (now Shaoyang City) in the last year of the Hongwu Regime. According to the elderly, Tancun Village was originally inhabited by the Liu family, the Huang family, and the He family. Up to now, there are many places named after these surnames, such as the Liujia Dam for the dam that irrigates half of the cultivated land in Tancun Village, the Liujia Mountain for the mountain behind Tiantang Village, as well as Huangjia Chong where the members of the Deng family have lived up to now. The number of immigrants from Jiangxi Province has been growing at a fast speed, while there are not so many indigenous residents who have lived here for generations, and it shows a declining trend. Some of the clans have even no offspring, and some have moved to other places to support themselves. Therefore, the old saying that no more members are born among the indigenous people still prevails in Tancun Village.

It can be seen from the preface of the Pedigree of Deng Clan that the Deng family in Huangtingshi regards Deng Yu, the Duke Gaomi of the Eastern Han Dynasty as the remote ancestor, Deng Helin in the Song Dynasty as the middle ancestor, and Deng Shi'an as the modern ancestor who first moved to Shaoyang. The remote and middle ancestors are just the imagination of the people of the local Deng family towards their ancestors, aiming to prove the orthodoxy of their identity as a distinguished family in Central Plains. However, after Deng Shi'an, who first moved to Shaoyang, there is a distinct family tree depicting the relationships among the ancestors for generations in the pedigree. Therefore, it is more reliable. During the Zhengtong Regime of the Ming Dynasty (1436-1449), Deng Shi'an moved to Huangtingshi, Wugang Prefecture, Hunan Province, because of his admiration for the scenic beauty of Nanyue Mountain, and the waterscape of Zishui River.

According to the elders of the Deng family, at that time, Deng Shi'an and his elder brother, Deng Shiji, moved from Taihe County, Ji'an Prefecture, Jiangxi Province, Deng Shiji settled in the current Longhui County, and Deng Shi'an settled in the current Shaoyang County (formerly under the jurisdiction of Wugang Prefecture). The two brothers changed their names to Shiji and Shi'an to commemorate their ancestral home, Ji'an Prefecture. However, Deng Shi'an didn't settle down in Tancun Village when he first came to Huangtingshi but settled down in Hongmiao Chong, Huangtingshi. In this regard, the eldest branch of the Deng clan in Huangtingshi lived in Hongmiao Chong.

As for why Deng Shi'an settled down in Hongmiao Chong, a geomantic legend goes among the local people. In that year, Deng Shi'an separated from Deng Shiji and came to Hongmiao Chong. Standing between the fields, he took a glance at the towering Yangwu Ridge on the left, and the high and steep Kunlun Mountain, where the peaks rise one after another. Furthermore, he saw the Wangting River flowing between the peaks. Hongmiao Chong is a long and narrow stretch of flatland surrounded by rivers and mountains. Deng Shi'an said that it is bound to give birth to great men in a remarkable place. So, he chose to settle down in Hongmiao Chong. So since ancient times, people in Huangtingshi have said that the location was so beneficial for the development of the Deng family that many intellectuals arose there. The members of the Deng family used to take pride in it, saying that many of their ancestors succeeded in the imperial examinations at the provincial level and in the highest imperial examinations. According to the pedigree of the clan, 52 scholars of the Deng family lived on government grants and passed the imperial examinations at the county level or higher since the Ming Dynasty, among whom three succeeded in the highest imperial examinations and one succeeded in the imperial examinations at the provincial level. Deng Shitang, who won second place in the imperial examinations at the provincial level in 1882 during the Guangxu Regime, is still regarded as a model for people to encourage their children to study hard.

And the Deng family moved to Tancun Village years later. It was not until the Qianlong Regime of the Qing Dynasty that Deng Yuanxuan, the 12th generation descendant of Deng Shi'an, moved from Hongmiao Chong to Tancun Village. According to legend, Deng Yuanxuan was born in a low-income family and got married to a woman surnamed Jiang, who came from the Jiang family in the Xiangche Village across the current Huangjia Village, marking the beginning of the connection between the Jiang family and the Deng family by marriage. At that time, Deng Yuanxuan moved to Tancun Village as a helper of his father-in-law's home. However, with the help of the Jiang family, Deng Yuanxuan's family began to prosper, and the number of family members increased gradually. With the growing economic strength, he asked his three brothers of the branch of the Deng family living in Hongmiao Chong to settle down in Tancun Village, and soon opened Huangjia Village and Tanshan Village. Because of the intermarriage relationship between the Deng family and the Jiang family in history, the two families have been able to get along well with each other in the long and narrow living space of Tancun Village.

After the founding of new China in 1949, the villagers of Tancun Village also devoted themselves to the socialist revolution and socialist construction in full swing. From 1952, with the successful completion of the land reform, Tancun Village, like other places in Shaoyang, carried out the movement of agricultural cooperation. It has gone through three stages from the mutual-aid team to the elementary agricultural producers' cooperative with semi-socialist characteristics, and then to the advanced agricultural producers' cooperative with fully socialist characteristics. By the end of 1956, it had completed the socialist transformation of agriculture.

On March 29, 1952, according to the Resolution of the CPC Central Committee on Mutual Aid and Cooperation of Agricultural Production (Draft) promulgated in December 1951, the people's Government of Hunan Province issued the Instructions on Promoting Mutual Aid in Work and Strengthening Organization, calling for the universal implementation of various mutual-aid forms in the rural areas of Hunan Province, such as the exchange of work points, help in farm work and work exchange between man and livestock. The mutual aid team is divided into the temporary mutual aid team and the permanent mutual aid team. The so-called temporary mutual aid team refers to the temporary transfer or exchange of work among the farmers during the production and labor work, while the farmers help each other during the busy season and engage in their farm work during the slack season. The permanent mutual aid team is a team of farmers that work together all year round with reasonable division of labor, simple production plans, a set of institutions, and a small number of accumulated public funds. Tancun Village is one of the first batches of villages that established the mutual-aid team for agricultural production in Shaoyang County.

In the spring of 1953, the government of Shaoyang County began to deploy the work of elementary agricultural producers' cooperative and held a series of training courses for a cooperative backbone. Six villages of Tancun Village took part in the training course in succession. The training courses for cooperative backbone were also offered in Huangtingshui District by which Tancun Village was governed. By early 1954, the movement of elementary agricultural production cooperation had been gradually implemented in a wide range in Tancun Village. In that year's spring plowing production, the villagers gave full play to the strength of the cooperative as a collective, implemented unified management and unified allocation of human resources and organized the production on schedule, so that a few farmers around who did not join in the cooperative took an active part in the movement of cooperation. In the elementary agricultural producers' cooperative, the members of the cooperative take private land as shares, conduct unified management, receive dividends in proportion to their land, and distribute the dividends based on labor. As for the distribution of dividends, some are based on the standard of 40 % for land and 60 % for labor work, while some are based on 50 % for land and 50 % for labor work.

In the winter of 1955, Tancun Village began to set up the advanced agricultural producers' cooperative, which incorporated all means of production, such as land, mountain forest, water pond, cattle, and farm tools, and canceled land dividend, implemented the method of distribution based on labor, accompanied by a large number of accumulated funds. Although farmers organize the advanced agricultural producers' cooperative voluntarily, it is still based on the natural villages where people live together. Most of the members who participate in the same advanced agricultural producers' cooperative are the relatives of the same clan. With a strong sense of family and belonging to the clan, the members can consciously help each other and trust each other in the process of production and labor, and constantly enhance internal unity and cohesion of the cooperative. Therefore, the advanced agricultural producers' cooperative played a positive role in the production and life of the villagers of Tancun Village at that time, and it allowed them to give play to the collective force to resist natural disasters, carry out basic reconstruction of farmland centered on water conservancy construction, and improve production conditions.

In 1954, Shaoyang County suffered a rare drought in one hundred years. The villagers of Tancun Village organized the members to successfully defeat the drought through the collective strength of the advanced agricultural producers' cooperative, which greatly reduced the loss arising from the disaster. At the same time, through the cooperative movement, it rapidly popularized advanced agricultural technology and promoted members to accept advanced experience in agricultural production consciously. For instance, the cooperative adopted the method of seed sorting by saltwater, deep plowing and intensive cultivation, even and compact planting and other advanced farming systems. In the spring of 1956, double cropping rice was cultivated in all the farmland, which greatly increased the yield of rice, and greatly improved the living standards of the members of the cooperative.

However, in the era of the planned economy, the villagers of Tancun Village had been living in poverty, and most of the families used to be worried about what to eat and wear. This situation did not change until the implementation of the household contract responsibility system after the reform and opening up. In May 1982, the villagers of Tancun Village contracted all the farmland to all households under the deployment of the local government. According to their recollection, the greet shoots of grains were distributed into the households at that time. From the second year of the distribution, agriculture had a good harvest year by year, and many families could resolve their food problems. Almost all the existing red tile-roofed houses were built after the implementation of the household contract responsibility system. But in a word, until the 1980s, Tancun Village was still relatively poor, because the local land resources were so limited that it could only allow the villagers to support their families. It was not until the 1990s that the economic situation of Tancun Village was fundamentally improved as a large number of rural workers went out to make money.

Section 2 Natural Environment of Tancun Village

Tancun Village, located in the branch of Yuecheng Mountains, is hilly and mountainous. As the saying goes, 50 % of the village is covered by mountains, the waters cover 5 %, 30 % is by the cultivated land, and the roads and houses cover the last 15 %. The hills are usually arc-shaped and round, mostly in the shape of steamed bun. The earth's surface is fragmented with many valleys. "The relative altitude of the peaks is mostly 60-150m, with a slope of 15 °C - 20 °C. Most of the peaks are composed of the Permian and Triassic sand shale rocks, with thick weathered crust and good soil quality (Editorial Committee on Shaoyang County Annals, 1993)." Moreover, there are lots of camellia oil trees and a large forest of pines, fir, and bushes. The slopes of the rolling peaks are developed into dry land by the villagers, which can grow dry grain crops and other industrial crops.

Yangwu Mountains, located in the southeast of the village, is well-known in Shaoyang County. On the one hand, the peaks are high with a beautiful view, and the highest peak is at an elevation of 511.9 m. In the past, there were green pines and verdant bamboos, where birds sang, and flowers gave forth their fragrance. On the other hand, the main reason is that the Yangwu Mountain built on the ridge has a long history with an endless stream of pilgrims. It echoed Liu Yuxi's lines of An Eulogium on A Humble Cell that a mountain needn't be high; It is famous so long as there is a deity on it.

In 1370, the third year of the Hongwu Regime of the Ming Dynasty, there were two temples on the top of the mountain. In 1672, the 11th year of the Kangxi Regime of the Qing Dynasty, more than a thousand statues of Buddha were made, with an iron stove for burning paper to the dead at a weight of 1,500 kg, a drum that can be heard within 10 km and a bell that can be heard within 15 km (Editorial Committee on Shaoyang County Annals, 1993). Elegant temples and clouds like the fairyland attracted numerous men of literature and writing to ascend the mountains, and then most of them wrote poems to praise the beautiful scenery. Lv Dianzhang, a poet in the Qing Dynasty, wrote in the poem Ascending Yangwu Mountains that "Thousands of ravines and mountains are broken and connected, and one peak is towering towards the clouds; The path is winding and dangling, the cliff is steep, and the man ascends the highest of the heaven like a roc (Records of Literature and Art of the Local Gazetteer of Wugang Prefecture during the Guangxu Regime)."

Here there are four distinct seasons, with an annual average temperature of around 16. 8°C. The hottest time of the year is July, and the extremely high temperature may be as high as 40. 1°C. Of course, there are not so many days at such a high temperature, while the temperature is about 35°C for only 22 to 25 days a year. The coldest month in the year is January, while the extremely low temperature may be less than or equal to zero. And it may snow in as many as fifteen days. But in recent years, under the influence of global warming, there are merely three or five days with snow in a year. There is abundant rainfall here, with annual average rainfall in the county of 1,255.3 mm, a maximum of 1,641.7 mm, and a minimum of 914.4 mm. The average number of rainy days is 161.8 days. The rainy days are mostly distributed from March to June, accounting for 41.5 % of the total rainfall of the whole year. In this regard, these months are also known as the plum rain season (Editorial Committee on Shaoyang County Annals, 1993).

Suitable temperature and abundant rainfall provide sufficient natural conditions for the development of the local rice-planting economy. The primary grain crop in Tancun Village is rice. Before the 1990s, the farmers had been growing the double-cropping rice. In the middle and last ten days of June of the lunar calendar, it is the rush season to harvest the early season rice and plant the late rice. At the busiest time of the year, the elderly, children, and even those working outside have to return to participate in farming as long as they have free time. As the saying goes, an eight-year-old grandmother is busy with the farm work, and even a three-year-old child has to be busy in the fields. It has manifested the busy scene during this period. Now, an overwhelming majority of the farmers grow the single cropping rice, because of the improvement of the economic situation, as well as a large number of young and middle-aged labor force going out to work and the decrease of the agricultural labor population.

Tancun Village is located at the lowest point of the Nipi Chong (The local people call the narrow valley between the two hills as Chong, and Nipi Chong is about 15 kilometers long from its starting point Chapu Village to Tancun Village) in Huangtingshi Town. The Wangting River originates from Chapu Village 15 kilometers away and flows down. Although the surface of the river is not wide, the flow of water is rapid. Tancun Village is located at the confluence of the Wangting River and Nanshui River. The Wangting River never runs dry all year round and has sufficient water, thus providing good water conservancy conditions for agricultural irrigation in Tancun Village and nourishing their land. However, due to the special location of the confluence, it tends to threaten the survival of the villagers of Tancun Village.

It is said that eight immortals travel to the cliff beside the Nanshui River, leaving eight figures here. Besides, because of the roundabout and deep water bottom of the Nanshui River, it is called the Eight Immortals Pool. According to the local older adults, when their ancestors first moved here, there were frequent floods. It was said that a dragon demon lived at the bottom of the Eight Immortals Pool and would come out to make some trouble every year. Later, Jiang Fayu, the sixth-generation descendant of the Jiang family, went to other places to study magic arts to eradicate the dragon demon and came back home three years later when he managed to learn the magic arts. That summer, the dragon demon came out to make trouble again. Jiang Fayu threw his robe into the Nanshui River and bound the dragon demon. Then, the people used a total of eighty-one big iron pots to press the dragon demon too heavily to move. Finally, Jiang Fayu practiced magic to press another mountain on the dragon demon, thus eliminating the floods.

Up to now, the mountain is like an iron pot upended on the ground, which is known as Yangming Mountain by local people, because Jiang

Fayu conquered the dragon demon and made a name for the Jiang family. As a result, Jiang Fayu has become one of the venerable masters that must be invited to practice magic among the local Taoists, masters, Meishan religious sects, and all those who know the sorcery. In history, there is indeed such a person named Jiang Fayu who learned magic arts. But the myth about his power and the legend of Jiang Fayu conquering the dragon demon is a kind of affiliation of the members of the Jiang family. It can also be said to be a myth built by the branch of the Jiang family who immigrated from Jiangxi Province to prove their historical achievements in opening up the living space, conquering nature, and eliminating disasters.

In reality, Tancun Village failed to eliminate the flood because of Jiang Fayu, a man of extraordinary power in history. According to the memory of some older adults, the pedigree and the notes of local literati, since the first year of the Republic of China, a total of 14 serious floods took place in Tancun Village, roughly in 1911, 1914, 1917, 1924, 1926, 1947, 1949, 1954, 1968, 1979, 1982, 1995, 1998 and 2001, respectively, among which seven floods broke out during the Republic of China and seven broke out after the founding of new China. According to an inscription in the village, the most serious flood disaster should be the flood in 1924, the 13th year of the Republic of China, as it was carved on the stone tablet that "A flood came to Tancun Village in 1924." According to the location of the stone tablet, the flood could inundate half of the houses and two-thirds of the cultivated land in Tancun Village.

The main reason for the vulnerability of Tancun Village to flood lies in the local landform and topography. First of all, when Nanshui River flows through the Tancun Village, it makes a big turn suddenly along the mountain, and the water flows in a circuitous way. Therefore, when there is a rainstorm in summer, the river easily floods. Secondly, because Tancun Village is at the valley bottom, it is known as Chongchong by the local people. There are continuous hills and mountains on both sides. When there is a rainstorm, the flood with silt will naturally rush to the farmland of the valley. Thirdly, the Wangting

River has a shallow bed and a narrow waterway, and the current is swift. The place where it enters the river is just the big circuitous position of the Nanshui River. Therefore, once the rainstorm occurs, the water flow is easily blocked in the estuary, leading to a flood. After the founding of the People's Republic of China, the government built two dams at the place where the Wangting River ran, coupled with the original Liujia Dam, and built a small factory integrating hydroelectric power generation and agricultural products processing at the place where the Wangting River of Tancun Village flowed into the Nanshui River. Since then, frequent floods have been fundamentally under control.

Section 3 Social Economy of Tancun Village

Tancun Village is a typical agricultural community where villagers have been making a living by agriculture for generations. However, due to the dense population and the small cultivated area per capita, villagers could only provide for themselves by farming. Taking the survey data of Tiantang natural village as an example, the paddy field area per capita is only 0.5 mu (1 mu = 0.0667 hectares), while the area of the upland field per capita is 0.2 mu, and the area of the dry soil is 0.4 mu. In the case of a famine year, it would be impossible for an ordinary family to stay alive. In the period of collectivization before the reform and opening up, local people used to worry about their food and clothing. Sweet potato, potato, melon, and vegetables were their primary food to make up for the serious shortage of rice. Even a coat or a pair of trousers can be even dressed by several persons from the eldest child to the second eldest child and finally to the youngest child. Therefore, it conforms to the saying that new clothes can be worn for three years, old clothes can be worn for another three years, and the sewed old clothes can be worn for another three years.

Rice planting is the most important agricultural activity in the region. In the past, villagers usually planted double-cropping rice. The annual gross yield per unit area of the double-cropping rice was about 650 to 700kg. But in recent years, single cropping rice has been planted in the region. And with the improvement of hybrid rice technology, the yield per unit area can generally reach about 450 to 500kg. The output of a large number of labor services not only reduces the tension between population and land but also rapidly alleviates the poverty of local people and then improves their standards of living. Because of the great achievements of reform and opening up, China's rural areas have been generally brought into a well-off society with prosperous markets and abundant products. It is also true for Tancun Village. Farmers can have access to sufficient and diversified food resources, and their dilemma of not having a full meal of cooked rice in the era of the planned economy is gone forever.

The yield of rice increases and farmers receive more income, while the amount of consumption is decreasing, so the vast majority of households have more surplus grain. People no longer measure the wealth of a family by the amount of grain in stock. And then the farmers' enthusiasm for growing grains has been much weaker than before. A large amount of paddy land has been used for other purposes or even lies waste. Moreover, the farmers have much looser dependence on the fields. Coupled with the low price of agricultural products, they can not even find the value of the fields. In this regard, it has become extremely common to rent the farmland at a low price. In 2007, a young man named Rong Hua rented more than 50 mu of paddy field to plant medicinal materials, and the rent was only 120 Yuan per mu. Besides, many rural families do not have enough young workers caused by the output of labor. The older people who stay at home are unable to cultivate the land. To avoid the land becoming barren, they tend to rent the fields to those families with plenty of workers free of rental.

The main industrial crops around Tancun Village are peanuts and camellia oil. However, due to the small per capita land area, peanuts and camellia oil could not produce much extra economic income except for self-sufficiency. If the local people wanted to plant more peanut and oil-team camellia trees, they had to reclaim the vacant land in the oil-team camellia hill, while the large area of the reclaimed vacant land on the oil-team camellia hill was planted with peanuts and peppers, which to some extent alleviated the pressure of land shortage. Oil-tea camellia trees are evergreen and wild fruit trees, which are grown all over the hills in the whole county. Original camellia oil with excellent quality can be pressed out from its seeds. According to the old custom, it is time to pick the oil-tea camellia fruits three days before the Cold Dew (17th solar term in China) every year. At that time, all the families will get up early and have breakfast before dawn, and then rush to the hills to pick the fruits.

As the oil-team camellia trees are uncultivated, each fruit-bearing forest has been contracted to each household, but the mature oil-tea camellia fruits that fail to be picked and carried to the home in time are bound to be stolen by others. It is also known as rush harvest by the local people, which can more aptly describe the busy scene of everyone competing against time in the harvest season of picking oil-team camellia fruits. Camellia oil extracted from oil tea camellia fruit is clear and tastes good. It is the first-class natural vegetable oil. In addition to the need for the cooking of the farmers themselves, some camellia oil can also be sold to foreign purchasers, who will sell the oil in other places. An ordinary family can sell 10 to 20 kg of camellia oil every year. Based on the purchase price of 44 Yuan per kg, a family can earn an income ranging from 440 to 880 Yuan every year.

Other agricultural products are mainly wheat, rapeseed, corn, potatoes, sweet potatoes, melons, fruits, and vegetables, which can support the farmers themselves, as well as be carried to the streets of Huangtingshi for trading. The farmers who engage in agriculture at home may also raise some pigs, chickens, ducks, geese, and other livestock. The prosperity of livestock and poultry, on the one hand, can improve the life of farmers, but on the other hand, it is also a critical source of income for a family. The local people have been accustomed to butchering pigs before the Spring Festival. The bacon, which is made of the pork hung on the stove and smoked with firewood, is a well-known specialty food in China.

The author conducted a simple sampling survey on the sales of several major local agricultural products in 2007, involving a total of 30 households with 111 residents. The results are shown in Table 1.1.

Table 1.1 Sales of major agricultural products

	Rice	Peanut	camellia oil	Pork	Rice	Sweet potato	Soybean	Vegetables
Quantity (kg)	4,064	2,865	416	2,348	720	83	135	5,233
Amount (Yuan)	5,689.6	9,120	18,304	11,035.6	1,008	116	378	4,481
Per capita (Yuan)	51.3	82.2	164.9	99.4	9.1	1.1	3.4	40.4

(Data source: It is the result of the household survey.)

It can be seen from the above table that in Tancun Village, the sales income per capita relying on pure agricultural production is 451.8 Yuan, which may be the amount of money equivalent to the value of the remaining agricultural products for the farmers after a year of hard work, except for their consumption. Thus, it can be seen that there is little chance that a surplus is available for the economic income of a household that is purely engaged in agriculture after the deduction of the family expenses. It means that if a family doesn't go out to work and obtain the economic income input, the family must be the poorest in the village.

From the overall situation of Huangtingshi Town, where Tancun Village is located, it also basically reflects the fact that the local economy improved with the growing number of migrant workers in the late 1980s. The following is the per capita net income of farmers from 1978 to 2002: 106 Yuan in 1978, 326 Yuan in 1983, 625 Yuan in 1988, 856 Yuan in 1993, 1,235 Yuan in 1998, and 1,568yuan in 2002 (Deng and Xiao). Since 1988, the per capita income has increased significantly. There is no doubt that it has something to do with the increase in the price of agricultural products and the improvement of agricultural production capacity, but the main reason is the increase in family income caused by the emergence of a large number of migrant workers.

Especially in recent years, almost all the young people and a considerable number of middle-aged people in the region go to the eastern coastal areas of Guangdong Province, and the income of these migrant workers has become the primary source of income for most families. In the survey, when asked about the income of the family, the respondents almost unanimously replied, "it mainly depended on our children working outside." Generally speaking, the families that have more persons working outside can live a better-off life. Since the 1990s, the migrant workers in the village have made primary financial contributions to the construction of most new buildings in Tancun Village. Generally, the monthly income of migrant workers is 800 to 1,500 Yuan, and the monthly income of a small number of people who work as executives in private enterprises or those who engage in technical work can reach 2,000 to 3,000 Yuan. However, there are only a few people that can earn such a high income. Even when they earn 800 Yuan a month, it is much higher than that of those who are completely engaged in agricultural work.

Deng Siping, who works in Shenzhen Youbang Factory, said to the author, "When I lie in bed at night, looking at every piece of furniture in the room, and staring at the floor and the wall, I think that Shenzhen Youbang Factory gives every brick and every piece of furniture in my house. Now all four members of our family work in the Factory. I sometimes worry about how I can support my family if the factory closes down one day." From his conversation, we can see the work is extremely important for the family to support itself. Despite various hardships at work, they are grateful to the coastal factories that allow them to work for money from the bottom of their hearts.

Therefore, on the one hand, we can see migrant workers leaving their hometown to work. They are the marginal persons of the city and at the bottom of society. And migrant workers have been a serious social problem in China at the present stage. On the other hand, we can see that almost all the people who come back from working outside agree with the jobs created for them in the coastal areas, and cherish their jobs very much. Just as He Qinglian described the positive effects of the tide of migrant workers in his book The Trap of Modernization, "The flow of rural labor is conducive to economic development and social progress. For the areas where the labor is output, it increases the income of farmers, and improves the level of their consumption and enhances the social purchasing power of the rural areas. As the saying goes, if one member of a family leaves home for work, his family, relatives and those around will be lifted out of poverty. Part of the rural labor force is transferred to non-agricultural areas so that the other part of the agricultural labor force that stays in the rural areas are able to access more agriculture resources (He, 1998)."

The money sent back by migrant workers not only increases the income of each family but also promotes the development of the local economy and society. Some people who have earned a sufficient amount of money by working in Shenzhen will return to their hometowns to invest in enterprises to provide some jobs for the farmers who are too old to go out to work. For instance, a group of young people who returned to the village after working outside for several years ran a river sand farm by the Nanshui River, where the workers could earn 22 - 25 Yuan a day. In 2007, several young people returned to the village and ran a firecracker factory with an investment of more than 200,000 Yuan, and they recruited nearly 100 employees, whose monthly salary could reach 1,200 Yuan. Tancun Village is rich in manganese ore resources, attracting local people for investment and development. At present, two small manganese mines have been registered, one of which is funded by some people in the neighboring villages who have returned after working outside for several years. In a word, rural migrant economy (Zhou, 2006) not only alleviated the poverty of the families in rural areas and boosted the development of society, but also revitalized the regional economy of Tancun Village.

Section 4 Cultural Ecosystem of Child Rearing

Anthropologists believe that things are interrelated. To carry out the ethnographic field survey of a small community, we should not only understand the meaning of its culture from the perspective of the natural environment but also put it into the social and cultural tradition. Only in this way can we not only know how it is but also understand why it is. According to the anthropological theory of cultural integration, a culture is a set of value matrixes with internal elements connected with each other, a set of means to understand and organize people's activities, and it is a basic standpoint of ethnography research to emphasize the correlation between various elements in a culture. Based on the ethnographic survey of the child rearing system in Tancun Village, we can see that the natural environment and cultural environment of Tancun Village are the cultural soil of its child rearing customs, constituting the cultural ecosystem of inheritance and transformation of the child rearing system for the villagers of Tancun Village. In the view of cultural anthropologists, the so-called cultural ecosystem generally refers to the unity composed of various cultural elements, such as the mode of production, lifestyle, customs and habits of specific or multi-ethnic groups in a certain region, while the unity is not only the outcome of the human beings' transformation of nature, adaptation to nature, and harmonious coexistence with nature, but also the result of human beings' handling of the relationship between man and man, between man and nature. To have a correct understanding of the child rearing system in Tancun Village in the overall context of culture, we need to first describe its cultural ecosystem before the formal exploration into the child rearing system in the village.

Folk Entertainment and Drama in Tancun Village

In the past, the main form of entertainment in the local area was watching plays. Flower-drum opera, puppet show, glove puppetry, Yugu (a percussion instrument made of bamboo, used to accompany the chanting of folk tales), sending the God of Wealth back and Lian Hua

Lao (one of folk art forms when blind artists made begging in ancient China) used to prevail in Tancun Village.

Glove puppetry, also known as finger puppetry, is a unique folk singing art in Shaoyang. In 1956, Liu Henggui, an entertainer in Shaoyang County, played a glove puppetry program Yang Xiao Fights the Tiger in the joint performance of folk literature and arts in Hunan Province. Then, he was recruited by Hunan Shadow Puppet Troupe and performed with the troupe in Europe, Southeast Asia, and other places. During the Cultural Revolution, glove puppetry shows were completely forbidden, and it was gradually restored after the 1980s, but only a few of the surviving old artists managed to perform on the stage with difficulty.

Yugu is also a popular folk drama form with local characteristics in Shaoyang. In the past, the villagers of Tancun Village used to invite Yugu artists to perform at any wedding or funeral, as long as economic conditions permit. A Yugu show consists of singing and accompanying, and usually, only two or three actors are required. A performer tends to play several roles in one show. The scripts are all stories about gifted scholars and beautiful ladies, or the heroes who get rid of the cruel and pacify the good people, or those who show excellent filial piety, or the scholars who passed the imperial examinations. But the tales are extremely close to the reality of people's lives and social expectations. Moreover, these tales are simple in plot and popular in the description, and they are completely performed in the local language, without any made-up literary scenes. Such rough and open folk art form not only brings the enjoyment of beauty to the daily life of the common people, helps them alleviate the pressure in their lives, but also becomes an important means for the common people to place their social ideals, promote social morality, and educate children and young people.

Sending the God of Wealth Back and Lian Hua Lao, which used to be like begging cultural behaviors in the past, can be regarded as a special begging culture. They mostly refer to the act that the performers sing and perform from door to door around the Spring Festival to get other people's alms. Furthermore, Sending the God of Wealth Back and

Lian Hua Lao are mostly held in festivals, especially during the Spring Festival. In the Spring Festival, every family has prepared a wealth of goods for the festival. In addition, Chinese people tend to do everything for luck during the Spring Festival, so the artists for Sending the God of Wealth Back and Lian Hua Lao are more likely to win the sympathy and generosity of the people when they perform during the Spring Festival. Every time they enter a house, they should not only play the Lian Hua Lao, and sing a song of blessing to please the host, but also present a New Year picture of the God of Wealth, which symbolizes that they have sent wealth to the host. It is said to be able to drive out evil spirits.

The most famous folk drama in Shaoyang is the flower-drum opera. In the county, Dongtian Chong in Jiugongqiao Town was known as the home of the flower-drum opera. The flower-drum opera in Shaoyang County is dominated by Nanlu Huagu, which is a semi-professional opera troupe that is gradually developed from a temporary opera troupe. In Tancun Village, the older people can mostly hum one or two flower-drum operas, and the CDs sold in the town's video shops also attract the older people to buy CDs with the flower-drum operas. The main traditional operas in the region include Shoot the Birds, Pair Up, Grind Soya Beans, Ask for Fees, Wang Laohu Snatches a Bride, Taoyuan Cave, Woodcutter Liu Hai, as well as the modern opera Play the Gong and Tinker the Pan, which have become the well-known flower-drum operas among the local people.

Since the founding of the People's Republic of China, the flower-drum opera has not been excluded by class struggle and ideology and has always been one of the major programs in the amateur literary and art performances among the masses. In the Mao Zedong era, it also served as the main propaganda tool of the rural propaganda team. In the 1990s, the Flower Drum Opera Troupe was officially established in Huangtingshi Town, where Tancun Village is located, becoming a profit-making and semi-professional folk flower-drum opera performance group. The troupe participated in various celebrations and ceremonies held in rural weddings or funerals. Especially in the funeral events, the flower-drum opera became an important folk event for local people to hold the funerals. If an older man dies, his family must invite the Flower Drum Opera Troupe to perform various programs. Otherwise, the bereaved will be considered the most disgraced in front of the local people.

In the local region, every clan has its folk band to teach the performance of traditional percussion music and Suona (a traditional woodwind instrument in China) and other wind music, which is mainly to cope with the weddings or funerals in rural areas. In 1994, the Western brass band appeared in Huangtingshi Town, and some families purchased a set of modern audio equipment, and thus the brass band with the modern audio equipment became the most t lively performance form in the local weddings or funerals. They mainly sing some popular songs with some traditional operas, such as singing the flower-drum operas and Yugu and making some songs and dances by themselves. In the funeral ceremony, to please the bereaved family and express their mourning for the dead, they also compiled some mourning songs, which were affectionate, extremely touching and tearful. Such a modern band usually consists of about ten performers, who are engaged in their own business at ordinary times. They will gather for the time being in case of a performance event, or they will gather together for rehearsal when they are at leisure. They usually charge employers 400-800 Yuan for each performance. In recent years, a group of the waist drum team composed of middle-aged and older women has appeared in the town, which has also added new colors to various ritual activities.

Folk recreational activities, operas, and quyi (Chinese folk art forms, including ballad singing, storytelling, comic dialogues, clapper talks, cross talks, etc.) are twin sisters of traditional ritual performance. Even for anthropologists, "rite is a kind of performance or cultural drama. Sir James George Frazer and other scholars of the Cambridge school in the 19th century believed that ancient Greek Tragedy, as well as the western drama derived from it, originated from ritual (Bowie, 2004)." Edward Burnett Tylor, a rationalist scholar, Émile Durkheim, a symbolist scholar, and Clifford Geertz, an interpretive scholar, all believe that there is no fixed, static, and distinct boundary between drama and ritual.

In the description of the rituals on the Bali Island, Clifford Geertz did not use the concept of ritual, but directly called a dramatic cultural performance, believing that the content of this performance is a ritual struggle. Clifford Geertz also replaced the dramatic cultural performance with drama and allowed us to see the scene of the drama, the role of actors, and the aesthetic effect of the drama. As for the connotation of the concept of "drama," he used, “For Balinese people, this kind of drama is not only a scene to watch, but also a ritual to perform. Here, there is no aesthetic gap between the actors and the audience, and the plot is not put in a state of vision and emptiness; by the end of the all-round fight between Rhonda (the terrible Witch) and Baron (the lovely monster), a majority, or nearly all, of the participants will be fully involved. According to the author's statistics on an example provided by Bello, sometimes a total of more than 75 performers of all ages and both sexes are involved in the drama, while it is common that thirty to forty people participated in the drama. As a type of performance, such a drama is not like the performance A Taste for Death, but like holding a grand Mass, which is to get gradually involved, not to look on and do nothing (Geertz, 1999).” From this concept, ritual and drama coincide. That is to say, in a specific space-time environment, drama and ritual can be converted to each other, and with the help of the ritual activities, drama can be repeatedly inherited and developed.

In Tancun Village, various rituals of weddings or funerals, whether it is traditional folk dramas or modern bands, all of these rural dramas embody the double meanings of the anthropological concept of drama, one is artistic performance, the other is social performance, while one is aesthetic significance, and the other is anthropological significance. In the same way, starting from the concept of performance, rituals also have the double meanings, one is ritual performance, and the other is drama performance, while one is anthropological significance, and the other is aesthetic significance.

From the description of the community history of Tancun Village, we can see that after a series of revolutionary movements since the founding of the People's Republic of China, especially the rapid development of modernization since the reform and opening up, lots of traditional folk dramas have died out in Tancun Village, and have been replaced by the modern cultural system with the television and films as the primary entertainment media. But it does not mean that there is no living space for traditional folk drama, including entertainment activities. It is precisely because the traditional folk drama is closely bound up with the rituals and lives of the local weddings or funerals, and is an integral part of the rituals activities. Moreover, traditional folk drama still shows tenacious vitality in modern times.

Festivals and Time System

The festival is the day set up by the folk according to a certain agricultural calendar, which appears in cycles and involves a specific meaning. Tancun Village is a typical agricultural community, where the traditional festivals and time system are formulated according to the lunar calendar in China. The concept of time in the lunar calendar represents the change of phenology. From the experience of production and life, people summed up the twenty-four moments of phenology change, so a year is divided into twenty-four solar terms (a day marking one of the 24 divisions of the solar year in the traditional Chinese calendar), each of which reflects the phenological characteristics of that period. According to the change of solar terms, people can decide when to sow seeds, when to transplant rice seedlings, and when and what crops to plant.

There are many festivals in various regions in China, according to the farming season. In Tancun Village, the important festivals valued by the villagers mainly include the Spring Festival, the Tomb Sweeping Day, the Dragon Boat Festival, the Mid-Autumn Festival and the Mid-July Days that is also known as the Ghost Festival, etc.

The Spring Festival is the grandest among the festivals in a year in China. From the beginning of the 12th month of the lunar calendar, people start to make preparations for the Spring Festival, including steaming wine, boiling sugar, smoking the meatballs and meat, purchasing furniture, buying new clothes, and new quilt, and buying fireworks and candies. There is a local song about purchasing the foods for the Spring Festival:

On the 21st day, do not worry;
On the 22nd day, go to the market;
On the 23rd day, buy the radish;
On the 24th day, offer sacrifices to the Kitchen God;
On the 25th day, grind tofu;
On the 26th day, butcher the pig;
On the 27th day, kill the capon;
On the 28th day, make Ciba (a traditional glutinous rice cake in China);
On the 29th day, prepare everything;
On New Year's Eve, eat the chicken drumsticks.

It should be the time for the Spring Festival since New Year's Eve. The villagers will have a year-end dinner on the 30th day of the 12th lunar month as the New Year's Eve and the first day of the first lunar month as the lunar New Year's Day, which means that the villagers should have breakfast before dawn on the two days. For the local people, they spend the Spring Festival on the 30th day of the 12th lunar month and the first day of the first lunar month. For the sake of good luck in the next year, the villagers are not allowed to say anything bad or have anything unlucky when having meals. For instance, they can not distinguish the fire or break anything. Therefore, several days before the Spring Festival, the adults will ask their children not to say anything stupid on the mornings of the two days. If the child accidentally said silly words, the adult would scold, "the hip is like the mouth, so talking is like breaking wind. " Furthermore, they believe that if they scold like this, children's silly words will not come true. But in that year, the adults would not feel at ease, but always worried about accidents.

Early in the morning of the lunar New Year's Day, people will go from door to door to wish each other a happy New Year, wishing each other good luck, happiness and wealth. New year's greetings should follow the principle of relatives to strangers. As the saying goes in the local region, they give new year's greetings to their sons on the first day of the lunar January, the sons-in-law on the second day, the parents of their daughters-in-law or sons-in-law on the third and fourth days, and the mother's brothers on the fifth and sixth days. When the people give the new year's greetings to a person, they should set off some big firecrackers before entering the person's yard and set off small firecrackers when arriving at the person's house, and then go in for tea and wine. People have been immersed in the festive atmosphere until the 15th day of the first month when the Spring Festival comes to an end.

The Tomb Sweeping Day is the time to have an outing in spring, sweep the grave and commemorate the ancestors. People should pay a visit to the tombs of the deceased ancestors and hang a string of paper flags on the grave to show that the grave has its owner and a successor. Before the foundation of the People's Republic of China, the Tomb Sweeping Day was bustling with noise and excitement. On the day, the clans and big families would organize the gathering to offer sacrifices to ancestors together, and gather all the male members in the ancestral hall to have a big dinner. At this moment, the consanguinity consciousness of the extended family was aroused again. Now, clan organizations no longer exist, and the rituals of ancestor worship have been scattered to all households. However, it is relatively common that the members of big families within five generations are organized temporarily to hang the strings of white paper to pay respect to the deceased at the graveyard.

The Dragon Boat Festival is on the fifth and the fifteenth days of the fifth lunar month. The festival is a leisure day after the busy spring sowing and before the Chufu (the first of the three ten-day periods of the dog days).

As for the origin of the Dragon Boat Festival, the local people all know that it is to commemorate Qu Yuan, the great poet and statesman of the State of Chu in the Warring States Period. Qu Yuan's story goes in Shaoyang County that Qu Yuan, as a minister loyal to his sovereign, admonished the King of Chu many times, but the traitor ministers framed him. At that time, the King Huai of Chu exiled him to Xupu County in Hunan Province. However, he had been concerned about the country and the people. Later, when hearing that the State of Chu was destroyed, he threw himself into the Miluo River on the fifth day of the fifth lunar month. The people rowed for his body on the river until finding it on the fifteenth day of the fifth lunar month. During this period, people were afraid that the big fish would devour Qu Yuan's body, so a large number of Zongzi (a pyramid-shaped glutinous rice dumpling wrapped in reed leaves) like saponin were put into the river to lure the fish away.

In this way, the customs of making Zongzi and rowing dragon boats came into being. Therefore, the Dragon Boat Festival involves two days, the fifth and fifteenth days of the fifth lunar month, also known as the minor Dragon Boat Festival and the major Dragon Boat Festival, while the way to celebrate the festival varies. The tradition of Tancun Village is mainly to celebrate the minor Dragon Boat Festival on the fifth day of the fifth lunar month. On the day, relatives and friends will present Zongzi, noodles, or the just mature chicken, ducks, fish and other food to each other.

The Mid-July Days, also known as the Ghost Festival, is the time to greet and send off ghosts and gods, lasting from the eleventh day to the fourteenth day of the seventh lunar month. As the traditional saying goes, the deceased ancestors would pay a visit to the house in this world from the nether world, and their family members would receive them warmly, preparing the banquets in the morning, middle and evening to pay respect to them every day. On the night of July 14th in the lunar calendar, the people in this world burn some clothes and paper money to their ancestors in the nether world. It was regarded as their respect for their ancestors. In recent years, as people have gained wealth to some extent, they will also make paper resembling money and television made of paper and burn them as the high-end presents to the ancestors, as well as prepare some vegetarian cakes for them as the solid food on their way back to the nether world.

The Mid-Autumn Festival falls on the 15th day of the 8th month according to the Chinese lunar calendar. It is a day for people to relax in autumn. At this time, many crops have been harvested, and people, with the joy of harvest, will gather with their families and exchange visits to their relatives, mainly presenting moon cakes, peanuts, and so on.

In the era of collective economy before the reform and opening up, the local people had accepted some festivals recognized by the government, such as the National Day, the New Year's Day, the International Working Women's Day, the May Day, the International Children's Day, the CPC Founding Day and the Army Day. Moreover, the popular solar calendar in the international community used to be the major time system for the local people. However, after the implementation of the household contract responsibility system, except for the National Day and the New Year's Day, which the local people will keep in mind but do not hold any ceremonies, other official festivals have no impact on the local people. Besides, young people may occasionally mention western festivals such as Valentine's Day and Christmas, while there are hardly any celebrations.

A new almanac is one of the most widely used calendars in the local region. The book of the new almanac is entitled to the Official Almanac of Wangxing Building by Li Fusheng, which was published by the Chetang Store, one kilometer away from the Zhouwang Store in the adjacent Longhui County. Almost every family in Tancun Village has a new almanac. New almanac not only provides solar terms and agricultural time but is also the only basis for local people to check the day for an important event. Whenever a villager in the village starts to build a house, holds a wedding or funeral ceremony, or takes a long journey or handles important affairs in other places, he or she will check the new almanac to see whether it is an auspicious day or not, or whether it is suitable for going out and handling affairs.

The new almanac roughly divides the days of the whole year into 12 characters, including establishment, tearing, filling, judging, determining, implementing, breaking, rooftop, completing, receiving, opening and closing, among which the days of the four characters, establishment, filling, judging and receiving, are inauspicious, and the days with the four characters, tearing, determining, implementing and rooftop, are auspicious. During the days with the characters of breaking and closing, it is necessary to avoid going on a journey. During the days with the characters of completing and opening, it is suitable for going out. Each day is matched with a star, and all the days corresponding to 28 stars, including horn, dipper, legs, well, neck, ox, bond, ghosts, root, girl, stomach, willow, room, emptiness, hairy head, star, heart, rooftop, net, extended net, tail, encampment, turtle beak, wings, winnowing basket, wall, three stars, and chariot.

Each star is annotated with a poem describing whether it is auspicious or not on the day. For instance, on the ninth day of the first lunar month in 2006, it is annotated on the almanac that "The ninth day is the day of establishment, in the star of heart." It means that the day is the third day of the establishment, which is an inauspicious day. And it says that "it is suitable to meet friends/relative, remove, raise the beam, sign contract, engage in business trading and encoffin," and it is the star of heart. On the star of the heart, it says that it is inauspicious to meet the star of heart. Whatever you do is most ominous. A funeral may suffer a heavy loss, or a marriage is indeed a false one. It can be seen that it is an extremely inauspicious day on the day, and any construction, marriage, or funeral is not suitable. Nowadays, local people use new almanacs most frequently in case of marriage, housing construction or residence relocation, funeral, and other situations. Even if young people do not believe in heresy at all, they must handle the rituals in the above aspects, following the new almanac.

Customs of Weddings and Funerals

In the case of an older man's death, the people should not say that the man died but should say that the man was deceased or passed away. When the older man died, all the dutiful sons and grandsons of the man at home had to go to bed to listen to the older man's last words. At this time, all the descendants expected to hear some auspicious words from the older man. Before the older man breathed his last, his family would burn a small amount of paper resembling money at the corner of the bed, which is called the last money, and prepare firecrackers. As soon as the older man died, his family would set off firecrackers to show that there was a deceased man in the house. At that moment, the older man's family members would rub the man with a wet towel, lift him on the floor of the hall and cover him with a mosquito net. That night, they would take the bed grass, sheets, clothes, umbrellas, shoes, and socks of the dead to the intersection outside the village and burn them.

Two types of religious persons mainly hold the funeral ceremony for the dead. One is a monk. Local people divide monks into two categories, one is monks living in temples, who are known as out-of-home monks, and the other is the monks living in the secular world, who are known as in-home monks, equivalent to the lay disciples. The in-home monks mainly hold the funeral ceremony in Tancun Village. The other is the Earth Immortal, also known as the geomancer. The Earth Immortal is mainly responsible for putting the deceased into the coffin, closing and moving the coffin, lifting the coffin out, dropping the coffin in the pit, and selecting the direction of the grave mound to determine the geomancy. Every procedure of the funeral ceremony must be strictly obeyed. And the Earth Immortal must determine the timetable for the procedures after he checks the date of birth and the eight characters of the deceased, the time of his death, as well as the match between the date of birth and the eight characters of the deceased and those of the immediate relatives. Once the specific time for these procedures is determined, it will be written on a blank paper and posted next to the obituary.

The rituals for the deceased by the monks mainly consist of guiding the way back home and to future life for the deceased, opening the hell and saving the deceased, saying mass for people, going around the coffin, and holding the sacrificial rites. The rituals of guiding the way back home and to future life for the deceased, opening the hell and saving the deceased, saying mass for people are all to chant the sutras to expiate the sins of the deceased. The monks should perform a group of religious rites and chant some scriptures. They intend to inform the ancestors of the clan, the god of earth, the Bodhisattva, and the ghosts and gods in the underworld to take care of the deceased all the way. Then, the deceased can reach the underworld calmly, and remove all the obstacles for the deceased to return to the underworld. The rituals of going around the coffin and holding the sacrificial rites are all aimed to mourn the deceased. When going around the coffin, the monk must, even in cold winter, walk barefoot in front of the queue and guide the descendants around the coffin. The monk chants the scriptures as he turns around. Every time he turns to the intense table in front of the coffin, he should give a bow, and all the descendants must do the same as the monk. When going around the coffin, all the descendants of the deceased must be arranged according to their birth order, and the eldest son should hold the memorial tablet of the deceased, on which there is a piece of red paper with the name, the date of the birth and death of the deceased written by the monk, placed on the sacrificial table tied with paper money and a leading streamer.

The ritual of holding the sacrificial rite is also known as the Wengong Rite or the Jiudian Rite. The family members of the deceased display the poultry, fish, and pig's head and fruits in front of the coffin. Under the guidance of the elders, the family members show their filial obedience to the deceased like taking care of the deceased's dinner during his lifetime. The sacrificial rites include starting the chant, singing the dirge, reading the rites, telling the rites, reading the oration, giving a salute, greeting the deceased with due respect, asking the deceased to have a meal, and performing the three kowtows and nine prostrations. It is also accompanied by gongs and drums, Qin and flute, the Suona horn, along with firecrackers to show the filial respect of the family members to the deceased. In the sacrificial rites, those who read and tell the rites mostly according to the Confucian classics. For instance, Zisi (Kong Ji, the grandson of Confucius) said that the coffin of the deceased must be moved to the grave within three days after the death. Anyone who bows to the deceased must be reverent and respectful to the deceased and never regret it. Confucius said that if for some time, a person had not changed his father's reasonable and useful principles about life after the death of his father, the man might be said to have fulfilled his filial duty.

During the funeral ceremony, relatives and friends of the deceased should stay beside the coffin all night long, and the family members of the deceased should distribute a piece of coarse white cloth about five feet long and three feet wide to all the relatives and friends attending the ceremony. The lineal relatives of the deceased within five generations and his collateral relatives within three generations or the in-law relatives within two generations must put the cloth on their heads, while the ordinary people put the close on their shoulders or tie them around their waists.

Before the founding of the People's Republic of China, the marriage customers of Tancun Village were quite tedious, which involved a large number of procedures, including exchanging the written marriage proposal on which are stated the year, month, day and hour of the birth of the bride and the bridegroom, sending betrothal gifts and money over to the bride by the bridegroom (also known as sending the eight characters or the written marriage proposal), presenting gifts to the bride's family before marriage, sending the bride's dowry to the bridegroom's house, going to the bride's home to escort her back to the wedding, performing the formal bows by bride and bridegroom, teasing the bride and the bridegroom on wedding night, the bride returning to her mother's home on the third day of the wedding and so forth.

Nowadays, the rites of presenting gifts to the bride's family before marriage, sending the bride's dowry to the bridegroom's house and teasing the bride and the bridegroom on wedding night and the bride returning to her mother's home on the third day of the wedding are continued, but other rites are no longer held, but some new procedures have been added, such as serving a cup of tea to the bridegroom, checking the potential groom's family conditions and his status by the matchmaker with the potential bride and her female relatives, and getting engaged. In general, when the matchmaker goes to the bridegroom's home with the bride and her close female relatives, the bride will make tea for the elderly in the bridegroom's family, check the groom's family condition and his condition and get engaged with the groom on the same way when the bridge is satisfied with the groom and agrees on the marriage. If the groom regrets after the engagement, he should not claim the money and things he has presented to the bride. But if the bride regrets, she must return the money and things presented by the groom to him. If the groom provides some labor services for the bride's family, it should be settled in money. As a result, if the bride cancels the marriage contract, the groom can claim to the bride's family, commonly known as getting even. About before the late 1980s, there had been the custom of crying marriage on the wedding day at the bride's home, and the elders had to present the gifts to the crying bride, but now we can no longer find a bride sing with tears on the wedding day.

Religious Beliefs

Shaoyang County, where Tancun Village is located, has long been affected by the religions. As early as the Tang Dynasty, Gaoxia Temple was built on the Gaoxiao Mountain of Wufengpu. It was the place where Li Xia, an Immortal in the Tang Dynasty, cultivated herself according to the Taoist doctrine.

In the late Tang Dynasty, a temple began to be built in Yangwu Mountains in Huangtingshi Town, where Tancun Village is located. In 1583, the seventeenth year of the Jiajing Regime of the Ming Dynasty, the Cha'an Temple in the current Cangzhen Town, had been at a considerable scale. Islam was introduced into Shaoyang County during the Hongwu Regime of the Ming Dynasty when a group of Hui people moved in with the troops and settled in the county. Qingcao Village in Yongxing Township, Huangtingshi Town is a Hui community, which maintains a relatively complete Islamic culture. Christianity and Catholicism were introduced into the county during the Republic of China. In 1913, the second year of the Republic of China, the United Methodist Church Mission and China Inland Mission were introduced into the county. Although the five major religions are available in the county, Buddhism is the only region that has the greatest impact on the villagers of Tancun Village.

According to the county annals, Yangwu Temple was first built in the Tang Dynasty, and renovated four times in 1370, the third year of the Hongwu Regime of the Ming Dynasty, in 1776, the 41st year of the Qianlong Regime of the Qing Dynasty, in 1887, the thirteenth year of the Guangxu Regime of the Qing Dynasty, and in 1919, the eighth year of the Republic of China (Editorial Committee on Shaoyang County Annals, 1993). Yangwu Temple has always been one of the important Buddhist attractions in the city and county where Tancun Village is located, and it has been widely reputed among the Buddhist pilgrims from the neighboring counties and provinces. Buddhist ceremonies will be held on the 19th day of the second lunar month as the birthday of Avalokitesvara, the 19th day of the sixth lunar month as the day of enlightenment, and the 19th day of the ninth lunar month as the day of starting to practice Buddhism. On the three days, all the devout men and women from the neighboring areas will come to the Temple to burn incense. Among the pilgrims, some even come from Guangxi and Guizhou Provinces. For the villagers of Tancun Village, they mainly engage in religious affairs by burning incense in Yangwu Temple, as they intend to pray for a son, safety, a scholarly honor or official rank, or for the Bodhisattva to help people in distress, and cure the diseases.

In terms of the origin of religion, Yangwu Temple is deeply affected by the Nanyue Chan sect. According to Shi Qingyuan, a nun as the abbot in the temple, the top Bodhisattva here is the Emperor of Nanyue Mountain, because Yangwu Temple is a branch originating from Nanyue Mountain. Therefore, Yangwu Temple is also known as the Little Nanyue among the local people. The Nanyue Chan sect is divided into the Southern Sect of Huineng and the Northern Sect of Shenxiu. Yangwu Temple belongs to the Linji School of the Huirang Branch in the Section of Caoxizong, under the leadership of the Monk Huineng of the Southern Sect. According to the elderly in Tancun Village, when the monk in Yangwu Mountain passed away in the past, he was honored as the Chan master XX in Linji in the generation XX in Caoxi or the saint XX in Linji. Because of the special relationship between Yangwu Mountain and Nanyue Mountain, there have been a group of Buddhist pilgrims on a pilgrimage to offer incense in Nanyue Mountain. As recorded in the Shaoyang County Annals during the Guangxu Regime of the Qing Dynasty, on the first and fifteenth days of the eighth lunar month, many people paid visits to Nanyue Mountain, Pingding Mountain, Shehu Mountain and Baiyun Rock to make offerings to the Buddha.

Compared with Buddhism, Taoism has less influence on the villagers. There are two existing Taoist temples in the county, one is the Jieyuan Temple, and the other is Gaoxia Temple, both of which are located around the county seat but are seldom known to the villagers of Tancun Village. As for the religion that has the greatest influence on the local people's beliefs, in addition to Buddhism, there are also some folk religious figures known as Yin Shi Gong, the Goddess, and so forth. From the viewpoint of the author, Yin Shigong should be a clergyman arising from the combination of Taoism and local folk religions in ancient times. However, through interviews with some Yin Shi Gong, it was found that they firmly deny that they are a branch of Taoism, but they also don't know in what sect they are. Some Yin Shigong claims that they learn the knowledge about the Yin religion, and some even claim that they learn the knowledge about the metaphysics (a philosophical sect in the Wei and Jin dynasties) or the heresy.

In ancient China, Tancun Village belonged to the State of Chu, where there had been evil spirits with an emphasis on the worship of unorthodox gods. According to Wang Yi's Chu Ci Zhang Ju, "In the past, in the county of the Ying, capital of the State of Chu, and between Yuanjiang River and Xiangjiang River, the people tended to believe in ghosts and be fond of worship. When offering sacrifices to the gods, the people must sing, dance and play the drums to please the gods (Hong, 1983)." It was recorded in the Geography Section of the Han Shu (History of the Former Han Dynasty) that the people in the State of Chu believed in the evil spirits and valued the worship of unorthodox gods.

The local Yin Shi Gong is engaged in various religious services, such as exorcism, soul retrieval, healing rituals for a frightened child and evil spirit elimination and so on. They have to mutter an invocation when they are performing religious rituals. From the perspective of the rituals by Yin Shi Gong, it should belong to one of the primitive religions in ancient times.

The Goddess is the most important psychic medium in the local area. Whenever the villagers encounter an unfortunate or abnormal event, such as a snake coming to their houses or one of their family members falling ill for a long time, they have to ask the Goddess for advice. In other words, the villagers should ask the Goddess for the reasons so as to invite the Yin Shi Gong to hold relevant religious rituals and eliminate the hazards. Therefore, the master of the nether world, the Goddess, and other gods have a great impact on the daily faith and life of the villagers of Tancun Village.

Finally, the Meishan Religious Sect also has a great influence in the local area. Meishan Religious Sect is a folk religion. As for the origin, the spirit tablet and myth of Meishan Religious Sect, public opinions are divergent, and people fail to come to an agreement. However, it is generally believed that Meishan Religious Sect originated from the ancient Meishan area, i.e., the now Xinhua, Anhua and the surrounding areas, but radiated to many surrounding areas. As described in the General History of Hunan, these areas are roughly located between Ningxiang, Shaoyang, Yiyang and Xiangxiang, with the center in Anhua and Xinhua. Xinhua is in the upper parts of Meishan and Anhua is in the lower parts of Meishan (Wu, 1994) . That is to say, in terms of geographical location, Meishan Religious Sect covers Shaoyang County, Yiyang City, Xinhua County, Anhua County and Huaihua City in Hunan Province.

The rituals of Meishan Religious Sect mainly consist of expelling the evil spirits for others, curing the diseases, making a vow and redeeming the vow to the god. They mainly offer sacrifices to Zhang Wulang, or Wu Gong Bai Jiang, especially the God of Hunters, indicating that the earliest human witchcraft is to regulate the hunters' hunting. Zhang Wulang is popular among the folk as the God of Hunters who turns the altar upside down and stands upside down. According to folklore, when he was hunting, he fought with the tiger in a desperate situation, and then he was accidentally knocked down the cliff and hung upside down on the tree to die. People remembered his heroic deeds and respected him as the God of Hunters. They graved a statue standing upside down and set up an altar for worship. The local Meishan Religious Sect was also deeply influenced by later Taoism. It was integrated with Taoism and borrowed from each other, becoming the original belief culture form of local people with the features of witchcraft, Taoism and Nuo rituals.

In the classification of the Meishan Religious Sect by the local people in Tancun Village, Meishan God is divided into three categories: upper Meishan, middle Meishan and lower Meishan. The three gods of Meishan are believed by three kinds of people, those who go hunting in the mountains, those who catch fish in the rivers and those who raise ducks. It is said that those who know the Meishan Religious Sect have great magic power. They not only master extraordinary skills of fishing and hunting, but can also cure many odd diseases. However, it is said that the Meishan God, who the local people adored, is eccentric and easily offended before they are unaware. Once someone offends the Meishan God, he will be teased by Meishan God and infected with an odd disease. Only when the person asks the Goddess or other people who know the Meishan Religious Sect to conduct a mass to ask for Meishan God's forgiveness, can his disease be cured.

It can be said that Tancun Village is a rural community where people believe in a variety of gods. Here, a person has to experience all kinds of religious sacrifice activities since he was very young, and different gods provide appropriate services for the local people. However, it can also be seen that in such a region with the cultural tradition of the belief in witches and ghosts, various taboo cultures, witchcraft beliefs, and ancient customs, such as calling back the spirits of the dead and collecting the spirits, have been quite popular. These witch cultures and ancient customs have a profound influence on the child rearing system that the author will describe in the following parts.

Chapter 3 Cultural Mechanism of Child-Bearing of the Villagers of Tancun Village

Culture is a pluralistic complex, which consists of a variety of material, spiritual and institutional forms. Birth culture refers to a complete set of material equipment, spiritual concepts and institution norms produced by people based on the practice of childbearing. Childbearing is a complex and risky process. In order to ensure the smooth reproduction of human beings so as to realize the continuity of life from generation to generation, people have established strict norms of conduct through a series of customs, which have been passed down from generation to generation and become a fixed cultural criterion, also known as a cultural mechanism. The cultural mechanism of childbearing refers to the standardized ways of act that people must follow in the activities of childbearing, including marriage, family structure, religious belief, taboo and values, institutions and norms, etc.

Section 1 Marriage and Ways of Spouse Selection

The marriage marks the beginning of generations of human beings. The act of marrying for two families is to join a young woman and a young man born in different environments and families, so that they can form a new family and fulfill the life responsibility of human reproduction. Therefore, a marriage institution is a part of the childbirth institution and an important institution to ensure the continuity of the race. The society gives the marriage institution special significance through the extremely complex symbolic system or semiotic system. Marriage refers to the combination of man and woman, but it is far more than the relationship between men and women, because the marriage is closely bound up with childbearing. Georg Simmel once wrote: "marriage involves sex, but it is far more than sex and goes beyond sex. Similarly, sex in marriage translates into something higher than physical behavior. Of course, objectively, sex is sex, but in marriage it is endowed with a completely different meaning. In marriage, sex is considered to be good, normal and conform to the interests of society, because it can help to breed and maintain the continuity of the race. Marriage is also a recognized method of granting children an identity, and the concept of legality or the recognition of legal father status prevails everywhere (Murphy, 1994)." Therefore, marriage has never been a cultural institution just for sex, but a social and cultural phenomenon that goes beyond physiological needs.

According to Fei Xiaotong, the significance of marriage is to establish the parental care system. In my opinion, marriage is caused by social forces, because as far as I know, there has never been a place in the world where marriage is regarded as a private matter between the parties concerned, and is not interested in by other people (Fei, 1998). Since the purpose of marriage is to establish the responsibility of parental care and ensure the continuous reproduction of human beings, marriage can not be regarded as a personal matter of the married couple, but a collective matter. The collective can either be the families of the married couple, or the clans of the couple, or even a country.

In the past dynasties of China, there were specific policies and laws on marriage to guide the process of people's marriage, although most of these policies and laws are created for the political purposes of rulers in different times, generally aimed at the population, war, economic and land development and other political purposes. In the Offices of Earth of the Rites of Zhou, The Pattern of the Family of the Book of Rites and other ancient books left by the people in the Zhou Dynasty, they all mentioned that the marriageable age was best at thirty for men and twenty for women. The Duke Huan of Qi, the first hegemon in the Spring and Autumn Period, once ordered that a husband should be married when he was 20, while a woman should be married when he was 15, and he also asked the maids in the imperial palace who had never been favored by him to marry out of the palace. Therefore, there is no old maid in the palace, and no unmarried men at marriageable age outside the palace.

At the end of the Spring and Autumn Period, Gou Jian, King of Yue (current Zhejiang-Fujian Area), ordered early marriage and encouraged childbearing to take revenge for the insult by the State of Wu. He stipulated that the men aged between 30 and 40 should not marry the older wives and that the older men should not marry the younger wives. If a woman does not marry at the age of 17, her parents are guilty, and if a man does not marry at 20, his parents are guilty. Not only that, but Confucian scholars also invented a complete set of rituals to ensure the smooth progress of marriage. As early as the Zhou Dynasty in the pre-Qin days (before 221 B.C. when the First Emperor of Qin united China), there was a relatively complete set of six ceremonies of betrothal and marriage that influenced the marriage of the Chinese people. According to the chapter Marriage of An Ordinary Officer of the Book of Etiquette and Ceremonial, the feudal marriage consists of six steps, namely, visiting the lady's family to formally seek a marriage alliance after the lady's parents agreed to consider a matchmaker's proposal, asking for the full name and time of birth of the lady through the matchmaker, engagement upon approval of the lady's family on propitious signs obtained through diving by the man's family according to birthdays, presentation of betrothal gifts to the bride's family, seeking approval by the bride's family of a wedding date selected by the bridegroom's family and the bridegroom's going to the bride's to meet her for the wedding.

These complicated rites show that people have created a series of cultural mechanism to ensure the smooth completion of the marriage and the stability of the families of both husband and wife, and made the wedding of a young couple legitimate. In spite of constant changes in the cultural mechanism, any human group always needs a specific marriage rite to implement the function of such cultural mechanism, no matter it is in ancient or modern times. These functions are roughly reflected in three aspects (Zhuang, 2002). First of all, it can maintain the stability of social groups. In most cases, marriage, as a norm, can reduce the conflicts among social groups arising from sexual reasons, which will be conducive to social stability. Second, it can provide suitable conditions, both social and economic, for the reproduction of the masses. Marriage is an underlying social cell that is characterized by the joint nurturing of offspring by female and male adults, so that it can provide a favorable environment for the growth of legal offspring and infants. Third, it can enhance the bonds between different groups, so that child rearing is not just a matter of individuals, but also a common concern of families and clans of both parents and even the entire community. At Tancun Village, there is a set of ongoing cultural mechanisms to guarantee the smooth completion of the marriage.

Marriage Forms

Strict Implementation of Exogamy

In southern China, most of the villages are inhabited by the members of the same family or clan. They are the descendants of the same ancestor, and there is an evident pedigree to record the kinship of the members. Therefore, they are brothers and sisters of the same generation or the cousins, aunts and nephews of two generations. They are strictly prohibited from relating to each other by intermarriage. Any relationship between men and women that goes against such a marriage institution can be regarded as incest.

Moreover, there are express provisions specified in the pedigree to restrain and punish such abuse. In the Guide to the Second Amendments to the Pedigree of the Jiang Clan, it is expressly stipulated that a man should not marry a woman of the same surname, which has been true in the ancient rites. In our clan, any family that gets the son or daughter married should avoid doing anything that may arouse suspicion and should not do as it pleases; otherwise, it will be contrary to moral human relations. Furthermore, it is stipulated that for anyone who violates the provision, the female should be sunken deep into the pond, and the male should take the risk of being driven out of the clan.

Since the founding of the People's Republic of China, people have transformed their thoughts and they are able to accept the marriage of a man and a woman, who are not relatives for at least five generations because the law only forbids the marriage between the lineal blood relatives and the collateral blood relatives within three generations. But they are still quite disgusted with the marriage of the same surname from the bottom of their hearts.

When asked about the opinion on the marriage of the same surnames in the interview, both the young and the old agreed that it should be forbidden. They are disgusted with the marriage of the same surname for several simple reasons. First, there have not yet been such rules for the previous dynasties. Second, they are afraid that they may get punished on their offspring, which means that the child of a couple of the same surname may be in abnormal conditions. Third, it may confuse the seniority in the clan, which means that an aunt may get married to her nephew, or an uncle may get married to his niece. In this case, the couple would not know how to call their relatives after marriage. The establishment of the marriage relationship is bound to lead to a change in the original appellations among the relatives that have been based on the pedigree. Owing to the above three reasons, they are generally against the marriage of the same surname up to now.

The first reason is apparently out of the intangible rule of traditional power, a cultural power, of people's thoughts and acts. The second reason is the product of modern scientific knowledge. In particular, the current genetic theory allows people to be convinced that consanguineous marriage will inevitably lead to the decline of the quality of future generations. Even the older people in the seventies believe firmly in the view. The third reason is out of the fear of incest taboos.

People have been living in a relatively peaceful and stable cultural order, while the consanguineous marriage is bound to lead to putting the original cultural order into a disorderly state. Even the most basic appellations that the new couple has called for their relatives must be completely renewed, which is less likely for people to accept in any case. As a result, the ancients regarded the marriage of the same surname as a type of incest and banned it. It was recorded in the Commentary of Zuo on the Spring and Autumn Annals that "do not marry those of the same surname, and attach importance to the human relations to prevent any dissolute or bestial situation. " In the section Name of Bai Hu Tong, it wrote that "why does a person have a name? It is to believe in love, attach great importance to kinship, stay away from beasts and distinguish the marriage. Therefore, people have been classified for centuries, and the couple loves each other to live and feel sad for each other when they die. The people of the same surnames should not get married, as we are highly concerned about human relations. " On the ground of the above reasons, there has not yet been a family in Tancun Village found to relate to another family for the marriage of the same surname.

Even young men and women of the same surnames will be strongly condemned by the villagers when they fall in love. In the 1970s, a young man and woman, both surnamed Deng, were the members of the militia in the village. They fell in love with each other at work, and finally developed into lovers. When the marriage relationship that they determined in private was made to the public, they were severely scolded by their parents. At the same time, they were all blamed for their love by the villagers, which was regarded as the biggest joke in the history of the village. It was rumored that the couple had sex when they were guarding the warehouse for the town, and then the woman got pregnant. The parents of the woman considered the incident as a scandal against the morals, and then they scolded her every day. In the end, the woman could not bear the heavy pressure from the outside world and threw herself into the river and drowned.

Marriage of Cross Cousins and Marriage of Parallel Cousins

The villagers of Tancun Village are strictly forbidden to marry those of the same surnames, and they believe that those who violate the rule may lead to retribution on their offspring, but they do not oppose the marriage of cousins. In other words, the children of a brother and a sister or the children of two sisters may get married, which is called cementing old ties by marriage. Cousin marriage is divided into the wedding of cross cousins and the marriage of parallel cousins. Marriage of cross cousins means that a man can get married to the daughter of his mother's brother or the daughter of his father's sister. Marriage of parallel cousins implies that a man can get married to the daughter of his mother's sister. However, the marriage between cousins reflects the wish of the brother's and the sister's families or the families of the sisters, but is not the dominant marriage form in Tancun Village, because the cousins have been too familiar with each other. The inherent blood relationship and the appellations among relatives that the cousins have determined since they were very young have made it impossible for the cousins to complete the transformation of the spousal relations.

In this aspect, Sigmund Freud's psychological interpretation makes some sense. According to Freud, brothers and sisters who grew up together may lack sexual attraction due to their shyness and familiarity, which can be regarded as the reason for sexual taboos. Therefore, In Tancun Village, the villagers speak highly of those families who cement old ties by marriage, cousin marriage has not become the primary form of marriage in the local area.

In the survey, it was found that the villagers of Tancun Village implemented the marriage of cross cousins or parallel cousins mainly in two cases. One is that a girl's mother's brother or sister has too low income to get the son married, and then the girl is married to the son of her mother's brother or sister to ensure the continuity of the offspring. The other is that the cousins fall in love and then the adults intend to make do as they wish. Among the fifty families randomly interviewed, when asked whether there is cousin marriage in their families within three generations, only three families said that they once had, among which one took place during the Republic of China, and the other two took place in the 1960s and 1970s. The young people who have received modern scientific education believe that the cousins are still close relatives and that the close relatives who marry may give birth to an abnormal infant. Therefore, there is no cousin marriage among the younger generation of the villagers of Tancun Village.

Levirate Marriage and Sororate Marriage

Levirate marriage is a type of marriage in which the brother of a deceased man is obliged to marry his brother's widow, and the widow is forced to marry her dead husband's brother. In the era of traditional familism, women are regarded as the private property of their husband's family, especially those who are engaged in mercenary marriage. Once a woman's husband is deceased, her husband's family tends not to let them marry a stranger and then her husband's family members forced her to marry her husband's younger or elder brother. Since the founding of the People's Republic of China, marriage freedom has been prevailing, while levirate marriage has been seldom seen. Even if there is such a case, it is based on the initiative of both husband and wife themselves, without any compulsion.

The author investigated that, in 1986, a family surnamed Luo had a levirate marriage. The woman named Yang XX, and her former husband was named Luo Ming, who worked in a private coal mine and died of the gas explosion. They had a son more than one year old. Luo's younger brother, Luo Hua, was 24 years old at that time, two years older than Yang, his sister-in-law. After the death of his elder brother, Luo Hua was also very sympathetic about Yang's situation as a widow. With the help of his family and neighbors, Yang agreed to get married to Luo Hua, her husband's younger brother, and Luo Hua was also willing to take care of his widowed sister-in-law and his young nephew. When the author asked Yang why she would marry her husband's younger brother, she answered, "it did not matter at that time. Anyway, my husband was dead, and our family was in a tough situation. I had to take care of my son over one year old. He did not dislike me, and he was more capable than his brother. Our family members were all trying to persuade me, and the neighbors were all asking me not to marry out, so I agreed to marry him."

It is the only levirate marriage in the current Tancun Village. It does not make any sense from the statistical angle, but it can show that the local people are not against the levirate marriage. The fact of the family can also, to some extent, prove that levirate marriage is the best way for children in an incomplete family because his or her new father is his or her uncle so that they will not get discriminated against in the combined family. Yang, a party in the levirate marriage case, said, "fortunately, I made a wise decision at that time and my son was not pitiful at all. Now, he is on good terms with his father (Luo Hua) and is obedient to him. After graduating from high school, he went to work in Guangdong Province. He earned more than 2,000 Yuan a month and sent the part that he saved to his father every month." From a sociological point of view, levirate marriage is an excellent way to mend the relationship of the incomplete families caused by the accidental death of some family members. As long as both parties involved in the marriage are on their initiatives, the new husband and the woman's children have a natural blood relationship as the uncle and the nephew, and it is more conducive to the upbringing of children than those newly combined families where the members do not have any blood ties.

Sororate marriage is a type of marriage in which a husband engages in marriage with the sister of his wife, usually after the death of his wife. However, the sororate marriage does not refer to the wedding of the deceased wife's sisters in anthropology, as in a sororate marriage, the elder or younger sister of the dead wife is not obliged to marry her brother-in-law, but they are voluntarily married to their brother-in-law out of some personal feelings or the matchmaking of their relatives, friends or neighbors. Two cases of sororate marriage took place in Tancun Village in the 1980s. In one example, a primary school teacher's wife died in childbirth, and her younger sister offered to marry her brother-in-law. The other case was that a self-employed man's wife died of illness, and he married his deceased wife's younger sister due to the matchmaking of his parents-in-law and many of his relatives. According to the two cases, we can see that the sororate marriage only occurs in those families who are in better economic conditions and in which the men are more capable. Otherwise, the woman, as a sister-in-law, will never marry her brother-in-law.

Medium of Marriage

Before the founding of the People's Republic of China, the villagers of Tancun Village used to get married by parents' orders and on the matchmaker's word. The matchmaker is an indispensable medium in a marriage. As the saying goes, it does not rain if there is no dark cloud in the sky, and the people will not get married if there is no matchmaker in the world. The matchmaker plays a role as a medium between the two families of two surnames to get two persons at the marriageable age of the two families married to enhance the relationship between the two families.

There was a record of the matchmaker in ancient China. In the Zhou Dynasty, there was an official position for matchmakers. In the Odes of Bin of the Book of Songs, it wrote, "how can we cut down a tree? It can not be done without an ax. How can a man get married? It can not be done without a matchmaker." According to the Summary of the Rules of Propriety in the Book of Rites, a potential bridegroom should not ask for the prospective bride's name, birthday and birth-hour without the help of a matchmaker. According to the section The State of

Yan in the Intrigues of the Warring States, "without a matchmaker, a maiden could not be married even when she grew old." It wrote in the Garden of Anecdotes that it was not what a man of noble character did when a scholar met a girl before passing the imperial examination and got married without a matchmaker. In Tancun Village, people not only think that the matchmaker is the tradition of Confucian ethics. Only in this way, the family of a couple will gain the face and will not be teased by others.

Moreover, they believe that being a matchmaker is to do a good deed to the next life and that those who have received the kindness from a matchmaker in this life must warn their offspring not to forget the goodness of the matchmaker for generations. As the saying goes, it is better to destroy ten temples than spoil one marriage. It can be seen that being a matchmaker is a magnificent deed to accumulate virtue.

In Tancun Village, both men and women act as a matchmaker. It wrote in the Children's Education Society that a male go-between is commonly known as a matchmaker and a female go-between is widely known as a woman matchmaker. But In Tancun Village, there is no clear distinction between the concept of matchmaker and woman matchmaker. As long as a man or a woman plays an intermediary role in a marriage, he or she is called a matchmaker. Local matchmakers can be divided into two categories, one is the semi-professional matchmakers and the other is the non-professional matchmakers. Generally speaking, the people who play such roles are the women aged at their forties or fifties. Semi-professional matchmakers are those who specialize in making a match for the young people of marriageable age to make a profit and survive. One of the critical purposes of the matchmakers is to get the cash gift from the man's family in the course of matchmaking. It is the service fee paid by the prospective bridegroom's family for the matchmaker in contributing to the marriage. The cost depends on the man's family's economic condition and his situation, ranging from 500 to 1,000 Yuan.

The most famous woman matchmaker in Tancun Village is Yang Siniang (杨四娘), as she is surnamed Yang (杨) and her husband is the fourth (四, meaning four in Chinese) eldest among his brothers. She said, "no matter how much the cash gift is, it depends on whether she can meet the clients who have good financial conditions, are generous and willing to spend money. If she is lucky to meet one, she can receive a cash gift ranging from 1,000 Yuan to 2,000 Yuan. But if she is unlucky, she can only receive three or four hundred Yuan. Last year, I made a match for a family in the Luojia Village in Shuangqing Township, Shaoyang County. The man of the family was a master of a coal mine. Their family was wealthy and generous. I did not tell him how much I wanted, but he gave me more than 2,000 Yuan in the whole process. He is the most generous client that I have ever met. We have to make a lot of efforts to manage to make a match when some men that we meet are not good-looking or have no ability, or are stupid or too lazy, or who overtly agree but covertly oppose so that the girls do not like them, or they are somewhat disabled and can not get married to a girl. If we manage to get the man married, it will be a great deed for his family. So the family will pay me more, at least one thousand Yuan. But the cash gift from ordinary families is usually around five or six hundred Yuan. As we know, the prices are so high nowadays, and then they can not pay us a little. Otherwise, we will not be willing to make a match. In this case, we will directly ask them for a reasonable price. In other words, if some families are in bad condition, we can ask less. As matchmakers, we are doing good deeds for the next life and expecting future generations to have a bright future."

According to Yang's words, we can see that, first of all, there is an essential criterion for the pay of the professional matchmakers in the local area, around 500 Yuan. Second, the minimum remuneration of matchmakers can not be negotiated; otherwise, the matchmakers will directly ask for a reasonable price regardless of the feelings of the man's family. Third, if the male clients are in better family conditions or the man has problems of his own, the matchmakers must be paid more. No matter how much the matchmaker is overpaid, she will accept it without hesitation. Fourth, after all, the position of matchmaker is moral, and the matchmakers tend to accumulate virtue for the next life.

As a semi-professional matchmaker, she tends to be an excellent negotiator. She has to deliver messages back and forth between the potential bride's and bridegroom's families, but there should not be any misunderstanding in this process. Otherwise, it will cause dissatisfaction between the two sides and affect the success of matchmaking. As a result, it is an essential skill for matchmakers to play language games (Zhang, 1999). As the local saying goes, the matchmaker is so eloquent that she can give an extravagantly colorful description of the potential bride and bridegroom. In the communication between the two sides, she should not only convey the intentions of the prospective bride's and groom's families to the other party, but should also be good at telling white lies to please and satisfy the other side. Therefore, matchmakers exaggerate embellishment to many details, while they can not let the potential bride's and groom's families grasp any errors in their words. Otherwise, in case that the couple does not get along well in the future, the matchmakers will be blamed.

Therefore, we should not believe too much in the words of matchmakers, which has been widely known for a long time in history. In the section Close Relatives of the book Models for the World, Yuan Cai, a scholar in the Song Dynasty, said that "as the ancients said, the people in the Zhou Dynasty disliked the matchmakers because they used to react from their words. When the matchmaker visited the potential bride's house, she would say the potential groom's family was wealthy. And when she visited the potential groom's house, she would say the bride looked beautiful. It became worse in modern times. On the one hand, the matchmaker told the bride's family that the groom's family did not expect a heavy dowry and would lend a hand in the preparations of the wedding. On the other hand, she told the groom's family about the high demand for the gifts from the bride's family and made a false declaration on the amount. If the potential bride and groom believe in the matchmaker's words easily and get married, they will gradually blame and hate each other, and eventually fall out. And even some couples may get divorced. Generally speaking, a marriage can not be done without a matchmaker, and the people can not believe everything the matchmaker tells them. It is better to observe at first. "

When a matchmaker visits the potential bride's house and tells the family about the prospective groom, she will discuss the prospective bride's parents, "his family is better off than many and worse off than some, but his parents are capable and treat their daughter-in-law very well. The man is in a good temper, lives a moral life, and treats others kind-heartedly. If your daughter marries the man, she will certainly live in ease and comfort. Their village has smooth water traffic, and it will not be affected even in the drought days. And there has been water in the paddy fields all year round." The matchmaker's words have two features, one is that the matchmaker is good at compromising the difficulties and shortcomings of the other side, and she neither conceals anything nor says everything out, and the other is that the matchmaker tends to boast about the family conditions of the other party, greatly publicizes the strengths of each other's families, such as right natural conditions, etc. It is precisely because the matchmaker's words can not be too believed, so there must be a custom of checking the potential groom's family conditions and his status by the matchmaker with the prospective bride and her female relatives during the blind date of the young people in Tancun Village.

Most of the non-professional matchmakers have ties of kinship or friendship with either or both parties of the husband and wife in marriage, or they are the acquaintances, friends, neighbors or classmates of the couple. These people usually make a match due to kinship, friendship or human relations, and most of them are female. In Tancun Village, if a man or woman in a family comes to a marriageable age but fails to find the right spouse, their parents will worry about their marriage. Then, the parents tend to ask their relatives or friends to pay attention to finding the right spouse for their children in daily life. Although economic interests do not drive these non-professional matchmakers, they will be paid by the groom's family at the same remuneration as the processional matchmaker according to the custom, as long as they manage to make a match. Actually, among the media of marriage, non-professional matchmakers play a leading role, and they have a higher success rate in making a match. As they are relatives or friends of either or both parties of the potential couple, the prospective bride or groom can trust them. It is precisely because of the cultural pressure of kinship, friendship or human relations that it is much easier for the non-professional matchmakers to make a match than professional matchmakers. Moreover, the non-professional matchmakers do not need to possess so many skills as professional matchmakers.

Changes in the Standard and Method of Spouse Selection

After knowing the intermediary role of matchmakers in marriage in Tancun Village, we can study how the young people in Tancun Village choose their spouses. Briefly speaking, spouse selection is the first procedure for establishing a marriage relationship. In essence, spouse selection is an act that a man and woman do based on their mutual attraction and choice. But the influence and restrictions of economic and cultural factors that make spouse selection transcend the biological instincts of human beings, thus becoming an extremely complex cultural phenomenon.

According to the purpose of spouse selection, it can be divided into satisfaction-based spouse selection and institution-based spouse selection. The former is aimed to satisfy the physical and psychological needs of individuals, and it is usually regarded as the modern trend of spouse selection. The latter is designed to set up a new family and give birth to a child, and it is usually regarded as the traditional trend of spouse selection. On the one hand, the spouse selection based on personal needs is generally performed by the individuals themselves. On the other hand, the spouse selection due to other factors except for emotions, such as establishing a new family and giving birth to a child, tends to be intervened with by different groups except for the individuals themselves, especially the relatives (Sun, 2005).

However, strictly speaking, the spouse selection of the young people in Tancun Village can not be classified as the traditional or modern type, because it has reflected both conventional and contemporary factors in the selection of spouse by the young people. The man and woman must be voluntary and in love with each other to get married, and love should be the prerequisite for the marriage. However, we must take the will of the potential couple's parents into account, and their parents must approve the marriage of the couple. No matter the couple fall in love freely or the couple's parents want the couple to marry, a matchmaker must be invited as a medium to go between the couple.

In Tancun Village, in many cases, a matchmaker is invited by the potential couple that is prepared for the wedding after negotiation to act as the chief witness at the wedding ceremony. During the survey, the author conducted a questionnaire survey for two items, the standards, and methods of spouse selection (see Appendix 1). The results are shown in Table 3.1.

Table 3.1 Changes in the standards of spouse selection for the villagers of Tancun Village (%)

	Before 1950s	1960s – 1970s	1980s – 1990s	Singles
Good-looking	10 %	64 %	78 %	80 %
High political status	16.7 %	92 %	8 %	—
Good economic conditions	16.7 %	2 %	84 %	92 %
High level of education	30 %	62 %	88 %	82 %
A virtuous and gentle wife	13.3 %	58 %	78 %	70 %
Upright and honest qualities	73.3 %	72 %	56 %	22 %
Strong capabilities	76.7 %	72 %	82 %	88 %
Filial piety to parents	80 %	4 %	42 %	38 %

The standards and methods of spouse selection have been continually changing with the reform of social institutions and the economy. Among the respondents, some older people in their seventies to nineties got married in the 1950s and 1960s, some middle-aged got married in the 1980s, and some young people married in the 1990s and in the 21st century. The author investigated the couples who got married in different periods from the perspectives of good-looking, high political status, economic conditions, high level of education, a virtuous and gentle wife, upright and honest qualities, robust capability and filial piety to parents, requiring them to make multiple choices for the criteria by which they chose their spouses at that time. The results are shown in Table 3.1. The samples in the survey involved 180 respondents, among who 30 got married in the 1950s, 50 got married in the 1960s and 1970s, 50 got married in the 1980s and 1990s and 50 did not marry. As the standard of spouse selection is a conceptual form and it is less likely to make a clear distinction between the people of different age groups, this paper just makes a rough classification of the respondents, including those who married before the 1950s, those who married in the 1960s and 1970s, those who married since the 1980s and 1990s, and those who reached the marriageable age but had not married.

Among those who married before the 1950s, they attached the most importance to three standards, filial piety to parents, strong capabilities and upright and honest qualities. Among the three rules, 80 % of the respondents chose the item of filial piety to parents, ranking first among all the criteria of spouse selection, which reflects the dominant role of the traditional concept of filial piety in the marriage behaviors of the people. From the perspective of the classification of traditional and modern standards of spouse selection, those who married before the 1950s can be mostly classified as the conventional type. They do not ask for too many changes in their marriage, but just want their spouses to focus on the family honestly, bear their due responsibilities and support the family. Therefore, 73.3 % of the respondents chose the standard of upright and honest qualities for the other side, and 76.7 % chose the standard of strong capabilities for the other hand.

We can see from the interviews that the standard of strong capabilities proposed by those who married before the 1950s is not like the standard of capabilities by modern young people, but it means that the husband should be able to support the family, and protect the parents, wife and children from cold and hunger. As a result, men with skills or expertise in production become the first choice for women to choose a husband. It is worth mentioning that, for those who married before the 1950s, the upright and honest qualities are the best evaluation for a person's character, which actually reflects the fundamental personality traits of farmers in China. Because of this, they do not pay much attention to the appearance of the spouse when making a choice. Of the thirty respondents, only three chose the item, good-looking, accounting for 10 % . Most of the respondents said, "at that time, before the wedding, the man and woman had not met each other, They got married at a young age and then they were so naive that they did not care about whether the husband or wife looked good.

Moreover, the man just thought of marrying a woman that could take care of household chores, serve her husband, be conscientious, and be obedient to his parents. It did not matter whether the woman looked good. No matter how the woman looked, she was a good choice as long as she could give birth to children."

It can be seen that, in the eyes of the older people, the purpose of marriage is to give birth to children and maintain the dominant position of men in the family. They get married mainly to satisfy the needs of the traditional cultural systems, but they have not considered the affections between the husband and wife before marriage at all. At the same time, among these older people, the political conditions have become the necessary criteria for them to choose a spouse. Among the thirty respondents, five chose the item, high political status, accounting for 16.7 % of the respondents, which indicates that the young people after the founding of the People's Republic of China were influenced by the class consciousness and that their marriage also became ideological. It is more highlighted in the practice of the people who married in the 1960s and 1970s.

Compared with the standard of spouse selection for those who married before the 1950s, those who married in the 1960s and 1970s gave priority to the political status of the spouse when making a choice of the spouse, which was the most prominent change. Among the 50 respondents, 46 chose the standard, accounting for 92 % of the total respondents, which reflects that the political life became the central theme of the times at that time, and then people were pulled to the track of political movements and ideology. Thus, political status became a critical value standard.

As the saying goes in Tancun Village, a dragon begets a dragon, a phoenix begets a phoenix, and those begotten by rats are good at digging holes. In the 1960s and 1970s, class identity was regarded as the dividing line between good people and bad people. A landlord and the descendant of a landlord got married and gave birth to a child, who was classified as the class of landlord, regarded as a bad person, becoming the object of dictatorship. However, a poor peasant and another poor peasant got married and gave birth to a child, who was classified as a good person, becoming the master of the state and society. Marriage is regarded as a manifestation of a revolutionary act. Therefore, in the marriage practices, it became the trend of the times that a person chose a spouse born in a better class to constitute a revolutionary family and then give birth to a revolutionary offspring. In this regard, poor peasants, Party members, militiamen, and cadres of the production team were the first choices for the women to find a spouse. Moreover, these people can easily get married. Even the girls, who were born in the families of landlords, rich peasants or other exploiting classes, would choose to marry the men who are poor peasants in order to evade the torture of the class struggle so as to get rid of their original status and seek political asylum. However, it is still an important standard to require the husband to be upright and honest, as well as highly capable, as 72 % of the respondents chose the two standards of upright and honest qualities and strong capabilities. At that time, the capable people were usually the cadres of the village committees and production teams, militiamen, party and League members. In the era of political leadership, the economic conditions of the husband or wife were mostly neglected. Only one of the 50 respondents chose the standard of economic conditions, which reflects that it seemed shameful to pursue a good economic status. Among the standards, the educational background had become a key consideration, as 62 % of the respondents chose it, which was related to the popularization of elementary education at that time.

It is worth noting that, at that time, people seldom considered whether their spouses were obedient to their parents when making a choice, as only 2 % of the respondents chose the standard of filial piety to parents. In this way, it shows that the traditional concepts were fading out at that time, and that all the thoughts and ideas of the feudal times were criticized as backward thoughts. During the numerous movements that broke the feudal thoughts, the filial piety culture, as one of the excellent traditions of the Chinese nationality, was also treated coldly. On the other hand, it has a lot to do with the production and social organizations at that time, as it was the collective era of the people's commune, villages and production teams. Moreover, the people lived a collective life, and the traditional functions of the family became inferior, and the elderly were taken care of by the collective, rather than by their families. Therefore, people did not need to worry about whether the spouse was obedient to the parents.

Since the 1980s and 1990s, the villagers of Tancun Village have changed their standards again when choosing the right spouse.

First of all, there are more diversified standards for choosing a spouse. The economic conditions, which were not valued in the 1960s and 1970s, become one of the most important standards, as 84 % of the respondents chose it. The educational background has become the top standard, as 88 % of the respondents chose it. At that time, the educated people could generally be assigned to better jobs, and even became public servants of the state and received a permanent income. Furthermore, it would improve the economic conditions of the families. At the same time, the standard of strong capabilities has also become a key index to measure the conditions of the mate, as 82 % of the respondents chose it.

Secondly, since the implementation of the system of farm output quotas fixed by household, the issues related to the elderly have been raised to a key position for the marriage life of the people. Therefore, the filial piety to parents has become a consideration again, with 42 % of the respondents choosing it. The concept of filial piety has faded to some extent compared with the older people who married in the 1950s, but there is an increasingly prominent trend of the young people selecting a spouse on the premise of satisfying their own needs, as they have been in higher pursuit of a personal life in the context of market economy. In addition, 42 % of the respondents chose the standard of filial piety to parents, which, to some extent, showed the return of the traditional cultural values.

Thirdly, due to the impact of the market economy, the standard of upright and honest qualities, which had been valued for a long time, became slightly less important, as only 56 % of the respondents chose it. With the cessation of the ideological struggle, people seldom took political factors into account in the process of choosing spouse, as only 8 % of the respondents chose it, mainly concentrated on the people who married in the early and middle periods of the 1980s. The party members and League members, who had been valued in the past, had no obvious strengths in the practical marriage activities.

For the singles, they tend more to choose an ideal spouse. Economic conditions rank first among the standards, which is indispensable from the value orientation of the people's pursuit of economic interests in the market economy. Moreover, the standard of strong capabilities has also become one of the most important ones. However, at present, the criterion of strong capabilities is mainly determined by the economic conditions, wealth and social status. Anyone who is rich, or has a highly paid job may be regarded as a capable person even if he has received little education. Then, the standard of educational background ranked third, showing that the villagers of Tancun Village have paid increasing attention to actual benefits and pursued better material conditions in the course of the marriage. There is no doubt that only a few women can marry rich people in the local area. For most of the single women, it is merely an extravagant hope in their minds to marry a capable and rich man, which is somewhat idealistic. Moreover, it has become necessary for the people at marriageable age to hope to find a spouse who looks good, has a nice character, and is virtuous and gentle. As for the standard of political status, none of the single respondents had chosen it. It seemed to be out of date to discuss the political conditions when they try to find a mate among the singles. It also reflects that the young people in Tancun Village tend to be more individualized when they are choosing the right mate, emphasizing their material and psychological needs.

With the change of the standards of spouse selection, the local people have also changed the way to choose a spouse. The author conducted a questionnaire survey on the following three methods of spouse selection for fifty women who have been married since the 1990s, among which one was that the potential couple first became lovers and then invited a matchmaker to arrange the wedding, another was that they were completely introduced by the matchmaker before the wedding, and the rest was that they became lovers and got married as they liked. The results showed that 22 respondents first became lovers and then invited a matchmaker to arrange the wedding, accounting for 44 % , that 15 were completely introduced by the matchmaker before the wedding, accounting for 30 % , and that 13 became lovers and got married as they liked, accounting for 26 % .

As can be seen from the survey, the experience of free love has become the leading trend, involving a total of 70 % respondents, far exceeding the proportion of the couples that were completely introduced by the matchmaker before the wedding at 30 % , indicating that the modern view of love and marriage has become the primary value orientation of the local people. In spite of this, they have not abandoned the traditional model of matchmaking. Of the 50 respondents, 37 went into marriage with the intermediary role of the matchmaker, accounting for 74 % . 15 respondents were completely introduced by the matchmaker before the wedding, accounting for 30 % . That is to say, since the 1990s, nearly one-third of the people who married in Tancun Village found their mates via the matchmaker. 44 % of the respondents were lovers before the wedding, but they still invited a matchmaker to arrange the wedding in the end. In the local area, the matchmaker has become a symbol of marriage, because most people believe that marriage without a matchmaker is a shame.

Thus, we can make such a conclusion that, in the context of modernization, free love has become a leading trend of the marriage life for the villagers of Tancun Village, showing a new social practice. Moreover, there has been an increasing trend of free love among the young people, but the matchmaking by parents' order and on the matchmaker's word still plays a role in the marriage of some people. At least, it is of some symbolic significance as a rite. The mode of free love is blended with the traditional marriage methods in an organic and harmonious way, complementing each other.

The villagers of Tancun Village advocate free love, but do not deny the arrangement by the matchmakers for a wedding, which indicates that they hold a rational attitude towards marriage. A young man and woman, no matter how deeply they love each other, should always respect their parents' opinions when deciding on the marriage affairs, and their marriage should be involved in the introduction of the matchmaker. Only a few people who work outside can become lovers as they like and finally get married. Most young people believe that their parents have rich social experience and can consider the conditions of the man and woman in an all-round way. Through the matchmaker, the man and woman can gain a better understanding of each other, especially the mutual understanding between their families. In this way, it can avoid the weak foundation for the marriage of the couples, and reduce the conflicts between the married couples. Marriage is not an elusive castle in the air, but a real life. It can not be divorced from reality, but is closely linked with reality, with the food, clothing housing and transportation, as well as the childbearing and raising.

According to the local people, with the involvement of the parents, the young people can learn about the potential husband or wife through various channels, including the family background of the potential husband or wife, and the ideological and moral qualities and capabilities of individuals, so that they can have a thorough understanding of the potential husband or wife. At the same time, they believe that only by arranging a match by parents' order and on the matchmaker's word and following the traditional marriage customs passed down from generation to generation, their marriage ceremony can be spoken highly of by the society, and the future families can be equipped with a solid foundation recognized by the public. Especially the woman thinks that only when the man asks the matchmaker to formally come to her family and make a match, she can gain face and establish her due status in her husband's family when she gets married in the future. Just like a woman who married less than two years ago told the author, "if my husband wants to bully me, I will tell him confidently 'it is not that I want to marry you, but that your parents asked the matchmaker to my mother's house and got me married into your house formally.'" It is a value principle from a psychological perspective, as well as the respect for the value of the woman. Therefore, the custom of arranging a match by parents' order and on the matchmaker's word has not been blindly thrown into the garbage of history as the dross of the feudal society in Tancun Village. On the contrary, it is integrated into modern marriage and plays an important social role in marriage activities.

Marriage and Bi-parental Raising

Marriage is to confirm the relationship between men and women through legal means to achieve the reproduction of the race. Therefore, the establishment of marriage has also announced the beginning of childbearing that conforms to the social norms. As a result, people of any nationality will take the trouble to implement a group of complex rites for the establishment of marriage to ensure the legitimacy of the marriage. Moreover, any irregular sexual behavior or method of marriage will be condemned and punished by society. Russell, M. a

British philosopher, said, “The primary purpose of marriage is to supplement the world population (Russell, 1988).” Sociologists and anthropologists all agree that reproduction is the primary purpose of marriage. They divide the purpose of marriage into three stages. “In the initial stage, it is dominated by the economic conditions, followed by reproduction and love; in the second stage, it is dominated by reproduction, followed by the economic conditions and love; in the final stage, it is first dominated by love, followed by reproduction and the economic conditions (Chen, 1961).” In Tancun Village, the way to establish the marriage among the villagers also reflects the development trends of the marriage purpose of human beings.

In ancient China, traditional ideas based on Confucius's thoughts have also confirmed reproduction as the purpose of marriage. It wrote in the section Meaning of the Marriage Ceremony in the Book of Rites that the man and woman who held a wedding ceremony would consolidate the ties between the two families to offer sacrifice to the ancestors and to give birth to children to ensure the continuity of the families. It also wrote in The Book of Changes that when human beings first arise in the world, there has been the distinction between the men and women, and then a man will marry a woman to emphasize the human relations and ensure the continuity of descendants for generations. These classics also warn the people that marriage is an essential rite for human beings to link the past and the future, to bear the responsibility of inheriting the family tradition of the ancestors and continuing the family line for the descendants. Therefore, it was strictly pointed out by Mencius that “Having no male heir is the gravest of the three cardinal offenses against filial piety (Li Lou Part Ⅰ, Mencius).” It also raises the reproductive purpose of marriage to the core of Confucian ethics.

Therefore, for the sake of children, for the sake of childbearing and raising, people have no choice but to get married. Marriage is a cultural mechanism to determine parents for the child. Thus, the marriage relationship between the man and woman far exceeds the relationship between both sexes. In the cultural traditions of many nationalities, sexual freedom is not restricted. At least, the sexual freedom before marriage is even encouraged by society. The girls of the Taliu people (a branch of the Yi Nationality mainly in Liude Township of Yongsheng County in northwest Yunnan Province), before they get married, all live in a room named the youth shed or boudoir, which is their private space to engage in social activities. Here, a girl may have sexual relations with the boy that she loves. Every girl is only qualified to marry after she enjoys sufficient sexual freedom before marriage. But once married, both the man and woman must be loyal to each other, be responsible for their family, and jointly bear the responsibility of raising children. Therefore, marriage can never be equated with the determination of sexual relations.

When a woman is pregnant and gives birth to an infant, the new life can only be recognized by society through a series of rituals. Under the patriarchal social system, such recognition first requires determining that the infant has a legal father. Therefore, most societies only recognize the children born by a married couple. For the children born out of wedlock, people will discriminate against and repel them, and call them bastards. As a result, marriage is to determine the relationship between men and women in a way that conforms to cultural standards, and also to determine the social relationship between the couple and the child. Finally, the man and woman who give birth to a child share the obligations and responsibilities of raising the child together. According to Fei Xiaotong, the marriage means that a man and a woman agree to share the responsibilities of raising their child, that there is no absolute connection between the marriage relationship and gender relations, and that the reason for the restriction of the sexual relations beyond the marriage is that it is necessary to maintain and guarantee the long-term care of the children (Fei, 1981).

It is precisely because of the responsibilities and obligations involved in a marriage that men no longer have freedom. They are under varied cultural pressure in terms of laws, morality, and customs and so on. In this regard, they must provide the pregnant wives with the comprehensive protective facilities, and share with their wives the expected interests of the fetus, because their wives give birth to heirs that enable their families to continue their family line.

From a biological point of view, the relationship between a child and his or her mother can be defined, but a father is needed to bring up the child, while marriage endows the father of the child with a legal role. It can be said that one of the purposes of marriage is to place the child in an institution of bi-parental raising. The children must receive bi-parental care, which requires the joint engagement of the father, the mother, the father's family members and the mother's family members. It means that "marriage is not a private affair. Before the wedding, various responsibilities that are performed by the potential husband and wife and their relatives, in our opinion, are of great significance to extend the marriage of two individuals into a matter where many people have to bear their responsibilities, as well as to expand the marriage from the affection and love between the husband and wife to all kinds of complicated social contacts. Among these obligations that must be performed, the most notable is a mutual service or presenting with the economic character, while these obligations tend to spread to the people other than the parties concerned (Fei, 2005)."

Bi-parental raising is accomplished in the family. Similarly, the stability of the family is based on the cultural needs of both husband and wife raising their children. Only when both parents are living, their children can grow up in a healthy environment. A lasting marriage and a stable family not only meet the material needs of the children during their growth, but can also satisfy their psychological and emotional needs, which will be conducive to the healthy development of children's personality. "Maternal love is more conducive to the development of such emotions as caring and feeling accepted, while paternal love is conducive to the development of children in terms of attitudes and values. In a sense, if a person enjoys these two types of love, he or she will absorb these aspects of human experience into his or her personality (Lugo, 1996)."

Section 2 Customs of Praying for Children in Rites

In the traditional patriarchal society, the purpose of marriage is to have children and to consolidate the ties between two families. For newly married couples, people were most looking forward to and concerned most about whether they have a child. It is the eternally immutable wishes for people to wish the couple have an infant immediately and have a son and a daughter. In traditional times, people believe that the status and values of women are reflected by their children, especially their sons. As the saying goes, having no male heir is the gravest of the three cardinal offenses against filial piety. It has become a traditional criterion to measure whether a woman is virtuous and capable by checking whether the woman has given birth to a child and how many children she has. Therefore, pregnancy and childbearing have been the greatest concerns for women who have been married but have not yet been pregnant, thus leading to great psychological pressure. In order to achieve the expectations for a new life, balance their mental anxiety and ensure the safety of childbearing, the local people have developed a variety of customs of praying for children. In summary, it can be roughly divided into three categories, praying to the gods for children, sending sons by other people and mediumistic praying for children (Zhong, 1998).

Customs of Praying for Children in the Wedding Ceremony

According to the villagers of Tancun Village, it is an inevitable logical process to get married and have children. After a couple gets married, it will be deemed as the greatest sense of well-being in their lifetime if they can give birth to many children, both sons and daughters, and then have both grandsons and granddaughters. It is also their ultimate value goal in their lives. As the saying goes, having no male heir is the gravest of the three cardinal offenses against filial piety. If a newly married couple fails to give birth to a child in two or three years after their marriage, it is bound to cause panic in the entire family. After getting married, the people tend to have an extremely strong desire to pray for children, and the resulting customs of praying for children are commonly seen all over China.

In Tancun Village, all kinds of customs of praying for children have been carried out consciously before the wedding ceremony. The basic premise for the marriage of a young man and woman is to ensure that the eight characters of the two are well matched. Whether the eight characters are matched is determined by the fortune-teller according to the match of the year, month, day and hour and the zodiac of the birth of the man and woman as well as the match of the five elements of the two persons. If a young man and woman are well-matched in their eight characters, they can not only live together to old age, but also have lots of children and grandchildren after marriage.

The villagers of Tancun Village believe that the Chinese zodiac is interlinked with human character and that the nature of the people is similar to that of the Chinese zodiac. For instance, it avoids a female born in the year of Tiger, because the tiger is born fierce, and the female may represent a bad sign for her husband or children. The Chinese zodiac itself is not good or bad, but the key lies in the match between the zodiacs, since the zodiacs may mutually reinforce or restrain each other. As the proverb goes among the people, the horse scares the ox, and the rat and the goat cannot live together to old age; the snake looks at the tiger like the knife file, while the pig is in tears when seeing an infant monkey. As a result, checking whether the eight characters of the man and woman are matched before the wedding is the most important part for the villagers of Tancun Village to treat their marriage cautiously, because the match of the eight characters not only affects the lives of the young man and woman, but also influences whether they can smoothly give birth to a child.

According to Valuable Prescriptions for Emergencies, "for those who intend to become couples, the husband and wife should reinforce each other in the eight characters and five elements, and it should be combined with morals. If the match of the eight characters of the man and woman does not lead to a decline or death, they are deemed to have a child. But if they restrict each other in the match of eight characters and it leads to a decline and even death, they are deemed not to have a child. Even if they accidentally have a child, it is bound to ultimately bring trouble to them. If the two reinforce each other and are privileged to meet a person of great morals and good luck, they should still avoid the taboos as prescribed in the Prescriptions, and then all of their children will become the perfection itself." Besides, according to the book On the Infertility, "there are three reasons for those who are infertile, one is that the location of the tomb has a bad influence on the fortune of the family, one is that the couple restrict each other in age, and the last is that the couple suffers serious diseases." It can be seen that the ancients attribute infertility to the reasons in geomantic omen, Chinese zodiac and disease. As a result, the villagers of Tancun Village much check the date of birth and the eight characters of the man and woman before engagement. The man will be engaged to the woman if their eight characters are well-matched, and will not if they restrict each other. It is indeed a cultural means in the wedding ceremony to ensure the smooth completion of childbearing.

When the wedding ceremony of an adult man is about to be held, his parents first have to make a new bed for their son and daughter-in-law. When making the bed, the carpenter will ask the master of the family loudly before giving the first stroke on the timber with an ax, "what is the size of your bed?" At this moment, the master will answer loudly, "the bigger, the better. It is best to accommodate many piglets and allow people to practice boxing together on the bed."

In fact, the bed for the newly married couple has a relatively fixed size in the carpentry industry. In general, the new bed is 5.7 feet long, 3.7 feet wide and 1.7 feet high. A remainder of 0.7 must be added to an integer, which means that, on the one hand, an adult is followed by a young one and then the new couple will give birth to a child. On the other hand, in the Chinese language, the character "Qi" (7, meaning seven in Chinese) has a homophonic word "Qi" (妻, meaning the wife in Chinese), which indicates that the man, with his wife, can have many children and live a prosperous life. But when the carpenters are cutting the timbre, they will deliberately ask the master of the family loudly for good luck. But it was also said that the carpenters deliberately had an evil idea, as the parents of the man must present a red envelope to the carpenter to chant the scriptures of Luban (an ancient Chinese carpenter, and the patron saint of Chinese builders) if they had not prayed for good luck before realizing it, so as to eliminate the possible adverse consequences. The term, piglets, in the master's answer, represents that the future daughter-in-law will have such strong capabilities of childbearing that she will give birth to as many children as pigs giving birth to piglets. Moreover, these piglets are born with good fortune and easily brought up, and they will be free from the attacks of ghosts.

Therefore, in Tancun Village, people will say "raise the new infant like raising piggy or doggy", when giving best wishes to a new infant of a family. If a kid in a family falls ill, others should not say that he is ill in front of the kid, but should say he is living like a dog these days. It means that, when a child falls ill, he will get better soon even without injection or medicine like the piggy or doggy. In the answer of the master, "practice boxing on the bed" also shows the people's psychological desire for boys, since only boys may get involved in the martial practice. At present, the newly married men and women do not have to ask the carpenter to make a new bed, but buy a ready-made Simmons bed in the furniture store in the town. At this time, the boss of the furniture store will give lots of wishes to the newlyweds, like "may you have many children," "may you have both son and daughter," and "wish you have a healthy infant next year." It has become an essential quality for an owner of a furniture store to be able to send such blessings.

In the wedding ceremony, the bride's mother should put some peanuts, soybeans, candies, Chinese dates, sunflower seeds, rice and other items in each piece of the dowry of her daughter. Peanuts, soybeans, Chinese dates, longan, sunflower seeds and rice are all prolific plants, which symbolize that the bride will become as highly productive as these plants. Moreover, these prolific plants brought from the bride's mother's house are more auspicious to some extent, which indicates that women's fertility can be passed down from generation to generation. At the same time, in Chinese language, the Chinese dates (枣, Zao), peanuts (花生, Hua Sheng), longan (桂圆, Gui Yuan) and sunflower seeds (葵花籽, Kui Hua Zi) can be connected as the homophonic word of Zao Sheng Gui Zi (早生贵子, may the bride have an infant soon), which is the wishes of the bride's mother's family to the bride and the bridegroom.

In traditional society, when a woman just got married to her husband, she had to serve as a slave to her mother-in-law. She could not become the master of the family until she gave birth to a son. Then, the bride's mother hoped most that her married daughter could give birth to a son for her husband's family as early as possible to truly become the master of the family, while what she was concerned most was that her daughter could not have a son for a long time. As a result, the bride's mother prepared these prolific plants for her daughter accompanied by blessings and worries, and she regarded these plants as sacred items. They said that when they put these items in the dowry, they should not have any distractions in mind. If any bad omen arose from their minds, they would call out "Amitabha" immediately to seek the blessing of Bodhisattva.

The customs of teasing the newlyweds on wedding night can be seen in all regions of China. The folklorists interpret the behavior of teasing the newlyweds on the wedding night as an interactive custom enhancing the interpersonal relations, a celebration event, as well as a mediumistic ritual of giving the best wishes to the newlyweds. Therefore, it can close the distance between the bride and the groom, enables the bride to quickly get rid of the maidenliness and reservedness when she is a girl, and accelerates the role transformation of the bride to adapt to the new environment in her husband's house as soon as possible. In the meantime, teasing the newlyweds on the wedding night is also a custom of sexual enlightenment and education, which is conducive to the harmony of the marriage life of the newlyweds. Because of this, such custom, which used to be regarded as morbid by the literati of all dynasties, has been prevailing for thousands of years despite repeated prohibitions (Shang, 2000).

The wedding celebrations in the bridal chamber involve a wide variety of entertainment activities, but most of them focus on sex and childbearing, with a strong mediumistic sense. The purpose is to allow the bride and groom to gain a harmonious sexual life and strong fertility through these mediumistic activities.

In Tancun Village, the custom most related to childbearing in the wedding celebrations in the bridal chamber is the bed-curtain hanging. On the night of the wedding ceremony, after a drink, three or five older women will flood into the bridal chamber with a large group of children to hold the bed-curtain hanging ritual for the newlyweds. These older women must have many sons and grandchildren and their husbands are all alive. It is said that such women are the most blessed, so it enables the newlyweds to share the good fortune of these women by inviting them to preside over the ritual of bed-curtain hanging. There is a taboo that can never be broken in this ritual, which is that those women who have no children, or the widows who have been remarried, or the women who have been remarried after a divorce are forbidden to enter the bridal chamber, because these people may bring some bad luck to the bride. Therefore, in the ritual of bed-curtain hanging, those women who have no children or remarry will avoid such situations consciously so as not to be seen by the bride in the ritual.

At the beginning of the ritual, these blessed older women will first stand around the new bed with a plate on their hands, filled with peanuts, Chinese dates, longan, sunflower seeds and candies. Then, they take turns to address some auspicious words to bless the bride and groom. For example, distribute candies at the wedding ceremony this year, and you will have an infant next year. If your head faces east when sleeping, your child will become a scholar in the future, and if your head faces west when sleeping, your child will become an emperor in the future. Hang the bed-curtain on four corners, and you will have many children.

If the curtain is hung high, your child will be born next year. If the curtain is hung low, you will have an infant next year. After taking turns several times, they will toss the peanuts, Chinese dates, longan, sunflower seeds and candies onto the new bed. At this time, the children in the bridal chamber will rush to the bed to grab the food. The whole scene is so bustling. The children will not be restrained, but they can roll and make noise at will on the bed. The more children there are, the happier the groom's parents will be, because more children on the new bed means that the newly married couple will have more children in the future.

Mediumistic Customs of Praying for Children

In Tancun Village, if the bride fails to be pregnant for more than a year after marriage, her family members will worry about whether they offend some god, and then hold some rituals to be forgiven by the god, hoping to get help from the god.

If the young couple worries that they can not have a child because they offend the gods, they can ask the Goddess for help under the guidance of their mothers or other female senior relatives. The Goddess, in fact, is a witch, but it can be said that she is the most reliable predictor in the local area. According to the local people, they can accurately indicate all kinds of bad omens that have recently appeared in the customer's home, and, on this basis, tell the customer that they may have offended some god, some ancestors or bumped into some ghosts. In general, the witch will tell the new couple that they can not have a child after marriage because they have offended their ancestors or the Local God of the Land. After the couple go back home, the experienced elder women in their family should put liquors, fruits, tobacco, meat, fish and other sacrifices in front of the shrine, burn a large amount of paper resembling money, and call on their ancestors, and confess to them they did not show enough filial piety to their ancestors. Moreover, they will ask their ancestors to forgive them, and promise to be reverent and respectful to them in the future. Then they will ask their ancestors to send a child to them for the prosperity of future generations, and bless the younger generations with a healthy and safe life. After that, they will throw a pair of hexagrams made of sheep's horn tips on the ground to judge whether the ancestors agree to their request. First, they will play a Yin hexagram, which means that the ancestors have accepted the sacrifices and the burnt paper from the descendants. Second, they will play a Yang hexagram, which means that the ancestors promise to bless their future generations and fulfill their requests.

If it is the Local God of the Land to blame, they also need to call on their ancestors as the above rituals, but mainly to put in a good word to the Local God of the Land. In Tancun Village, the tablet of the Local God of the Land is placed below the shrine in every family, and God tends to be worshiped by the people as frequently as their ancestors. The couples who fail to have a child offer sacrifices to all their ancestors and the Local God of the Land, wishing that they would send a child to their families, and burn the paper resembling money to make a vow. Then, if a couple really has their child in the future, they will hold a ceremony to redeem the vow to the gods. In addition to praying to the Local God of the Land for children, some villagers will pray for children to the god in the temple of the god of the earth at the entrance to the village. In Tancun Village, the Local God of the Land is regarded as the god of sending children. In general, the mother-in-law takes the young daughter-in-law to offer sacrifices to the Local God of the Land to pray for children. Before that, the mother-in-law may first ask the carpenter to make a box wrapped in red cloth, which is an exquisite square box made of timbre, wrapped in red cloth, and filled with some offerings, such as vegetarian cakes, tofu and some cooked pork. After offering sacrifices in front of the temple, they will burn some paper resembling money and set off a string of firecrackers.

In the process of praying for children, the box wrapped in red cloth made of timbre is of great cultural significance, as the box symbolizes the womb of a pregnant woman with a fetus, and the red cloth outside the box symbolizes the blood. The local people attempt to achieve the effect of making something by setting its analog by using such imitative witchcraft, thereby receiving a child from the Local God of the Land. In the view of modern science, it is completely ridiculous and unfounded witchcraft. In the primitive mentality structure, it is full of convincing and reasonable imagination. "The primitive people, even the members of the society which has been considerably developed but still retains more or less primitive thinking mode, believe that the art image, whether it is a portrait, a statue or a sculpture, is as real as the individual being modeled. The Chinese people believe that the association between the image and the existence has become identical in both substance and spirit (Lucien, 1995)." In the view of the villagers of Tancun Village, the box wrapped in red cloth is the statue of a woman's womb. With the article, the child sent by the Local God of the Land can be transformed into a fetus in the womb.

Among the customs of praying for children in various regions, the custom of sending melons to pray for children is a universal, mediumistic and recreational activity. According to the section Eating Melons for Children in the Chapter Superstition of Qing Bai Lei Chao, "on the night of the Mid-Autumn Festival, people in the Huizhou region would send melons as a present to the couples who had not had a child for years after marriage. First, the relatives stole a white gourd from the vegetable farm, and painted the face of the woman who had not been pregnant for years with some colors on the gourd, and covered it with a coat. On the night of the Mid-Autumn Day, an older person of the family was recommended to hold the gourd to the woman's house, accompanied by some people beating the gong and setting off firecrackers. Then, the older person put the gourd on the bed, and covered it with the quilt, chanting, 'plant melons and get melons, sow beans and get beans (Pan, 2001).'" It has been earlier recorded in the Book of Songs that melons are used to symbolize a woman giving birth to a child. The section Continuity of the chapter Greater Odes of the Kingdom of the Book of Songs begins with the line that your family can grow and prosper like spreading melon vines. Wen Yiduo holds that "because melons have numerous seeds, it is the best symbol for the reproduction of offspring, and it can be compared to a woman giving birth to a child (Wen, 1954)." In Tancun Village, the custom of sending melons to pray for children had been prevailing by the 1950s. Although the procedures are roughly the same as those in other areas, the villagers of Tancun Village lay more stress on the similarity between the melon and the infant in appearance when making it.

The parents of the couple who has not had a child may express their ideas when drinking with others, or complain deliberately in the yard, "my son has been married for a long time, but they have not had a son yet. No one cares about it." In this way, others will understand what they mean. The kind-hearted neighbors will come to give a hand. They agree to pick a white gourd in a vegetable garden, and then make a long and thin towel gourd into the feet and hands of a doll, pick an eggplant and put it on the top of the white gourd as the head of the door, and poke a hole below the white gourd, fill the white gourd with water and then insert and plug a red pepper (referring to the male genital). After making the white gourd into a doll, the people, led by an elderly man, will flood into the house of the family where the young couple has not had a child yet, setting off firecrackers and winding the trumpet. As soon as they enter the door, the leading older man says, "Congratulations! Now we send you a healthy son, and you will have another younger son this year." The master of the family will bow and offer cigarettes to the men present to thank everyone for their kindness. While talking to each other, they will put the doll made of the white gourd on the bed, cover it with a quilt, pull out the pepper at the bottom of the white gourd, and then the water in it will flow out. All the people present laugh, "it urinates! It urinates!", making the bed a mess. Seeing this, the master will serve a banquet to entertain the people there, instead of feeling unhappy.

In the customs of stealing melons and sending children, the pepper is the symbol of the male genital. In the traditional customs of all ethnic groups in southern China, pepper is regarded as the symbol of male. Among the Dong and Miao people, when a new infant is born, the family members tend to hang some articles besides the gate in order to warn the strangers not to enter the house, and they will hang the pepper if a boy is born, and hang the cloth if a girl is born. According to the myth of Muliujia among the Zhuang people, when Muliujia created human beings, the clay figures that grabbed pepper became boys. Therefore, even up to now, pepper is still regarded as the symbol of the male genital among the Zhuang people.

In traditional society, the most basic value appeal of the rural people in China is to pursue more children and more blessings. In the past, if a woman could not have her second child a long time after giving birth to the first son or daughter, she would look like a weight that could not float up any more once falling into the water. In Tancun Village, the first son or daughter is called a weight son or a weight daughter, which means that the first child, like the weight, oppresses the younger brother or sister so much that the mother could not have a second child. The solution is that the woman has to go back to her mother's house and asks for eggs from door to door, and writes down the names of the persons who give eggs to her on a piece of red paper, which is also known as recording the gifts. After receiving the eggs, the woman should cook the eggs and the weight in the pot and eat them together. She should eat one egg at a time and three times a day. In this way, the woman could be pregnant again. The way of eating the eggs with weight is like the popular customs of begging for food or cloth from door to door. It is called the way of gathering auspiciousness (Gao, 1993). Here, eggs become a crucial mediumistic tool for people to pray for children.

In China, it has a long history of considering eggs as a mediumistic tool to pray for children to promote the childbirth rate and serve as a therapy for infertility after marriage. For instance, in the ceremony held for a new-born infant on the third day after its birth, the relatives and friends will come to celebrate the birth of the infant, and put red eggs in the bathtub. The infertile women will ask for the red eggs, as they believe that they will be pregnant by eating these eggs.

In ancient China, on the Shangsi Festival (also known as the Double Third Festival, on the third day of the third month of the Chinese calendar), there was the custom of floating eggs by the waters, which is also a symbol of praying for children. Later, it is renamed as date floating and wine cup floating, which is described in some poems. Moreover, the customs of egg floating and wine cup floating all originate from the belief in egg-aided fertility. There is also the custom of taking eggs as a kind of witchcraft for marriage to pray for children in many ethnic regions in China. In Leishan County of Qiandongnan Miao and Dong Autonomous Prefecture in Guizhou Province, an infertile Miao couple in Guizhou Province would go out with a duck's egg in the midnight. They would pile many stones on the land for children, and lay the egg on the stones. After offering the sacrifices to the god, they would engage in sexual relations below the branch of a big tree, and go back to their house with the egg on their back before dawn. It represents that they carry their son back to their house. In the Xiangxi Tujia and Miao Autonomous Prefecture in Hunan Province, in the mediumistic activities to pray for children, the witch would hold a tube filled with rice and a duck's egg on the rice, and put a male penis pasted with cloth paper in the tube to tease the seven fairies in the heaven, so as to pray for children.

Nowadays, those who are infertile or hope to have a son mainly offer sacrifices to Avalokitesvara, who is the Bodhisattva that can help the needy and relieve the distressed. In the eyes of the villagers of Tancun Village, Avalokitesvara is the most powerful and efficacious god. As a result, on the 19th day of the second lunar month as the birthday of Avalokitesvara, the 19th day of the sixth lunar month as the day of enlightenment, and the 19th day of the ninth lunar month as the day of starting to practice Buddhism, those who ask Avalokitesvara for help would burn incense in the nearby temple on Yangwu Mountains. Under the guidance of the nun, the people who pray for children would first make a vow to Avalokitesvara, and pay the temple an amount ranging from 500 to 800 Yuan according to their financial strength. If they finally have a child in the future, they must redeem the vow to the temple on time. When redeeming the vow, they have to take the incense, candles, paper resembling money as well as a banner to thank Avalokitesvara for its effectiveness. With an infant in the arms, the adults should set off firecrackers at the gate of the temple to report the good news. Then, under the guidance of the nun, they present the money for redeeming the vow to Avalokitesvara and make divination to judge whether Avalokitesvara has accepted the money. In many cases, the nun will tell the pilgrims, "Avalokitesvara is so kind-hearted, since you were originally pregnant with a daughter, but it replaced the fetus with a son." Then, the people who have a son as they like show their sincere thanks to Avalokitesvara. Moreover, many parents also ask the nun for a name for their new-born son, or identify Avalokitesvara as the adoptive mother for their son, hoping to obtain aura from gods and divine figures, so that their son will always live a safe and peaceful life.

Section 3 Taboos in Childbearing

The taboo is a preventive measure to avoid the gods' anger or misfortune. If the witchcraft tells us how to do something, taboos tell us what can not be done. The word, taboo, comes from the Polynesian word, tabu, which refers to the people or things with some supernatural spirits that are beyond the reach of ordinary people at a specific moment. There are two reasons why they are beyond the reach, one is that they are sacred, and the other is that they are unclean or inauspicious. The classification of taboos is complicated among the people. In the book Golden Bough, James George Frazer divides taboos roughly into four categories. The first is the taboos about behavior, the second is about mankind, the third is about articles and the fourth is about vocabulary. In Tancun Village, villagers also have many taboos relating to childbearing. Generally speaking, it can be divided into three categories, taboos in behavior, taboos in diet and other taboos.

Taboos in Behavior

In a family, a young woman's pregnancy is the most important and happiest event in rural areas. Therefore, a woman's pregnancy is also known as Youxi (Chinese: 有喜, a happy event). Then, a pregnant woman needs special care, and a group of cultural institutions needs to be set to ensure the smooth delivery of the fetus in the woman's womb. Taboos are the major cultural institutions to prevent a pregnant woman from emergencies. In Tancun Village, there are a lot of taboos for the childbearing of pregnant women in terms of daily life, the mode of behavior and diet, and the norms of sexual behaviors.

Pregnant women are regarded as people with low Yang Qi, so there are taboos for pregnant women going out in the morning and returning in the evening. In other words, pregnant women should not go out in the early morning or come back home till late at night, especially not to walk around at night. The ghost who dies in childbirth is the most dangerous ghost for a pregnant woman. Therefore, pregnant women are forbidden to enter the room of a woman near the time of labor to avoid the invasion of the ghost dying in childbirth. If someone dies, a pregnant woman is usually not allowed to attend the funeral ceremony, unless it is the funeral of her relative. But she must avoid temporarily when her relative's coffin is being carried to the cemetery so as not to offend the evil spirits. During the funeral activities, all kinds of ghosts may come and go at any time. Especially the wandering souls may take the opportunity to ask for the paper resembling money. Pregnant women have low Yang Qi, and they are easily offended by ghosts and their souls may be hooked. At the same time, there are various scenes to worship the ghosts and gods, where pregnant women are so easily frightened that it may affect the fetus in their womb.

Pregnant women are considered to have low Yang Qi, so they are also deemed to have a bad fortune. If a man goes on a long journey or asks for someone for help but he first meets a pregnant woman on the road, it is considered as a bad omen, which indicates that the man will have a bad luck and the person who he asks for help will undoubtedly be less likely to manage to handle the relevant affairs. Pregnant women have bad fortune, so they are strictly prohibited from crossing the shoulder pole of a man. If the shoulder pole across the roadblocks the way for a pregnant woman, she may either walk around the pole, or ask the owner of the shoulder pole to take it away. If the pregnant woman goes across the shoulder pole, she will be scolded by the owner of the shoulder pole, and she has to put it on her head and press it gently. Besides, pregnant women are not allowed to sit with a bowl at the gate or make carping comments with others.

A pregnant woman is also called a four-eyed person in the local area, and she is not allowed to hold a new-born infant in her arms. Otherwise, the infant may have diarrhea due to the four-eyed disease. If a pregnant woman makes the infant of other people suffer diarrhea due to violating the taboo, she will be scolded by the people around her for no conscience. The local people believe that if an infant has diarrhea, there is no way to cure it even if it is taken to the hospital, and that it is difficult to ultimately cure diarrhea by injection or medicine. Instead, they must ask those who know the Yin religion for a bowl of water to feed the infant. Those who know the Yin religion are usually middle-aged and older women. They first hold the infant, who suffers diarrhea, in their arms and give three bows outside at the door of its house, and then carry a bowl of water and say some incantations to outside the door. Finally, they draw a magic figure in the water with a chopstick. The entire ritual is very simple, and the reward is very low, as long as one kg of sugar or 0.5 kg of pork is sufficient.

In the views of the local people, pregnant women are unclean as the women during the menstrual period, with something silted. They may block the good luck of the men due to any carelessness. During the menstrual period, a woman can not take a bath with her husband in the same bathtub, or the husband must take a bath first, and then it is the wife's turn. After taking a bath, the wife should clean the bathtub with a basin of clean water and then put the bathtub upside down on the ground, so that it will not block the good fortune of the husband in the next night. As the women during the menstrual period, pregnant women must follow these taboos. Otherwise, they will be teased by the people around them. More seriously, they may be blamed by their mother-in-law.

Since the pregnant women are silted to some extent, in pregnancy, especially when it approaches the time of labor, the couples are not allowed to engage in sexual relations, and even some couples are ordered to sleep in separate beds by the older people. Until the child is born and is one month old, the couple can engage in regular sexual relations. After the couple sleeps in separate beds, the mother-in-law will sleep with the pregnant woman every night, and take care of the pregnant woman every night.

Taboos in Diet

Pregnant women have various forms of taboos in diet, most of which are a manifestation of people's thoughts of avoiding harm. They avoid leading to a risk of childbearing due to their diet. Moreover, the taboos of pregnant women in diet involve some mediumistic ideas, believing that their children will be what they eat in pregnancy.

Pregnant women are not allowed to eat rabbits, because rabbits have three-lip mouths. People believe that if a pregnant woman eats the rabbit, the mouth of the newborn will have the three-lip mouth or open mouth, while the local people call the children with such lips as a child with scars. It wrote in the Chapter of the Meaning of Life in the book Lun Heng (by Wang Chong in the Eastern Han Dynasty) that a pregnant woman who eats rabbit meat gives birth to an infant with a harelip. It can be seen that, as early as in the Han Dynasty, there was a custom that pregnant women should not eat rabbit meat. Chicken and ducks are the best food supplements in rural areas. Pregnant women should eat more chicken and duck meat, but not eat the chicken and duck gizzards. Gizzards are so fat that a pregnant woman who eats them may give birth to a child with upturned lips.

Moreover, pregnant women should not eat ginger, because ginger has many branches. A pregnant woman who eats ginger may give birth to an infant with five fingers on one hand. Lily is also a multi-petaled plant, and pregnant women should not eat such multi-petaled food. Otherwise, they may give birth to an infant with double-layer teeth. Pepper is the most commonly used ingredient in Hunan cuisine. People in Hunan love to eat pepper, but pregnant women are not allowed to eat spicy dishes. Even if they can have spicy dishes, they are allowed to eat only a little, as the people hold that if the pregnant woman has too much pepper, she may give birth to an infant with red eyes. Besides, pregnant women are not allowed to take fruits with them, as the people worry that the newborn may suffer a tumor. The pregnant period of donkey and horse is longer than that of mankind, so pregnant women are forbidden to eat donkey or horse meat. Otherwise, the pregnant period of pregnant women may last more than ten months and even reach twelve months like that of the donkey and horse.

Snake, turtle, terrapin and other animals are considered to have bad luck. It is believed that once a pregnant woman eats them, it will bring bad luck to the fetus, and more seriously, it may even cause the infant to be disfigured. Pregnant women are not allowed to eat crabs, as the newborn may smack the bubbles and drool. They should not eat the cock, as the newborn may not be able to sleep well and cry at night after birth. They can not eat shrimps or eel, as the infant may not be able to speak.

The food that pregnant women eat may exert the corresponding impact on the fetus, which means that there is certain telepathy between the fetus and its mother or even its father. Lucien, L. B. explained such a phenomenon of primitive thinking with the law of participation. "In many primitive ethnic groups, such essential co-existence and mutual infiltration exist between the infant and its father, between the infant and its mother, and between the infant and its parents. It is part of those taboos or preventive measures that should be observed by the father, the mother or the parents of the infant from the date when the mother is found pregnant to the time when the infant is born (Lucien, 1995). "The ancient Chinese explained the mysterious links between the pregnant woman and the fetus with the theory of the external world affecting the internal fetus.

"According to the previous theories, when a woman is pregnant for three months, everything in her body changes while the character of the fetus has not been fixed. Therefore, when a woman is pregnant for three months, she can watch rhinos, elephants and wild animals, or pearls and jades, or visit the persons of virtue or the masters of great kindness. She can watch the ritual music performance, or the bell and drum show, or the ceremonies to worship the ancestors, the military furnishings. She can burn the incense to worship celebrities, chant the beautiful poems and books, proverbs and commandments both in ancient and modern times. She should live in a simple and quiet place, and sit in a proper way. She can play some musical instruments to regulate her state of mind and neutralize her personality, and control her hobbies and desires, and keep a peaceful attitude towards everything. In this way, her children will all be kind-hearted, loyal and obedient to their state and parents, live a healthy and long life, with a benevolent and intelligent mind. It is precisely the antenatal education (Sun and Gao, 2004)."

In addition to the theory of external world affecting the internal fetus, it can also achieve the effects of antenatal education by guiding the pregnant women to conduct some positive actions, such as listening to music, seeing the sages, chanting the poems, controlling the hobbies and desires and eating regular food. Moreover, the mental state of pregnant women also has a great impact on the fetus. In the Chapter of Qi and Life in the book Lun Heng, it wrote that "when a woman is pregnant, she must walk and sit up upright, and keep in a good mood. She should not be subject to her changing moods. If she is too happy, it will hurt her heart and her Qi will disperse. If she is furious, it will hurt her liver and the Qi will rise. If she thinks too much, it will hurt her spleen, and the Qi will stagnate. If she worries too much, it will hurt her lungs and the Qi will gather. If she fears too much, it will hurt her kidney and the Qi will go down. When the Qi of the mother is hurt, the Qi of the fetus will be hurt accordingly. If the newborn is blind, or deaf or dumb, or suffers dementia or epilepsy, it is caused by the inadequate natural endowment."

Therefore, it is of vital importance for a pregnant woman to keep a good mental state for the healthy growth of her infant. Therefore, it is reasonable to prohibit pregnant women from eating spicy food. Spicy food may make pregnant women fussier from excessive internal heat. Meanwhile, pregnant women are not allowed to eat snakes, turtles and other terrifying food, since they may easily lead to the inner fear of pregnant women and affect the development of the fetus.

The taboos in diet reflect the cultural regulation of primitive eugenics. Through the taboos of pregnant women in diet, it can not only ensure the health of the mother, but also ensure the provision of adequate nutrition to the fetus. Parts of the taboos are of some scientific value, but the taboos are mysterious and superstitious to some extent.

Other Taboos

After the delivery of a pregnant woman, the placenta of the infant can not be thrown casually. If it is eaten by someone or other animals, it will endanger the life of the infant. The infant's clothes, diapers and other articles can not be exposed outside at night, because these items are used by the child next to its skin. If they are not recovered at night but are exposed to dew outside, it may be like that the infant has not returned home, and is vulnerable to the invasion of the ghost wandering at night, which will be harmful to the infant. The diapers of children under one year old can not be exposed to the sun, as people are afraid that the sun gets so furious that it affects the yield of the fields. Children tend to be warned by their parents not to damage the swallows' nest. Otherwise, the children will have scabies on the head. The swallows' nest is built in the corner of the roof bean, like an upside-down head with blemishes on the surface, which is similar to the scab in appearance to some extent.

Adults educate their children to protect the ecological balance through the resemblance between the scab and the swallows' nest. If a child suffers from pinkeye or another keratitis, it will be teased for peeing at a woman going to the bathroom. In fact, it is to use the taboos to teach the children about the ethics and gender awareness of the principle that it is improper for men and women to touch each other's hand in passing objects.

After marriage, the couples should bear the burden of childbearing and raising. The sexual affairs between couples become an inevitable process to give birth to children. In Tancun Village, there is a saying about the frequency and time of the sexual life for couples that the couple expects the time to blow out the lamp before sleeping at their twenties, and waits for the night watchman to sound the night watches at their thirties, and engages in sexual affairs about once a month at their forties, and has sexual relations every a few months like spending the festivals in their fifties, and engages in sexual life once a year like giving New Year's greetings at their sixties. It means that, as people grow older, they engage in fewer and fewer sexual affairs. As for extramarital sexual affairs, it has been a taboo in the local area. As some saying goes in the local area, gambling is like stealing, and rape is like murder; those who enjoy extramarital affairs are deemed to die; amour comes from the gambling house, and deaths come from the houses of courtesans. Even when it comes to the sexual affairs between the couple, there is a lot to pay attention to. It is not suitable for couples to have sexual intercourse when they are exhausted, ill, traveling far, bored, hungry, full, frightened, or suffer from rheumatic fever, or when it is gloomy and cold. It is completely forbidden to engage in sexual affairs in the ancestral halls, ancestral rooms, temples, Taoist temples, former residences, or by the tombs and coffins.

The delivery of pregnant women is a critical moment concerning happiness or sadness. If both the mother and infant are doing well, the whole family will feel delighted. But if it is a difficult labor, it may lead to a tragedy. Pregnant women are forbidden to deliver at their mother's house. In case it is about to labor, the husband's family should ask Yin Shi Gong to hold the ceremony to thank the mother-in-law's family one month after the birth of the new infant. It is more forbidden to give birth to other people's houses. When a pregnant woman is giving birth to her infant, her husband and other pregnant women are not allowed to enter the delivery room. After the infant is born, its placenta can not be thrown casually, but should be put into a tile jar and buried deep underground. If it is not handled properly, it will lead a disaster to the new infant. When the umbilical cord of the infant is cut, it should be air-dried and wrapped with paper. If the infant suffers from abdominal pain, inflammation of the navel, or cries at night, it can be treated by grinding the dried umbilical cord with water. The lying-in woman should not be extremely happy, or sad, depressed or nervous in the first month after the childbirth. She can not be exposed to cold water, frost and wind. And she is not allowed to visit other people's houses in the month.

As for the duration of pregnancy, it is believed among the people that the premature infants who are born when they stay in the fetus for seven months can still survive, but it is difficult for those who are born when they stay in the fetus for eight or nine months to survive. In addition, there are also taboos on the time to give birth to the infant. As the saying goes, a boy fears to be born on the first day of the lunar month, and a girl fears to be born on the fifteenth day; it is inauspicious to give birth to the infant on the first and fifteen days of the first lunar month and on the Mid-July Days.

It will be regarded as a curse of the parents, because the parents expect to take a break during the Spring Festival, the Lantern Festival, the Dragon Boat Festival or the Mid-Autumn Festival but the infant is born at this moment. At the same time, these festivals, which are the most important for Chinese people, should have been celebrated. But if children are born in these festivals, they can celebrate their birthdays but can not spend the festivals. The traditional villagers of Tancun Village prefer sons to daughters. As the saying goes, a family will succeed in every field if a son is born, but the family will go poor year by year if a daughter is born. It means that giving birth to a son is a blessing to the family.

In terms of infant feeding, mothers should not feed their babies at the breast after they suffer excessive heat, cold, tiredness, anger, sorrow, drink or sexual affairs. The infant's diapers and swaddling clothes are better made of old cloth rather than new cloth. It is said that the best diapers and swaddling clothes are made of the old cotton-padded jacket and quilt of the older people with long life, so that it enables the infant to live a long life. The swaddling clothes can not be too thick, as it is commonly said to easily lead the infant to have sores, or easily make the infant weak and fear cold. If the swaddling clothes are dirty and washed, they cannot be exposed to the sun at a high place. At night, they should be taken back to the indoors. Otherwise, it is commonly believed to be followed by ghosts, frightening the infant. It is not allowed for adults to go below the swaddling clothes or diapers of the infant, which is believed to make the infant less blessed. Babies should not wear trousers until one hundred days after their birth, and they should be swaddled into a quilt to make it flexible to move their legs and feet, which is conducive to their development. In this way, it is believed that even when the infant dies, it can go to the next life quickly. Twins should wear the same clothes, since it is God's will to make them look identical. What God will no frost can kill.

Three days after the birth of the infant, it is necessary to take a bath for the infant according to the customs of the local people. And the water for washing the infant can not be poured randomly, as it is said that the god of the child is still wandering around the infant's house within one hundred days after its birth. Therefore, people should be cautious everywhere. On the third day after the infant's birth, the relatives and friends of the family will come to celebrate the infant's birth. The infant's maternal grandparents will present the bay's full clothes, hats, shoes and socks to the infant. The infant's paternal grandparents will have a banquet to receive the guests and distribute red eggs to the guests. However, people in white, the relatives of the deceased and those who wear straw sandals are not allowed to attend the ceremony.

When an infant is newly born in a family, the first person who comes to the house is called "the newborn's visitor". If a man visits the infant girl's house, it is considered that the infant girl is blessed and can smoothly grow up. If a woman visits the infant boy's house, it is considered that the Yin Qi is so strong that the infant boy will be feeble and sick. The cradle of the infant should not be shaken when the infant does not stay in it. In the house where a boy is born, the infant boy is often said to be a girl, as it is believed that the girls are inferior and can be easily raised. When the wife gives birth to the child, the husband must go to his mother-in-law's house to report the happy news to his parents-in-law. If the infant is a boy, the husband should carry a rooster to his mother-in-law's house. If the infant is a girl, the husband should carry a hen. The infant should have his hair cut for the first time thirty days after he is born, but the hair in front of his forehead should be retained to cover the fontanel. In fact, it is to protect the infant from getting a cold.

To give an infant a name, people tend to use the surname of its father, followed by the Chinese character representing his position in the family hierarchy and another Chinese character in the end, and then it becomes the formal name of the infant. Some people ask the fortune-teller for help. If an infant lacks one of the five elements (metal, wood, water, fire and earth) in the date of its birth and the eight characters, it will be supplemented in his name. If an infant lacks the earth element, one character in his name must be composed of the radical of Tu (Chinese: 土, meaning earth). As for the pet name for a child, it is mostly such names as Gouyazi (Chinese: 狗伢子, meaning puppy dog), or Niuyazi (Chinese: 牛伢子, meaning calf), because it is believed that the child with a bad name can grow up in a stable and smooth way. Some children are born with bad eight characters, which must be resolved by acknowledging someone as the adoptive father. And it is best that the adoptive father is a solitary old man, or a beggar, or a fortune-teller, as people believe that these men live a miserable life and then they can bear the misfortune instead of the children. Some babies are born with special eight characters, so they must acknowledge one hundred adoptive fathers. But it is relatively troublesome to acknowledge them one by one. Therefore, the children acknowledge a cypress tree (Chinese: 柏树) as the adoptive father. In the Chinese language, the character Bai (Chinese: 柏, Bǎi) is a homophonic word of Bai (Chinese:百, Bǎi , meaning one hundred). Besides, some children acknowledge stone lions, or stone statues of Buddha as adoptive fathers.

According to the local people, the time of the birth of a person is closely bound up with its eight characters and fate. If a child is born at a good time, it will bring good luck to the child's future. But if a child is born at a bad time, it will cause numerous disasters to the child's life, so it must experience many tough times. Therefore, the time of birth is of great importance to a child. Adults should never neglect the time of the birth of their children. Traditionally, the time of twelve o'clock in the day is set at noon and twenty-four o'clock in the evening is set at midnight. On this basis, a day is divided into 12 two-hour periods as follows:

Zi Shi (Chinese: 子时): from 11 p.m. to 1 a.m.

Chou Shi (Chinese: 丑时): from 1 a.m. to 3 a.m.

Yin Shi (Chinese: 寅时): from 3 a.m. to 5 a.m.

Mao Shi (Chinese: 卯时): from 5 a.m. to 7 a.m.

Chen Shi (Chinese: 辰时): from 7 a.m. to 9 a.m.

Si Shi (Chinese: 巳时): from 9 a.m. to 11 a.m.

Wu Shi (Chinese: 午时): from 11 a.m. to 1 p.m.

Wei Shi (Chinese: 未时): from 1 p.m. to 3 p.m.

Shen Shi (Chinese: 申时): from 3 p.m. to 5 p.m.

You Shi (Chinese: 酉时): from 5 p.m. to 7 p.m.

Xu Shi (Chinese: 戌时): from 7 p.m. to 9 p.m.

Hai Shi (Chinese: 亥时): from 9 p.m. to 11 p.m.

It is divided according to the modern precise timing tools. In fact, in the folk, people had to judge and record the time by experience when all kinds of timing tools, such as watches and wall clocks, have not been widely used. In Tancun Village, the birth of a child means that he or she begins the journey of his or her life. And under the control of the fatalism, people believe that the future and destiny of a person are doomed at the moment when it is born. As the saying goes, life is determined by the eight characters, and the future is determined at the moment of childbirth.

The fortune-teller is the predictor of the child's destiny. They can know the fate of the child according to the time of its birth. They can predict when he or she suffers from a disaster, when he or she goes smoothly, when he or she can enter a higher school, and when he or she should evade risks, when he or she suffers minor ailments, and when he or she gets married, when he or she has a child, whether he or she has a happy marriage, and whether he or she has a bright future. In the past, the watch was a rare luxury for ordinary people, and people had to judge the time based on their experience. In this way, it formed a unique system of local knowledge, which was passed down in the form of songs or proverbs from generation to generation. In Tancun Village, people judge the time according to the song that it is Zi Shi in the midnight, and people have the first sleep in Chou Shi, it is dark in Yin Shi and Mao Shi, there is shadow in Chen Shi, it is noon in Wu Shi, the sun declines toward the west in Wei Shi, it is Shen Shi to see the sunset, and it is You Shi to light the candle, Xu Shi to work and Hai Shi to go to bed. With such songs, people can roughly remember the time when their children were born. Therefore, when mothers or grandmothers go to the fortune-teller for their children or grandchildren, they usually report some living scenes when the children were born, rather than the specified time. They will tell some specific situations to the fortune-teller to determine the time, as they may say roosters crowed when the child was born; it was daybreak about a quarter after the midwives finished washing the newborn infant; when we just lit the candle, she had labor pains and then, she gave birth to the child after we had a meal.

Besides, there are many taboos for child-raising. It is not allowed to scratch the arch of the infant's foot, or pinch its cheek, or pull its ears. When describing a good-looking or fat infant, people should say it is ugly, and it is forbidden to say the infant is heavy when people hold the infant in the arms. It is forbidden to say that the infant is not sick, because it may go against the auspicious words and then the bay may be feeble and sick. If an infant cries frequently at night, the parents can write a letter that "to the God of Heaven and the God of Land, my infant cries at night. Please read the letter, and make it sleep sound every night" on a piece of red paper, make 100 copies of the letter, and post them everywhere. Children are not allowed to eat pigs' brains; otherwise the children may have premature white hair. Children are not allowed to eat fish row; otherwise, they may be illiterate in the future. Children are not allowed to count the stars in the sky; otherwise, they can not count when they grow up. Children are forbidden to point at the moon; otherwise, they may suffer an ear sore.

On the one hand, the cultural meaning of taboos lies in that it is a preventive means and concept in the beliefs and customs, and it is the mysterious and traditional thinking and behavioral habit in the subconscious, which has been constantly inherited, repeated and patterned by people from generation to generation. According to such thinking habit, people can know what to do and what not to do, and consciously succumb to the constraint of taboos to coordinate their behaviors. Prior to the establishment of the modern scientific system, the villagers of Tancun Village had developed a number of strict taboos in the course of the inheritance, accumulation and learning of the birth culture, which was the control measures they had adopted in the face of diseases and disasters and the resulting misfortunes. Even up to now, with the development of the increasingly developed science and technology, they still adhere strictly to these taboos, as it is better to believe the worse and be pleasantly surprised, than to be optimistic and learn the worst. Thus, we can see that the strong sense of life of the local people has been always accompanied by serious anxieties. It can be even said that it is their inability to control the continuity and reproduction of life that makes them adopt the taboos as a means to alleviate their anxiety and balance their panic.

On the other hand, the cultural meaning of taboos also lies in that the taboos go deep into the cultural system of the groups as a cultural gene that is passed down from generation to generation. Closely combined with the lifestyle, value judgment, words and deeds of the people, taboos constitute the common knowledge authority proposed by Geertz, C. (Geertz, 2004). Taboo is regarded as a piece of general knowledge, and people do not need to demonstrate its scientific basis, as long as they know what they should do or what they should not do. Each taboo has always been reasonable for the local people, so no one will doubt, argue about or ponder over the taboo, but observe it in a habitual and natural way.

Taking the witchcraft of the Azande and the common knowledge of the Azande in the book Witchcraft, Oracles and Magic among the Azande by Sir Edward Evans-Pritchard as an example, Geertz, C. explained the reason why witchcraft obtained mysterious forces. The Azande hurt their feet by a stump when they are walking, or keep the rules and do not engage in sexual relations with their wives but the pottery is still broken, or they eat too many bananas, leading to a stomachache. It is originally the common sense in the eyes of Sir Edward Evans-Pritchard, as everything is natural and normal. However, in the eyes of the Azande, these bad things are all caused by the addiction to the sorcery, which is a general knowledge for the Azande. The general knowledge is beyond all doubt. The mysterious belief in witchcraft is an integral part of the world outlook of the Azande, and they believe that it is mystical, which is the truth that they have elaborately made and maintained according to the cause that they put themselves in the place of others. Because faith becomes common sense, everything becomes well-reasoned, and things are no longer mysterious, while it is not the primitive metaphysics, which is the cultural authority. The general knowledge endows the witchcraft with some meanings and forces.

Women in Tancun Village, for the sake of childbearing, have been cautiously following the witchcraft beliefs that have been passed down from generation to generation in the whole process from the beginning of the wedding ceremony to the adulthood of their children, even for young people who have received modern scientific education. In these specific occasions, rationality becomes feeble in front of witchcraft, because it is believed that these taboos are general knowledge, and are the outcome of the repeated practices by their ancestors. Nowadays, the villagers of Tancun Village do not exclude science, as modern medicine is the primary means that they can depend on to ensure the safety of pregnant women. However, science can be foreseen and controlled, while taboos and witchcraft are unknown. As a result, the present villagers of Tancun Village rely on science and modern medicine on the premise of abiding by taboos and witchcraft. In their minds, science and tradition are not mutually exclusive, but the two can be coordinated with each other, jointly protecting their faith of having a flourishing population.

Section 4 Qi Shui and Shu Wan

Pregnancy and childbearing are both difficult and dangerous for women, which is called going through the gate of hell by the villagers of Tancun Village, especially when the medical conditions and childbearing technology were extremely backward in the past. For this reason, people need to create a set of local cultural institutions to guarantee that the local pregnant women can give birth to their children smoothly. Otherwise, it is impossible for the women to assume their responsibilities of having children to perpetuate their families, and there is less chance for the new generation of family members, as the continuity of the family, to survive. According to the author, these cultural institutions that ensure the smooth progress of women's childbearing are designed for a specific region, which are the effective cultural rules that are accumulated and developed from history by the people from generation to generation in each region, and practiced by the local people for a long time. These cultural rules are accompanied y the whole process from the pregnancy of women to the growth of children. Since they are local cultural rules, it is not necessary to have a modern scientific basis for demonstration, as long as the local people believe them.

Tancun Village is deeply affected by the Meishan Culture, where the people worship witches and ghosts. Therefore, witchcraft is a prevailing means to solve the problem of witches and ghosts causing trouble. In particular, the witchcraft that interferes with children's birth and growth has been deeply believed by the people there.

According to the villagers of Tancun Village, the pregnancy of women and the birth and growth of babies not only need to be blessed by the gods that are widely worships among the people, such as Avalokitesvara and Supreme Lord Laozi, but also need to be protected by the local gods, including the Bodhisattva of Temple King, the God of Land and the God of Ancestors.

According to the local people, the Bodhisattva of Temple King is in charge of the population changes in the local area. In the past, anyone who has to obtain the legal status of a member of the local area, such as a newborn, must pay a visit to the Bodhisattva of Temple King, inform him and be approved by him.

The Local God of the Land is the local god in charge of maintaining the social order in the area, and he is equivalent to the chief executive in the world to protect the people in the area from the interference and invasion of external wandering ghosts. As a result, The Local God of the Land is an essential god in the local area. There is not only a public temple in the village to worship the Local God of the Land, but the tablet of the Local God of the Land can be seen on the shrine of every household. God has been frequently worshiped together with the ancestors of the villagers. However, the Local God of the Land is easily offended and furious. Especially, the villagers can not interfere with his peaceful life at will. The local people believe that, anyone who digs ditches to build canals, or breaks ground in starting building a house, or even moves the furniture or living tools in the house may disturb the God, which may lead to serious consequences. The disturbed Local God of the Land may play tricks on the pregnant women or the newborn babies in the village, causing the pregnant women to give birth to premature babies, and causing the babies to cry and not to drink milk. Therefore, if there are pregnant women or newborn babies in the village, the ceremony of Qi Shui must be held to worship the Local God of the Land for his approval before a building project starts, so as not to make pregnant women give birth prematurely and the babies feel sick. But if someone accidentally offends God and causes chaos and panic, the people who know the Yin religion must be invited to perform the magic arts of Shu Wan to pray for the forgiveness of God.

Qi Shui Ceremony

In the view of the local people, any construction activities, such as building houses, digging channels, repairing the pigpen or cattle pen, moving the furniture or cleaning the house, may disturb the Local God of the Land and interfere with his peaceful life, which may cause serious discontent of the God. Human beings live in peace with the gods under normal conditions, as human beings live and work in peace and contentment in this world while the gods live a happy and contented life under the ground. With the balance of Yin and Yang, the two refrain from invading each other. Any form of destruction to such structural harmony is illegal unless it is agreed by the other party, accompanied by some ritual compensation. It is the cultural function of Qi Shui.

The Local God of the Land depicted in many folk operas is a humorous, kind-hearted and amiable god. However, in the views of the villagers of Tancun Village, the Local God of the Land is moody and easily offended. The offended God tends to take revenge on the most disadvantaged groups in the world. He may make the pregnant woman give birth prematurely, or let the newborn cry, eat or drink nothing. The villagers of Tancun Village hold the Qi Shui ceremony before construction mainly to pacify the Local God of the Land and to bribe or make up for him.

The Qi Shui ceremony is divided into the Large-scale Qi Shui ceremony and the Small-scale Qi Shui ceremony. The Large-scale Qi Shui ceremony is a ritual activity to maintain the public security and regional order, aiming to protect the people other than the villagers of the village from being blamed by the Local God of the Land. When engaged in the repair or construction of public facilities and religious sites in the region, such as channels, temples or ancestral temples, villagers need to perform the Qi Shui ceremony to the local gods other than in the village, so as to obtain the permission of the gods and free themselves from the punishment of the gods. The local gods include Bodhisattva of Temple King, the Local God of the Land, the God of Mountains and the God of Waters, God of Ancestors and so on. The place where the ceremony takes effect is centered on the site of the ceremony and radiates to the surrounding area at a distance of five kilometers in diameter.

As the saying goes among the local people, the Large-scale Qi Shui ceremony can take effect in the surrounding area at a distance of five kilometers in all directions. The figure "five" here is an abstract number, rather than an accurate one, which implies that the Large-scale Qi Shui ceremony can take effect by radiating to a large area, so as to prevent the pregnant women and newborn babies from being blamed by the Local God of the Land. The site to hold the Large-scale Qi Shui ceremony should be determined according to the area of the space that needs prevention. If it is only to guard against the Local God of the Land and other gods in a natural village, the ceremony should be held at the entrance to the village. But if it is to guard against the Local God of the Land and other gods in a large area, the ceremony should be held in public space, such as ancestral temples, temple gates, the intersection of multiple roads and so on. Bronislaw Kaspar Malinowski wrote, "Witchcraft is a public institution from the perspective of its primary form (Malinowski, 2003)." The publicity of ritual activities lies in that it can safeguard the security of the groups, and maintain the continuity of cultural integrity and the normal operation of cultural order in the region.

The family of the Local God of the Land is an extremely complex and populous system of gods, as the descendants of the Local God of the Land can be found in every corner of the world, ranging from the cross-regional space, such as the town god, to each household. In Tancun Village, the god that has jurisdiction and control over the household is called the God of the House, which shares equal status with the ancestors of the family. Therefore, the God of the House is closely related to the population reproduction, economic prosperity and safety of the domestic animals of the household.

If the head of a family intends to build a house, or repair the pigpen or cattle pen, move the furniture or clean the house, or clean the pigpen or cattle pen, which is only involved in the internal affairs of the household, the family only needs to hold a ceremony for the God of the House within the household, so that it can avoid the possible disasters to the family members. In this case, the Qi Shui ceremony held is called the Small-scale Qi Shui ceremony, which is to be held in front of the shrine in the central room of the house, indicating that the Small-scale

Qi Shui ceremony is only targeted at a limited scope of small households. The Large-scale and the Small-scale Qi Shui ceremonies only vary from each other in terms of the site where the ceremony is held and the scope of jurisdiction, while the procedures of the ceremony are simple and the same. But the ceremony must be presided over by the professional religious figures who know the Yin religion, as they have the psychic powers. According to the procedures of the ceremony taught by their masters, they can communicate with the Local God of the Land and convey the requirements of the human beings in the world so as to evade the possible disasters.

At the ceremony of Qi Shui, the masters who know the Yin religion will place a stool in front of the entrance or in front of the shrine in the household, put three small cups of spirits on the stool, and insert three incenses and two candles into the ground, and then incant silently. According to the masters, the Qi Shui Incantation chanted by the people learning from different masters is roughly the same, but the magic figures and the techniques may be slightly different. The masters said that, no matter what religious ceremonies or activities they preside over, they must think of the appearance of their masters in their minds before calling the gods. Otherwise, the magic they perform will not work. It is the same important as the incantation and magic figures.

Therefore, even if the person who presides over the ceremony learns the incantation and magic figures but he had not learned them directly from the master, which means that his master did not agree that he could perform the religious rites when he was alive, it will not achieve the purpose of the rites even if he has learned how to incant or draw the magic figures. Therefore, at the time of every Qi Shui ceremony, the person who performs the magic has to incant and draw the magic figures and perform other magic arts, but he must be aided by his master, namely, the founder of the religion. Therefore, at the time of the ceremony, the person who performs the magic must think of the look of his master in his mind, and always talk about his master in his mind to ask for help, and then chant the Qi Shui Incantation silently:

To the divine gods: XX, an ordinary person and believer, is here to burn the incenses to call up the gods and Buddha of Confucianism, Buddhism and Taoism in Kunlun Mountain, Huoshao Plateau and Xiaolin Plateau to attend the ceremony. Beg your forgiveness, and please ask the Supreme Lord Laozi, Hua Tuo, the Ancestor of Snow Mountains, Avalokitesvara, the Xuantian Heaven Emperor, the Master of Zhenwu to attend the ceremony. Please ask the Bodhisattva of Temple King, the souls of the previous landlords, the gods in the nether world, the God of Xinglong Land, the Goddess of Wangxiang, Bhaisajya-raja, the Songzi Avalokitesvara, as well as the general guarding the house, the Xingxiu on duty, Tai Gong Wen Jun, and the god of land in charge of the mountains, the god of land in charge of the roads, the god of land in charge of the ponds, the god of land in charge of the houses to bless the family. In the house, the men and women are safe and healthy, and the domestic animals are all thriving. The members go to each other for something, and they do not address each other casually for nothing. The gods can return to your palaces, and they all come with their mounts. Where the golden hoe moves, nothing is a taboo.

Once the divine Patriarch Pu'an arrives, the construction starts, the phoenix bird is both the heaven and the earth, and it sets up the stars determining killings on heaven monster, on earth monster, on a yearly monster, on a monthly monster and on an hourly monster. And there are no taboos on heaven, on the earth, on the year, on the month, on the day and on the hour. Devils should all be retreated. When Patriarch Pu'an comes, nothing is a taboo.

After chanting the incantation, the master killed a rooster quickly, and took out a red magic figure, pasted chicken blood, and burnt it with a handful of paper resembling money on the ground. Next, the master pulled his fingers on both hands to show the symbols of the corresponding magic. Suddenly, he shouted "God bless" and threw down the divination made of the tip of the sheep horn abruptly. To this point, the ceremony came to an end.

Qi Shui Incantation is a sacred language. In the course of the ceremony, the person who performs the magic can only incant silently in an ambiguous tone. His pronunciation and intonation are in fixed patterns, which can only be imitated from his master, and can not be incanted in a standardized tone which is widely used now. The use of the ambiguous and irregular or simple voice and tone increases the mystery of incantation, which is a basic pattern of the primitive incantation. This pattern is also shown in the primitive incantation of other places in the world. In the analysis of primitive thinking, Lucien, L. B. pointed out that "the songs, scriptures and incantations used in the witchcraft and even in the religious rites, which can not be understood by the audience and sometimes even by those who chant, show the mystery and power of the words. As long as the songs, scriptures and incantations are passed down orally in the traditional language of worship, they can be considered effective. Herbert Spencer and Francis Gillen pointed out that in the tribes of central Australia, the aborigines mostly did not know the meaning of the words in the ceremonies to worship the gods, and the words were passed down from their ancestors in the era of Alche Ringa in a fixed form (Lucien, 1995)."

Shu Wan Ceremony

Pregnant women and newborn babies are the most vulnerable groups in the families, and they are most subject to accidental interference. In the era with less developed medical technology, people used to be particularly worried about some inexplicable supernatural gods attacking pregnant women and babies. Therefore, in daily life, if the villagers of Tancun Village accidentally offend the gods to avoid the pregnant women or babies being blamed by the gods, they used to hold the Shu Wan ceremony to remedy it.

In rural areas, the most fundamental production life for people is to have some dealings with the god of the land and ask the god of land for the materials of living, so they almost have to work on the fields every day. Therefore, it will inevitably disturb the god of land or other gods. As a result, it is often found that some pregnant women or babies cry for no reason, feel ill, or even suffer from abortion or premature delivery, while the villagers of Tancun Village generally attribute these unconventional phenomena to the people offending the Local God of the Land. It is found in the survey that a large number of people said that they had experienced or witnessed such situations. The author can not give a specific figure to explain the universality of this situation, but many of the women interviewed claimed to have undergone such misfortune.

In the local conceptual terms, the phenomenon that pregnant women are teased by the god of the land and thus give birth prematurely or the babies are teased by the god of the land and do not eat or drink, or cry constantly is collectively known as Wan Dao (晚倒). All the pregnant women that are teased by the god of land may suffer from abdominal pain like giving birth to the child, but it has not reached the expected date of confinement (commonly known as "full term") and the infant can not come out. Then, the pregnant woman may be tortured to the extreme, and more seriously, the woman may give birth prematurely or suffer from abortion. If the infant is teased by the god of the land and does not eat or drink, it may close its eyes all day long and keep crying. According to the local people, if the pregnant woman and the infant are teased by the god of the land, it will not work even if they are injected or take medicine. The only solution is to hold the Shu Wan ceremony.

The Shu Wan ceremony is usually held in front of the shrine in the central room. But the time for the ceremony is not fixed, either in the morning or in the afternoon on the evening. The person who performs the magic of the Shu Wan ceremony is the one in the above Qi Shui ceremony, and the procedures and offerings used in the ceremony are completely the same as those in the Qi Shui ceremony. But the Shu Wan ceremony is targeted at the pregnant woman or infant victim in a household, and there is no ceremony targeted at the village or the areas other than the village. Therefore, the Shu Wan ceremony has always been held in front of the shrine in the central room of a household.

At the time of the Shu Wan ceremony, the sorcerer should chant the Shu Wan incantations. Its religious rites are consistent with those of Qi Shui. The incantation of Shu Wan is as follows:

To the divine gods: here the mortal has a request to welcome you. There are numerous gods in heaven. The mortal does not invite the gods in other prefectures or counties for help, but sincerely invites the Patriarch Pu'an in the eastern and northern palaces and the Patriarch Anxian in the southern and western palaces to receive the offerings and incenses at the Shu Wan ceremony. Here respectfully invite the deceased ancestors of the branch XX in this clan, the holy god in the Dongshan Mountain, the holy goddess in the Nanshan Mountain, the previous landlords, the gods in the nether world, Guan Yu, the God of Wealth, and the infinitely merciful and compassionate Avalokitesvara to receive the offerings and incenses at the Shu Wan ceremony. Invite the God of Xinglong Land, the Goddess of Wangxiang, the God of Longevity, the fortune boy, the God of Jinbao to receive the offerings and incenses. Invite the God of Life and the God of Kitchen in heaven, the god in front of the house, the God of Procurators and all the gods to receive the offerings and incenses at the Shu Wan ceremony. Invite the Three Eternity Emperors in charge of the gods of heaven, earth and water, the civil and military officials, the Emperor Zitong to receive the offerings and incenses at the Shu Wan ceremony. Invite the Emperor of Herbs, Hua Tuo, Avalokitesvara and the Ancestor of Xueshan.

There are countless ancestors and gods, and the disciple can not invite all of them even in thousands of days, and can not offer sacrifices to all the sages even in tens of thousands of days. Invite the first sage, and thousands of sages will come. Invite the second sage, and tens of thousands of mounts will come. First communicate with the gods and then tell them the request orally. Today it is XXXX XX XX (YYYY-MM-DD), and here the believers sincerely prepare the offerings available to the ancestors. The disciple here requests humbly the Ancestor XXX, the Master XXX, the Du Shi XXX (reading the birth of the person aloud), the Master XXX (reading the birth of the person aloud), to attend the Shu Wan ceremony. (at the same time, first make a

Yin hexagram, and then a Yang hexagram, indicating that all the masters and gods are willing to come and give a helping hand. Then, the master took a bowl half-filled with water and drew a magic figure in the water with a piece of burning incense inserted in front of the shrine as a pen. At the end of the ceremony, the pregnant woman or infant could drink the water and then all problems could be solved.)

With the incense going above the censer, the ancestor issues an order, and the master changes it into a mystery solution, and then into a magic figure (drawing a magic figure in the water again with the incense and making some magic symbols). The hand turns into an arrow and the wind turns into a fairy wind. It is afraid that it may offend the signs of the childbirth by the heaven, by the earth, by the gods, by the house, by the gods in front of the house, by the God of Kitchen and by the piled woods and stones.

The disciple has retreated the stars determining killings on earth monster, on heaven monster, on month monster, day monster and hour monster. The disciple has retreated the Wuji about heaven, the earth, the year, the month and the day, and all the devils should be decapitated. Patriarch Pu'an comes here, and then nothing is a taboo. (drawing a magic figure in the water again with the incense) First report to the wood element in the east, and then report to the fire element in the south, the metal element in the west, the water element in the north and the earth element in the center. Inform the Patriarch Pu'an in the eastern, southern, western and southern palaces. See the Immortal of Pan Gu in the Upper, Middle and Lower Proterozoic, the Immortal of Jiu Niu in the Yang and Yin worlds, and the Immortal of Feishan Zoushi. Then, report to the Blue Dragon, the White Tiger, the Rosefinch and the Tortoise. And inform the god of land in all mountains and in all directions, and the Dragon King, and all the family members of the God of Land. Dab the head of the dragon if it is offended, the waist of the dragon if it is offended, the tail of the dragon if it is offended and the claw of the dragon if it is offended. In seven days, dig a pit and pile up woods and stones, and then Ancestors will come on the day they inform. Patriarch Pu'an comes here, and then nothing is a taboo. (drawing a magic figure in the water again with the incense and make a Yin hexagram. To this point, the ceremony comes to an end.)

Whether it is the Qi Shui ceremony or the Shu Wan ceremony, neither of them involves a scientific basis in modern times, but in Tancun Village, the villagers have been inheriting and holding the ceremonies from generation to generation.

As long as any abnormal situation occurs to pregnant women or infants in the family, even the people who are not superstitious at ordinary times have to take great pains to hold ceremonies with the idea of preferring to believe it to be true in their minds to avoid the unnecessary disaster. In the whole process of the ceremony, what can best show the magic power of the master is the incantation that he chants, which is also the most mysterious part of the whole ceremony. Incantation is a phenomenon of linguistic worship. "From the perspective of the practical and utilitarian purposes of religions, some folk languages and phenomena have been deified and endowed with some extraordinary mysterious power to stimulate the people to believe in them in the corresponding psychological conditions of a cultural environment, thus making it leads to artificial linguistic superstition effect (Qu, 2002)."

Those who know the Yin religion possess such linguistic witchcraft that is not known by the ordinary people, and they are believed to have some supernatural and mysterious power, forcing the ordinary people to follow these witchcraft rites. The author found in the survey that there were the members of the Communist Party, cadres of the village committee and teachers who had held Shu Wan ceremonies in their houses, most of whom have received junior or senior high school education and can be regarded as intellectuals. But when talking with them at ordinary times, the author found that they are all atheists. They did not want to talk about too much about the Shu Wan ceremonies in their homes and showed only a little interest, but they all told the author that "I do not know why. Anyway, everything goes well after we believe in it and hold the ceremony."

Bronislaw Kaspar Malinowski used the concept of magic power to illustrate the efficacy of the ceremonies when discussing the simple witchcrafts directly performed in some ceremonies. The magic power is the common virtue of all the witchcrafts, and exists on the items where the witchcraft is performed. Incantation is considered as the core and the most important carrier of the magic power, and it enables the person who performs the witchcraft to achieve its emotional purpose.

Bronislaw Kaspar Malinowski pointed out that, "when studying the formula of incantation of the primitive witchcraft, we found that three standard components were related to the belief of magic power. First of all, it is the effectiveness of sound, which is to imitate the sound in nature. Second, the primitive conjuration magic is expressly displayed in language and the language is needed to launch, describe or command the intended purpose. Third, almost every incantation involves an element that can not be found in the ceremony, which is the introduction of myth, the ancestor and / or the cultural hero of witchcraft (Malinowski, 1987). "

The Qi Shui and Shu Wan ceremonies in Tancun Village also indicate that the magic power must be displayed with the aid of the carrier, incantation. The incantation of the sorcerer has a tradition of inheritance from the masters, involving ancestral worship. Moreover, most of the invited gods are the cultural heroes in the history of China. Only with the help of the power of these figures, the sorcerer can deliver the magic power. In the Qi Shui and Shu Wan ceremonies, the incantation of the sorcerer must also match the hand knack, while the former has the ability to strengthen the magic power. Incantation is a type of linguistic worship, and hand knack is a show entertaining the gods or the symbols of battle actions. Through the performance of hand knack, it expresses the cultural meaning of the sorcerer defeating or controlling the gods.

Religious piety is a highly complicated emotion, which contains love and unconditional obedience to a specific article that is lofty, mysterious and supernatural. There is a strong sense of reliance for protection, fear, reverence, gratitude, hope for the future, or other elements. Unless a person has progressed to a relatively high level of reason and moral capability, he can never feel or express such a complex emotion (Darwin, 1986).

Both the Qi Shui and Shu Wan ceremonies are just the remedies adopted by the villagers of Tancun Village for some acts that may offend the gods in daily life. The present villagers do not believe in these ceremonies, but such ritual activities have been frequently aroused. When people are faced with some crises beyond control, these cultural symbols will always be remembered, practiced and created again. In daily life, these rituals, which are dismissed as superstitions, tend to endow the people with unexplained trust under special conditions. In this case, the superstitions become credible.

Section 5 Leisure and Work of Pregnant Women

Daily life is the most common mode of the culture in a region, and it is also a topic that needs to be carefully investigated for anthropologists, folklorists and ethnographers. The daily life contains the superficial and in-depth cultural meanings of a region. From the daily life, we can have insight into many fundamental cultural criteria and basic values that the local people have observed. The daily things seem to be simple, but they involve all aspects of the culture. Leisure is an important part of daily life, and the change in the leisure life can reflect the change in the lifestyle of the people in a region. However, the meaning of leisure life is understood in different ways in academic circles.

According to Dumuzedier, J. (1962), "The leisure is the general term of the casual activities that an individual, when liberated from the duties assigned to him or her by his or her job, family or society, engages himself or herself in the society spontaneously and gives full play to his or her free creativity, in order to relax himself or herself, to take a rest, or to cultivate his or her knowledge and capabilities without any stake." Thus, it can be seen that Dumuzedier distinguishes the leisure life from the general work and obligation, and emphasizes that the essence of leisure is to liberate the people from labor to control themselves at their freedom. Therefore, leisure life refers to all the activities that people engage in their spare time, including reading, entertainment, sports and social activities other than the housework, labor and sleep. However, Dumuzedier defines leisure due to his observation and reflection on industrial society. But in rural communities such as Tancun Village, it is actually difficult to really separate leisure from the daily work and housework. The leisure life they claim is just to steal a moment of leisure from a busy life. Especially, women can never be liberated from the heavy housework.

Work and Leisure in the Collectivization Period

In the era of the planned economy, the family, as the fundamental production and distribution unit, was replaced by the production team. In the past, each person was attributed to a specific family. In the family, its interpersonal relationship network mainly depends on the close relationship with other members of the family. In the production team, its social identity is subordinate to a specific collective production team, and its production and life are completely dependent on the coordination and regulation of the production team, while the family loses part of its inherent social functions. In the production team similar to an extended family, the leadership of the production team acts as a parent that has to manage every social member of the team in an all-round way. The team leader becomes the chief executive of the rural community, as he can ask each social member about any detail of their acts. Under such a system, individuals do not have the freedom they should have, and they can only be arranged by the team leader or other senior executives to arrange the daily work, assign the tasks designated by the superiors and distribute the public assets and basic consumption materials. Moreover, all social members enjoy equal rights under a unified workpoint system.

The former leader of the Tiantang Production Team recalled that, at that time, an ordinary male worker could obtain ten workpoints a day, and that an ordinary female work could obtain seven workpoints. If some workers did more work or engaged in high-intensity work under the arrangement of the leader, the workers could obtain 11.5 or 12 workpoints. At ordinary times, female workers obtained seven workpoints when working for one day, but they could obtain ten points during the period of rush-harvesting and rush-planting. The workpoints are the major basis for each member of the production team to get paid. The higher workpoints the member obtains, the higher pay he or she will gain from the collective income. On the contrary, the lower workpoints the member obtains, the lower pay he or she will gain from the collective income. However, the number of workpoints is directly related to the number of mature labor workers in a family. In the same way, the amount of income of a family depends on the number of mature labor workers in the family.

Thus, it can be seen that it is the priority of priorities for each family to earn workpoints, because it is directly related to the primary income for a family to eat, dress and consume. For the sake of workpoints, people are not willing to see a doctor even when they are ill, let alone to ask for leave to stay at home. The people work hard to earn workpoints as much as possible, while the custom of confinement for lying-in women, which has been passed down from generation to generation, has become indifferent. The people are alienated as machines to work. A lot of pregnant women may be working in the fields or paddy fields even when they are about to give birth.

In traditional concepts, local people generally do not advocate that pregnant women are divorced from labor work. They believe that pregnant women should take part in more labor work during pregnancy, and move the waist and abdomen more, so that they can prevent the fetus from growing too strong, thereby reducing the pain and danger of pregnant women to give birth and guaranteeing that the mother and the infant can do well. It is also believed in modern medicine that appropriate activities during pregnancy can exercise the physical strength and endurance of pregnant women, accelerate blood circulation and promote metabolic function, and enable the fetus to grow normally and the pregnant woman to give birth smoothly.

However, during the collectivization period of Tancun Village, pregnant women did too much high-intensity work. Thus, it was common that pregnant women suffered from abortion or premature delivery as they participated in the production work as much as ordinary people to earn more workpoints. Some villagers joked that the infant automatically came out when the pregnant woman was engaged in production work.

When there was no electricity, no TV or other modern media, the primary leisure activity for pregnant women was to watch others gather in the laneway and gossip with each other and tell stories and legends. The stories are mostly to advocate filial piety and conscience and to warn the young people to understand the truth that good is rewarded with good and evil with evil. There are also some stories about the characters and plots in the classical novels, such as the gods and monsters in the Journey to the West, the heroes on the Wagang Village in the Romance of the Sui and Tang Dynasties and the heroes in Liangshan in All Men Are Brothers. These folk storytellers are usually eloquent and tell stories in a humorous way, but they do not care about the authenticity and historicity of the stories they tell. Therefore, it is a common matter for them to tell the plot that Zhang Fei killed Yue Fei, but it does not affect the strong interest of the audience. As the saying goes in the local area, when hearing the story of the Monk Xuanzang in the Tang Dynasty, the villagers delay the time of planting in spring. It vividly describes the eloquence of the storyteller and the infatuation of the hearers with the story.

In the slack season, pregnant women can relax for a moment during the work, and they have to prepare necessary clothes, shoes and socks for the children to be born. Most of the cloth that is made into clothes, shoes and socks is the old coats and trousers, and even some of them were worn by their husbands when they were very young. As the saying goes, a son wears his father's clothes, and his children wear his clothes. In the era of collection economy in which materials are in short supply, even the old cloth is precious. Pregnant women clean the old cloth that can be used at home first, and then patch the cloth layer by layer, and add the old cotton wadding to the interlayer. Then, a thick warm coat is made. The self-made diaper is a single layer of rectangular old cloth, which is called Tie Bu (贴布, underclothes) by the local people. It is also an essential standard for the local people to evaluate whether any pregnant woman is capable and virtuous by judging whether she can get these necessities for a newborn prepared. In addition to preparing clothes for the infant to be born, the pregnant woman must also learn to stitch the shoe soles and make cloth shoes.

Watching films was the rarest event at that time. In 1952, the No. 46 Film Team of Hunan Province began to show films in the county seat of Shaoyang County. In 1955, the open-air film was shown in Huangtingshi Town, where the Tancun Village is located, for the first time. The films are mostly about the War of Liberation (referring in particular to the Third Revolutionary Civil War in China) and the land reform, such as Reconnaissance Across the Yangtze River, attracting thousands of spectators every time (Deng and Xiao)□. In order to appreciate a rare film, pregnant women, regardless of the taboo that they were not allowed to go out in the evening, would rush to watch the films like going to the fair even in the midnight. For the reasons why pregnant women dare to go out at midnight, on the one hand, the materialist ideology was thoroughly carried out in the vigorous movements against feudalistic superstition at that time. On the other hand, films were extremely attractive to the people and it was a rare chance for the people to see a film. "In 1973, all the people's communes under the jurisdiction of Shaoyang County set up film teams, and the film projection management sub-stations were established in all the districts (Editorial Committee on Shaoyang County Annals, 1993). " Since then, it has become more convenient for the villagers of Tancun Village to see films, and daytime films and overnight films tend to be constantly shown. Thus, it becomes a routine for people to see a film in daily life.

Compared with films, the broadcast industry developed faster after the founding of the People's Republic of China, becoming an essential part of people's leisure life. Through broadcasting, people could have access to the political trends of the state, the international situation, learn all kinds of revolutionary songs, comprehend the truth of revolution and receive political and ideological education. In 1955, Shaoyang County People's Government renamed the original radio state as Shaoyang County People's Radio Station. By 1958, all districts and townships had set up radio stations, which not only rebroadcast the news from the China National Radio and Hunan Broadcasting System, but were also used to publicize the excellent deeds and models arising from the county in the course of socialist construction. In the 1970s, the broadcast industry reached its peak. According to the instructions of

Chairman Mao Zedong that the broadcasting network must be set in rural areas, the broadcasting network was vigorously set up in various regions, which led to a straight-line increase in the coverage rate of loudspeakers. In 1957, the coverage ratio of loudspeakers in Huangtingshi Town was only 2.5 % , and it reached 20.4 % by 1972 and 50 % by 1975 (Deng and Xiao). At the initial stage of the implementation of reform and opening up in 1981, the coverage rate of loudspeakers was as high as 63 % . The radio station broadcast for 400 minutes every day, among which 180 minutes is for the self-made programs. It broadcast three times a day, in the morning, at noon and in the evening. And the program Requests from Listeners was set (Editorial Committee on Shaoyang County Annals, 1993), thus providing a platform for the ordinary people to engage in the development of the broadcast industry. It has become a national event for the people to listen to the radio in their leisure time.

With the vigorous development of films, broadcasting and other modern cultural technologies, a lot of traditional folk arts have developed accordingly, becoming an important part of adjusting the work and life of the people. In Tancun Village, the most popular folk art performances are divided into two categories, one is the Qiyang opera, which is commonly known as Daxi (大戏, large-scale opera) among the local people, and the other is the flower-drum opera. Every time when it came to the Spring Festival or the production team held a celebration, the villagers of Tancun Village would invite the folk art troupes to perform the Qiyang opera. Before the founding of the People's Republic of China, the local operas performed among the people were mainly some serialized theatrical plays, such as Xue Gang Fan Tang, Generals of the Yang Family, General Yue Fei, The Pearl Pagoda, and The Heroine of the Yangs and so on. After the founding of the People's Republic of China, these costume plays were seldom performed, but some modern revolutionary operas were adapted and performed, such as The Red Lantern, Raid on the White Tiger Regiment, Taking Tiger Mountain by Strategies, Shajia Village, The Red Guards on Honghu

Lake, Red Detachment of Women, Fly away from the Luding Bridge, Rent Collection Courtyard, The Azalea Mountain and so on.

The traditional Qiyang opera in the local area has become a form of art that promotes the revolutionary spirit and carries forward the revolutionary culture. It is a typical way for the cultural form of national awareness to obtain legitimacy in the local area in the form of folk arts.

In Tancun Village, the flower-drum opera is mainly dominated by the flower-drum opera troupe in Shaoyangnan Road. "It was transformed from the flower-drum operas that were performed by a Xiao Dan (小旦, the female character type in the opera) and a Xiao Chou (小丑, the clownish role in the opera) or by a Xiao Dan and a Xiao Sheng (小生, the young man's role in the opera), and the troupe gradually developed from a temporary Shehuo (社火, a folk art performance given on traditional or religious festivals in China) troupe to a semi-professional troupe. " "Since Wang Chunsheng initiated the Wang Family Opera Troupe in Shaoyang County in the late 20th century, the flower-drum opera performances have been thriving in the county (Editorial Committee on Shaoyang County Annals, 1993)." Traditional operas include Shoot the Birds, Grind Tofu, Ask for Fees, A Bride for A Ride, Taoyuan Cave, Woodcutter Liu Hai and so on. After the founding of the People's Republic of China, the flower-drum opera was also reformed, becoming a form of folk art to publicize the socialist construction. The opera Tinker the Pan, which is even known to women and children, tells the new spiritual look of the people in the course of building the socialist countryside in China with the unique the witty tone and jocular common sayings of the flower-drum operas.

Evolution of Daily Life and Leisure Activities in Contemporary China

Since the reform and opening up, with the implementation of the household contract responsibility system in rural areas, the social function of the family, as the fundamental production and distribution unit, has been restored, and farmers can freely control their time for activities again. At the same time, with a large number of rural workers flowing to the coastal areas in eastern China, it has not only greatly improved the economic development of rural areas, but also injected some modern thoughts into the rural areas. The daily life and leisure activities of pregnant women have undergone dramatic changes in terms of scheduling and the content of activities.

First of all, leisure time increased significantly. After the implementation of the household contract responsibility system in rural areas, the enthusiasm and responsibility of farmers in labor work were dramatically improved. In the past, the peasants worked for the collective, and their actions were carried out under the political encouragement and the administrative encouragement of the superior leaders, and they were forced to work to ear workpoints and obtain the consumption materials required for their lives. After the reform of the rural system, the autonomy and consciousness of farmers in labor work have been enhanced. Moreover, farmers are no longer subject to the unified command of rural cadres, but they have the freedom to decide their legitimate labor work and manage their time as they like. Besides, pregnant women are once again cared for by their family members. In the slack season, they do not need to work in the fields, but they can stay at home and do some housework, or chat with the older people or other women in the village. Even in the busy season, the pregnant women who are near the time of labor can still care for their safety. When asked about the changes in the living conditions of pregnant women after the reform and opening up in the interviews with some older women, they always sighed, showing their sincere envy for the present pregnant women.

Grandma Zhang, 64, said, "Those days were so miserable for us. There was no difference between pregnant women and ordinary women. If you were pregnant but you wanted to have a rest or do something simple when you were busy with farm work in the fields, you would be scolded by other people. At that time, in the busy seasons, we used to leave for the fields before dawn. Except for returning home to have lunch for more than two hours at noon, we had to go back home until it was completely dark in the evening. A lot of pregnant women suffered from abortion or premature delivery due to excessive labor work. After the reform and opening up, pregnant women live a better life. Their husbands can prepare whatever they want to eat, and if their husbands can not, they can ask their parents-in-law or parents for help. In their families, the members will try their best to cook the dishes that suit the taste of pregnant women every time. During the busiest seasons, in families with only a few mature workers, pregnant women are just helping others. Anyway, it is their own businesses. They just need to work in the fields for a few more days, while it is not a big deal. They do not need to be compared with others as before. In the past, other people used to stare at pregnant women to see whether you did less work or simple tasks. Now, it is better. No one will compare pregnant women with others, and no one will compete with them. If you want to do something, just do it. It does not matter whether you do it well or not, but it is up to you. The husband will never let his pregnant wife suffer because of the heavy farm work during the busiest seasons."

In the 1980s, the villagers of Tancun Village seldom went out for work, and the villagers were mainly dependent on the fields. It was a typical rural agricultural society at that time. JBZ was the first in Tancun Village to go out for work. He went to Bao'an District, Shenzhen City in 1985. After that, the villagers began to go out for work, becoming a member of the floating population. At present, few of the young and middle-aged people stay at home in the village, and most of the people make a living by working in other cities as migrant workers. The fertile fields and other fields of their families are managed by their parents or other seniors, or completely deserted. In the past busiest seasons, the peasants are no longer busy with the farm work. The local people used to grow the double-cropping rice, but now they grow the single-cropping rice. Moreover, in the past, due to the small amount of land area per capita, people had to make use of every piece of land, even the corners of the fields, but now they grow the single-cropping rice. Because of the small land area per capita, people had to grow all kinds of crops on every piece of fields, even in the corners, and reclaim barren hills, and even reclaim the oil-tea camellia forests to plant peanuts, soybeans and other crops.

Now, a large number of young people do not work in their hometowns, and those who are left behind in the hometown are the older people. Thus, the tension between man and land has been alleviated, and the land seems to be less precious. Much of the dry land was deserted, and even the best paddy fields were neglected, but every family had plenty of grain in stock. It was found in the household investigation that most of the pregnant women who are staying in the village wait for delivery after returning from Guangdong or Zhejiang Province. They are all dressed in fashion, no longer like the women who used to work in the fields in the past. Many of them have been strangers to their parents-in-law as they have been working in other cities all year round after marriage. In this case, it becomes a rare opportunity for the daughters-in-law who return to their hometowns to give birth to get well along with their parents-in-law. As a result, pregnant women become the rare or honored guests in their families, as they are taken the utmost care of and warmly received by their parents-in-law, and they do not need to do any manual work.

A statistical survey was conducted on the average daily time spent on different activities of ten pregnant women in a week. The results are shown in Figure 3.1, indicating that the present pregnant women in Tancun Village can manage an average period of 660 minutes, i.e. 11 hours, as they like, except for doing housework, sleeping, having meals and taking care of and educating their children, accounting for 45.8 % of a day's time.

Of the discretionary time for individuals, playing mahjong, cards and poker are the main entertainment activities for pregnant women, accounting for 34.8 % , followed by watching TV and VCD, accounting for 28.8 % , while the time of pregnant women chatting with the elderly people is also up to 100 minutes, accounting for 15.2 % . It is worth noting that the Internet has begun to affect the lives of the locals. In the survey, it was found that four of the 10 pregnant women knew how to surf the Internet. And they spent four hours a week chatting with their husbands or other friends who work in Guangdong Province and other regions online.

Table 3.1 Daily Activities of Some Pregnant Women in A Week (Unit: Minute)

Doing housework	110	Watching TV, VCD, etc.	190
Making telephone calls	10	Watching films	—
Sleeping	510	Going sightseeing	2 0
Having meals	40	Taking physical exercises	40
Taking care of and teaching children	120	Gossiping with others	100
Playing mahjong, cards and poker	230	Other activities	56
Surfing the Internet	14		

Pregnant women are not only free to spend more time, but they have a variety of ways to spend their leisure time. The main ways of spending the leisure time include playing mahjong, playing poker, playing cards, watching TV and CD, reading books and newspapers, listening to music, chatting with others, visiting relatives, and shopping on the streets, among which playing mahjong is the most popular entertainment activity. It is a gambling game involving four players.

According to the local rules, winning in a game is divided into a large winning game and a small winning game. In a small winning game, the winner can gain six Yuan, which means that the other three players lose two Yuan, respectively. If a winner wins with all paired tiles or pure one suit, the scores will be two times, which means that the winner gains eight Yuan from each of the other three players. It is the most basic chip in a gambling game. There is no doubt that the players can discuss the times of the scores. Even according to the basic gambling chip, it is very common to lose one or two hundred Yuan in a morning if the player has a stroke of bad luck.

However, playing mahjong involves low technical standards and it is highly accidental. For the players who often play together, there is an equal chance for them to win or lose in the end. In general, if a player loses one day, he may win the next day, or he may win in the afternoon if he loses in the morning. Such a form of the roulette game is very attractive in the local area, and all the villagers, regardless of age and sex, can play it. As the result of the mahjong game depends mainly on the luck of the player, which also means the chance, the people feel it is an exciting game and then they do not think that they will lose a lot of money. It is impossible that a player always plays mahjong with bad or good luck, so every game is a fair game, which is consistent with the thoughts of the local people in trying their fortune.

Modern media tools, such as TV sets and DV players, are quite popular in Tancun Village. There is a color TV set in almost every household, so watching TV becomes the primary activity for the villagers to spend their slack time and nightlife. Young pregnant women have no special preference for TV programs, but few people are concerned about the children's programs. However, the villagers are highly interested in the entertainment programs on Hunan TV. Pregnant women will never miss an episode of the programs like Happy Camp in their spare time. In addition, TV series, such as romance dramas, fairy tales, historical plays and costume plays, cater to the public's interest.

In a word, with the improvement of economic conditions, the present women live in a relaxed and pleasant environment compared with those in the past. Not only are they taken the utmost care of by their family members in material life, but they also gain a relative degree of freedom in the spiritual life. Due to the reduction in agricultural activity, the increased time for free allocation and the diversification of leisure mode, it has greatly reduced the likelihood of affecting the physical health of pregnant women due to pregnancy. In the interviews with young mothers or pregnant women, they all said that they feel relaxed and happy during their pregnancy. And when the author had talked with the middle-aged and elder women about how they felt during the pregnancy in the past, they all sighed quietly that they had undergone so many hardships that they gave birth to and raised their children to the present, and they were extremely envious of the life of the present pregnant women.

Chapter 4 Child Rearing as An Economic and Cultural Factor

For the reasons why human beings give birth, biologists hold that it is the outcome of physiological impulse, and biological evolutionists think that it is the need for natural selection, and anthropologists think it is a social and cultural behavior, and economists think it is a behavior of production and consumption. There is no doubt that, to give birth to and raise children, human beings must invest some capital in giving birth to and raising their children like being engaged in economic activities, including material, money, energy and emotional capital.

In this research field, the representatives are Ribinstan and Gary Stanley Becker. They offer an effective way to explain the behavior of human reproduction by regarding the childbearing as consumer behavior, so that it can be calculated according to the cost-utility logic of economics. The cost of a child refers to all the expenditure of the parents giving birth to and raising the child, as well as the shadow price of the time invested by the parents in the process. In other words, the cost of a child not only contains the direct costs (according to the normal standard of society, the cost of the basic necessities of a child's life, the cost of education, the cost of cultural and recreational activities, and the cost of marriage that is formally paid or subsidized by the parents), but also involves indirect costs (the loss of the opportunities of parents receiving education and gaining income due to childbearing and upbringing, also known as opportunity cost or time cost).

In addition to the concept of the child, they also proposed the concept of the net cost of a child, which is the difference of the sum of the direct costs and indirect costs minus the present value of the monetary income and service that the child provides for the family. A famous hypothesis is that if the net cost of a child is positive, the amount of child rearing paid by the parents is higher than the amount of income offered by the child, and then the demand for a child will decrease. On the contrary, if the net cost of a child is negative, the amount of child rearing paid by the parents is lower than the amount of income offered by the child, and then the demand for a child will rise (Becker, 1987).

In 1992, Gary Stanley Becker, a winner of the Nobel Prize in Economics, interpreted the theory of cost-utility of the childbearing behavior from the perspective of the fundamental theorem of economics that the quantity of demand for any kind of commodity is in negative correlation with the value of the commodity. He pointed out that, "in practical terms, the theorem is extremely important. From the angle of social sciences, the theorem is one of the most significant and general theorems (Becker, 1987). " That is to say, the higher the price of a commodity is, the lower the amount of its demand will be; on the contrary, the lower the prices, the higher the amount of its demand will be.

Gary Stanley Becker, on the basis of the fundamental theorem, put forward the view that the children are equated to the durable consumer goods and the durable product. He said, "for most of the parents, the child is a source of material income or satisfaction. From the viewpoint of economists, children will be regarded as consumer goods. In case that the child may offer some monetary income sometimes, the child is also a product. I attempted to clarify that, in the analysis of the demand for children, the demand theory for durable consumer goods was also a useful structure (Becker, 1985). " In other words, when the cost of raising a child goes beyond its utility, the child can be regarded as the durable consumer goods; when its utility exceeds its cost, the child can be regarded as a durable product.

However, when the theory of Gary Stanley Becker was applied to the analysis of the childbearing behavior of Chinese people, especially when anthropologists entered a specific rural community to conduct a survey on the child rearing behavior, we found that the demand of the peasants for childbearing did not involve too much rational calculation of economics. In the views of the Chinese farmers, the man and the woman must have children after they get married, and it seems to be the logical outcome of anthropological marriage to give birth to and bring up children. More than that, the community survey shows that most of the rural people believe that they need to give birth to a son. As a result, childbearing can not be seen as a purely economic behavior, but a cultural behavior that contains economic input.

In the field survey on Nanyang Village in Yuyao City, Zhejiang Province, Li Yinhe pointed out that " From a micro point of view, economic factors have little effect on reducing farmers' impetus to childbirth. That is to say, no matter how rich a farmer has become, he still has a strong impetus to childbearing, and money does not lead to an automatic reduction in his desire to have children. Therefore, we can boldly judge that Gary Stanley Becker's theory does not apply to the childbearing behavior of Chinese farmers at the present stage (Li, 1994) ."

The theory of the cost-utility of the child may take effect in the individual-based society or culture of the West, because such society regards the family as a rational decision-making unit and women can make decisions on whether to have children or not on their own in accordance with the principle of the market. However, " in China, where the family is a standard, the childbearing behavior is far from an economic behavior operating according to the laws of the commodity economy, but tends to show the nature of ignoring the possible economic consequences (Li, 1994). " This chapter will describe the childbearing behavior of the villagers of Tancun Village from both economic and cultural perspectives.

Section 1 Economics of Child Rearing in Tancun Village

The economic theories of child rearing have been widely studied in the fields of microeconomics and population economics. Gary Stanley Becker, a well-known economist and the winner of the Nobel Prize in Economics, is the authority in the field. In China, a lot of scholars have conducted an economic analysis of the cost of childbearing (Li, 1992; Du, 1990). Here, by making an ethnographic description of the financial costs of raising children for the villagers of Tancun Village, we can see that the family is required to make a huge investment in raising a child, which also affects the childbearing behavior of the local people to some extent.

The economic investment in child rearing is the economics of daily life. On the one hand, it indeed involves a specific amount of money. On the other hand, it is a process of scattered consumption that can not be measured. In addition, it also involves the emotional investment, time, energy cost of the parents, as well as the loss of the resulting opportunity cost. In brief, the opportunity cost refers to the greatest value of the things to be abandoned for the sake of obtaining something. For example, raising a child means that a mother must ask for maternity leave or quit a job, and then the mother may be unable to work for money as she can only stay at home to take care of the child in two or more years. Therefore, it is difficult to calculate the cost of raising a child. However, children also mean that the lives of the parents when they are old can be guaranteed. Especially in countries such as China, where the family pension is still the primary pension model, the child is equivalent to wealth.

In rural areas, raising children is an investment, because the child is not only the continuation of the parents' life and bears the family line as a cultural symbol of successors, but it can also satisfy the expectation for the parents to be provided for when they are getting older. Parents will never calculate how much it may take to bring up a child, but they will feel fortunate in having a child so that they live a happy and reliable life as seniors. In the survey, when asked "how much do you think will be spent in raising a child", none of the respondents could give a concrete number, because, in their opinion, they do not need to calculate it. JBP, at his fifties, briefly talked about how he thought of the cost of raising a child.

He said: "It is beyond calculation and I do not have made accounts. When my children were young, I did not need to pay their tuition fees, but I had to spend a lot on their lives, including the food, the clothes, the daily necessities and the charges for medicine if they were sick. When HX, my eldest son, was very young, he was much feebler than the children of other families, as he got sick every two or three days. It did not matter if we spent a lot of money, but we worried about him too much. When he grew older, he had to go to school, and it took at least 12,000 Yuan to support him in the three years of high school studies. Now he is twenty-five or twenty-six years old, but he has not got married, and he hardly has any savings after working in Shenzhen for years. In the future, when he gets married, he will ask us to subsidize his wedding. If he is asked to repay us, I don't think he will be able to do it for the rest of his life."

It can be seen from these simple words that the opinions of the local people on the economic investment in raising a child are reflected in four aspects: first of all, the cost of raising a child can be divided into computable and incomputable costs. For instance, education costs can be accurately calculated, but living expenses can not be calculated. Second, the cost of raising a child also includes the devotions that the parents have made to the child, such as paternal love and maternal love. Third, in the course of raising a child until he gets married, the most important and the largest amount of expenses are the expenses on the wedding and education for the child. Fourth, in the views of the parents, the expenses of child rearing can never be repaid by their children throughout their lives. Therefore, if child rearing is regarded as an economic topic, it is an economic proposition that can never be expressed by a mathematical formula. If an ethnographic survey is conducted on the economic issues of child rearing, the result can just be an estimated and relatively approximate figure.

The cost of raising a child needs to be examined before the child is born. When a young mother is pregnant, her family members need to take special care of her in order to ensure the smooth delivery of the child. Thus, the family members need to spend an extra amount of expenditure, while the pregnant woman has to give up many opportunities to make money during her pregnancy.

This year, a boss from another place planted more than 100 mu of medical herbs in Tancun Village. The herb is called incised spleenwort, also known as wide cypress among the local people. From late May to mid-July, the boss hired more than 30 women every day to harvest the herbs, with a daily salary of 25 Yuan. However, pregnant women could only give up the most convenient opportunity to make money. In this case, pregnant women lost the opportunity cost of more than 1,300 Yuan in nearly two months. Other women, who work in the river sand farm by the Haoshui River on the south of the village, can make a profit of 22 Yuan every day, and they need to work for about 18 days in a month. That is to say, they can earn 396 Yuan every month. Assuming that a pregnant woman can not do heavy work for at least eight months of pregnancy, she has to lose an opportunity cost of more than 3,000 Yuan.

Before the infant is born, his family members should begin to be busy preparing his birth. It is mentioned above that, about the daily life of pregnant women, in traditional societies before reform and opening up, a virtuous and capable young woman should be able to make good use of the old cloth to stitch it into the coats and hats of the child to be born. Now, young mothers are no longer busy making clothes for the infant to be born, while only the grandmother, who is idle at home, may prepare some necessities for her grandson to be born, such as internal hats, external hats, diapers, shoes, socks, thin coats, and cotton-padded clothes.

However, the present older women have no longer stitched the old cloth, but purchased new cloth to make new clothes for their grandchildren, while the young mothers hardly think that their mothers-in-law are capable in this aspect. Instead, they think that their mothers-in-law are mean. The young mothers, who have been working in open coastal areas, are economically capable, and they have had modern consumption ideas. So they will never be stingy with the money spent on the child to be born. All the necessities they have prepared for their children are ordered from the cotton yarn shop in the town. According to the owner of the cotton yarn shop, it takes more than 100 Yuan to prepare a full set of clothes and hats for a child. In general, they need to order five or six sets of clothes, so they need to pay five or six hundred Yuan. It is only a part of the large number of clothes that they prepare for the child. And a large number of expenses can not be calculated in detail.

The family members of a pregnant woman pay much attention to the nutrient intake of the pregnant woman, so that the infant to be born can develop well and lay a solid physical foundation and the pregnant woman can give birth normally. The elderly women said, "nowadays, the people are more finicky compared with us at that time. Those days, we did not have any delicious food, and we could not even eat our fill. Fortunately, it was so strange at that time that we could give birth to our children in a short time, and bring them up well. But now, people may complain that they lack nutrients once they live a slightly poorer life. They claim that they need to eat meat and nutritious dishes every day. The dishes must suit their appetites. Currently, the people live in a prosperous era and they earn money, so they do not need to suffer a lot."

In most families, older people are only responsible for preparing the daily necessities for pregnant women, and the money spent is paid by the pregnant women themselves. It is common to eat fruits, but there are only a few kinds of fruits in the tow. And pregnant women eat more apples, oranges, grapes, bananas and pears. Generally speaking, a family with a pregnant woman has to spend an extra amount of 500 Yuan a month than before on their daily expenses. However, pregnant women can not be treated specially in every month. In general, the closer it is to the expected date of childbirth, the higher the cost of living will be. As family conditions vary, the spending is different. Families with relatively poor conditions spend an extra amount of 100 Yuan a month, and those with better conditions may spend an extra amount of 1,000 Yuan a month. There is no doubt that these figures can not accurately reflect all the extra expenses of living for pregnant women during their pregnancy, since the life is a day-to-day account, and on one is forced to work out the accurate amount of money spent, while they can not draw a clear distinction between the expenses on the lives of pregnant women and other expenses.

Assuming that a pregnant woman spends an average extra amount of 500 Yuan in her daily life, she and her family members need to spend an extra amount of 5,000 Yuan until she gives birth. The amount makes up for more than one-fourth of the annual income for the husband of a pregnant woman working in Guangdong Province, as the monthly salary of a man from Tancun Village working in other cities tends to be between 1,500 and 2,000 Yuan. Moreover, for the women who leave their hometowns and work in other cities for years, they may suffer greater economic losses due to childbirth. They usually need to take leave for about six and seven months at home, and they have to suffer a loss of one to two thousand Yuan a month. Given that it takes at least a year for a pregnant woman to be confined in childbirth and raise the infant, they may lose about 30,000 Yuan in order to have a child.

The villagers of Tancun Village believe that they do not need to increase huge spending in bringing up a child. As the saying goes in the local area, they are only worried about giving birth to children, but not raising them. It means that it is more difficult to give birth to a child than to bring him or her up. In rural areas, the children are mostly raised roughly. Therefore, in the eyes of the villagers of Tancun Village, it takes a low cost to bring a child up. As the saying goes, a yellow dog can be fed if everyone eats a little less; it is just a matter of another pair of chopsticks if a new family member comes out. That is to say, a child can be easily raised on the premise that the original living expenses remain unchanged. As a result, it seems to be a silly job to figure out how much money is needed to bring up a child in rural areas.

For this reason, the local people are extremely confused about the survey on the cost of raising a child. In their opinions, it is free to have rice, and the vegetables are planted by them in their fields, so it is unnecessary to calculate the cost of the rice and vegetables, because one less person in the family does not mean that the food left for the person can be exchanged for money.

It is a common phenomenon in the rural areas of China, where there are both the natural economy and market economy. The traditional model of the natural economy is the economic root reason for rural people to spend no or little money raising their children. The economic approach and the idea of the cost of raising a child that is determined by the approach have made it difficult to exercise effective control over the childbearing behavior of the villagers of Tancun Village for a long time. And the family planning work of the local government has been plagued.

Tancun Village is a rural community with a large number of migrant numbers, and most of the people who are left behind are the older people above fifty years old and the children under eighteen years old now. Therefore, in most families, the actual guardian of a child is not the child's parents but the grandparents of the child. The service charges, the maintenance and living expenses of the left-behind children and their guardians, which are to be studied in Chapter 6, are the economic liabilities that the young parents are obliged to assume.

The NEET (Not in Education, Employment or Training) groups are not commonly seen in rural areas, but a lot of people have to bring up their children and even their grandchildren. Thus, older grandparents need to take on heavy economic burdens. In general, young parents who leave their children at home need to send the basic living expenses for not less than 150 Yuan a month to their children, and they also need to pay the children's grandparents at an annual fee ranging from 500 to 1,000 Yuan. The fee involves double meanings. On the one hand, the grandparents, who serve as guardians, have made extra devotions to raising their grandchildren, so they need to be economically made up for by the children's parents. On the other hand, it is the money paid by the children's parents to support the grandparents, which is the embodiment of filial piety by the young people in the form of money.

For many young couples, they are most concerned about the economic burden when deciding whether to give birth to the second or third child. It was found in the survey that, the more economically capable the family is, the more likely it is to have more children, but the poorer the family is, the more scared it is to have one or more children. It is evident that the case is contrary to the view that the traditional thoughts of more children and more blessings and the fact of population explosion used to be attributed to economic poverty. The survey in Tancun Village showed that it did not support the hackneyed and stereotyped view that the poorer the family was, the more children it would have.

In the various costs for the preparation of the son's most important events in his life, the parents spend the most on preparing his wedding ceremony and building a house for the son to get married. In Tancun Village, it takes about 6,000 to 12,000 Yuan to prepare a wedding ceremony, while most of the villagers spend about 8,000 Yuan. Some villagers say that, "it takes at least 10,000 Yuan to prepare the wedding ceremony." Some say, "there is no fixed standard for the expenditure of the wedding ceremony. It is enough that the poor may spend five or six thousand Yuan, while the rich may spend more than 10,000 Yuan. " According to the author's investigation of the newlyweds' families in 2006, the cost of the wedding ranges from a maximum of 12,000 Yuan to a minimum of 5,500 Yuan. Here are TWO CASES to give a brief description of the costs of the wedding of the villagers of Tancun Village.

Case **4.1** JYY's wedding costs: JYY met his wife via the introduction of his aunt in the first lunar month of 2004. His wife, Yang XX, 22, worked in Guangzhou Province for six years after graduating from junior high school in 2000. JYY, 26, is the son of the boss of a firebrick (known as red bricks among the local people) yard in Tancun Village, and his family was in better condition. He also worked in Guangdong after graduating from senior high school. His marriage to his wife was largely determined in the first lunar month of 2004. And then the two families completed most of the ritual procedures of the marriage in just a few days. After two years of close contact, the wedding ceremony was formally held on the eighth day of the first lunar month in 2006.

(1) Checking the potential groom's family conditions and his status by the matchmaker with the potential bride and her female relatives: Also known as a blind date, it refers to the process that the man and the woman and their families determine whether to agree on the marriage. On the day, the matchmaker goes to the man's house for a blind date with the woman and her close female relatives. It is for the first time that the relatives of the woman visit the man's house. If they are satisfied with the man, the woman and her relatives will have a meal in his home. But if they do not agree, they will immediately go back after a small talk. In the process of the blind date, the man's parents should give red envelopes to the woman and her relatives.

In this case, JYY's parents presented 2,668 Yuan to the woman, 888 Yuan to her mother, and 268 Yuan to the woman's aunt and sister-in-law, respectively. The aunt, as a matchmaker, earned an extra matchmaking fee of 128 Yuan. It amounted to 4,220 Yuan. JYY's parents were so generous that they won a good reputation far and near for the family. The amount of money in the red envelope can also be used as a basis for the woman and her family to determine the family conditions of the man.

(2) Serving a cup of tea to the bridegroom and getting engaged: In tradition, the man should be engaged to the woman three or four months after the woman checks the man's family conditions and his status with the matchmaker and her female relatives, and the woman should make tea for the elderly in the man's family. It is one of the most important rituals in marriage. Through the ritual, the marriage between the man and the woman can be determined, and the families and clans of the

man and the woman are formally connected with each other by marriage. If the woman and her female relatives are satisfied with the man and his family and the woman agrees to marry the man, the woman can serve a cup of tea to the man after having the meal, and then the man drinks the tea and puts a red envelope in the tea tray. Thus, the marriage is determined, and it is equivalent to the man sending betrothal gifts.

However, nowadays, young people all go out for work, and the time systems of enterprises make the man and the woman too busy to perform these tedious marriage rituals. In general, the rituals of serving a cup of tea to the bridegroom and getting engaged are completed two or three days after they check the groom's family conditions, or even on the same day.

In this case, JYY gave the woman a red envelope with more than 1,000 Yuan.

(3) Presenting at ordinary times and during the Spring Festival holidays: In the two years after JYY's marriage was determined, they spent two Dragon Boat Festivals, Mid-Autumn Festivals and two Spring Festivals together, and celebrated his father-in-law's fiftieth birthday. As JYY had been working outside for years, the presents for his parents-in-law were prepared by his parents for the most important festivals and his father-in-law's birthday. They spent about forty Yuan buying presents during the festivals. During the Spring Festival, they spent one or two hundred Yuan purchasing New Year's gifts. At JYY's father-in-law's fiftieth birthday, he gave presents worth about three hundred Yuan. Thus, the expenses of gratitude were nearly eight hundred Yuan.

(4) Moving into the husband's household upon marriage: On the eighth day of the first lunar month in 2006, JYY and his wife held the wedding ceremony. At this stage, the man's family must send betrothal gifts to the woman's family. JYY's parents sent more than 4,000 Yuan and more than 56 kg of pork and other gifts to the woman's family, which were worth more than 5,000 Yuan.

(5) Giving a wedding banquet: It took more than 2,000 Yuan.

(6) Purchasing furniture: It took more than 4,000 Yuan.

JYY and his parents spent a total of 17,000 Yuan preparing for marriage. The expenses of purchasing the dowry, TV set and VCD and other electrical appliances for his wife's family were about 5,000 Yuan. With the amount of 5,000 Yuan subtracted, JYY and his parents actually spent more than 12,000 Yuan.

Case **4.2** LLW's wedding costs: LLW and his wife WZJ's marriage was a lightning marriage, as it took only over one month for them from having the blind date to the wedding ceremony. They met in the blind date on the twelfth day of the twelfth lunar month in 2005, and held the wedding ceremony on the eighteenth day of the first lunar month of 2006. Their wedding ceremony was very simple and covered low costs.

(1) Checking the potential groom's family conditions and his status by the matchmaker with the potential bride and her female relatives, serving a cup of tea to the bridegroom and getting engaged: The three rituals were completed at one time, covering a total cost of more than 3,200 Yuan.

(2) Presenting at ordinary times and during the Spring Festival holidays: The two spent the Spring Festival together once, covering a cost of more than 80 Yuan.

(3) Moving into the husband's household upon marriage: LLW sent WZJ's family more than 3,800 Yuan to purchase the dowry.

(4) Giving a wedding feast: LLW and WZJ did not give a grand feast but had dinner with their families, with a total of four tables set, covering a cost of around 500 Yuan.

All in all, the wedding cost LLW and his family a total of 7,580 Yuan. As his wife's family purchased the dowry with about 2,000 Yuan, LLW actually spent more than 5,500 Yuan.

It is worth mentioning that there is a convention in Tancun Village that the cash gift sent by the man's family to the woman herself in a number of rituals before marriage may be generally taken back to the man's house as private assets when they get married, thus becoming part of the economic foundation for the new family of the newlyweds. Except for only a few families with better economic conditions like JYY's family, the men in Tancun Village should bear most of the wedding costs by themselves, because most of the young men have been working in other cities, who are the high-income groups compared with their parents who have been engaged in farm work in their hometowns.

In practice, the young people are tired of their work, and they have been taking the cumbersome rituals of marriage less seriously, while a considerable number of people have pledged to marry without the permission of their parents when they are working in other regions. Many women tend to attach less importance to the financial condition of the man's family, but more important to the individual capabilities of the man. There is a local saying that the woman who has good taste checks the ability of the man, while the woman who does not have a good taste checks the region when choosing the right spouse. Now, it is easy for a young but capable man to get married. As a result, the man who meets such a good chance can get married to a desirable wife without too high costs.

As can be seen from the above descriptions, the villagers of Tancun Village have to spend a huge amount of money in various procedures from the birth of the child, to his adulthood, to the support of his life and education, and to the marriage of the child. Under the influence of the concept of market economy, the youth of Tancun Village had to consider the economic cost of raising a child, which changed the traditional concept of childbearing to some extent and made childbearing behavior more and more rational.

Section 2 Milk, Food and Blood: Patterns of Infant Feeding in Tancun Village

The life of a newborn is so fragile that it can grow only with the careful care of its mother, which is a biological motive for all primates. However, for human beings, the pattern of infant feeding is not only involved in simple food feeding, but also contains a special cultural choice. Furthermore, whether to carry out breastfeeding or how long breastfeeding takes reflects the mother's review of her value, because the breastfeeding for the child is bound to damage the interests of the mother herself, such as going against beauty and body shape. Breast milk, involving the realization of blood ties, tends to be regarded as the medium of life, emotion and physical ability between generations. In the same way, the logic of the villagers of Tancun Village about breast milk and blood is the biological basis for the Confucian ethics of filial piety to be rationally inherited, because, from a cultural perspective, the life of the offspring is derived from the mother's milk, and the milk produces the blood of the offspring and determines their physical qualities. All patterns of infant feeding are centered on the cultural functions of life extension.

Cultural Functions of Breast Feeding

After the birth of the first infant, women complete the transformation of their social identity, declaring that they have formally become a mother from a girl. The primary obligation of the mother is to meet the physiological needs of the infant for food. Breastfeeding is the bounden duty of the mother, while sucking is the natural instinct of the infant. It is called physiological breastfeeding for the time being. Since Fei Xiaotong divides child rearing into physiological nurturing and social upbringing, the functions of the mother and the father can be distinguished in the bi-parental system from the perspectives of biology and culture. The infant should be weaned twice when he grows up, one is physiological weaning and the other is social weaning (Fei, 1998).

Therefore, in this book, the stage that the infant's food can not be done without the mother's milk is called physiological breastfeeding.

Soon after birth, the child who closes its eyes begins to hang down his head and look for its mother's nipple. But at this point, the mother's colostrums can not be immediately fed to the infant, which is considered as a taboo by the women in Tancun Village. The older women will cautiously warn their daughter or daughter-in-law, who just gave birth, of the taboo. It is hard to say whether there is a modern scientific basis for the argument, but they insist that the first milk is yellow, which must contain toxins, and that it may be bad for the health of the child. Therefore, the mother, who just had an infant, must use her hands to squeeze her breast that begins to have more milk, and then expel the yellow liquid in the middle, so that the infant can suck the white milk from its mother as it likes.

In order to ensure that the lying-in woman has enough milk for the physiological breastfeeding of her infant, her family members must design a special diet for her so that she can absorb good and sufficient nutrients. In Tancun Village, the requirements for the diet of a lying-in woman seem to go against the concepts of modern medicine in many ways. According to modern science, the basic practice of ensuring the absorption of good nutrients to get the lying-in woman to get enough protein every day, so eggs are seen as the ideal nutrients. But in Tancun Village, eating eggs is the greatest taboo of a woman who has just given birth in diet, which is also a principle of dietary culture that is dominated by the traditional concepts of Yin and Yang in China. A woman who has just given birth is extremely weak and is thought to suffer excessive deficiency fire in her liver and kidney, and it is difficult for her to absorb highly tonic and hot food. Eggs are hot food. If a woman who has just given birth eats eggs, she will inevitably get inflamed, and suffer an imbalance of Yin and Yang. It may also lead the woman to suffer anorexia, constipation and debilitation during her confinement in childbirth. More seriously, she may be unable to return to the physical state that she used to be.

Therefore, according to the custom of Tancun Village, women are required to be vegetarian for five to seven days after childbirth. During these days, the lying-in women are not allowed to eat any hot food, including pork, chicken, eggs, etc. Even in the dishes they eat, oil and salt should be added as little or no as possible. As a result, the lying-in women mainly eat light vegetables, clear soup and rice gruel in the first few days after childbirth. They can not eat all kinds of delicious meat dishes until the deficiency fire in their bodies is removed, including chicken, lean meat, eggs, pork tripe, pork chops, sweet rice wine, brown sugar and so on.

Breastfeeding, for a young woman who has just become a mother, is a conflict and pain that is accompanied by the change of the role. With the reform and opening up, society and economy are changing, people's ethics and ideas of chastity have also undergone profound changes, but it is so embarrassing for a young woman, who has just given birth, to feed her infant in an imposing manner. In a few days after the birth of the child, the mother can not dare to feed it until there is no one around, but her mother, as an experienced woman, will inadvertently and playfully teach her, "you are an apple in our eyes before you are married, but you will do like a pig or dog after you have a child." That is to say, before a woman gets married, her breasts are too precious to be exposed, but as a mother she has to feed her infant like a pig or a dog feeding their children. It is natural for a mother. In this way, the young lying-in woman's mother tells her daughter not to be shy. Then, after the woman suggests herself many times, she can change her emotional feelings and feed her infant more and more naturally and boldly.

When the mother feeds her infant boldly, casually and naturally, her infant can drink the sweet milk at any time and get the necessary nutritional supplement. When a child lying in its mother's arms cries in a crowd, the first that its mother will do is to naturally lift up her clothes and put her nipples into the child's mouth, regardless of the men around. Furthermore, no one will criticize such public behavior of women. It is a common emotion of human beings to child rearing.

Newborn babies are the most vulnerable of all primates, and the only safe way for babies to get food is through breastfeeding.

The importance and legitimacy of breastfeeding for newborn babies can be understood from both biological and cultural angles.

First of all, newborns can not take the initiative to seek food, but their vigorous metabolism requires plenty of nutrient-rich substances for energy, and breast milk is the best nutrient. Breast milk is highly nutritious and easily digested. According to the analysis, breast milk contains 1.5 % protein, 3.7 % fat and 6.9 % lactose, with 68 calories per 100 milliliters. At the same time, breast milk also has many advantages such as economical feeding, health, convenience and suitable temperature and so forth. The various immune antibodies contained in it can enhance the resistance of infants to some diseases, which makes the breast milk unequaled by all the man-made nutrients.

Second, breastfeeding is far beyond its biological significance. As Dr. James P. Grant, Executive Director of the United Nations Children's Fund (UNICEF), addressed, "the role of breastfeeding in children's survival and healthy development is far more significant than we imagined (Grant, 1994)." The assertion by James P. Grant warns us to pay attention to the importance of breastfeeding on the personality, psychology and socialization of babies. Psychologists have shown that the formation of a person's personality and emotional qualities are interrelated to the pattern of infant feeding in the earlier infant stage. Newborns can listen and look at another person who loves them when they are 10 weeks old, and participate in the process by the feeling, physical contact and gentle action. The tendencies, expressions and actions are consistent with those of the people they love and accompany. Babies seek eye contact and can imitate the movements of the eyes. It is the initial mutual subjectivity or the basic mutual awareness between person and person. Such communication has been confirmed, and the dual organization of the self and other reflected in the infant's brain when it is prepared to feel a real partner has led to some emotions, which are conducive to the development of the infant's brain.

The superiority of breastfeeding not only provides a guarantee for the physical health of the infant, which is the basic material premise for the infant to engage in socialization, but also creates a favorable condition for the interaction between the mother and the infant. Such interaction is the original interpersonal communication and initial emotional communication after the birth of the baby, which includes not only physical contact, material giving, but also kinship expression and skill cultivation, with plenty of psychological and social connotations. All of this is a combination of natural connections between the mother and the baby and the uniqueness of the baby from significant others at present and in the future, thus making breastfeeding of unparalleled significance for the socialization of the baby. Breastfeeding is not only conducive to the intellectual development of infants and the cultivation of positive social emotions and the cultivation of initial social consciousness and ability, but also enables infants to learn all kinds of basic skills and initial social rules (Wang, 1995).

Basic methods are emphasized in breastfeeding for infants. For example, a mother can not feed the baby lying low so as not to choke the baby. If a young mother always gets her child choked in breastfeeding, she may gain a bad reputation among the women in the village and be teased by others for her inability. In order to avoid the child's choking, the mother tends to squeeze out a little milk on the ground before feeding the child if she has too much breast milk. When feeding the child, the mother must put the child's head higher than the foot, and incline slightly to prevent the milk from flowing into the child's weasand and choking the child. If the mother comes back from farm work in the hot sun, she is not allowed to feed the child immediately, because she is internally hot and her breast milk is also hot, which may lead to the child who eats it to suffer from diarrhea due to the unbalance of cold and heat. And in the eyes of the locals, the resulting gastrointestinal problems of the baby tend to be cured in a long time. So, in the summer, the mother should first take a rest after coming back from farm work in the fields, and wash the nipples until the sweat on her body dries, before feeding the child. The mother is not allowed to feed the child if she falls sick. According to the local people, breast milk is made from the mother's blood, so if the mother falls sick, her blood will become unclean and the child will suffer from the same disease as its mother if he is fed by its mother.

There is a custom of borrowing breast milk in the local area. If the mother of a child can not produce enough breast milk during lactation due to congenital hypoplasia, the child can only borrow the breast milk from the mother of its peers. The mothers have so much breast milk that their children can not eat it up, so they can feed the children who have no sufficient milk from their mothers. But it is more out of their maternal kindness. In general, such a mother will consciously feed her child with the milk in her left breast, and feed the child of another family with the milk in her right breast, because they believe that the milk in the left breast is more nutritious than that of the right one.

Mothers during lactation must be mindful of their diet and physical health because it is known to all that the diseases can be easily spread via breast milk. In general, the more and the better the mother eats, the higher the quality of the milk produced will be, and the more beneficial it will be to the growth and development of the child. On the contrary, if the mother lives a poor life or eats nothing due to a bad appetite, it is bound to affect the constitution of the child. Therefore, the family members of the mother will try their best to meet the nutritional requirements of the mother during lactation.

Local people believe that the dishes that promote the lactation mainly include chicken broth, lean meat broth, pork tripe broth, pork chop soup and poached egg in fermented glutinous rice soup, so that the family members of the mother must invest a lot of extra expenses in purchasing these ingredients during the lactation period. If a child is sick during the lactation period and sees a veteran doctor of traditional Chinese medicine, the doctor makes a prescription for the child, requiring the mother to take the Chinese medicine together with the child. On the one hand, it is to prevent the mother from being ill to aggravate the child's condition. On the other hand, it is believed that the medicine that the mother takes will be dissolved in the breast milk, so that the child can be treated while it is breastfed.

Breastfeeding is also a way for a mother to coax a child to sleep. When the baby cries, the mother can calm the child down in three ways. First, the mother can hold the baby in her arms and gently pat the baby's back, and repeatedly make some buzzing sound in her mouth, so that the child can sleep unconsciously accompanied by the pleasant music. Second, the mother can go back and forth with the baby in her arms, and shake it gently up and down, so that the baby may feel like moving and stop crying. Third, it is the easiest way to get the mother's nipple into the child's mouth and induce it to sleep. The above three ways are the most effective baby hypnosis for the local people. The young mothers experience the toil and happiness of raising a child in the course of feeding, delighting and getting off the child to bed. It is the process of frequent cultural interaction and integration. With their parents' emotional and physical investments day by day, children have accumulated the identity of blood relationship between them and their parents in their subconscious since they were very young. The relationship between father and son, the relationship between mother and son and all the cultural relations arising in this aspect constitute the basic structures of all family sociology, such as the initial emotional, ethical, moral, legal and material relations, in the process of child rearing.

Weaning and Feeding by All Types of Food

The villagers of Tancun Village believe that breast milk is the best tonic to the human body, so that the children who drank a lot of breast milk are deemed to have a solid physical foundation, which means that such people are generally in good condition with a strong body and unusual strength. Therefore, the mother will try to extend the breastfeeding time for her child, and increase the times of feeding, so that they can drink more breast milk. In general, children just drink breast milk for about one and a half years, because mothers have to stop breastfeeding in order to continue to have children. The weaning process is described by Fei Xiaotong as the physiological weaning. However, this pattern of weaning is temporary. .After a year or so, the mother gives birth to the younger sister or brother, and then the weaned child may be able to share the sweet breast milk with the younger sister or brother once again. In this way, children can drink breast milk for a long time. It is common for children to be breastfed until they are three years old, and some are even breastfed until they are seven or eight years old. It is often joked by the villagers that some children are breastfed until they wear underpants, that the kids have dinner with the bowl in the hand while being breastfed by their mothers, or that the pupils may put down the schoolbag and ask for breast milk after returning from school. Thus, it can be seen that some children are breastfed for an extremely long time.

Therefore, for many children in Tancun Village, the last weaning comes when the mother does not have breast milk anymore or when the child grows up and feels so shy that it does not want to drink the breast milk of its mother. Physiological weaning also involves the root of social weaning. For example, because of the strict implementation of the family planning system, mothers have to end their reproductive tasks early and no longer have lactation as they have fewer children. So children who are growing up can not have the chance to recover the physiological breastfeeding as their previous generation. Nowadays, most of the villagers of Tancun Village have two children, but there is a longer and longer interval between the births of the two children, usually around three or four years. As a result, when the second child is born, the mother is back in the lactation, while the first child is already four years old. The idea of shyness begins to be injected into the child's mind, and drinking breast milk has been less attractive to them. Thus, in Tancun Village, the present children have been physiologically weaned at a younger and younger age. The author learned that, among the five children over one year old, who had recently learned to walk, one child was weaned latest when it was eleven months old, and one was weaned earliest when it was seven months old.

On the one hand, the early completion of the physiological weaning for current children is closely related to the fast-paced work and life of the young mothers nowadays, because they must end the breastfeeding as early as possible to work in other cities. As discussed earlier, women have lost a lot of opportunities to make money due to the birth of their children. Especially as a member of the migrant workers in developed areas, mothers also worry about being fired from factories if they do not return to work for a long time. So, while they are still at home, they will first get their children weaned, and then train their children to develop the habit of drinking milk, so as not to make their children unable to be separated from them.

On the other hand, the early completion of the physiological weaning for current children is inseparable from the improvement of people's living standards. Milk products of high quality are readily available to the weaned children. Most of the families in the village mainly purchase the Nanshan Milk Powder produced in Nanshan Pasture in Chengbu County, Hunan Province. Nanshan Milk Powder is usually sold at about thirty Yuan per bag in the market. The families in better conditions buy the Liduojing Infant Milk Powder at more than eighty Yuan per barrel. In addition, the food, such as soy milk, nutritious rice flour and the fruit juice processed by the mothers themselves, have become common food for infants. As a result, children rely less on breast milk than their predecessors.

It is a tough and painful process to wean the children physiologically. The children who have been accustomed to drinking breast milk are forcibly deprived of the right to enjoy the sweet milk in their mothers' arms, while they tend to cry all night in protest. No mother is cruel to see the child crying but does not feed it. Therefore, it is extremely difficult to wean the child while holding it in the arms. In Tancun Village, a common way to wean the child is to separate the child from its mother for a week. During this period, the child is usually taken care of by its paternal or maternal grandmother, who will be patient with the child and reconstitute powdered milk by adding water or make fruit juice to the child once it cries from hunger.

Moreover, during this period, the mother of the child should try not to hold the child. The women told the author, "if the child was just weaned for only a few days but its mother carried it in the arms, the child would immediately seek for its mother's breast for milk, as if it knew the woman was its mother." After the hardships for a week or so, the child will largely become accustomed to drinking milk or eating other things. To this point, the child can be taken care of by its mother again. During the weaning period, if the baby cries piteously for the breast milk, the mother will try anything possible to make her child hate or fear breast milk. Their solution is to coat the nipples with Coptis juice or chili powder, so that the child will be too scared to drink breast again any more if its moth touches its mother's nipples. From then on, the child will gradually manage to be physiologically weaned.

It is a universal cultural mechanism to conduct physiological weaning of the child. As the child becomes physically stronger, it can not meet the needs of the child's metabolism only by drinking breast milk. Therefore, it is necessary to cultivate children to accept all the food sources of the living environment in the community as one of the means of social nurturing.

In Tancun Village, through social weaning, the children can get rid of the dependence on breast milk and adapt to more food choices step by step. This cultural pattern is not exclusive to the villagers of Tancun Village. Among the vast ethnic groups in southwest China, people all complete the painful process of getting the children weaned roughly in the same way. For example, for the Naxi people in Baidi Village, Shangri-la County, Yunnan Province, "the way to get the child weaned is to separate the child from its mother for one week. During this period, the child may either sleep with its paternal grandparents, or be sent to its maternal grandparents' house. On the one hand, the mother tries not to get exposed to its child as less as possible. On the other hand, the mother coats her nipples with the things with a bitter taste, such as wormwood juice, chicken gall and pig gall, so that the child will be no longer willing to suck. Some mothers even draw some pictures threatening the children on the breasts (He, 2001)."

After the child is weaned, its parents begin to train it to eat coarse food grain. According to the villagers of Tancun Village, two things are the most nourishing to the human body, one is breast milk and the other is rice. As the saying goes, anything else is not as nourishing as rice. The villagers believe that children should eat all types of food since they were very young. It means that children have to eat much food, and should not be fastidious about what they eat. To feed all types of food to children is to eat rice, vegetables and meat. Before all the teeth of the child come out, the adult will usually feed the child after chewing the food up in his mouth and then putting it onto the chopsticks and into the child's mouth. It does not look very hygienic, but in the views of ordinary older people, it is a habit but it is not dirty.

The rice is ground into flour and then mixed with water into the paste, which is the best food for the children. The tool used to grind rice is the traditional stone mill. The flour that is ground with such a tool is thick but highly sticky, and tastes quite delicious. However, ready-made rice flour products are now available in the market. Only a few older women are able to adapt traditional methods to grind some self-made rice flour to the children.

Cultural Logic of Breast Milk and Blood

In the views of the local people, the blood flowing in the human body is not easily come by, and it comes from drinking the breast milk of the mother in childhood. Breast milk and blood have acquired an idealized connection. The blood is transformed from the breast milk of the mother drunken in early childhood, so it is naturally considered precious. As almost every older person says, blood is more expensive than gold. However, young people in the village do not think so because they know a little bit of modern physiology. When the child fights with another child, it will seldom arouse the conflicts between the adults as long as there is no bleeding. But if a child is bleed, it will provoke the anger of its parents even when it is just a slight skin injury. Due to the special cult of blood, it is hard to convince them that drawing a small amount of blood will not affect their health.

On December 26, 2006, a blood donation vehicle came to the middle school of the town where Tancun Village is located, which was organized by the Red Cross Society of Shaoyang County to advocate for the people to donate blood voluntarily. Although the doctors had made great efforts to publicize blood donation and the school teachers and leaders also convened students to have meetings and encourage people to donate blood, in the end, only the headmaster and several young teachers who had received a college education in the middle school donated blood.

During a routine physical examination of students organized by the town hospital, the author learned that a considerable number of students did not take the physical examination, although the examination fee was very cheap, at 5 Yuan per person. Part of the reason these students did not take the physical examination is that some students' parents argue that drawing so much blood for no reason will hurt the body of their children as their children have no pain or disease. In their opinions, the child's blood is transformed from the breast milk that the child drunk when it was very young, and it is accumulated from countless food the child has eaten. And they hold that the blood can not be drawn until there is no alternative, and that the blood will be reduced once it is drawn. In their opinions, blood is the symbol of life, and one of the prominent signs of the vitality is the plentiful animal spirits. According to the view of traditional Chinese medicine, blood is generated when the body is filled with Qi, and all the diseases will be eliminated. It can be seen that the local people's worship of blood reflects their logical thinking on the healthy growth of life, as blood is the source of life and the foundation of health.

The local people's cultural awareness of blood reveals the life bond of the consanguinity between the mother and the child. The logical relationship between blood and breast milk indicates that blood is the root of a living body, which means that the blood is equivalent to the living body, and that the blood is transformed from breast milk, which means that the breast milk is equivalent to the blood of the child as well as the living body of the child. The concept has laid the simplest biological foundation for traditional filial ethics in China. The child's life not only belongs to itself, but also is the continuation of the mother's life, as well as the foundation for the reproduction of the next generation of life. What the mother passes on to the child through her own milk is blood, which is also the sustenance of life, declaring the moral principle that kinship is deeper than blood. It is the justification for the existence of Chinese filial piety culture in Tancun Village. Confucian filial piety ethics contains some profound philosophies, but the simple villagers of Tancun Village have given a local cultural understanding of the Confucian filial piety ethics, which is that the rationality of the filial piety lies in that the blood of the children comes from the breast milk of their mothers, which is the justification of the natural law that any child must show filial piety to its parents.

The local understanding is in line with the explanation of filial piety in Confucian classics. When explaining the relationship between the human body and filial piety, Confucius, the founder of Confucianism, said, "Our skin and hair are given by our parents and we should protect and cherish them and not get any slightest damage. It is the beginning of fulfilling our filial duties. In the world, we should follow the morality of benevolence and righteousness, make great achievements, show our fame to the later generations and make our parents show their glory. It is the ultimate goal of filial piety (General Introduction of the Book of Filial Piety)." In other words, Our body, hair and skin are given by our parents, so we must cherish it and take good care of it, because a healthy body and mind is the most basic condition for being a man and doing things. So we should cherish it and love it, which marks the beginning of showing filial piety to our parents. Moreover, we should grow up in a healthy way, and do things according to the right principles, and make our name respected by the future generations, so that the future generations will know that our parents taught us well and raised an excellent child. It is the ultimate goal of filial piety. In this sense, the worship of the villagers of Tancun Village for the blood indicates the cultural meaning of the ethics of filial piety to the parents and the ancestors.

Section 3 Children's Games: A Metaphor of Society

As a form of entertainment, games have always been studied by folklorists and anthropologists. When scholars come to the field, they pay a great deal of attention to the way the game is played in an indigenous tribe which is different from that in their cultures, describe the rules, participants, time and place of the game in detail, explore the origin of the game, and track its evolution and differences in tastes and interests. However, they are more concerned about the religious implications of the game or the cultural functions of the community. Clifford Geertz, the famous American anthropologist, gives a deep description of the cockfight game of the Balinese in his masterpiece The Interpretation of Cultures, and opens a path to the deep cultural interpretation of games. He divides cockfight into deep and shallow. Through meticulous observation and the deep description, he believes that the deeper the game is, the better it will show the dramatic nature of the status and relationship of the local people. Cockfight itself is only shallow, but through the deep observation of the cockfight process and the participation of the participants, the cockfight can reveal the psychological experience of the Balinese. And it is found that the true cultural significance of cockfight is the ability to explain the psychological experience of the local people. By participating in cockfight games, the Balinese can learn about the psychological experience that a Balinese person should do (Geertz, 1999). In this section, the author will describe the mode and changes in children's games in Tancun Village, and analyze their deep cultural metaphors.

Game Participants

It is a common nature of humans and animals to play games. It can even be said that before human beings came into being, or before the human culture came into being, the game had been widely available in the animal world. Because the most fundamental impulse of the game is the reaction from animals to external stimuli, the game is the instinct of biology and human beings, for biologists and physiologists, and no matter what the purpose of the game, the game is first derived from the psychological mechanism of going from stimulus to reaction. However, human beings are rational animals, far beyond animals. Human culture is the only creation of all biological circles. For this reason, it is entirely impossible to summarize the nature of the game by simply attributing the game into the roots of biology. So, for the anthropologists who specialize in the study of culture, they believe that the game is a process that the infants acquire the cultural rules, and that the infants can imitate the behavior patterns and thinking concepts of adults through the game. However, the sociologists believe that the game is a process that the infants are socialized and acquire the principles of conduct, and that the infants are repeatedly molded into those who conform to the rules of standardized behavior in a particular community through the game.

In ancient China, people paid great attention to the cultural function of the game, and they regarded the game as an experience beneficial to scholarly research and advocated the properly relaxing modes of games. In the Record on the Subject of Education of The Book of Rites, it wrote that "therefore, a gentleman should learn the main course well when learning, and learn all kinds of skills while resting at home." The positive value of games was also affirmed in The Analects, which wrote "Is not there the games of gambling and chess? It is better to do this than to be idle." Confucius even thought that "in terms of aspirations, we need to be lofty, to establish our aspirations with the realm we want to achieve; in terms of words and deeds, we need to restrain ourselves with good moral norms; we need to keep our inner goodness and benevolence, act with tolerance and love; meanwhile, we need to be able to master the six arts of propriety, music, archery, riding, writing and arithmetic," which expressly pointed out that the work and rest should be properly balanced and that games are beneficial for physical and mental cultivation.

In addition, in Yanshi Jiaxun (The Family Instructions of Yan), Yan Zhitui argued that, "Playing chess is also an elegant game in modern times, and it enables the people to relieve the loneliness and grief, and it can be played from time to time." Wang Shouren, a thinker of the Ming

Dynasty, regarded the game as a child's nature, and emphasized the importance of the game to the children's psychological education. In the article "The Teaching Rules for Children to Liu Bosong and Other Mentors", Wang wrote "generally speaking, children are naturally fond of playing and scared of being restricted, just like when plants and trees start to sprout, they will grow rapidly and flourish if they are allowed to grow freely, but they will wither quickly if they are destroyed. Now, to educate the children, we must make them develop in line with their interests, encourage them more, so that they will feel delighted from the bottom of their hearts, and then they can naturally make continuous progress."

Therefore, the game was carefully recorded in the works of the literati in ancient China. According to the Annual Customs and Festivals in Peking, "With the bound bamboos as the skeleton, the kite is pasted with paper and made into the images of a red-crowned crane, peacock, swallow and tiger, involving extraordinary painting skills. If a child flies a kite in the sky, it will be the most attractive one. " "The shuttlecock is based on a coin and leather, lined with a copper coin, and bound with eagle plume and a leather belt. If a child kicks it, it will help to invigorate the circulation of blood and protect the child against the cold." "The mouth of the glass trumpet is like the wine cup, and the handle is about two or three feet long. By breathing with the trumpet, the child can clear the Qi in its body." "The child of a poor family carved stone into a ball and kicked it with his feet. He won by attacking the counterparty back and forth (Annual Customs and Festivals in Peking, Tun Li-ch'en)."

Games are a common form of entertainment for human beings. Even after a long time, many folk games, which first appeared in ancient China, are still popular in rural China, such as tug of war and rope skipping. "Now the children, in two teams, stand at both ends of the rope, and pull the rope until one team drags the other over a line on the group, and the former team will win and feel delighted." "With a long rope, two children turn the handles at each end, while the rope turns around so fast that makes it difficult for the children to stare at it.

It looks like hundreds of ropes but actually, there is only one rope. A group of children tries to jump over the rope in turn when the rope moves, and those who can jump over the role are winners (Customs of Amendments to Past Events in Peking, Ying Lian, et al.). " These games are no different from today's children's games in terms of form, rule or cultural function.

At this point, we need to give a scientific definition of games. In this regard, many folklorists have made research conclusions. For example, Wu Bing'an holds that "folk games refer to the recreational activities spread in the lives of the masses. Games are the most common, the most universal and the most interesting recreational activity among the folk recreational customs. It is mainly popular among the children and in the recreational programs of adults during festivals." And he divided the games into four categories, indoor life games, courtyard games, merry-making games and all kinds of gambling games (Wu, 1985). In the book The Handbook of Folklore, Zhong Jingwen argued that, "folk games refer to the recreational activities that are popular in the folk and mainly aimed to have fund and while away the time. From the perspective of spatial activity form, games can be divided into indoor games and courtyard games. From the perspective of the nature of the game, games can be divided into intelligent games, physical games, and both intelligent and physical games (Zhong, 1998)." In these definitions, the game is still regarded as a custom phenomenon, and the scientific connotation of the game is not defined from the angle of culture.

Different from the above two definitions, the definition of the game by Johan Huizinga, a famous Dutch anthropologist, is more widely accepted in the circles of sociology and anthropology, and he lays more stress on the cultural function of the game. In his book Homo Ludens: A Study of the Play-Element in Culture, he pointed out that the game is a crucial cultural phenomenon. Games can be found everywhere. Gaming is a distinctive behavior that is diverse from ordinary life. "The game is an activity that is carried out in a specific time and space. The game presents an obvious order, follows widely accepted rules, and has no necessity for the trend of the times and material utility. The mood of the players is jubilant and enthusiastic, depending on the situation, or holy, or festive. In a game, the players feel excited and nervous, accompanied by dancing with joy, and happy laughter and cheerful voices. Subsequently, they may get completely carefree and joyful (Huizinga, 2007)."

Johan Huizinga's definition of the game allows us to see the purity of the game. Each game form is formed due to the performance of the people in a specific temporal and spatial context, while playing the game is a way of expressing our emotions out of compliance with the rules. Some games are performed in an extremely cheerful and relaxing state, and it is the way for the people to seek the content of the mind, to let the negative moods out, and to have fun; games are filled with fun. Some games are extremely serious, such as football and Chinese chess, and are demonstrated in extremely solemn situations. As for the most primitive ritual games of sacred ceremony, sacrifice and offering, it is hard to see the people burst out laughing non-seriously and festively.

Games exist in all aspects of human behavior and can be staged whenever and wherever possible. With the help of the game, people can express their likes and dislikes and aesthetic tastes for values and duplicate social structures and political competition. Games educate the next generation of mankind. Furthermore, the game also contains sacred religious sentiment and ritual solemnity. In a word, the game is also a culture, a condensed form of the great civilized life. In this sense, games are sacred. As a result, Johan Huizinga even exaggerates: "the true and pure game is one of the foundations of human civilization.

Thus, it can be seen that compared with all other cultural activities, games have extremely prominent features.

First, the game is voluntary. No matter what kind of game it is, players are willing to participate in the game.

Second, the game is neither an ordinary nor real life. It steps out of real-life and enters into a temporary field of activity, with its own tendencies. The game is a function of culture, and the expression of the game satisfies various public ideals.

Third, the game is isolated and restricted. This feature is more prominent in the field of festivals and rituals. The game is played within a specific time and space. The game has a starting point. At some point, it stops dead and goes to its end. In the process, everything is moving, changing, alternating, following, linking and separating. And as a cultural phenomenon, games have a fixed form. Once played, the game is preserved as an innovative form of the mind, ultimately becoming a treasure in memory. Games can be repeated at any time. Whether it is children's games, chess games or regular mystical rituals, it can be repeated.

More interesting than time limits is the limitation of the game in space. The performance and existence of all games are limited to the pre-designated field and the marked boundary. This boundary can be either a matter's boundary or a boundary of imagination, either a consciously marked boundary or a boundary taken for granted. In the playground, an absolute and unique order plays a dominant role. The game creates an order, and the game is order itself. The game creates a temporary and limited perfection to the imperfect world and the chaotic life. The game demands an absolute and supreme order. All games have corresponding rules, which determine the power to control the situation in a temporarily defined playground. At the same time, the rules of the game cannot be doubted, because the principles hidden behind the rules are unshakable truths (Huizinga, 2007).

Major Games for Children in Tancun Village

Games, as an integral part of the culture of a region, are closely bound up with the social and economic structures of the region. Through the children's games in a region, we can gain a perspective on the social and economic conditions, values and lifestyles of the people in this place. In the era of planned economy and the 1980s when the people groped the way out of the planned economy, children's games mostly appeared in collective form, reflecting the cultural impact of political and economic life on children in their minds at that time. In the production organization structure at that time, all the adults were energetic members of the production team, and their production and living behaviors were collectively incorporated into a specific group organization, while the underage children took the production and life of the adults as the model and played some games involved in groups.

According to the survey of young and middle-aged people born in the 1960s and 1970s, it was found that the game they played most during their childhood was fighting field battles. Fighting is a military affair, a political act organized and carried out by the troops. But in Tancun Village, the children living in the era of the planned economy became the soldiers in the game. Organized by the older children of the village, they served as officers and officials at all levels of the army, such as scouts, sappers or guards.

In general, when playing the game, the children of the whole village .organize a so-called military organization under the leadership of a very prestigious big boy, who is hailed as the commander by other children. The boy tends to be the leader of the Children's Corps of the primary school in the village, such as squadron leader or battalion chief. The commander then appoints his subordinates, who are appointed according to the military establishment that they know. The children who can be appointed by the commander are usually those who do well in school, serve as student cadres, or behave very bravely at various gatherings in the village.

Every evening, the commander organized all the children in the village to take part in military training or combat exercises. Before the training, the commander would gather all the cadres of the children to his headquarters, the entrance of the village, which was also a public place for adults to gather. Here, the commander would deploy the training program or launch a battle against the children of a neighboring village. By this time, the children's parents who were working late had mostly just returned from the fields. They were busy registering the workpoints at the teller of the villager or cleaning the farm tools and preparing the dinner. Then, they had neither time nor energy to interfere with the children's affairs. Therefore, the commander of the children became the mastermind of organizing one funny evening after another.

Meanwhile, the commander would organize the children to crawl on their belly in the open fields, or organize them to attack a specific hill, or divide the children into groups, so that they could learn how to fight as a guerrilla at the ends of the village, or in the lanes, or in the wild.

DC, who used to be the commander of the children in Huangjia Village recalled,

"When we were young, our parents seemed not to care about us. .At that time, the children seldom saw their parents all day long, and most of the time they went out in the early morning and came back till late at night. Our childhood was mostly spent with other children in the village. What impressed me most was that as long as it didn't rain, we would go to the entrance of the village every evening and fight field battles, especially in the summer and autumn evenings. Before being arranged by anyone else, all the boys in the village would automatically gather at the entrance. We had seen many war films, such as The Red Guards on Honghu Lake, Zhang Ga the Soldier Boy and Guerrillas on the Railway, so we imitated those revolutionary heroes to fight field battles in the village.

There are three types of field games that we play the most. First, we attacked a hill and conducted field training. Second, we engaged in street battles and ran all over the village. The commanders of all the sides commanded their men to hide in the woodpile, in the corner of the house, in the cowshed, or in the pigsty in the village. When they saw the enemy pass by, they would suddenly jump out, pointing at the other side and shouting 'Bang', which indicates that the enemy had been hit by a bullet. Third, we had the most intense field training, which usually took place in battles with children from other villages.

When we were very young, we used to fight field battles with the children of the Jiang family from Xiangche Village, while our battles were quite vivid and fierce. After the harvest season in autumn, we used to engage in field battles with the children from Xiangche Village in the agricultural hillock in front of the village with the fields as a barrier. As the children came from Xiangche Village and we were not from the same village, we could fight them boldly and confidently. We hit them with mud, and some even used pebbles as weapons. It was strange at that time that it did not matter if any of us was hurt by the weapons. The child who was hurt would not tell his parents, while his parents took no interest in it. But if a child in the village was injured, we would avenge him. Sometimes we would engage in hand-to-hand combat with the children from other villages, right in the middle of the field, fighting each other, soldiers versus soldiers and generals versus generals. In this way, we would fight each other until our parents called us at the entrance to the village to go home for dinner."

When it comes to the games of field battles during their childhood, the respondents at their thirties or forties were all brightened up with great joy when talking about those days, while they seemed to take pride in having spent an adventurous and courageous childhood. JDS, who went to the Sino-Vietnamese War (the Third Indo-China War), told the author, "when we were young, we used to fight field battles in the village. I was not afraid of death, so I often led our troops. Once, I was hit with a stone by a child of the Luo family and my forehead was bleeding. I rushed up and caught him, while other children in our village took him as a prisoner and asked the children of his family to surrender to us. "When the author asked him if these courageous childhood experiences had any impact on his later performance in the Sino-Vietnamese War, he replied, "When I was young, we fought field battles. It trained my courage for not being scared to death. So, of course, I was easily motivated by officers on a real battlefield." He was also granted with the Merit Citation Class III for his bravery in the war, and was appointed deputy secretary of the party committee of the town supply and marketing cooperative after he was discharged from active military service.

JBD, the former secretary of the party in Tancun Village, told the author, " When we were young, we fought field battles completely inspired by the stories of some heroes. At school, our teachers used to tell us the stories of the Eighth Route Army and the People's Liberation Army. At home, our parents also told us the stories of revolutionary heroes. For example, we heard many stories about Mao

Zedong, Zhu De, Xu Shiyou (a general in the Chinese People's Liberation Army), Yang Dezhi (commander in China during the Sino–Vietnamese War or Third Indochina War) and other revolutionary leaders. Stories of heroes could be frequently heard on the radio in every household. As a result, when we were very young, we worshipped the revolutionary heroes and the Chinese People's Liberation Army, often imitating the images of the PLA soldiers that we saw in the films. When we engaged in field battles, we would make hats out of sticks and grass and put them on our heads as camouflage. "

It can be seen from the interviews with the respondents that the children's game of field battles reflects the mental outlook of the post-revolutionary era and it is a practical means by which the revolutionary cultural hegemony can model children's personality. The primary function of games should be to entertain, but as children grow up, it is bound to have an important impact on their socialization. The first premise of the game of field battles is that the children should have a field for group life, while the collective economic organization provides the necessary social basis for the formation of this field. In the era of collective economy, all mature labor workers are incorporated into the collective labor organizations, and they have no time or freedom to take care of their children in separate families. As a result, the children spontaneously gather in their communities to engage in group activities, thus becoming an inevitable choice for them during their childhood. Through field battles, each child is trained in his or her own children's organization, so that he or she can be socialized.

On the one hand, children must gain a recognized position in the group organization. The child must learn to get along with others, and be well coordinated with other members of the group. Otherwise, he will be isolated by other children in the village and excluded from the group. In this way, he will not only lose his partners, but also have difficulty in gaining the qualification to participate in the group game.

In addition, through participating in such group games, children are cultivated in the spirit of collectivism, which enables them to form a sense of group honor and develop the courage to make contributions to the collective. For this reason, in the field battle game, the children will not give up because of a slight injury. Whether it is the training of crawling in the field or the battle with the enemy of the children from other villages, the children will show a spirit of being courageous to sacrifice and not being scared of death. Therefore, the children who were born and lived in this era do not have the bad habits of being pampered. As mentioned above, JDS said that "When I was young, we fought field battles. It trained my courage for not being scared to death. So, of course, I was easily motivated by officers on a real battlefield," while these experiences of field battle games in childhood allow the children to cultivate a brave and dedicated personality in the course of socialization.

Finally, in the 1960s and 1970s, ideology was the theme of the political life of the state, when the revolutionary discourse encouraged the people to learn from heroes and soldiers. At that time, in the countryside, the mode of decentralized production and management for thousands of years was also broken, and the semi-militarized management of production and life was carried out, which was bound to exert an imperceptible influence on the growing children, thus guiding them to worship the soldiers and to be curious about the war. The collective organization of the production team provides a social picture for children to have an opportunity to get together as an army to organize various training programs. The field battle game of the children is exactly the extension of revolutionary consciousness and revolutionary discourse in children's lives, and it also provides a good way to train the descendants of the revolutionary undertakings and the new generation of revolutionaries as successors.

If the boys born in the 1960s and the 1970s mainly played the game of imitating the soldiers' field battles, the girls with their age played the game of field hopping (similar to hopscotch), a game of enclosure and the accompanying symbolic ceremony of fighting against the landlord. Land is the foundation of farmers. It has always been the lifelong goal of every farmer to be able to possess more land. However, after the victory of the democratic revolution, land became the main basis for classifying the social status of the people. People who own too much land may be classified as landlords, and they may be regarded as exploiters in the countryside and forced to accept the revolutionary transformation of poor peasants. The process of such an agrarian revolution has been deeply interpreted in the girls' game of field hopping, so that the new generation who did not experience the revolutionary struggle can receive the education of class consciousness in the routine game activities.

As for the basic rules of field hopping, first, a piece of multi-layer vacant land in the shape of Tu (土, soil in Chinese) is marked out on the plain (see Figure 4-1), and then eight areas are divided and named as B, C, D, E, B', C', D' and E', representing eight fields. This game is usually played in pairs. The player should start from the area A and hop the areas one by one from B to C to D to E and from B' to C' to D' to E'.

The basic tool of field hopping is a shuttlecock strung with abacus beads. Standing at A, the player throws the shuttlecock to area B, and hops to a little in front of the shuttlecock with one foot. Her heels could not touch the line. Then, she kicks the shuttlecock hard to A and jumps out on one leg and returns to A. Then, she takes the shuttlecock between her heels and throws it up behind her. Before the shuttlecock falls to the ground, she should catch the shuttlecock quickly with both hands. So, she passes the area B. During the jump, she could only stand on one foot, and if the other foot touches the ground a little, it is considered a failure. The shuttlecock thrown can not stop on the line, and her heels can not stop on the line when she jumps to each area. Otherwise, it is considered a failure. When kicking the shuttlecock back to A, the player can only put forth her strength once. If she fails to kick it back to A, it is a failure. At the same time, the player must put forth her strength properly. Otherwise, if the shuttlecock is kicked too far, she can not catch it with both feet after returning to A, which is also regarded as a failure. Finally, she should throw the shuttlecock from behind with her heels and catch it with her hands. Otherwise, the game would be a failure. This game mainly trains the skills of the feet, requiring the players to have high strength of the legs, as well as perseverance and judgment.

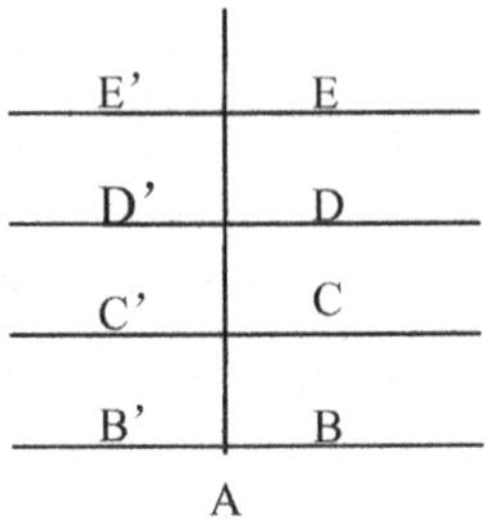

Figure 4-1 Rules of field hopping

When the player finishes all the areas according to the rule, she is eligible to buy the fields. The rule for buying the field is that she should first announce to other players which area or field she intends to buy. Then, with her back to the vacant land in the shape of Tu, she throws the shuttlecock to the field she is going to buy, and then turns back and kicks back the shuttlecock according to the rule of field hopping. In this way, the field becomes private property. If the shuttlecock she throws behind her fails to fall on the field to be bought, the game will be considered a failure, or it is also a failure if she does not complete all the procedures in accordance with the rule of field hopping.

The field that the player "buys" has the property of "ownership" in the following game. Once the player buys the field, the subsequent players must jump over the field when they jump and land on the ground with one foot. Otherwise, it is a failure. Therefore, once a player buys the first piece of field, it will be easier for her to play the game subsequently. And she will buy more and more fields. However, the players who fail to buy a field must jump over the fields that have been bought. Thus, it is more and more difficult to play the game. Finally, the player has to become a poor peasant or a landless person. The game comes to an end when all the fields are bought.

Finally, the game enters into the stage of fighting against the landlord. The player who buys the most fields will be classified as a landlord at the end of the game, who will be criticized and denounced by other players who have no or fewer fields. However, the struggle is symbolic, as the players who have no or fewer fields will pinch the hand of the player classified as landlord gently, chanting the nursery rhyme that "the landlord, with no conscience, exploits the peasants and ordinary people." In the end, everyone starts a new game in the riot of laughter.

Compared with boys' children's games, girls' games focus on the cultural projection of land reform and class struggle in rural areas. The stigma of this particular social context can be found in any of the other games for girls. For example, in the rope skipping game for girls, the nursery rhyme goes that "the tractor has four feet, parents go to work, and the elder sister buys apples back home. The apple is so sweet and free of charge. The people's commune holds a meeting. Long live, Chairman Mao!" This is a nursery rhyme that praises revolutionary leaders and communism, and another song praises that "Liu Hulan, 15, joined the revolutionary guerrillas. She died for the revolution, and Chairman Mao praised that she did the right thing! Well done!" Nursery rhymes inspire us to learn from the heroes' dedication to the revolution at the cost of their lives.

The social metaphor reflected by the girls' field hopping game should be pondered. The rules of the whole game are very difficult, which is a metaphor for the process that farmers suffer many hardships before buying the land. The rules of the game are fair to every one, since every player must rely on their own ability to overcome one after another difficulty, and ultimately they can get the qualification of buying the field, which teaches the children to know that they must work hard to gain something and dare to compete. After the fierce competition, the winner obtains the ownership of the fields. Therefore, according to the rules of the game, she can prohibit other players from passing through her fields, so that she can acquire more fields. However, the resulting series consequence is that she separates herself from her partners in an asymmetrical class relationship, while the winner becomes a landlord, but the losers become poor peasants.

Thus, the game became a structural event, and the two poles that formed the structure were winners and losers, landlords and poor peasants, exploiters and exploitees, the criticized and criticizers. The final struggle and the nursery rhyme are more symbolic, allowing the children to have fun in the game as if they experience a class struggle in rural areas. As Levi-Strauss C. said, "it seems that the game has an effect of separating the players. At the end of the game, a distinction is made between the players or teams, but at first there is no inequality between them. When the game ends, the players or teams are divided into winners and losers. So, for games, symmetry is predetermined; and it's structural because it comes from the principle that the rules of the game are the same for both sides. In this way, asymmetry is created by people; it must come from the nature of chance, while the latter itself should be attributed to the intention, fortune and talent (Levi-Strauss, 1987)."

Functions and Meaning of Games

In the period of economic underdevelopment, there are a variety of children's games. In addition to the aforementioned field battle game, field hopping and other group games, individual or small games are also very diverse. For example, flying a kite, playing hide-and-seek, playing house, beating spinning top, rope skipping and walking on stilts have played a significant educational role in the growth of children. Moreover, these games enable them to learn to obey the rules, distinguish right from wrong, get along with others and develop social skills. The training of these abilities is natural and simple, much of which is conducted without the involvement of adults, but it is all about survival skills that can never be developed by any type of preaching.

Of the traditional games of children, two kinds of games are the most important. One is the parent-child games in family life, which usually take place between parents and their children, while the games similar to the parent-child games also arise between the adult relatives and the children of blood relations. The other is the outdoor games, which are a better means to cultivate the social interaction of children.

By participating in various game activities, the children can be culturally cultivated, and affected by the traditional culture, ethics, etiquette, rules of conduct, interpersonal communication and even religious concepts of the community, and gradually achieve cultural acculturation, and internalize what they have learned from the game into their internal system of traditional knowledge, thereby becoming a social person that conforms to the cultural criteria in the community.

Parent-child game is an activity between parents and children based on parent-child affection. A large number of research results show that the parent-child game is of great significance to promote the development of children, especially in psychological development. Parent-child games can promote the development of children's cognitive ability. Games between parents and infants can arouse the attention of infants, thus promoting their continuous activities and exploratory behaviors (Rubin et al., 1983). At the same time, the parent-child game can promote the development of children's social skills. Parents who often play games with their children and lead happy lives to play an important role in promoting the social development of their children, while the children who have no opportunities to play games with their parents and lead unhappy lives are not good at interacting with others in the game activities (Bronman, 1982). Moreover, the better the parents are at games and the more positive the emotional expression and game stimulation is in the parent-child game, the more positive the response of children to their parents and their playing behavior will be. In particular, in symbolic play, "the more active the mother's physical play behavior (such as gestures, language, and interpretation of the play activity) is, the better the infant will like the symbolic play (Damast et al., 1996)." However, the parent-child game is more about influencing the formation of children's personality and psychology, and laying a profound and unconscious foundation for blood identity. In terms of social interaction, to promote children's inheritance of community culture and internalization of standardized cultural patterns, it is necessary to get the children involved in a wider range of outdoor games.

Outdoor game is a spontaneous activity in which children of different age groups compete with each other based on their luck and skills, under a more flexible rule that may slightly vary according to the changes in the time and place. It is free in form, and focuses on entertainment and the physical and mental exercises. It is highly linked up with life, with a strong flavor of life. In the description of children's games at Tancun Village, we mainly focus on the cultural significance of the traditional outdoor games because the cultural imprint left by outdoor games on every villager has never changed, and the outdoor games can evoke the memories of the respondents most in the survey. Whether it is a field battle game or field hopping, these outdoor games enable the children to be self-taught in socialization through their personal experience and behavior imitation. In this sense, the outdoor game is an experiential activity for children. Outdoor activities play a role in outdoor education for the growth of children.

Compared with school education, outdoor education, though an unjustified and irrational mode of traditional education, is the most effective method of socialization in terms of language, moral and cultural life. Psychological research suggests that outdoor education, or game experience, is an inevitable process for the children aged between six and fourteen, because they need to learn the language of life and master how to resolve the conflicts between an ever-changing civilized society and an almost eternal nature of human beings. On the contrary, today's children, most of who tend to play alone in front of civilized machines indoors, fail to fully develop their language of life that is essential for their lives in terms of the ability to think, perceive, imagine and perform. Despite the fact that the information machines represented by television can entertain the public and provide information, they also make children become isolated, and weaken people's inheritance and perception of traditional culture. In this way, people all become modern people who break away from tradition and have no history.

However, the morals, the language, the criteria for social conducts and customs and habits, which have been passed down from generation to generation by the ancestors of the community, have become less likely to be fully inherited by today's children, which undoubtedly has an impact on the formation of the children's personality in adolescence. For this reason, it is still of some cultural value for today's children to get out of their houses, and enter into the community, and develop and inherit the traditional outdoor game activities.

There is no doubt that the game plays an educational role in children's development, which is a basic consensus among anthropologists. When studying Chinese civilization, Marcel Granet, a famous French sociologist and Sinologist, even attributed the formation of the social system in China to the primitive customs. He argued that the cultural traditions of the Chinese people could be continued from generation to generation in the traditional customs embodied in games. With extremely lively and compelling words, he depicted how people are civilized in ritual games and competition.

"The clans in the rural areas held festivals in the form of contests, while the organizers of the contests expected to have many children and have an abundant harvest of all crops. As is known to all, such ideas are hidden behind a majority of primitive rituals. The ancients were deeply convinced that their clans had been blessed by the gods if each of their rituals was successfully completed, they had won every game or competition, and they had seen propitious omens in every sacrificial ceremony. Moreover, they believed that when the cult or nuo (傩, local drama from Anhui Province, featuring masked dancing) dance came to a perfect end, everything would be fine, which indicated that the gods were on their side, so that the order of the universe was safeguarded, and the benefits of their culture and other cultures were guaranteed. It is a life experience in which the feelings of satisfaction are crystallized into faith and faith takes shape in the mind. In ancient China, almost every activity took the form of a ritualistic contest. And the component of the game can be seen in various activities, such as wading in the water, climbing mountains, cutting wood and plucking flowers (Huizinga, 2007). "

In the period of traditional society, the more the game is associated with the daily life, the production and spiritual life, the more diversified outdoor games there will be, and the more powerful the educational functions of the game will be. In addition, games are also the cultural force to shape the common value and the shared historical memories of the people. In the ritual games year after year, people have learned consistent customs, habits, moral codes, public order and religious beliefs, and mastered how to conduct themselves, so that culture can be passed down from generation to generation.

In the thick description of the children's games of fighting field battles and field hopping among the villagers of Tancun Village (Geertz, 1999), we can see that there are some structural differences in the outdoor games of boys and girls. The basic temperament of boys is bravery, struggle, heroism, impulsiveness and passion, while the field battle game cultivates boys' masculinity. In the era of Mao Zedong that advocated the revolutionary heroism, the discourse of the times, such as worshipping the soldiers, preparing for war and protecting our homes and defending our country, taught the boys of that time through games. Then, the national consciousness and historical memory became the common values of the men of Tancun Village who grew up in that era. Girls, who are structurally contrasted to boys, need to have the feminine temperament of patience, industry, compliance with the rules and housework, and the field hopping game is clearly conducive to the cultivation and formation of this temperament. Through the games, girls can understand that only by working hard can they make their families wealthy. It is the general expectation of farmers in agricultural society to have an abundance of land. At the same time, the historical scenes of the agrarian revolution and the rural class struggle were incorporated into the girls' games, and the subsequent game of fighting against the landlord allowed the younger generation to receive the education of the outlook on class struggle.

However, with the reform of the rural economic system and the implementation of the household contract responsibility system, the household was re-established as an independent production and living unit, and the production activities in rural areas changed from collective activities in the past to separate and scattered household labor, and thus the children were incorporated into the labor forces of the daily work in the household by their parents, and lost the opportunity to play as they liked in the era of collective economy. During that time, whenever children were at home from school, they would be ordered by their parents to put cattle out to pasture, mow green feed for pigs, chop wood, or water the vegetable garden, while the children had to be responsible for most of the farm work other than the work involving heavy physical labor in the household.

As a result, some group games for children in the past, such as fighting field battles and field hopping, began to decline. One of the main reasons for this decline in traditional games is the decline in group activities among villagers, which has deprived children of the archetype of imitating the group activities of adults, and given the children fewer opportunities to get involved in group activities.

It was found in the survey that the open-air well built near the village, which had been an indispensable source of the drinking water for villagers in daily life, was abandoned, becoming the place where the people did the laundry and washed their feet, because every household had dug a groundwater well and installed the tap water machine that was powered by the electric pump. The public co-operation of villagers in the past began to fade, which inevitably led to the decline of group play among children. Nowadays, children are rarely found playing games in the village. Occasionally, there are only simple games involving one or two children, such as playing glass balls, kicking the dire shuttlecock, skipping the rope, and playing house and so forth. The game that the boys play most is a game called Ba Pa (砸啪, pinyin: bápà in Hunan dialect, meaning playing the cardboard). Pa (啪,

originally meaning the exclamation of bang, but now referred to as the cardboard) is the tool for the boys in the game. Three or four pieces of paper are folded into a square cardboard. Since it bursts with a bang when one player throws his cardboard on the cardboard of another player, the cardboard used in the game is named Pa (啪). There are usually two players in one game, who throw the cardboard on the cardboard of the component. As long as a player gets the cardboard of the other player upside down, the former can take possession of this cardboard.

As for the decrease in the outdoor games of children groups, it is not only related to the reduction of group activities among the adults since the implementation of the household contract responsibility system, but also has to do with the enrollment rate of children and the younger age of school admission.

At Tancun Village, children usually become students when they are five or six years old, and some children are even admitted to the kindergarten more than one kilometer away from the Village when they are four years old. Thus, the children have to go to school and do homework every day, depriving them of free time to play games. At the same time, school education has been further developed and strengthened, which makes the space of children's games shift from the village to the school. If the traditional children's games in the village are spontaneous, wild and closely connected with nature, the games at school are competitive and regulative, and many of them are world sports, such as table tennis, badminton, volleyball, basketball, horizontal bars and parallel bars and so on. Children's play has been increasingly divorced from nature. There is no doubt that these sports activities can also get the children trained well, so that they can be exercised in both body and mind. However, these activities are not randomly designed, but the rules have priority over anything else, and the players can not design the rules themselves. As a result, these activities are devoid of life, and the children feel less relaxed and delighted when engaged in these activities.

One of the universal effects of scientific and technological civilization and modernization on the rural life is that the leisure life of the people begins to be dominated by television, VCD, various game machines and computers and other modern machines. Children have also been increasingly indulged in animation films, game machines and other modern entertainment activities. It is one of the reasons for the decline of traditional outdoor games for kids at Tancun Village. The children leave home for school one by one after seven o'clock in the morning, and do not get back home at half past five in the afternoon. They spend up to 10 hours a day shuttling between the school and home and staying at school. With less freedom and more regulated time consumption, children have to seek for fun from virtual games on TV and computers at the cost of the outdoor games in groups.

Nowadays, in our rapidly changing technological civilization, all aspects of the social life give priority to economic activities, so our life has always been uncoordinated, filled with anxiety and suspicion, highly tense and bustling. And while children imitate the adults around them who have no stable values and outlook on life, they adapt to the information civilization created by science and technology far more actively and proficiently than the adults.

Morita Yuzo, a folklorist in Japan, has noted with concern that modern technology has led to the decline of traditional games for children in Japanese society. He declared, " Regardless of the age, children imitate adults, grow up in the confusion and hesitation and develop the unique features of their times. However, in order to adapt to a scientific and civilized society with diversified values, adults have become more confused than children, so that children can no longer imitate them. In this way, they can only imitate what they see on the TV, video games, the Internet, anime and other phenomena around them (Morita, 2006)." Now we can not predict whether it will have any adverse effects on their development when the traditional group games that are lost in the growth of children are replaced by the electronic products and virtual games, but we can firmly assert that under the mold of electronic products, now the children have been increasingly away from nature, and they have gradually lost the experience of the diversified joys in life.

Section 4 Medical Pluralism of Child Health

Since the publication of the book Suicide: A Study in Sociology by Émile Durkheim, a great French sociologist in the 19th century, the scholars of social studies have paid close attention to the relationship between mental stress, pain, disease and social structure in the new industrial society. Even in the study of so-called primitive or traditional societies, anthropologists have long noted the cultural significance of medical knowledge and etiological explanations. The most common research perspective in this field is mainly about the research on religious rituals and body and emotions, and the relationship between them and medical treatment, and scholars have taken the medical treatment, disease, and pain and body cognition in different cultures as an integral part of cross-cultural research.

Levi-Strauss, C., a master of structuralism anthropology, studied the witchcraft treatment in South America, explored how the power of the faith relieved the pain of women in childbirth through detailed description, and pointed out that the witchcraft treatment takes effect when the body and emotions of the receiver are associated with its social and cultural knowledge (Levi-Strauss, 1963). Turner, Victor W., a representative of symbolic anthropologists, studied the healing rituals of the Ndembu tribe, describing how its people explain the local knowledge about the causes of diseases and how they treat the diseases (Turner, 1964). In the World Ethnographic Survey and Human Relations Area Files, the most renowned ethnographic material in the international anthropology circles, different types of disease views, treatment methods and social roles of medical workers were also collected. The interests of anthropologists in the fields of medicine, health, and the spread of the disease have expanded the applied field of anthropology and thus a new branch of medical anthropology has arisen.

In medical anthropology, ethnic medicine or folk medicine is the most well-known field. In the process of development, various regions and ethnic groups have developed their unique disease belief and treatment practice with their cultural features. The study on these disease beliefs and treatment practices is known as ethnic medicine or folk medicine, which reflects the emphasis on the non-western medical systems in anthropological studies.

Rivers, W. J. H., a famous anthropologist, was one of the first anthropologists to study the non-western medical systems. In the book Medicine, Magic and Religion published in 1924, he divided the world views of human beings into three categories, magic views, religious views and naturalistic views. He argues that every world view gives rise to a set of related etiological ideas, and that the therapies vary due to the difference in etiology (Rivers, 1924).

In fact, the folk medicine system, like other aspects of culture, is subject to different cultural environments. In the course of adapting to their respective ecological environment and lifestyles, people have created their unique cultural patterns, as well as produced the folk medical knowledge exclusive to their cultural environments. That is to say, different folk medical systems may come into being under different cultures. According to Arthur Kleinman, an anthropologist at Harvard University, all cultures involve the understanding, diagnosis and treatment methods of the causes of diseases. By expanding this model of cultural interpretation, we can see that it also contains the behavior of seeking treatment, the practical utility of folk medicine, and the study of differences between different medical systems (Kleinman, 1980). It is the major field of the culture-medicine research related to anthropology to carry out a cross-cultural comparative study on the medical systems of different ethnic groups.

In order to better explain the differences in the folk medical systems arising from different cultures, many anthropologists proposed the concept of medical pluralism, which means that, under the same social background, a variety of medical interpretation systems and treatment systems coexist in parallel, such as traditional Chinese medicine and western medicine. The classic ethnography by the anthropologist Crandon- Malamud, L., depicted the medical pluralism in Bolivia in the context of social and political changes, and he found that how patients choose a medical discourse or medical model tends to be a realistic strategy, not only for economic reasons, but also for essential political factors, which is bound up with the ethnic identity and class rise of the local people (Crandon- Malamud, 1991). Medical pluralism is such a flexible concept that it can better explain that folk medicine is actually an instrumental choice that is used by people to solve the health problems, and that no matter what medical method or knowledge system it is, it can be adopted by people as long as it can remove the hardship and danger posed to the physical health of human body.

Therefore, medical pluralism reflects the adaptive mechanism that multiple cultures coexist and interact with each other, which allows people to develop a wider range of means for the treatment of diseases. By studying the changes in the medical system of Tancun Village, this chapter intends to illustrate the logic of medical treatment of antidote of both witchcraft and medicine by the local people for the health problems of children by exploring the medical pluralism of Tancun Village.

Development of Western Medicine in Tancun Village

As in other parts of China, traditional Chinese medicine has always been very well developed in Tancun Village, where the people generally worship the traditional Chinese medicine. However, as a representative of modern medicine, western medicine was introduced to the county where Tancun Village was located as early as 1923. At that time, Christian Zeng Junhou set up western medicine shelves at the Gospel Hall at the current Tangdukou Town, Shaoyang County (Editorial Committee on Shaoyang County Annals, 1993). Affected by the Christians in the county seat, Chen Wangyun, a Christian from Huangtingshi Town, where Tancun Village was located, opened the Renji Hospital in 1933, the twenty-second year of the Republic of China. It was a special western medical hospital, where Chen Wangyun worked as the doctor and nurse simultaneously. As the older people recalled, the opening of the hospital did not exert much influence on the local people, because they did not believe in western medicine and regarded traditional Chinese medicine as the most reliable medicine. "At that time, people were afraid that there were opium cigarettes in western medicine and they claimed that western medicine was used by the imperialists to cheat and hurt the ordinary people in China." DSF, 92, said.

During the period of the Republic of China, therefore, the villagers of Tancun Village went to the doctors of traditional Chinese medicine or folk herbal doctor, commonly known as the herbal practitioner, once they fell sick. Chen Wangyun's western medical hospital had to close down only four years later. It was not until 1945, the 34th year of the Republic of China that the hospital was restored, as the Japanese troops invaded in the local area and a large number of wounded soldiers and wounded poor people in the anti-Japanese battles needed timely rescue and treatment from western medicine. The hospital gradually won the trust of the masses when it cooperated with the mobile medical team that was re-established from the Wugang County Health Center at that time to rescue and treat the wounded. "When the Japanese retreated after the defeat, Renji Hospital was opened again. At that time, the medical teams from the county government lived in the town. But only the brave dared to see the doctor in the western medical hospital." DSF said.

It can be seen that, at that time, people were generally suspicious and wait-and-see about western medicine. Western medicine was not recognized by the locals at Tancun Village until the founding of the People's Republic of China. Under the active promotion and publicity of the new government, western medicine was ultimately rooted in such a remote rural community as Tancun Village.

In 1952, after the founding of the People’s Republic of China, the three great remold movements were carried out like a raging fire, and the socialist transformation also began in the medical and health industry. The individual and decentralized traditional Chinese medicine clinics that existed before the founding of the People’s Republic of

China and the western medicine industry were integrated into joint clinics. At that time, both traditional Chinese medicine and western medicine were respected and utilized by the government. If the cadres of the people's government and the teachers of the school fell ill, they were willing to go to the doctors of western medicine, since western medicine had quick effects.

In this context, the villagers of Tancun Village also began to believe in the efficacy of western medicine. During the interviews, the author found that many elderly people could clearly remember Doctor Yang and Doctor Luo who were engaged in western medicine in Huangtingshi Town Joint Clinic in the 1950s. Among them, Dr. Yang was born in a landowner family. His medical practice was under surveillance of the poor and lower-middle peasants. Moreover, at that time, he could not make house calls freely, and every time he saw a patient, he had to ask the leader for approval. From the narration of the old people, it can be seen that the western doctors at that time had won a high reputation in the minds of the common people and were recognized by the local people. However, it seemed that, at that time, the villagers of Tancun Village who dared to ask the western doctors for medical advice were mainly limited to adults. And when it comes to treating children's diseases, the villagers do not believe much in western medicine.

In this regard, it can be illustrated with the following two cases.

Case **4.3** ZYE, 75, told the author about the unexpected death of her first daughter. She said that her first daughter was very lovely and well behaved. It was around 1953 or 1954 (she could not tell exactly what year it was, since she had nine children in her lifetime, and then she could not know the specific time when her first daughter died). One summer morning, after her daughter had followed her to pick some melon vines in the vegetable garden, she asked her daughter on a small bench and talked to her while she peeled the vines. Suddenly, her daughter said she was itchy, but ZYE did not pay much attention to that. Less than an hour later, her daughter suddenly fell on the ground with her eyes half-closed, saying nothing. Mrs. Zhang said she was in a hurry to take her daughter to the Joint Clinic's traditional Chinese medicine department, Deng Benfan, for treatment. Deng asked her to go to the western medicine department, Dr. Yang, because her daughter's life was in danger.

Mrs. Zhang and her husband went to the western medicine department with her daughter in the arms. Unfortunately, they met several villagers on the way. They all told ZYE at once, "your daughter will take an injection if you go to the western medicine department and it will go into the blood. The child of XXX is ill, but XXX dares not to go there." Some said, "your daughter may have a sunstroke, and you should scrap her neck, chest or back immediately. Otherwise, she may die." These people made ZYE and her husband completely lose their heads. They wanted to go to the western medicine department but they feared that it would be not effective for their daughter. Finally, they had to carry their daughter to get scrapped by the well. Two of the villagers who were good at scrapping helped them on the side, and they told ZYE and her husband that her daughter's sunstroke was so serious that she needed to be blood let.

Hence, they found a small piece of porcelain to let blood on the finger of her daughter. After that, the little girl was much better, and cried out that she was hungry and wanted to eat something. Mrs. Zhang happily took her daughter back home and cooked for her, but she fell unconscious as soon as she took a mouthful out of the rice bowl in her hand. She died before she was sent to the hospital.

Looking back on this, Mrs. Zhang is still very regretful up to now. "We were so stupid," she said. "if we had gotten to Dr. Yang earlier, my daughter would not have died." There is no way to know for sure what was wrong with the child at the time, and Mrs. Zhang, based on the current knowledge, concluded that " it could have been something poisonous that she had eaten in the wild and that she had been poisoned." If this is the case, if she could have listened to the advice of Doctor Deng in the department of traditional Chinese medicine and turned to western medicine, maybe it would not have caused such serious consequences. However, eventually, Mrs. Zhang did not dispel her misgivings about western medicine, and they obeyed the villagers by mistake, while their daughter died. It reflects how western medicine was seriously resisted by local medical knowledge in the early days of its introduction to Tancun Village.

Case **4.4** The second case is just the opposite of the above case. When the child was ill, his parents first turned to western medicine, but the western medicine department could not treat him. Finally, the traditional Chinese medicine department cured him. DCC, 85, told the author that his oldest son almost died of meningitis when he was a child. DCC said "My eldest son was seriously ill and he was completely in a daze about whether he was in the nether world or the living world. The children at that time were not as finicky as those at present. So we left him alone, just let him lie in bed, groaning with pain. To their surprise, in the afternoon, he began to tremble from head to foot and cramp, and his teeth chattered. I quickly took him to see Dr. Yang of the western medicine department. He listened with his stethoscope, opened the child's eyes, and told DCC that his son had meningitis. It was too late to save him. I was not reconciled at all. So I took the child to Dr. Deng Benfan of the traditional Chinese medicine department. After checking his situation, he said nothing but went out with a hoe. As a result, he dug up dozens of earthworms with a hoe, crushed them with the handle of the hoe, poured a bowl of water, and then squeezed my oldest son's nose to fill his mouth with water. After the child drank the earthworm water for less than half an hour, his spasmolysis was suppressed."

As this case shows, western medicine is not a predominant and all-purpose medical system. Western medicine may be at a loss of what to do in the face of complicated diseases, but traditional Chinese medicine and even local medical knowledge still have incomparable advantages.

Western medicine and traditional Chinese medicine have existed side by side in the town where Tancun Village was located for a long time. However, for most of the masses, their concerns about western medicine have not been allayed. It was not until the 1950s that this situation gradually changed with the establishment of the health worker system of agricultural cooperatives and the health room in the production team by the state.

In Tancun Village, the first health worker called LQW was trained in 1956. He was a veteran, with rich knowledge, deep insight and high-class status. So the villagers trust him very much. Under his guidance, a health room was set up in the village, which treated diseases mainly based on western medicine, supplemented by traditional Chinese medicine. The drugs in the health room are not quite complete, but as long as the health worker dispenses some drugs and gives an injection to the patient, most of the common diseases can be cured. With the establishment of the new social system and the implementation of the new medical methods, people were not really open-minded to western medicine until the mid- and late 1950s, and then the medical pluralism of the villagers of Tancun Village, from an anthropological perspective, was ultimately determined. And it has been further improved with the constant perfection of the medical system reform of the government.

In Mao Zedong's era, the most historic measure taken by the state to improve the health care conditions in rural areas was the establishment of the rural cooperative medical center. In order to supplement the technical forces of the rural cooperative medical center, the government devoted greater efforts to training the barefoot doctors and maternal and child health care workers in rural areas in the 1960s and 1970s. Since then, a relatively complete medical and health system was established in Shaoyang County, where Tancun Village is located, ranging from the cooperative medical centers in villages, to the hospitals in the towns, the people's hospitals in the county seat and the traditional Chinese medicine hospital. If women and children get sick, they can have access to conventional treatment.

The barefoot doctors and maternal and child health care workers of the village, who live with the villagers and are both farmers and doctors, are very responsible for their work. They, coupled with the surrounding villages, are all members of the acquaintance society, and they are familiar with each other. So, it is as common as the everyday life for them to go from door to door to treat the patients, which has greatly improved the medical and health conditions of the villagers of Tancun Village. JJZ, who used to work as a barefoot doctor for more than ten years, said, "it is urgent to treat the patients. Sometimes when I just came back from the fields, I would be called out without even washing my feet, while I had to go because it was my duty. It is not uncommon to be called for treatment late at night. If a child had a high fever, its parents did not dare to treat it lightly because the high fever may easily lead to polio. Then, as doctors, we should assume more responsibilities." From his few words, we can see how busy the barefoot doctor was at that time and how simple the professional ethics of a rural doctor is.

At that time, the village medical center is generally a combination of traditional Chinese medicine and western medicine. The barefoot doctor is engaged in the diagnosis and treatment of both western medicine and traditional Chinese medicine, and he also needs to work as a nurse. He is an all-round doctor, but he tends to focus on western medicine. JJZ said, "I usually prescribe western drugs for patients, and the patients also prefer to take western medicine, because it is quick and convenient to eat. It is not as troublesome as traditional Chinese medicine, as traditional Chinese medicine cures the disease for a long time and needs to be decocted in an earthenware pot."

The author interviewed 50 patients in JJZ's current clinic and asked them whether they would like to be prescribed western medicine or traditional Chinese medicine if they were ill. As a result, 35 patients answered that they were willing to be prescribed western medicine. Only six answered they wanted to prescribe traditional Chinese medicine, as they gave a reason that "western medicine cures the symptoms, but not the disease, while the traditional Chinese medicine, though taking effect slower, does not have side effects, and it can affect a radical cure the disease. And traditional Chinese medicine was much cheaper." The rest nine said that "it depends on the actual situation. Traditional Chinese medicine is prescribed if it has better effects, and western medicine is prescribed if it has better effects." Thus, it can be seen that patients generally are more willing to accept western medicine treatment, but on the whole, the villagers of Tancun Village are willing to accept the medical methods of both traditional Chinese medicine and traditional medicine. In the medical pluralism pattern, the choice of treatment method depends on the understanding of the disease and the need for treatment.

With the implementation of the reform and opening-up policy, "the rural medical system has also been further reformed, changing from the medical protection and health stations and the health care stations in the 1980s to the village clinics in the 1990s (Editorial Committee on Shaoyang County Annals).

Furthermore, the medical system in rural areas has become more flexible and the practice of many barefoot doctors has become market-oriented, with private hospitals, clinics and for-profit village clinics becoming the main force of medical care in rural areas. There are three private medical institutions in Tancun Village. One was the clinic of the former barefoot doctor, JJZ, but his clinic at Tancun Village had been relocated to Huangtingshi Town. It is said that his clinic is the best-known hospital in the town because of his excellent medical skills, especially in treating children's diseases, and his reputation in the town. The other two were set up by doctors who returned to the town after graduating from Shaoyang City Nursing School in the 1990s, and one of them does not yet have a doctor's license but operates on the sly.

With the improvement of medical conditions, women and children received better health care. For example, in the early 1990s, women still mainly relied on the birth attendants that received short-term training while today's young pregnant women generally give birth in the hospital, thus reducing the risk of pregnant women giving birth. In the past, people said that women had to go through the gate of hell to have a baby. Now no one worries about the dangers of giving birth to a baby. JCE, the birth attendant in Tancun Village, joked, "Now I am almost unemployed. Although I have been delivering babies for so many years and have gained a lot of experience, people are getting more and more concerned about themselves. The pregnant women will go to the hospital ahead of the due date. The rate of hospital births among women in the town in recent years can attest to what I say. About 62.8 % of pregnant women gave birth in hospital in 2000, 76.8 % in 2003, 78.8 % in 2004 and 87.7 % in 2005 ."

The improving medical environment for pregnant and lying-in women has also greatly reduced the risks of childbirth. According to the Statistical Yearbook of Shaoyang County 2005, even in 2000, the year with the highest maternal mortality rate, the mortality rate was 49 per 100,000, compared with 3.2 per 100,000 in 2004, the lowest year (Department of Statistics of Shaoyang County, 2006) . Infant mortality was generally low, falling from 20.7 per thousand in 2000 to 12.1 per thousand in 2004 to 10 per thousand in 2005 (Department of Statistics of Shaoyang County,2006).

There are as many as eleven public and private hospitals in the neighboring towns of Tancun Village, as well as four pharmacies, which make it very convenient for people to get timely treatment once they are ill. It has created the conditions for young mothers to leave their babies for their parents-in-law to take care and go to work in southern coastal cities. As soon as the child is slightly unwell, the grandparent will take the child to the hospital to get infused or take drugs. But a lot of people also complain that "now the medicine is less effective than before, because even if the child has a slight cold, it has to take a lot of medicine and take an injection for a few days. Of course, it's hard to say whether it is because the drug does not work now or the virus has evolved, or whether people have become too dependent on drugs and lost their sensitivity to them. However, it is certain that with the development of medicine and the economy, people have become more and more inseparable from science and technology. In terms of children's medical care, a large amount of effective folk medical knowledge, which used to be commonly used, has been gradually forgotten because of the infiltration of modern western medicine.

Folk Therapies for Children's Health and Herbal Practitioner

There was no such thing as inflammation in the folk medicine of Tancun Village, where villagers believed that any wound would not be festered or inflamed if it had been burnt or rubbed with tung oil, as was evident in the treatment of umbilical cord of newborn babies. In the past, after the birth of a baby, the midwife would burn the scissors on the tung oil lamp and the cut off the afterbirth five inches from the umbilical cord, wipe some tung oil, and cover the umbilical cord with some cotton cloth and cotton to prevent the umbilical cord from inflammation and cold. In the absence of antibiotics and anti-inflammatory drugs, tung oil is the best anti-inflammatory drugs. Even up to now, the villagers of Tancun Village also like to apply the tung oil on the part where it is red and swollen and massage gently, as it is said that the method is very effective for reducing swelling. According to tradition, the dried umbilical cord that falls off after the baby's umbilical hole is closed should not be left lying around, but should be carefully preserved, because if the baby is crying day and night because of inflammation in the umbilicus that has just fallen out of the umbilical cord, acquiring water from the baby's own umbilical cord can cure the inflammation in the umbilical hole. These folk therapies seem not to have any scientific basis, but they have been used by the villagers of Tancun Village all the time. To this day, pregnant and lying-in women still follow the convention of keeping their babies' umbilical cords in this way after giving birth in the hospital.

During the rainy season from March to May, children playing outdoors tend to get their clothes wet and suffer a typhoid fever. In this case, the local people prevent their children from catching a cold by warming the children by straw fire. They would call together a few children who had been caught in the rain and burn a pile of straw. In the midst of the fire and the thick smoke, the children would warm themselves and sing nursery rhymes like "warming by the straw fire, releasing the cod, and eating rice with fermented black beans and chilies." The children, in high spirits, were heated by the fire, and the cold from the whole body was driven out by the fire. Even if a child has a slight cold, it can also be exempted from the pain of injection and the bitterness of medicine.

"Cupping therapy" is a universal treatment method suitable for both young and old in the local area, and it is believed to be a remedy for all diseases. It can also be found everywhere in the fields of modern Chinese medicine. As long as the villagers of Tancun Village have dizziness, nausea, weakness of limbs, cold, chills and other symptoms, they all prefer to get a cupping jar in the forehead, which is jokingly called printing a "sun" among the local people. The basic method is to use a small vacant bottle with a suitable neck, remove the cap, and then ignite a small piece of paper and put it into the bottle, and immediately put the mouth of the bottle vertically to the forehead, or other parts of pain. Then, the bottle can be quickly adsorbed on the skin under the action of air pressure. When the heat in the bottle dissipates, the person can remove the bottle and leave a round red mark on the forehead, so it is called the "sun" by the people. If the patient has a cold, he should drink a large bowl of soup made with spring Onions, shredded ginger and peppers after the cupping therapy. In general, the patient is required to drink the soup while it is hot, get warmed all over, and keep sweating, and then sleep on the bed. In this way, the cold virus can be forced out of the body.

Heatstroke, though not a serious illness, may lead to death if it is not treated well. The heatstroke can be easily cured. As long as there is a basin of cold water, a person scraps the patient's skin with its index finger and middle finger along the back spine, chest, neck, wrist and all the joints. It is known as Che Sha (scrapping) in the local dialect, but is literally known as "Gua Sha" (刮痧).

Almost all of the villagers in Tancun Village know a little about scrapping. According to the older people, there are many types of symptoms of heatstroke on the skin, such as loach shape and cattle shape and so on. The people who are experienced in scrapping and highly skilled tend to learn from the masters and get well trained. They can not only identify the types of the symptoms of heatstroke on the skin, but also scrap at the corresponding acupoints for different symptoms of heatstroke on the skin. The tools they used are mainly copper coins, embroidery needles and sharp pieces of broken tiles. Under normal circumstances, they scrap the skin with their fingers and copper coins, but in serious cases, they must use the embroidery needle to pick the corresponding acupuncture points to get some spots of blood out, and even use the broken tile to scratch the finger to get it slightly bleed. The medicine, 10 drops (十滴水, a popular medicine for summer ailments) and Huoxiang Zhengqi Liquid (藿香正气水), is commonly used to cure the heatstroke in modern medical practices, but the villagers of Tancun Village hold that, if someone has a serious heatstroke, and it is of no help even by taking an injection or taking medicine, the traditional scrapping techniques must be adopted to cure him.

Infantile malnutrition is one of the most common diseases for infants and young children in Tancun Village in summer and autumn. There are many medical explanations for the disease, but local people believe it is mainly due to high temperatures, dietetic hygiene and food retention. Children who suffer from infantile malnutrition tend to be restless and crying and suffer from dyspepsia and anorexia, and more seriously, the children may be all skin and bones. The doctors in the hospital mainly depend on traditional Chinese medicine to treat infantile malnutrition, but many people complain that "the children who take medicine prescribed by the hospital doctors may suffer infantile malnutrition soon after being cured, and it is better to take a handful of herbal medicine from Zhang Shilian." A handful of herbal medicine here is a folk medical concept in the local area, which is to prescribe a few herbs at will. Zhang Shilian, at her fifties, is well-known as an expert in treating infantile malnutrition for children. But she does not make a living by practicing medicine, and she just intends to do a good deed by curing the infantile malnutrition for children, while she does not charge any fee. The herbs that she mainly adopts are the herbs called tender-flowered hedyotis (Hedyotis is a genus of flowering plants in the family Rubiaceae) herb and Chinese lobelia, supplemented by some unknown herbs and roots. The herbs and roots are mashed and wrapped with black cloth to apply on the wrist. New herbs and roots should be changed about every three days.

Those people who can cure infantile malnutrition or are experts in scrapping can be regarded as extremely active folk medical workers in the local area, but they can only treat one disease. And a group of folk medical workers who are more capable than them is called herbal practitioners by the locals.

Herbal practitioners are actually the most common folk semi-professional medical workers in the areas where Meishan Culture prevails. They usually engage in farm work at ordinary times, and they have no fixed place to practice medicine or charge a fixed amount of medical fees. In general, the patients will come to see the herbal practitioners, but occasionally they make house calls to the patients. Herbal practitioners seldom store stale herbs in their houses. Usually, if a patient comes to them, they go up the hill to gather herbs and make a proper prescription instantly. For this reason, herbal practitioners have to pay attention to any place and remember the locations of the herbs on the hill and in the wild. In this way, they can gather the herbs required for the prescription in a short time. If they make a house call to a patient, they need to search for herbs as they go, in case the patient needs them.

Herbal practitioners in Tancun Village mainly treat unknown pyogenic infections, injuries from falls, fractures, contusions and strains, burns, scalds, and snake wounds, gynecological diseases and unspecified incurable diseases that can not be cured in hospitals. The local people are convinced that herbal practitioners are more capable of treating these diseases than regular doctors in hospitals. Like the treatment of unknown pyogenic infections, the common unknown pyogenic infections include the shrimp-shaped pyogenic infection, the boil on the nape, soft-shelled ulcer and so on. From these frightening terms, it can be seen that it can be extremely painful for anyone to have any of these unknown pyogenic infections. For example, the shrimp-shaped pyogenic infection is a kind of pyogenic infection on fingers or toes, and it is red and swollen. And it is impossible for people to endure the itching and the patients tend to be unable to fall asleep all night. A teacher surnamed Chen in the town middle school had a shrimp-shaped pyogenic infection, but he was not getting better even after half a month's treatment in the hospital. In desperation, he turned to a herbal practitioner, and then he was cured only after taking the medicine of three prescriptions.

In July 2006, a four-year-old girl was scalded by a pot of boiling water. After she was sent to the hospital, the doctor used hydrogen peroxide to clean the child's scald, and then applied a special ointment that was designed for scalds and then gave an infusion for diminishing the inflammation. After being treated in the hospital for three or four days, her scald was not getting better but began to get broken and festered.

At that time, someone in the village suggested that the girl's parents try to turn to the herbal practitioner. On their first visit to the herbal practitioner's house, they bought the only 1kg of pork and about 1kg of eggs. After carefully examining the wounds and asking when she got scalded, the herbal practitioner went up the hill with a hoe to dig for herbs. About half an hour later, the practitioner brought back a lot of herbs. He divided the herbs into two parts, one of which was crushed on the spot, and the other part was chewed up by the practitioner's teeth. The two parts were mixed together. Then he smeared the paste over the wound and covered it with a piece of black cloth (as the practitioner said it was better to use black cloth). The rest herbs were taken home, boiled in a cauldron and cooled to wash the wound. In general, the wound should be washed three times a day for about half an hour each time. These herbs look like leaves and roots, but they are highly effective in curing the scalds. The little girl's wound healed in only half a month.

Meishan Religion, Witch Doctors and Faith Healing

Academic discussion of folk religious culture has been going on for a long time, but the scholars either study the worship of the gods and ancestors of Taoism among the Han people as well as the related folk customs and beliefs, or study the primitive religious beliefs of various ethnic minorities. However, little attention has been paid to the study of the Meishan religious culture in and around central Hunan Province. According to the current research results, it suggests that Meishan is a compound god with archetypal connotations of the goddess, god of men, god of hunters, the god of ancestors and god of fertility (Wu, 2004).

Some scholars hold that Meishan is a religion established by Zhang Wulang, a mythological figure that is related to Chiyou (蚩尤, mythological warrior engaged in fighting with the Yellow Emperor) and Panhu (盘瓠, the ancestor of Yao people, and also the ancestor god worshipped by the Yao and She people too), and that the religion is deeply affected by the Zhengyi Sect of Taoism and is a quasi-religion which lies between the primitive religion and the institutional religion. Its adherents are mainly Shi Gong (Shi Gong, meaning Taoist priests), as well as hunters, cowherds, duck watchers, herbal practitioners, sailors, martial artists, and fishermen (Chen and Li, 2004). Some researchers believe that Meishan is a geographical concept, and that the Meishan Religious Sect is a primitive religion originating in the area.

According to the section Meishan Cave of Volume 494 Minority Nationalities of The History of Song, Meishan Cave belongs to the ethnic groups, and was not connected with the Central Plains. It was adjacent to Changsha on the north, Shaoyang on the south, Yuanling on the west and Changde on the north, while Meishan is located between the four cities. According to the section Records on Ancestors of Meishan in the Local Gazetteers of Baoqing Prefecture, compiled during the Daoguang Regime of the Qing Dynasty, The History of Song wrote that, in the beginning, there were 14,800 households registered in Meishan with 19,080 residents in total.

Researchers, specialized in the studies of the Yao nationality, argue that Meishan Religious Sect is a branch of Yao Taoism, and it is the outcome of the acculturalization and fusion between the primitive religions of the Yao people and the ethnic groups in south China and the Taoism of the Han people. Professor Zhang Youjun of Guangxi University for Nationalities believe that Meishan Religious Sect, also known as the Meishan Branch of Taoism, Martial Arts Sect, Fa Religion or Shi Gong Religion, is a religion believed by the people of the Han people, the Yao people, the Zhuang people, the Mulao people, the Maonan people and the Dong people and other nationalities in south China (Zhang, 1994).

Dr. Jacques Lemoine, former director of Institute of Southeast Asia and Southern China, French National Academy of Sciences, discusses the historical process of Taoism's introduction into the Yao nationality area and its interaction with the original religions in the area from the perspective of similarities between the religious rituals of the Yao people worshiping Panhu and other gods and the Taoist rituals of the Han people, and pointed out that the Meishan Religious Sect is a branch of Yao Taoism (Lemoine, 1987).

Hu Qiwang et al. also argue that the representation of the Yao Taoism is Meishan Religious Sect, which is the product of a Taoist belief that blends the worship of the Yao's ancestors with their primitive beliefs, with a large number of Shi Gong and Dao Gong as its missionaries (Hu, 1994).

It can be seen that although the research viewpoints of Meishan and Meishan Religious Sect are diverse, scholars have basically reached consensus on the following aspects: first of all, Meishan is regional religion and is believed by the ethnic groups and the Han people within the region; second, in the process of cultural transmission, it is reflected in the fusion of Taoism and local primitive religions; third, the religious rituals are closely bound up with the folk-like and witchcraft culture; fourth, its missionaries are more diversified, mainly including Shi Gong, Taoist priests, hunters and duck watchers, etc. Tancun Village is located in the area that is affected by the Meishan religion culture, and the worship of Meishan God has a profound impact on the religious life of the local people, especially in the customs of Meishan witchcraft and treatment relating to child health. The Meishan religion that is prevailing in Tancun Village establishes the cultural scenarios for the discussion of the magical healing of child health in this chapter.

Hunan people have always believed in ghosts and witchcraft, and emphasized the excessive religious activities. According to the Preface of Present to Doctor Tang Bogao in the Collected Works of Jie Xisi, "People in the State of Chu have commonly believed in a witch, which has been the case since the Xia, Shang and Zhou Dynasties, especially in the present stage. People who suffer from a disease, regardless of the time of onset or the severity of the disease, will throw the medicine away once they take it one time but it does not work. As for witchcraft, even if they try it dozens of times but it does not work, they will never regret but will bear the blame and reproach themselves. Moreover, they will exhaust all of their properties and energy to go to witch doctors, but it eventually does not take effect, and they pass away. At that moment, they will accuse each other, 'It was the doctor's fault to make them delay in applying witchcraft.' They even do not say a word to blame the witchcraft at the last moment." In the Song Dynasty, Wang Shiyu, Magistrate of Changsha County, submitted a memorial on the request to ban the witches, saying "I heard that the people in the State of Chu have believed in witches since ancient times, especially in modern times. The most serious case is that there is a gate guard while the people firmly believe in him, declaring that all the affairs of the family are under his control. So, people dare not to see a doctor when they are ill but believe in the witches."

In the Zishui River basin, such as Xinning County, "people invite the witch to their houses at an auspicious time in the Winter Solstice (22nd solar term in China), play the ox horn, sing, and play whirling dance to celebrate the god, which is called to redeem the vow to the god in Baoshan Temple. The people will give a banquet to entertain their relatives and friends and invite each other to have a drink together at the end of the day (Xinning County Annals of the Guangxu Regime of the

Qing Dynasty)." Children are the most vulnerable group in the village and must be taken special care of by adults. But as long as the child is ill in hospital and is not cured for a long time, its parents in Tancun Village will seek the antidotes of both witchcraft and medicine to ensure the safety of the child's life and body.

Magical Healing

Anthropologists believe that "medicine in the world can be divided into three major systems: personalistic, naturalistic, and scientific medical systems. The national medical system generally refers to the personalistic and naturalistic medical systems. The personalistic medical system holds that diseases are caused by agents such as supernatural beings (deities, etc.), non-human beings (ghosts, ancestors, etc.), and humans (sorcerers). The naturalistic medical system holds that diseases are caused by external factors that upset the balance of the body (Shi, 1996)." In the areas with Meishan Culture, the national medical systems, other than the scientific medical system, still play an irreplaceable cultural function for the health of children. Thus, it requires us to explore the significance of folk witch doctors outside modern medicine, which is condemned as "superstitious" by the world, and the faith healing in the medical care for children.

In Tancun Village, the methods of magical healing mainly include Qi Shui, Shu Wan, Chu Shen, healing rituals for a frightened child, binding up the soul, retrieving the soul, Chong Nuo, burning paper money in the evening, Xie Di and so on. Magic users tend to choose the corresponding rituals according to the symptoms and the severity of the disease of the child. Among the magical acts, the most representative cultural features are magic figure, incantation, mystery solution and hand knack.

According to the investigation, the magic figures and incantation applied by the Meishan disciples in various regions vary from each other to some extent, but they all follow a scripture called fundamental scriptures. Fundamental scriptures are the transcription, and only the disciple who is directly taught by the master can copy it and it will not take effect until the sealing of hexagrams (a ritual for the disciple finishing his apprenticeship) of the master. Fundamental scriptures mainly record some magic figures, incantation and mystery solutions in the Meishan Religious Sect. Mystery solution is the water in which the Meishan disciple chants the incantation and draws a magic figure, like homeostatic liquid, bone setting and analgesia solution, bone-melting liquid and evil spirit collection solution and so on. The magical figure is a phenomenon of character worship. It is a symbol drawn with some Chinese characters or combinations of Chinese characters, such as the figure of Jing (井, meaning the well), the figure of Lei (雷, meaning the thunder), the figure of Chang (猖, meaning the evil spirits), the figure of Zhan (斩, meaning beheading). The incantation generally adopts the Rush As Imperative Order, which is a kind of speech worship used in conjunction with a magic figure.

In terms of incantations of bone setting and analgesia solution, the incantation is that "Sincerely invite Hua Tuo to wear the golden armor, with a gold sword in hand, to conquer demons and save the God. Show the supernatural spirit and your special prowess with great strength. In the past, in the Cave of Yuhuang Mountain, Hua Tuo's mother surnamed Zhang was born. On the fifty-seventh day of the forty-seventh year, Hua Tuo was born during Chen Shi (from 7 to 9 in the morning). Good men and women invited Hua Tuo to operate to set the bone, showing his supernatural spirits. During the operation, Hua Tuo used a bowl of cool water to show his prowess. Invite Supreme Lord Laozi to rush as imperative order." Then, the mysterious figure of the Chang is drawn with the finger on a bowl of water, and then the water is called a mystery solution. When performing the magical power, the Meishan disciple must apply the magic figure, incantation and mystery solution simultaneously so as to achieve the goal of healing.

Healing Rituals for a Frightened Child

If a child becomes thin, anorectic, weary, weak in limbs and timid, or dreamy when sleeping at night, the adults argue that evil spirits have attacked the child's soul, and they need to hold a healing ritual for the frightened child. All the villagers of Tancun Village believe that all the folk religious people who have studied the Yin religion can hold the healing rituals for the frightened children, and such religious people include monks and Taoist priests, Shi Gong, the geomancer, the witch, and so on. In general, a more complex healing ritual for a frightened child should be performed by the witch. Before the healing ritual for a frightened child, the family members of the child need to prepare a coat of the child, one cup of rice wine, an egg, seven strings of twines in white and black, and a liter of rice with a red envelope on the rice, which is the fee paid to the witch. The witch burns three sticks of incense on the rice. She chants scriptures and invites the god while burning the paper and then draws magic figures on the wine, rice and egg, and incants. After the ritual, she wraps the cup and the egg with the coat, and binds it up with the twines, and places it beside the pillow of the frightened child for three nights. After three nights, rice and eggs are mixed and cooked into rice or porridge, and given to the child, but if the child can not eat it, its mother may eat it. In this way, the soul of the child that is traumatized due to fright can be repaired.

Other folk religious people hold the healing rituals for the frightened child in a simple way, as long as they incant for a while and draw several mysterious figures. When performing a healing ritual for a frightened child, Shi Gong drew a figure on the palm of the frightened child's right hand with his finger, and then drew the figure on the top of the child's skull, back of his neck and chest while telling the ghost the child's name. Then, Shi Gong covered half of his mouth with his right hand and blew into the palm of the child's hand as he incanted. Here, Shi Gong's Qi blown becomes the medium for delivering mana: incantation delivers mana to Qi through the mouth, which in turn delivers mana to the child. The child receives the mana of Shi Gong at its right shoulder. After chanting, Shi Gong could deliver the mana, and then cover the child's right shoulder with his right hand after each blow. After repeating the procedures three times, the ritual came to an end. If the child was too frightened, Shi Gong would take out a yellow paper figure and fold it into a triangle for the child to wear on his chest or in his pocket until it was lost before the child realized it.

If the local people were interviewed, they would say that the healing ritual for a frightened child is just a kind of superstition, but once someone suffers from something that is not a disease with the above symptoms, almost everyone will hold such a healing ritual. For the modern people who are controlled by both scientific and traditional thoughts, the ritual is just a practical choice, and it is a temporary and practical witchcraft-based behavior that is adopted by people in the face of challenges under a normal state of life, so that they can keep the normal living order. When describing the cultural functions of magic, Bronislaw Kaspar Malinowski pointed out that, "No matter how much knowledge and science can help a person meets his or her needs, they always have some limitations. There is a vast field in human affairs that goes beyond the reach of science. It can not eliminate disease and decay, or resist death, or lead to a substantial increase in the harmony between people and the environment, or establish a good interpersonal relationship between the people. The field is always outside the domain of science, but it is within the domain of religion (Malinowski, 2002)."

It is because modern science fails to fully meet the needs of human beings, that the religion, or even superstition, can exist in the world in case people need it. Under normal, none of the villagers of Tancun Village will believe in such a superstitious matter like the healing rituals for a frightened child, but once the normal is interrupted, the superstition has to get the people believed. It is the dialectics of religion for the villagers of Tancun Village.

Inquiring of God and Practicing Divination for Causes of Disease

If someone falls sick but is not cured after long-term treatment, the villagers of Tancun Village will naturally guess whether the person has offended a ghost or Guai Zai (怪哉, the name of an insect in prison according to the ancient legend). Hence, it is rather common to inquire of the god in the local area. The purpose of inquiring of the god is to find out what reasons lead to illness. The Goddess acts as a psychic between the god or ghost with mankind, and it is highly active in Shaoyang County and its surrounding areas. She is actually the witch. The author interviewed two of the Goddess in the town where Tancun Village is located, one of whom called herself the disciple of Meishan God, and the other did not know which sect she belonged to and had no classics. They said they did not know why they had mana and became psychic. According to the local people, inquiring of the god is a kind of divination that can predict what has not yet been known. At the time of inquiring of the god, the Goddess is able to accurately tell when and why the family members of the person who falls sick but is not cured after long-term treatment offended a ghost, a soul or one of their deceased ancestors. Then, guided by the Goddess, the person should reconcile the conflicts between mankind and the ghost by holding the corresponding religious rituals.

In the process of inquiring of the god, the soul of the ancestor, through some divine and mad rituals, enters into the body of the Goddess, and is integrated with the human body of the Goddess. At this time, the original individuality and autonomy of the Goddess no longer exist, but it is combined with a god, so that the spirit of the god can be materialized into a visible individual that can talk to mankind. Meanwhile, the Goddess is not the one she used to be, and the god becomes the dominant force in her mind. With the help of the body of the Goddess, the god can gain the power of a spokesman, and it is the teacher of the Goddess. As an interactive medium between the two, the Goddess also uses the medium of the god to gain the ability to predict the future.

In the ritual of inquiring of the god, the Goddess leads the person inquires of the god into a specific scene in the past by performing or reproducing the language, actions and consciousness of the ancestor or the god, and illustrating the abnormal phenomena that can be commonly found in real life, and then guides the person to recall and make a strained interpretation for all kinds of inauspicious omens that occurred to the person himself or herself or to his or her house. In this regard, the Goddess in a divine and mad state is to treat her patients in the context of a ritual that reconstructs reality (Roseman, 1991). Therefore, faith healing is also a history, as the procedures that it has performed lead the patient and the person who inquires of the god into the scene in the past and transform the reality and the scene in the past into historical symbols, so that the patient and the person who inquires of the god will go into the strained facts, and be convinced that the Goddess has found the causes of the disease and the means to eradicate the disease, and that the patient can be recovered from the disease as the relevant rituals are held.

The Goddess, as a psychic between man and ghost, advocates the initiative of the god, reflecting the universal theme of the use of power from outside by the psychic. "Danger originates from the outside, but it is also a power and can be socialized (Strathern, 1999)." The dominant force of the god on the body that it is attached to gains the power of frightening and convincing the people, and allows the Goddess, a talented woman, to gain a high reputation among the people due to its ability to predict the future as she acts as the spokesman for the gods, in the course of further socialization.

Section 5 Adoption: The Continuity System of Childless Families

In the traditional concepts of the Chinese people, the purpose of childbearing is to offer sacrifices to the ancestors and continue the family line, which means that the fundamental purpose of childbearing is to perpetuate the family, so that the deceased ancestors can be worshipped, and the lives of the parents can be continued in the next generation. It is also a basic proposition of human reproduction that childbearing is to keep the metabolism of human society from suspending. Therefore, the Chinese people attach great importance to the meaning of childbearing in inheriting the family line, and regard it as an expression of filial piety. As the saying goes, having no male heir is the gravest of the three cardinal offenses against filial piety. The absence of male offspring is regarded as the most serious filial disobedience of a person to his ancestors. It can be said that this is the ethical and moral root of the Chinese people's efforts to have children and then have more sons. But if a person fails to have a son in his life to continue his family line, he must take an alternative measure to make up for this defect in order to ensure that his lineage will be carried on. It is the continuity system of childless families, which is commonly seen among the people.

The continuity system of childless families means that individual families have no successor, and adopt a child or a young relative, so that their families can be continued and they can be cared for by this world after death in the underworld. It is the material core of the family culture in China. From a biological point of view, the continuity system of childless families refers to the cultural mechanism that an individual family adopts a child from the next generation in the clan and establishes a fictitious family (Ma, 1999), because its blood relationship will break and the integrity of the family will no longer continue. From a sociological point of view, the continuity system of childless families is a flexible mechanism to ensure the inheritance of property and the family supporting in paternal families. Precisely because the continuity of childless families is a cultural means to solve the problems of blood relationship, property and pension, the continuity system of childless families, which is the most popular among the people in China, must adhere to the principle of kinship, which means to adopt a child from the clan to continue the family lineage.

The basic legal basis of the continuity of childless families is the pedigree, which allows the people to specify the method of adopting a child from close relatives according to the distance of the kinship recorded in the pedigree. "For example, if A dies but has no biological heir, he may, in the sequence recorded in the pedigree, choose one of the closest relatives in the next generation according to the family tree. The person may be the son of A's brother in our society, so all the peers may be the candidate heirs of the uncle. There are more detailed rules on the adoption of the brother's son. If A is the eldest brother but has no son, the eldest son of the second eldest brother B has an obligation to be adopted by his uncle. But if B has no son, the eldest son of the third eldest brother C has the obligation. If B has no son, but A has two sons, the second son of A has an obligation to be adopted by his uncle. It is because the patriarchal principle involves the prerogative provisions of the eldest son. As the eldest son and the eldest grandson are the authentic heirs of a family, they can not be adopted by anyone else (Fei, 1998)." It is a general practice for people in the rural areas, including Tancun Village, to adopt a young relative to continue the family lineage according to the principle of kinship, so as to make up for the defect of no son.

As of the 1980s, in Tancun Village, the families with no son had mainly solved the absence of an heir by adopting a young child from the relatives of the same clan. The reason why they adopt a child from the relatives of the same clan as the heir because they intend to ensure the purity of their bloodlines and prevent the outflow of the property of the members of the clan. The adoption of a young relative is recorded in the pedigree of the Deng family and the Jiang family in Tancun Village. It is in line with the feudal ethics and rites to adopt a son. However, the eldest son has only one son, so there is no reason for the son to be adopted. In this case, according to the affinities of the relatives, a child of a relative should be adopted if there is a proper candidate, but if no, a worthy child should be adopted. It is possible to choose a child from the clan as long as the child is among the younger generation of the adoptive person in the clan. But in the pedigree, it should be noted about the seniority of the child in his biological father's family and it should be specified that the child was adopted by the adoptive person. Moreover, it should be noted in the adoptive father's family about whose son was adopted by the father. As for the adoption of a child from other clans to break the rules of the clan, it is strictly banned to include the adoptive son in the pedigree (excerpted from the Pedigree of the Clan of Jiang).

The principles of the adoption system of young relatives in traditional society have been made clear in the preceding paragraph. First of all, the adoption of young relatives is in line with the feudal ethics and rites. Second, the adoption must ensure the purity of the bloodlines of the clan, so a child from another family can not be adopted and the position of the adopted son and the adoptive father should follow the order in the pedigree. Otherwise, the adopted son can not be included in the pedigree and can not obtain a legal identity as a member of the clan. Third, the adoption must abide by the principle of affinities.

However, it was found in the investigation that the adoption of young relatives in villagers of Tancun Village is about the coordination of the interests between the adoptive and the adopted, but not completely related to the feudal ethnic code. In general, for the couples who have no children or those who have daughters but no sons, it is in line with the feudal ethnic code to adopt a son from relatives, which means that they can have an heir to offer sacrifices to them and their ancestors after their death. But they mainly expect to be supported in their old age. In other words, being supported in old age is the fundamental motive for the childless couples to adopt a son. It is the reasonability of the young people to support the older people in their old age, which is an act that needs to be realized under the constraints of filial piety, conscience and morals.

Therefore, childless couples should try to select their heirs according to the principle of affinities. First, they select a proper heir from the closest nephews. If they can not find the right one, they can find one from the sons of the male cousins. Centered on themselves, they can adopt a child from close relatives to distant relatives to support them in their old age. The closer the blood relationship is, the better the relationship between the adoptive father and the adopted son will be cultivated and the more the adoptive parents can be recognized by the adopted son. Once the adopted son is found, an older man in the clan comes forward to prove the fact that the adoptive parents adopt a child from the child's biological parents. At the same time, the child's biological parents must write a Letter of Adoption, which is equivalent to a contract for adoption, and it shall be legal after it is supervised and signed by the persons present. If any accident occurs to the adoption in the future, the Letter of Adoption will become a legal basis, and the older people in the clan will uphold justice and protect the rights and interests of the adoptive parents.

Since the practical purpose of the childless families in Tancun Village adopting young relatives is to support them in their old age, the culture of filial piety will have mercy on the families when the family members are aged. Therefore, if a family in the clan has no son and intends to adopt a child, people are not opposed to adopting children from other clans. But if they adopt children from other clans, they must buy a child from his biological parents to buy out the custody of the child, so that the relationship between the adoptive parents and the child can be determined as the adoption of blood relation by means of social nurturing. This approach is contrary to the principle of patriarchal society in China's traditional society, but it is also a countermeasure. Tanaka Issei, a Japanese scholar, once paid attention to the phenomenon in the study of the clan culture in southeastern China. He collected a copy of the contract for buying a child of another clan as follows:

Here a contract is concluded. The husband XX and the wife XX have a son named XX, XX years old. Now due to the poverty of the family, the couple is willing to sell their son after deliberate discussion, and first find a family to adopt him. Now it is to entrust the middleman XX to the house of XX to speak for them. They agree to buy the child as an adopted son to inherit the family lineage. In the face of the two families, it is expressly stated that the alimony fee for the child is XX Yuan in full. On the date of the conclusion of the contract, the money shall be paid to the couple XX via the middleman. On the same day, the child shall be taken back home by XX and adopted as the son. When the child grows up, gets engaged and married, his children and grandchildren shall be permanently the descendants of XX, and his biological parents and relatives shall not regret or make trouble. If the child flees in private, his biological parents shall, with his adoptive parents, find him out and send him back to the adoptive parents' house. In case of an accident, it is up to Heaven. It shall have nothing to do with XX. And it shall be mutually consented by the two families. In fear of a mere verbal statement being no guarantee, a contract is reached to prove the fact. The copy is saved for future reference (Issei, 1996).

It can be seen from the contract that even if it is a countermeasure, the adoption of a person from another clan to inherit the family lineage is still subject to many restrictions. First of all, the relatives in the clan have the priority to adoption, and only when a child has no one to rear among the relatives in the clan and it is agreed by the relatives in the clan, the child can be sold to a person from another clan for adoption. Second, the adoption of a child from another clan must be carried out in the form of purchase through a market-oriented means. Third, the adopted child and his descendants must be surnamed the same as his adoptive father to inherit the family line. Fourth, the adopted child should be divorced from his biological parents in terms of rights and obligations. These constraints actually guarantee the permanency of the social father-son relationship between the adoptive father and the adopted son, and lead to the practical completion of the establishment of the fictitious family in the continuity system of childless families. As

Liang Zhiping pointed out in the study of the customary law of clans in China, the adoption of a child from another clan to inherit the family line may be agreed by the relatives and then the adoptive parents have the right to pay an amount of money to include the adopted child in the pedigree. When the custom grows strong, the relatives, both the distance and the close, including the peers in the clan, may not intervene with the adoption as they like, or they can not actually look into the relevant affairs (Liang, 1996).

Most of the biological parents adopt their children to other families because their families are financially difficult and have many children while they can not afford to raise them.

Getting a child adopted by another family can relieve the family burden, which is equivalent to providing the child with a better environment for his growth. Generally speaking, the family condition of the adoptive parents is better than that of the biological parents, while the biological parents can gain a certain amount of benefits from the adoptive parents. Otherwise, no one is willing to give their child to another person. According to the rules, the adopted child can bear no responsibility for his biological parents, and it means that the biological parents completely lose the child. For this reason, it is their rights and interests to obtain the necessary compensation.

JPS, 50, said, "I was adopted by my uncle (JPS's father's younger male cousin) when I was seven years old. It was so hard at that time that a family that could have something to eat in the early 1960s was a rich family. When I was adopted by my adoptive parents, they gave a dou (1 dou equals 10 liters) of rice to my biological parents. I have many brothers and sisters, and we often had nothing to eat. After I went to my adoptive parents' house, I lived a better material life and sometimes I smuggled some food to my younger sisters." It can be seen that the adoption of a child reflects the coordination of the interests between the two families. Because of the interest involved, it is bound to complicate the relationship between the two families in case of any change in the interest. Here are three cases from the field study on how the adoptive relations develop around the interests in Tancun Village.

Case **4.5** The adoptive parents have been working hard and living frugally in everyday spending and trying to save every penny all their lives. On the one hand, they start to accumulate pension funds when they are young, so that they can gain some economic strength to support themselves when they are old. On the other hand, they do everything they can to meet the needs of the adopted son, giving him a sense of superiority and putting fewer burdens on him, lest the adopted son abandons them. According to the villagers, it is actually a measure taken by the adoptive parents to guarantee their future lives. HLY and his wife in Tancun Village are like this.

HLY adopted a child surnamed Luo when he was thirty-four years old. The villagers all said that they did not waste anything at ordinary times, as they would eat the peanuts half by half, for fear of eating more peanuts. But they were willing to pay for their adopted son. They not only built a house for him and got him married, but also paid for the clothes their grandchildren wore in daily life. As a result, Luo's family, including his son and daughter-in-law, all respected and showed their obedience to HLY and his wife. Although Luo himself did not live quite well and did not offer many benefits to his adoptive parents in material life, he did indeed regard his adoptive parents as his biological parents. He was on good terms with HLY. Now, HLY and his wife are both in their seventies, and they live a happy life. Luo gives the 600 kg of grain that he should offer to his adopted parents in time every time. On the birthday of the old couple, he will kill chickens and buy fish to give a banquet for the celebration. In 2004, HLY almost died from an illness, and he was recovered from the illness with the meticulous care of Luo, who carried HLY on his back if necessary. The local people said, "Luo has a bad temper, but he is very filial to HLY, and he is much better than some natural sons." In this case, the virtue of diligence and thrift of the adoptive parents and their favor and virtue to the adopted son make the adopted son do a lot to return their kindness. In the giving and returning of such affection, the adopted son and his adoptive father were originally from two strange families, but they really become the father and the son, thus achieving the transformation of the social father-son relationship.

Case **4.6** Some adoptive parents work hard, diligently and thriftily in order to provide the adopted son with more material benefits. However, the giving in the material does not get the expected return in spirit. Some adopted sons begin to turn their backs on their adoptive parents when they grow into adults and are able to earn their own living. They not only do not repay their adoptive parents materially, but even deny they are adopted, as they attempt to get rid of their obligations as an adopted son. As a local saying goes, he is your son when he asks you for help and he will be your father when he no longer needs you.

GDH is one of those people. He is the nephew of his adoptive parents. When he was a child, it was his adoptive parents who fed him, dressed him and sent him to school. Even when he got married, his adoptive parents opened their purse to prepare for his wedding ceremony. In the first few years after they lived apart, he was somewhat obedient to his adoptive parents. But as his own children grew up and the family burden mounted, he began to turn his back on his adoptive parents in an attempt to get rid of his obligations of supporting his adoptive parents when they were old. "He often scolded his adoptive parents very badly," said the villagers. Through the abuse, he kept distancing himself from his adoptive parents, and used to neglect the lives and health of his adoptive parents in bad faith, on the pretext of disharmony with his adoptive parents. Although some in the clan denounced him, even an upright official finds it hard to settle a family quarrel. Who can restrain him under such an obligation that depends on morality and conscience? Although it is illegal for him not to support his adoptive parents, there is no way to resolve such disputes between the father and the son in daily life from a legal point of view. In the summer of 2005, after his adoptive father died, he refused to take responsibility for the funeral, and later only paid more than 1,500 Yuan under the mediation of the elderly members of his family, while the cost of a local regular funeral ceremony is usually between 10,000 and

12,000 Yuan. In the end, with the help of his relatives and clansmen, some money was collected for the funeral and a fairly simple funeral ceremony was held.

This case shows that when the adoptive parents are young and able to support themselves, they can bring benefits to the adoptive son, and their adopted son still needs to rely on them to grow up, get married and start a career. At this point, the adoptive parents become lucrative targets for the adopted son. Hence, they do not show any disgust with their adoptive parents. But when the adoptive parents are troubled by their old age and sickness, they will become the economic burdens to their adopted son. Hence, the adopted son will begin trying to get rid of the burden. Therefore, the adoption of a young relative or a stranger involves some risks. In the case of a morally bankrupt adopted son, adoption merely means a nominal process of upbringing. In this case, for the adoptive parents, the only consolation they can get is that they have an adoptive son under their names in the pedigree to carry on the family lineage, and have a tablet on the shrine of their adopted son as a soul after their death.

Case **4.7** JJ and JY are blood brothers. After discharged from military service in the 1960s, JJ was appointed as a worker in the town supply and marketing cooperative, and he became an urban resident consuming commodity grain. JY had always been a farmer living in the Huangjia Group in Tancun Village. JJ and his wife only had a daughter, while JY had four sons. In the 1980s, JY, who lived in the countryside, got into a financially difficult situation, and agreed to get his third son named CQ adopted by his elder brother, JJ. In the era of the planned economy, the supply and marketing cooperative was the best unit in Huangtingshi Town. So, CQ, as a farmer, was undoubtedly willing to be adopted by his uncle, JJ, because once he became the adopted son of his uncle, he could consume the commodity grain and become the urban resident. Moreover, he could take over from the supply and marketing cooperative after his uncle retired. When the Letter of Adoption was written, it was signed by the village chief and the oldest and most senior member of their family present.

But later, due to the reform of the national economic system and urban household registration system, CQ had not been brought to the town by his adoptive parents. With the closure of the supply and marketing cooperative, his adoptive parents also lost their jobs. CQ was adopted by his uncle, but he had been living with his biological parents, and his adoptive parents just provided some tuition fees, living expenses and the expending on clothes, shoes and socks. In order to obtain the special allowances of the government for the households in hardship and the households enjoying the five guarantees (food, clothing, medical care, housing and burial expenses by the people's communes), as well as the minimum living allowances for the urban households in difficulty, JJ and his wife had never admitted that they adopted a son in the neighborhood committee, because if he admitted, he would have a son and a daughter and then he could no longer enjoy the special living subsidies granted by the government.

In 1996, when the Deng family revised the pedigree for the third time, JJ asked to write CQ's name under his name as his descendent, but was refused by CQ. JJ showed the Letter of Adoption and CQ also admitted that he had been adopted by JJ, but CQ refused to recognize the legality of the Letter of Adoption on the grounds that he had not received any benefits from JJ. In the winter of 2004, JJ died of illness and did not make a will to leave the family property to his adopted son CQ. It was said that JJ had left more than fifty thousand Yuan and told his wife to give the bank book to his daughter before he died. Before the funeral, CQ had asked his adoptive mother to consider a portion of his inheritance, but was denied. On the Tomb Sweeping Day in 2005, JJ's daughter made a tombstone for her father, on which were engraved the names of CQ and his son as JJ's son and grandson. CQ got so mad that he threatened to use a chisel to chisel out the words on the tombstone, but finally he did not chisel. It's just that JJ's tombstone was somehow smashed in two. The villagers said that CQ did, but was firmly denied by CQ. The author found that on the primary tablet of the shine in the central room of CQ's house was CQ's biological father, while the tablet of JJ was invited to the shrine of CQ's family as an uncle, a collateral relative within five generations.

If the first two cases are both the adoptive parents' attempts to gain the adoption son's recognition of the status of the adoptive parents through active and dedicatory means, the third case embodies the orientation of the interest balance in the traditional customs of adoption of young relatives. The devotion of the adoptive parents to their adopted son is actually a risk-taking investment behavior. Their contribution may achieve the traditional cultural presupposition, so that they can not only be provided for in their old age, but also guarantee the continuity of the family line after their death. However, it may also be all in vain to suffer a loss. Therefore, it is just an ideal cultural state to achieve the purpose of continuing the family lineage of childless families by adopting a young relative or a child from another clan, while whether the relationship between the ultimate rights and obligations lasts forever depends on two factors of economic condition and morals.

On the one hand, the adoptive parents themselves need to have as much economic power as possible. If they are economically capable, they will not impose too much burden on their adopted son, or even make their adopted son able to make some profits, and then the adopted son will seldom abandon his adoptive parents.

On the other hand, the conscience and morals of the adopted son himself is the key to maintaining the fictitious family composed of the adoptive parents and the adopted son. The adoptive parents may live a happy life in their old age in case they adopt a conscientious child. But if they adopt a discredited child, they may only get a nominal son, which is a case of rearing that thoroughly helps others at their own expenses (Fei, 1998).

Because of adoption of young relatives or children from other clans is a highly risky investment behavior, the adoptive parents in the third case, after the balance of interests, believe that it is better to depend on their own efforts and the government's allowances to spend the rest of their lives than to adopt their nephew at a high risk. They are not willing to spend too much in the process of adoption, and they do not invest in the corresponding emotional and economic costs like the biological parents, and the Letter of Adoption, which had been originally recognized by the society, also becomes a mere scrap of paper.

The above discusses the adoption of young relatives or children from other clans under the traditional continuity system of childless families for the villagers in Tancun Village, which reflects the coordination and conflict of interests behind such behavior and the three situations manifested by it. However, no matter what the situation is, the following features can not be neglected in the study of the traditional continuity system of childless families: first of all, the purpose of adoption is to provide for the elderly and continue the family line, so only the boys can be adopted; second, the basic principle of adoption is the principle of affinities by extending our own feelings to others; third, the biological parents of the adopted child must have far more than one son.

However, with the implementation of the national population and family planning work and the promulgation and implementation of the Adoption Law of the People's Republic of China, it is evident that the traditional adoption system would eventually become unsustainable. Due to the government's control over childbirth, the number of children has been correspondingly reduced. Both boys and girls are precious to every family. According to the local people, both boys and girls are the treasure of the family. No one wants to get his child adopted by others. Radical changes have taken place in the adoption of children since the late 1980s.

Just as the political, economic, social and cultural phenomena arising from modernization inevitably change, in Tancun Village, the continuity system of childless families has also undergone profound changes with the modernization of the economy and national population policy. In the 1980s and 1990s, people had the hardest time suppressing childbirth. On the one hand, people wanted to have and rear many children and have more sons. On the other hand, the state implemented the family planning system, and the birth of extra-plan babies was an illegal act. Local officials from towns to villages had been mainly engaged in two jobs, one was to implement the family planning and the other was to collect various taxes. Officials took severe punishment methods to make villagers give up the birth of extra-plan babies. Therefore, any couple who wanted to have more children had to face huge risks. Every extra child out of the family planning they had came at a necessary cost.

In such a population policy context, it is impossible for the couples that have no children or have daughters but no sons to adopt a child from their brothers or clansmen, because they have no more sons. The traditional continuity system of childless families no longer exist. However, it has made another mode of adoption relatively easy to adopt unwanted baby girls.

Every time a baby girl was abandoned, it would draw a lot of attention from the villagers. They showed deep sympathy for the poor girl and fed her to keep her alive as long as possible. Finally, some kind-hearted people would adopt an abandoned baby girl. In general, the biological parents who abandoned the baby would place a sheet of paper in the baby's swaddling clothes to record the year, the month, the date and the hour of the birth of the baby, along with dozens of Yuan left by its biological parents. All the information about the baby was recorded on the piece of paper. No one knew which village the baby was from and who its parents were. For the adoptive parents who adopt a child, if they bring up such a baby girl, she will be their daughter forever, and they will be her only parents because it is impossible for her to keep in touch with her biological parents.

It is fully different from the traditional model of adoption. In terms of the traditional adoption acts, it must be achieved through the negotiation between the adoptive parents and the biological parents or through the purchase by the adoptive parents, and the purpose of the adoption is to continue the family line of the households who have no children or have daughters but no sons. At present, the villagers of Tancun Village adopt abandoned babies mainly out of the humanitarian moral power

In the views of the villagers of Tancun Village, the adoption of abandoned babies does not violate the Family Planning Law of the People's Republic of China. Because adoption is not equivalent to extra birth of children, they believe it is a good deed to adopt an abandoned child. It does not violate the law of the state, but allows the families to have a child for free. However, according to relevant laws and regulations of the state, adoption must also comply with the provisions of the Adoption Law of the People's Republic of China and relevant laws. According to Article 6 of the Adoption Law of the People's Republic of China, adopters shall meet simultaneously the following requirements: first, childless; second, capable of rearing and educating the adoptee; third, suffering no such disease as is medically regarded as unfit for adopting a child; and fourth, having reached the age of thirty. According to the law, the adoption of all the adopters who do not meet simultaneously the above requirements is deemed as illegal. However, the law of the state is not equivalent to the law understood by the common people. In the eyes of the villagers of Tancun Village, as long as the couples with children have better standards of living and they can assume the responsibility of rearing and educating the adoptee, their adoption should be deemed as reasonable.

In fact, there are currently five adopted girls at Tancun Village, while only one of the adopters meets the above requirements and the other four groups of adopters have their children, but live in good families, while they want to have one more child but have had sterilization operations. In accordance with Article 43 of the Regulations on the Population and Family Planning of Hunan Province, illegal adoption of children is subject to the same collection of social maintenance fees as illegal extra-births, as "If an extra child is born illegally, it shall be levied at twice the gross income of the previous year; on this basis, for everyone more child, the levy shall be increased threefold in turn." In practice, however, the officials engaged in family planning work are more lenient in collecting social maintenance fees for the couples who are not qualified for adoption.

Chapter 5 Power Structure of Children's Education

In the concept system of sociology and anthropology, authority is closely related to power. Generally speaking, authority is built on the basis of power, which means that those who have power must have authority. On the contrary, power also depends on authority. From the perspective of the theory of power dynamics, power in the sociological sense refers to the control, dominance and influence possessed by an individual or a group. According to Max Weber, if a person enables another person to do something against his will, the former will have power over the latter (Weber, 1997). In order to achieve his power, a person must rely on some means or tools, such as the use of force, manipulation, persuasion and other means, which will result in the asymmetry in social relations. The party that has power dominates the other party that has no power in an unequal way. The theory of social exchange believes that one person can control another person because he has the social resources that another person needs but can not obtain anywhere else, so that the person who does not have such social resources has no choice but to submit to him in exchange for the resources he needs (Blau, 1988).In this sense, power is in direct proportion to the possession and distribution of social resources. That is to say, the more social resources a person has, the greater the power he will have in the social structure and the more social authority he will show in the social relations.

In most societies, the social resources that a person possesses have something to do with his status in the political, economic and cultural circles, and are guaranteed by certain institutions and customs. For example, some elders in traditional societies or parents in traditional families are congenitally endowed with power by customs. As long as the social resources owned by a person are recognized by institutions and customs, its power will obtain the basis of legitimacy, and authority will come into being accordingly, which is manifested in the approval and recognition of the owner of the power by those who submit to the authority.

As Francis Fukuyama, an American scholar, points out in his analysis of the cultural roots of paternal authority:

In western societies, the authority of the father must compete with the authority from other places, such as the child's teacher and boss, the state, and even the supreme God. In the United States, children's rebellion against their parents' authority has long been internalized into a part of the country's culture. Only when teenagers experience this stage, they can truly grow up as adults. Rebelling against parents becomes a ritual in the United States. This phenomenon in the United States is absolutely inconceivable in traditional Chinese society. It is never easy for the Chinese people to understand the western Christian idea that they should obey God's will, even if they have to disobey their families. After all, in Chinese society, filial piety to parents is a sacred act that no individual consciousness can transcend or contradict (Fukuyama, 2001).

Max Weber divides power into three types. First, it is the rational and statutory power, which is the power to appoint according to law and give executive orders. Obedience to this power is a hierarchy established based on the law, which is to submit to the power to confirm a post or position. Second, it is the traditional power, which is ancient, traditional and inviolable based on the legitimacy of the status of the people who exercise power. Third, it is the transcendent power. It means that this power is based on the cult of the individual and superstition. The hypothesis of this type of power has a far-reaching influence on the scholars in China, guiding the people to study the features of the social power of the different cultural traditions from the perspective of the status and role of the authority.

The type of power of the Chinese people basically belongs to the second type of power according to Weber's theory, which is summarized by Fei Xiaotong as the elder authority (Fei, 1985) , while other scholars call it folk authority (Wang, 1997) or local authority (Wang, 2000).

According to Fei Xiaotong and other Chinese scholars, the power and authority of the Chinese people are embedded in the traditional social structure system of China, which is composed of the family system, the customs system, the belief system, and the traditional discourse and educational systems. As a force in the process of child rearing and socialization, the family, social opinion and the behavior of the elders, in the initial stage, depict the cultural looks of the children all the time. When children reach the school-age and enter the school, teachers and the education system depict the knowledge system of the children according to the standardized norms, and run through the whole process of children's socialization in the form of power. That is to say, from birth to adulthood, a person must accept the cultural modeling of three forces in order to become a qualified member of a specific society that conforms to the norms of the society. These three forces are the family, the society and the school. Foucault M. called the three forces as three disciplinary powers in the course of children's socialization (Foucault, 2003). Moreover, they do not exert an influence in an isolated way, but interweave with each other, so that every child is inevitably affected by such power structure.

Disciplinary power, invented by Michel Foucault, a French sociologist, can be understood as a microscopic concept of power, because it has been deeply rooted in every aspect of society and is closely related to the body. The disciplinary power is more effective and more common than traditional punishments, and they play an irresistible role in the complex and turbulent network of social relationships. No matter it is the family, the society or the school, they all exercise the symbolic hegemony over the children as the objects of discipline, shaping the personality of the children according to their criteria.

The family, the society and the school constitute a relationship network to discipline the children, through which we can see that there are a variety of power relations, between all the points of the social body, between men and women, between members of the family, between teachers and students, between knowledge and ignorance, while they are more than the mere projection of great ruling power on individuals; they are concrete, they are constantly changing, and they are the soil on which the ruling power takes root, while they make it possible for the ruling power to play its role (Foucault, 1997). As a result, when discussing children's education, we must place it in the network of the family, the society and the school, so that we can have a panoramic view of the forming mechanism of children's personality and the cultural process of children being shaped into social persons.

Section 1 Family Education and Parents' Discipline

Michel Foucault believes that discipline refers to a ubiquitous and omnipotent power technology. In the investigation into the history of new power forms since the nineteenth century, Michel Foucault pointed out that discipline, as a kind of power, is more widely applied and necessary than the power in the past era of torture, because discipline has been deeply embedded in society itself and in every field of life. Discipline, proposed by Foucault, not only means a subject that people study, but also refers to the practice of making people obey rules or standards of behavior, and punishing them when they do not. By using the term discipline, he mainly refers to a special power technology generated since modern times, which is not only a technology for power to intervene with, train and monitor the body, but also a means to produce knowledge. Normalization is the core technology of technology. For this reason, "discipline is neither a system nor an institution. It is a type of power, an orbit for exercising power. It consists of a number of means, techniques, procedures, application levels, and objectives. Disciplinc is the 'physics' or' anatomy 'of power, as well as instructional technology." The new power technology takes the domestication of the human body as the core, and applies symbols, words, peep and other means to manipulate and dominate the body and mind to achieve the purpose of discipline. The human body is manipulated, molded and disciplined, while it obeys and cooperates, thus becoming nimble and muscular.

Therefore, the core concept of discipline is submissiveness. The body is tame and can be harnessed, used, modified and improved (Foucault, 2003). In the fundamental stage, a child is raised up in the family, where the family culture and the individual values of family members have been engaged in the peeing and monitoring of the physical and mental conditions of the child all the time. Adults, especially parents, instill the traditional cultures that they have understood in their children, so that the children will become those who conform to the traditional norms. However, all this happens when the children are completely in the dark and have no way to resist. The lifestyle and moral norms in the community, the concept of family, religion, etiquette and parent-child affection have been imprinted on the memory of children in the form of silent discipline. In the end, a standardized social person takes shape in the culture.

Family Life and Kinship Terms

The family is the basic cell of society and the basic social unit on which every child grows. In Tancun Village, the main family structure is a nuclear family. As the saying goes, the tree will have branches when it grows old, and the family will be separated when the children grow up. Each newlywed couple usually holds a separation ceremony about three months after marriage to become an independent family unit. Therefore, newborn babies usually live in a nuclear family. But because of their fragile vitality, they need to take special care of the adults to grow up safely. In this regard, after the baby is born, the new nuclear family after separation is again connected with the original nuclear family of the baby's grandparents around the growth of the baby.

A child's grandmother is one of its protectors only second to its mother. In the first month after the child is born, its grandmother is one of the main caregivers, as the grandmother not only needs to sleep with her daughter-in-law during the confinement period, but also need to be busy with arranging the life of her daughter-in-law, imparting the knowledge about raising the child, and taking care of her newborn grandson. Every day, the grandmother will hold her grandson in the arms, smile at the baby who can just open his eyes to look around, and keep talking with her grandson tirelessly. She may joke, "little fool, do not get naughty, or you will get spanked, doggy!" Such illogical words reflect the message code of the grandmother's care and happiness, while the child may generate symbolic interaction out of its instinct. When saying that, the child may burst out crying, and its grandmother will pretend to apologize, "Stop crying. Now you know nothing, why is your temper so bad? Grow up quickly, and then I will spank your ass." Then, the grandmother will put the feeding bottle into the child's mouth in a roar of laughter.

The grandmother and the mother observe how the baby changes every day, and feel happy to see the baby grow better day by day. As long as female relatives and friends come to their houses, the grandmother and the mother will ask them "did the ugly baby change these days?", the guests will carry the baby in their arms, and first play with it, and then complement, "he grew stronger. Look, how bright his eyes are! It seems that he has known me."

When women get together in a newborn's house, they mainly talk about who the baby looks like, which is also the favorite topic among neighbors, family and friends when it comes to complimenting the host of the family. "Look, the baby looks just the same as his father when he was very young. His nose and mouth are exactly alike those of his father." Next, the women will judge how the baby looks one after another. At this moment, the baby's father tends to listen to them on the side, while he seldom gives a response, just smiling with contentment. But if someone says the baby looks like a relative of the baby's maternal grandparents, such as the baby's maternal uncle, the grandmother sitting beside will argue and even get annoyed. At this moment, the baby's mother may say "The baby looks like his father, but his mouth and nose are like those of his maternal uncle. It is not bad if he looks like his uncle, as his uncle is much better than his stupid father." Then, they care for the baby in the laughter, feeding him, changing the diaper, or stretch his legs to make the baby pee, which is the beginning of cultivating the baby's health habit.

With the care of the grandmother, the mother and their female relatives and friends, the children learn to get along with these relatives from an early age, rely on the care of these people, especially the mother and grandmother. In a home with an infant, the author could see the infant's mother or grandmother has a meal with the child in the arms, while the father or grandmother has a drink on the side. The father or grandfather seldom holds the infant to make the mother or grandmother have a meal at ease because the villagers of Tancun Village believe that it is the duty of women to carry the infant in arms during meals. It originates from the traditional pattern of division of labor in China's rural areas that males are in charge of outside affairs and females are in charge of the house affairs.

It is time to teach children to develop good eating habits after they are weaned. In the eyes of the villagers of Tancun Village, a good eating habit is not to be picky about food. As the saying goes, the grass is thrown into the cattle pen, which means that children should eat like a cow eating grass no matter whether it is delicious or not. Adults tend to request their children to eat whatever food they provide, and they believe it is a sign of the good physical condition of the children. Moreover, they are convinced that eating more meat, eggs and tuber crops is the most beneficial to physical health.

They encourage their children to eat more, and if they eat four or five meals a day, it will make their parents happy. Children like to play in the neighbor's house and they frequently have a meal in the neighbor's house, while their parents do not object. It seems that raising a child is not a private matter, but a shared responsibility of the society. A number of actions that are centered on caring for children can boost the harmonious interactions among neighbors and strengthen social integration. In this regard, the children in Tancun Village are not as lonely as those in cities, who are locked up in tiny houses or fixed to their parents and not allowed to meet the people around them.

But, like many children from the countryside, the children of Tancun Village are not very concerned about hygiene, and it is common that the children at two or three years old urinate or defecate anywhere. Such unhygienic behavior is not criticized by adults. On the country, the parents of those children may say that their own shit does not smell, without any intention of blaming the children. Toilets can be found in every household, but the toilet is simply built, which is generally a pit dug beside the cattle or pig pen next to house with two pieces of boards on the pit and enclosed by straw or broken bricks. It is not safe for young children to enter such a latrine pit. Moreover, few children are taught to wash their hands after the toilet. And children are frequently seen to sit at the table without washing their hands full of mud.

Children are taught to be polite, trained to respect their elders and to develop their communication skills when they are just learning to speak. The first batch of vocabulary that the child learns after they can speak tends to be dad, mum, grandpa and grandma, followed by the names of the articles and food in daily life, such as tea, apple and bench. Children first learn to use the traditional kinship terms to call their closest relatives, which embody the intimate relationships between the children and their relatives with whom they have been together from morning to night. It can also make the elders satisfied with the wise performance of the children. Many of the children's grandparents or parents told the author, "When we have a baby, when the baby is not yet born, we are most worried about having a stupid, dumb or deaf child. Now that the baby can call grandpa, grandma, dad and mom, we eventually feel relieved." Since the children learn to use kinship terms, they begin to accept the training of courtesy. Whenever they met elders in the village, they will address the elders under the guidance of their mothers or grandmothers. The idea of the kinship system begins to take shape at this time.

The kinship terms used by children to address all the elders in the village are consistent with those to address the immediate family members of their families, and they address all the people in accordance with the seniority in the family.

If the child meets a villager in the generation of his grandfather in the family, he should address the villager Diadia (爹爹, Pinyin: diādià in Hunan dialect, meaning the grandfather). If the villager is young, the child's mother or grandmother will tell the child, "this man has in the generation of your Diadia, so he is also your Diadia but a young Diadia." As a result, the children in the lower position in the village may even address those who are of similar age as grandfather.

In the same way, the children must address all the women in the generation of their grandmother as Nini (奶奶, Pinyin: nīni in Hunan dialect, meaning the grandmother). To distinguish between the Diadia and Nini, the children usually add some prefixes to the kinship terms, like Da (大, meaning the eldest), Er (二, meaning the second eldest), San (三, meaning the third eldest), as well as Wan (晚, meaning the youngest), which are determined according to the ranks of the men or the women's husbands among the brothers. For instance, for the appellation of Er Diadia (二爹爹, meaning the second eldest grandfather), not only do his grandnephews address him that, but all the grandchildren in the village address him that, because he ranks the second among his brothers. For the appellation of Da Diadia (大爹爹, meaning the eldest grandfather), it shows that he is the eldest among his brothers. The appellation of Wan Diadia (晚爹爹), it means that he is the youngest among his brothers.

Similarly, children address everyone in their parents' generation in the same way that they address the sisters and brothers of their parents. These kinship terms are also determined according to the ranks of the men or the women's husbands among the brothers. If the man ranks first, he is addressed Dada (大大, meaning the eldest uncle). If the man ranks second, he is addressed Erye (二爷, meaning the second eldest uncle), and so on, but the youngest uncle should be addressed as Wanwan (晚晚). In daily life, children are required to address their elders in the village according to these kinship terms. Otherwise, the villagers will think that the children are poorly educated and in a bad manner, so the parents will lose face in the community. A child who addresses his elders intimately every time he meets them will be highly praised by the villagers, who consider him to be a polite, promising and eloquent child. There is no doubt that an eloquent child is more likely to receive the care of many of the clansmen in the village.

As for the address of the peers with the children, the villagers of Tancun Village have not set too rigorous rules. In general, the children address their brothers and sisters as elder brother, younger brother, elder sister and younger sister. But in daily life, only the younger are required to address the elder according to the appellations, while the elder directly calls the names of the younger. For instance, a younger brother must address his elder brothers as Da Gege (大哥哥, meaning the eldest brother), Er Gege (二哥哥, meaning the second eldest brother) and so on, while the elder brothers do not need to address the younger brothers as Er Di (二弟, meaning the second youngest brother), San Di (三弟, meaning the third youngest brother) and so on, but they directly call the names. The terms of the children addressing their brothers and sisters can be extended to their cousins and all their peers. The rules for the kinship terms for the cousins and peers are the same as those for the brothers and sisters. The younger brothers must address the elder brothers as Da Gege (大哥哥, meaning the eldest brother), Er Gege (二哥哥, meaning the second eldest brother) and so on. That is to say, the kinship terms of the villagers of Tancun Village in daily life are extended according to the kinship terms in a nuclear family, which is also used to address the children of the mother's brothers and sisters.

It is generally believed that the kinship terms of the Han people in China are similar to the Sudanese type in the classification of kinship terms proposed by the anthropologist G.P. Murdoch of the United States

(Zhuang, 2002). However, in fact, such classification can be merely limited to the written forms of address, which can be illustrated in the table of kinship terms of the patrilineal families of the Han people formulated by Lin Yaohua in detail.

But according to the practice of the daily life of the villagers of Tancun Village, the author holds that the kinship terms of the local people in daily life are more similar to but not equivalent to the Eskimo type. Its most striking feature is the importance it places on the cohesion of the members in the nuclear family, which means that the special appellations for the members of the nuclear family are extended to those for all the people in the clan. And the appellation is recapitulatory. The phenomenon that the kinship terms of the nuclear family are extended to those of all the people in the clan in daily life can be called repressed kinship terms. The use of such kinship terms can enhance the consanguinity identity between the children and the people in the clan, and boost unity within the community. In this way, parents can train their children's awareness of respect for the elders, so that they can learn to respect their elders and behave in harmony with the people in the clan.

Anthropologists have a basic consensus on the study of kinship system that a specific system of kinship terms is closely related to the social structure and family form of the community. Tancun Village is mainly inhabited by the Jiang family and the Deng family. Moreover, since the Ming dynasty, the two families have lived in the areas within the boundaries relative to each other. It can be said that every small natural village is made up of the common ancestors and descendants, who share the same clan with each other, while many of the villagers in a natural village are the members of a big clan who are relatives for more than five generations. The repressed kinship terms reflect the fact that the parents have taught their children about the consciousness of an extended family, so that the children can know the origins of their families from an early age. The villagers of Tancun Village are mainly composed of nuclear families, and each small family is separated from an extended family. But since the clans live together, the public living space and countless blood ties will integrate all the small families that are separated from the extended family. Because of such family structural form that involves separation, and then continuity and integration (Ma, 1999), the children can adopt the repressed kinship terms in daily life so as to keep intimate with no distinctions between persons. Such intimacy also indicates the strong kindred spirits of the villagers of Tancun Village.

Hegel, G. W.F. argued that the eternally immutable spirit of the Constitution in China is the kindred spirit (Hegel, 2001). As a matter of fact, this spirit occupies an important position in the history of Chinese thought. It not only had a wide and far-reaching influence in ancient times, but is also deeply rooted in the concept of Chinese people today. Nowadays, if the children in Tancun Village fail to adopt correct kinship terms because they can not tell, among the villagers, who are in the generation of their grandfather and who are in the generation of their fathers, they may be condemned as motherless children or underbred or even ridiculed as mentally retarded children. On the contrary, the children can address the elders in the clan in a polite and well-behaved manner, they will be unanimously praised by the people in the clan and win a good reputation.

Cultural Training and Parents' Discipline

At Tancun Village, parents have no intention to discipline their children. Children are free to get involved in all community activities, but only if these activities are absolutely safe. All kinds of behaviors that involve potential safety problems are fully prohibited. Parents tend to conduct safety education on their children when the children are very young by means of inducing or intimidating them. In the community activities, the behaviors, such as swimming, climbing onto the vehicles and climbing high walls and trees, are all banned as dangerous, and children's spirit of adventure and consciousness of challenge are not encouraged by parents. Parents attach great importance to safety education, mainly because they have fewer children and almost every child has become the emperor of its family in China. According to the local people, the kids are more precious now, and all the parents are scared of an accident occurring to their children. Furthermore, it is necessary to foster the awareness of children towards safety. But because parents worry too much about their children, they spoil them a little, and the children also become timid and overcautious.

Tancun Village is located by the Haoshui River in the upper reaches of the Zijiang River. In the past, children used to be good swimmers. Most of them could swim across the Haoshui River, three to four hundred meters wide. But now, few children can swim. Of the more than 20 primary and secondary school students interviewed, only three said they had taken a bath in the river, and believed that they could swim across it. Though it is difficult to determine whether it is adverse to the formation of the bravery of boys, it is at least possible to think that children may spend boring days in their children if they enjoy only the tenderness of their elders and do not engage in many activities that challenge nature.

Here is an example from the field survey, which shows how gruff the parents of Tancun Village raised their children and how much they doted on them. A boy, more than five years old, fell and hurt himself after climbing on a tractor. Although it was only a skin injury, his parents got all in a panic for a while. When the child's mother learned that the child fell from the tractor, she ran all the way to her child madly. When seeing the child safe and sound, she first felt rejoiced that her child was delivered from a great danger, while checking the injury carefully and repeatedly expressing her thanks to the ancestors for their blessings. After making sure that the child was not seriously injured, his mother got angry and hit him hard on the bottom. A democratic education was considered unnecessary by the parents in Tancun Village, as they do not think that more words of praise are as useful as a beating.

However, the beating by his father was more violent. The badly frightened boy who fell off the tractor came back home but his pitiful experience did not receive his father's sympathy. The child's father shouted angrily at the child, questioned the child whether he wanted to die, while holding a kitchen knife to the child and threatening to cut off a finger to the child, lest he climbs onto the vehicles again. The father's rudeness was only to frighten the boy, so that he could keep it in mind and never do such dangerous things as climbing onto the vehicles in the future. It was a form of education that used corporal punishment in disguise, but the harsh forms of education like this were common at Tancun Village. As was known to the villagers, there was an accident three years ago where a child died from falling when he climbed onto a vehicle. Parents' rudeness is only a superficial phenomenon, and their practical purpose is to educate their children to develop their awareness of safety and their habits of safety.

Here we can see an example of disciplinary violence. The child judges what is right and wrong in the world out of his curiosity, but the curiosity can not conflict with the values of a rough father. Children can only behave in the manner prescribed by their parents. Otherwise, the parents will teach them under the guise of care for them. Such education may be mild, but more often it is brutal. Violent symbols such as reprimands, beatings and injuries are used as basic means of exercising the disciplinary power of parents.

In fact, parents at Tancun Village seldom resort to persuasion and education when their children make mistakes. Instead, they treat and teach them in a rough way. Unlike children in the city, their parents are able to educate them in a democratic and equal manner to learn about the mistakes and correct them. Especially for fathers, what children are afraid of most is to make their father angry. Many children, behind their fathers' backs, nicknamed them explosive packages.

Tonnies, F. believes that the relationship between the father and the child is closely bound up with the power, since the father's love is different from the mother's love and it exists as an intense affection. "The relationship between fathers and their children is also more likely to be perceived as a form of pure power and violence that governs those who are not free." "The father's position is the most purely to clarify the concept of the rule from the perspective of community: ruling does not mean that the use and control of the power are beneficial for the master, but it means that the father plays a role in completing the tasks of giving birth to and raising the children, and educating them, and imparting a large amount of personal life experience, which can only be reciprocated gradually as the child grows older and establishes a true interactive relation between the father and the children (Tonnies, 1999)."

It has become a common way for parents in rural areas, especially fathers, to force their children to accept their education and deal with various relationships in accordance with the code of conduct that is prescribed by them. Coercion is a kind of traditional discipline power. Here, the father represents the ruler of discipline, who is rude, scolds and rebukes his children and cares for the physical safety of his children, interwoven with the close combination of cultural training and emotional cultivation. They exercise their powers as the disciplinary executives, because the parents at Tancun Village regard their children as part of their body, an extension of their body. It can be well illustrated by the saying among the villagers of Tancun Village that "since I can give birth to you, I can beat you to death", indicating that the parents seem to control the life and death of their children in their hands. But it is in this saying that it involves the value judgment of the villagers of Tancun Village in strictly educating the children. They believe that only by beating the children they can change from beastie children to qualified persons, while the beastie children here mean that a newborn baby is still a biological person and must be socialized to become a cultural person. They believe that the stricter they are with their children's education, the more promising and filial they will be in the future.

As Fei Xiaotong put it, "to be a parent, one must regard the child as a part of himself, and take responsibility for his work with no complaints; They should use their power on behalf of society to turn a beastie child into a member of society. Children are bound to feel less happy under control. But even when they feel unhappy, they are still willing to submit to their father. Even if they have a hatred of their father, they have to contain it in their subconscious. It is because, on the other hand, sons have grown up in their mother's arms and lived in their father's eyes, and they have developed deep feelings in their long-term close contact (Fei, 1998)."

The most important peacemaker in a family is the grandmother. The grandmother would try to teach every grandson and granddaughter who had made a mistake with her greatest patience, and she never agreed with her son to beat or scold her grandchildren. Some of the more virtuous grandmothers, though temporarily not to be partial to their grandchildren in front of their sons, tended to give the best comfort to their grandchildren who were scolded after that. The grandmother may take out the candies that she could not bear to eat at ordinary times to her grandson who was scolded and tell him not to make mistakes anymore in the future. With tears in the eyes, her grandson would nod in mistake as he ate the candies.

Prior to the 1990s, it had been quite common for children to get engaged in housework, which marked the beginning of rural people training their children's work skills and developing their habits of doing manual labor. Children at five or six years old used to carry the baskets to the wild to collect the green feed for pigs with their elder brothers and sisters. At that time, these children were generally familiar with the folk classification of a lot of plants, and knew the names of common plants, and they also knew what plants could be fed to domestic animals, what was poisonous and what was not. It is a routine task for all the older children to cut wood in the wild, and they are partially responsible for supplying the heat energy of their homes.

Before the reform and open policy, it had been the preferred way for the villagers of Tancun Village to save their household spending by taking resources from nature. As for the firewood cut back by the children, it is used for heating in daily life, and every household also needs to use all kinds of leaves, thatch, mosses and other plants to pad the cattle or pig pens so as to be used as fertilizer in the future. Girls are the mother's best helpers. They began to learn to cook and feed pigs at an early age, and they were able to knit wool and stitch soles or insoles when they were fifteen or sixteen years old. The children are familiar with farming because they have to get involved in various types of farming activities when they are very young, such as transplanting rice seedlings, pulling up weeds and applying fertilizer and so forth.

With the improvement of social and economic standards, children in rural areas today do not need to participate in as much housework and agricultural production as their predecessors. They are the closest to nature, but now they begin to become as unfamiliar with nature as the children in cities. Tancun Village is a labor-export rural community, and the outflow of a large number of young and middle-aged workers has relieved the pressure of the population on the local natural resources. The agricultural production activities of the villagers of Tancun Village are also declining step by step. The villagers who are left behind at home no longer need help from their children, based on the principle of doing as much farm work as they can.

When it comes to the topic of children doing housework and getting involved in farm work, many parents or grandparents told the author, "There are a lot of firewood on the mountain now, so we can get just part of them so that we can burn for a long time while our children do not need to help us." "Nowadays children live a better life, so they do not need to suffer and we just do all the housework." "Children should go to school. It is OK as long as they get high scores. Now the farm work is not much, and we can easily do it, so the children do not need to get involved. "As economic conditions have improved, local children have been partially freed from housework and farming, but as a result, the children have a boring time during childhood. They do not need to go up the mountain in groups to chop wood, or go out to pasture cattle in small groups, while they do not have the life experience of running all over the mountains to fight field battles. Instead, children spend a lot of time watching TV, watching DVDs and spending their golden childhoods in the animation world.

It should be the duty of the school to teach children to write and read, but the parents of Tancun Village, who have studied at school for several years, will consciously start teaching their children to read when they are two or three years old. They usually start by teaching children how to write their own names, and then teach the names of the articles that the children are often in contact with during their lives, such as a mountain, stone, field, earth, home, grandfather, grandmother, father, mother, etc. Nowadays, the Chinese characters' table for children is pasted on the walls of many houses where there are children, and the parents will teach their children to read these common words in their leisure time. The villagers of Tancun Village speak highly of education, and the adults tend to frequently teach their children some concepts in the era of imperial examinations.

As the saying goes, to be a scholar is to be the top of society, which is the primary classical basis for parents to encourage their children to study hard. The villagers all regard the children who have high academic records as examples for their children and they also envy the parents of the children who get high scores in different subjects. People, when they are talking with these parents consciously or unconsciously, "How fortunate you are! Your children win so much credit for you, and they are not only excellent in their academic studies, but also do well in their work. " "The cemetery and house of your family work so much that there are numerous talents in your family." "Oh my god! The ugly children in my family are so lazy that he goes to school so hard like killing him, if only he could do half as well as your child." It can be seen from these words that these parents praise, flatter and envy the parents who have excellent children, but they also regret that their children have not studied hard to bring credit to them.

In practice, the neighbors are accustomed to comparing with each other secretly, especially when their children are peers. They will compare which of the children in the two families is more diligent, who is more polite, and who obtains higher scores in the tests. If a child does well in everything, the villagers will praise that the child is more competent, while the neighbor next to the door may feel not convinced in private. Especially the mother of the neighboring family will be determined to encourage and spur her child to catch up with and surpass their neighboring child in every aspect. For this reason, the children develop a sense of competition in the power game of favor and face among adults (Huang et al., 2004). To win glory and credit for parents has become the driving force for many children to study hard.

This sense of competition also manifests itself in children's interactions with their peers. The villagers of Tancun Village advocate the morals of respecting the aged and taking good care of children, which is one of the excellent cultural traditions in China that have been passed down for thousands of years. Parents will teach their children to be polite to their elders. According to the local people, children should not be impolite to their elders, but should be well-behaved in front of the elders. However, when conflicts occur between children and their peers, parents either ignore them or encourage their children not to be modest and show too much cowardice in front of other partners. In their daily lives, parents often encourage their children to have the courage to be competitive and aggressive. And they often quote the famous saying by Mao Zedong that "We will not attack unless we are attacked; if we are attacked, we will certainly counterattack" to teach their children how to get along well with their partners.

In the common living space, it is common for children to quarrel and fight. Parents always say to their children, "no matter who you play with, you can not mess with the older one, and you can not bully the younger ones." The personality type of the children cultivated under such education mode is that they are not aggressive in getting along with others, but have a strong sense of self-protection, and that they are straightforward, loyal to their friends and principled in handling affairs. But it also causes the children not to be willing to lose.

Section 2 School Education and Teachers' Discipline

Discipline exercises the omnipresent power of education and gives a perspective of Michel Foucault's acute vision of micro-power. The core logic of the production of such power is the unity of opposites of power-knowledge. Michel Foucault's power theory has made it clear that knowledge is power, power produces knowledge, and it is the subject that links knowledge and power. Through external action, the subject internalizes knowledge in the body and thus becomes the master of truth, and generates power through the structure of the truth. In the views of Michel Foucault, the school is the field where knowledge is produced and then power is produced. In schools, as in prisons, hospitals and other fields, the disciplined are subject to the control, snooping and punishment of the subject, and all behaviors that violate the rules are excluded.

Here, the school facilitates the formation of disciplinary means, and teachers act as the subject of discipline that masters the power. The school has established a system of hierarchical surveillance and standardized adjudication, thus producing obedient and well-behaved children and disciplining naughty and disruptive rebels. Through discipline, teachers allow their students to become receivers and disseminators of knowledge, and make the cultural appearance of students show historical characteristics, which means that the education in every era creates the students of that era. Through school education, children become the product of knowledge and education is imprinted on the memory of generations of children, thus forming the cultural traditions of a specific community.

The school education for the villagers of Tancun Village can be traced back to the prefecture-run schools and county-run schools in the feudal times. Since then, the children of Tancun Village have received a formal, standardized and institutionalized school education. The logical relationship between knowledge and teacher has been deeply rooted in the thinking structure of the villagers of Tancun Village, thus forming the tradition of emphasizing education and advocating studies. The saying that "To be a scholar is to be the top of society" has become a family motto for parents at Tancun Village to teach their children. It is the outcome of educational discipline. Describing the development history of school education at Tancun Village plays a positive role in enhancing our understanding of the educational concepts of the villagers of Tancun Village and the succession of their concepts in history and space.

Old-style Private Schools and Education during the Republic of China in the Folk Memories

Tancun Village was governed by Wugang Prefecture from the Song Dynasty until the eve of the founding of the People's Republic of China. Wugang Prefecture is a remote area in southern Hunan Province, but education has been flourishing in earlier days. During the Song Dynasty, the central government established the educational institutions here, including the prefecture-run school. The prefecture-run school was originally located outside the Xingxian Gate in the south of the prefecture, and relocated twice during the Chongning and Shaoxing Regimes of the Song Dynasty. But it was destroyed in the wars in the late Yuan Dynasty. In 1370 during the Hongwu Regime of the Ming Dynasty, the school was relocated to its former site. From 1450 to 1456 during the Jingtai Regime of the Ming Dynasty, it was expanded. Since it used to be invaded by the tyrants, its ultimate scale could not be considered as a prefecture-run school. Therefore, it was rebuilt in 1472 during the Chenghua Regime of the Ming Dynasty.

Thus it can be seen as Tancun Village has been a place of enlightenment for the central dynasty as early as the Song Dynasty. Tancun Village is located on the edge of the two major economic and economic centers in southern Hunan at that time, the easternmost of Wugang Prefecture and the westernmost of Baoqing Prefecture. However, according to the Pedigree of Deng Clan, we can see that, in the whole era of imperial examinations, the Deng family had always been a notable family in Huangtingshi Town. Since the Hongwu

Regime of the Ming Dynasty, of the family members, 52 had official ranks in imperial examinations, including 3 Jinshi (进士, a successful candidate in the highest imperial examinations) and one Juren (举人, a successful candidate in the imperial examinations at the provincial level in the Ming and Qing dynasties). So, Tancun Village had a deep tradition of imperial examinations. In the last years of the Qing Dynasty, the imperial examinations were abolished and new-style schools were established throughout the country, but the new-style schools started very late at Tancun Village and the traditional education of old-style private schools in the era of imperial examinations had been retained in the Village.

It was not until 1922 that the first new-style school was established in the town where Tancun Village was located, Weiyi Primary School, the predecessor of the present town high school. The school was privately founded by one of the Deng family's patriarchs and was later accepted by the government of the Republic of China as a public institution. According to the older people, the school used to be relatively small, with only six teachers in total. Three of them graduated from Wugang Normal College and received a modern education. But the other three were changed from the teachers in the traditional old-style private schools. The school offered courses in Chinese language and literature, arithmetic, health, citizenship, history, geography, nature, physical education and music to teach students modern science and technology.

Ouyang, who studied at the school in the 1930s, recalled, "the teachers were excellent at that time, and all of them were experts in calligraphy. They taught the Chinese language and literature and mathematics very well. I had been studying in an old-style private school at home. Then, I came to the school and attended the senior classes, while I had never studied mathematics before that. Fortunately, the teachers were so patient that I could finish my primary school studies." It can be seen that the old-style private schools co-existed with the new-style schools in rural areas at that time. As a matter of fact, the students who could really go to regular schools were usually from the landlord families with better economic conditions, while the students in poor households had no choice but to study in the old-style private schools.

At that time, the education administrative department of Shaoyang County Government strictly banned the old-style private schools (Education Bureau of Shaoyang County, 1986) . For example, around the sixteenth year of the Republic of China, the Education Bureau of Shaoyang County Government issued an announcement and made a resolution to ban the old-style private schools, as follows:

1) An improved private school is allowed to be established in the area where there is no new-style school within two kilometers and a half, and its teachers must be certified by the education commission and submitted to the education bureau for approval;

2) No private schools are allowed within 1.5 km of the new-style school;

3) If a private school is closed due to the violation of the provisions in the preceding two paragraphs, the owner of the private school and teachers shall be fined at least five Yuan, respectively. In the case of centralized administration, the teacher and all the students shall be fined at least five Yuan. If the private school is resumed immediately after being closed, its fine shall be doubled and it shall be used for the education of the public in the area;

4) The education bureau shall order the education commissions of the districts to carry out the ban on private schools effectively. In case of disobedience, the education commission shall apply to the education bureau to transfer it to the county government for severe punishment; and

5) If necessary, the district governors and standing teams may be requested to assist the education bureau of the county government in closing down private schools.

However, as of 1949, the Deng family at Tancun Village still regularly invited a Xiucai (秀才, one who passed the imperial examination at the county level in the Ming and Qing dynasties) as the teacher of the old-style private school. Old-style private schools can be divided into private elementary schools and Confucian classics school. Children from ordinary families just study in private elementary schools for one or two years. The tuition fee for the private elementary school is one load of grain a year. The textbooks used in old-style private schools roughly include the Three-Character Classic, the Book of Family Names, Thousand-Character Classic, The Whip and Spur, The Wisdom of Ancient Aphorisms, The Children's Knowledge Treasury, Sheng Lv Qi Meng and The Four Books (The Great Learning, The Doctrine of the Mean, The Confucian Analects, and The Works of Mencius) and The Five Classics (The Book of Songs, The Book of History, The Book of Changes, The Book of Rites and The Spring and Autumn Annals). Teachers at private elementary schools only ask students to recite, and they do not explain any of the contents. Some old people who used to study in old-style private schools are even able to fluently recite the beginning of the Confucian Analects, but have no idea what it means.

School Education for Children at Tancun Village since the Founding of the People's Republic of China

School is the most institutionalized and formal place for children to be fully socialized, and also the main channel for children's socialization. Unlike individual family education, school education for children is collective and normative. The school will carry out planned, purposeful and strategic training for students in accordance with modern curriculum requirements and training objectives, so that students can become workers that conform to the needs of the state and society. What's more, families have to rely more on the school to develop their children into successful members of society.

Before the founding of the People's Republic of China, it was not easy for the children to go to school since Tancun Village was on the edge of the town. Coupled with economic difficulties, few families could afford to send their children to schools to receive modern education. Therefore, a large number of children are illiterate. In the first few years after the founding of the People's Republic of China, the new-style school did not develop at Tancun Village. Although the school was established in the ancestral hall of the Jiang clan at that time, there were only two teachers in the whole school, and both of them came from landlord families. They had to be criticized by the poor peasants from time to time, and then the regular teaching in the school used to be forced to suspend, and students could not receive a formal education, resulting in extremely low quality of education. Therefore, the majority of children in the 1950s are illiterate and semiliterate.

The author conducted a sampling survey of thirty villagers aged between sixty and seventy years old, 15 males and 15 females, who were just at the school-age of elementary and middle schools at that time. The results showed that only five of them attended junior high school, accounting for 16.7 % of the total, while one of the five was female, accounting for 20 % of the junior high school students; seven graduated from higher primary schools, accounting for 23.3 % of the total, while three of them were females, accounting for 42.9 % of the total higher primary school students; eleven attended lower primary school, accounting for 36.7 % of the total, while six of the eleventh villagers were females, accounting for 54.5 % of the total lower primary school students; the rest seven villagers had never studied at school or just studied at school for one or two semesters intermittently, accounting for 23.3 % of the total, while five of them were females, accounting for 71.4 % . If the villagers with a degree of higher primary school or above are regarded as literate persons, those with a degree of lower primary school or below are illiterate and semiliterate. According to this, of the thirty respondents, eighteen are illiterate and semiliterate, accounting for 60 % of the total, among which eleven are females, accounting for 61.1 % .

It is worth noting that more than 60 % of the respondents were illiterate and semiliterate, and most of them were women. Grandma BL,

67, told the author, "At that time, I had many sisters and brothers at home, and my family was also poor. Our parents could not afford to send us to school, but cared about us as long as there was something to eat. My father looked up to men and down on women. But every family was like this at that time. People said that it was no use of women studying at school for years, as long as they could read their names and count numbers. Anyway, the females would get married one day, and to pay the daughter for education was to pay for her future husband. I just went to school for one semester and a half, as I studied for a semester in the second grade and half a semester in the third grade. I studied the mid-semester of the third grade until the teacher asked me to pay the tuition fee. At that time, the tuition fee was low, but my father was reluctant to pay it. There was so much housework to do at home, and my parents asked me to take care of my younger brother at home. So I dropped from school at that time." It can be seen that the economic backwardness, the preference for sons over daughters, the marriage system, the inheritance system and the housework undertaken by females are the main reasons why females are unable to receive normal education.

The serious consequences and social problems of female dropouts have been frequently discussed in the academic circles. Yang Min and Zheng Xinrong believe that " girls' education is a comprehensive reflection of various social problems in education, such as human rights, population, women, ethnic minorities, religion, poverty and so on. At the same time, it is also a natural measure of social progress and educational development in a country or region (Yang and Zheng, 2000)." A large number of girls are deprived of education, resulting in a low level of education and poor qualities of women. It is accompanied not only by poverty and ignorance of families, but also by excessive population growth and a high rate of people having many children, which forces more girls to be deprived of the right to go to school. It also leads to a vicious circle from difficulty in girls' education, to poor quality of women, to poverty and ignorance of families, too many children in a family, and finally back to the difficulty in girls' education

(The National Key Research Project Group of the Eighth Five-Year Plan, 1994).

Wei Yu analyzed the economic reasons for girls' unemployment, and pointed out that, in a self-supporting economy, women do the most work, work longer hours a day than men, and contribute more to the family than men. In fact, there is a growing trend to deprive the right of girls to go to school since girls are requested to share the burden of their mothers' housework in many regions. In the end, girls are at a disadvantage compared with their brothers (Wei, 1996).

These findings explore the underlying causes of girls' dropouts and analyze the social consequences that they will inevitably cause. In Tancun Village, it was very serious that girls did not have equal access to education in the past, which also bothered the development of women themselves in Tancun Village. Even after the reform and opening up, these illiterate women were unable to work in the coastal areas of Guangdong Province, and as the grandmothers of left-behind children, they were unable to offer effective family tutoring for their grandchildren.

However, in the early days of the founding of the People's Republic of China, it was so terrible that not only the girls were unable to receive school education among the children in Tancun Village, but also the boys were. As a higher primary school student is an intellectual among the villagers, it can be seen that the children have extremely backward cultural qualities as a whole at that time. JYK, 64 told the author that he went to the higher primary school at that time, but attended the classes intermittently, with a break of two semesters. Although he was a student from a higher primary school, he did not know many words. He later attended several literacy classes and several evening classes for farmers, so that he could read newspapers and write letters.

After the Great Leap Forward in 1958, the Shaoyang County government attended to conduct a great leap forward in the education sector to vigorously set up private secondary schools and primary schools to implement comrade Mao Zedong's educational policy on the all-round development of morality, intelligence and physique. At that time, Tancun Village and the neighboring Zhushan Village co-founded the Zhushan Private School, consisting of more than 10 classes for primary and middle school students. The headmaster was headed by the then head of the Huangtingshi District Office, but in practice the government assigned DSF, a poor peasant, to take charge of regular administration. The funds for building the private school were all allocated by the district government, and the townships and villages undertook the purchase of necessary building materials and sent them to the construction site. The workers were mainly the villagers from Tancun Village and Zhushan Village, but a lot of work was completed by the students of the school.

DCC, in his eighties, recalled, "when I was assigned to take charge of building the private school, Zhushan School was just a hillside, and I called in the students from Tancun Village and Zhushan Village to level the ground. These students did a lot of hard manual work. At that time, primary school students were very tall and some junior high school students were rather strong. At that time, I was most afraid of any accident occurring to the students. There was almost an accident while we were building the third classroom building. As soon as the house was finished, hundreds of students were asked to pass the tiles. The tall students, led by the experienced construction workers, covered the roof with tiles. With so many people standing on the roof, the building could not bear the load. As soon as I found a crack in the wall below, I asked all of them to hurry down. About a quarter later after they came down, the building collapsed." From this brief account, we can know how difficult it was for students to found the school by themselves. The primary task of the students was to study, but the students at that time had to give priority to productive work.

"There was a farm behind the private school," DCC told the author, "students had to do manual work in the farm while studying at school. During the busiest seasons, the students and their teachers were required to help with the farm work and agricultural production. What's more, students were not concerned about who got higher scores in studies, but about who worked more actively and who had a better family background." Thus, it can be seen that the students were actually studying while doing manual work at that time. Although students went to school free of charge, they had to frequently take part in agricultural production, so they generally made poor academic performance.

DSY, a teacher who just retired from Huangtingshi Town Middle school, said, " I was the only person at Tancun Village in the 1950s and 1960s who was admitted to college through the formal college entrance examination. At that time, students were not requested to go to school, and they were reluctant to go to school. And the time for study at school was not guaranteed, so it was difficult for us to obtain higher grades even if we wanted to attend more classes." It can be seen that in the decade after the founding of the People's Republic of China, the children at Tancun Village had more opportunities to receive education and the children here had equal access to education, but according to the results of children receiving education, school education was still extremely backward during that period. And most of the students could only read some words, far from having high cultural qualities.

The ensuing Cultural Revolution caused severe damages to rural education in which some achievements had just been made. Tancun Village had a poor foundation for running schools. After the founding of the People's Republic of China, the primary school was established in the ancestral hall of the Jiang clan in the Village, but it was demolished by students as a building with feudal superstition during the Cultural Revolution. So, in the early 1970s, the primary school at Tancun Village didn't even have a schoolhouse, and it had to offer classes in the main assembly hall of the brigade Party branch at that time for three years. It was not until 1974 that the primary school of Tancun Village was constructed. As a result of the political movement in the school, the propaganda and education of the class struggle, the revolutionary consciousness, and the class consciousness became the primary tasks of the school.

At that time, there were two factions of Communist Red Guards in the town where Tancun Village was located, one was Xiangjiang Wind and Thunder and the other was the Faculty Union. According to some retired teachers, the two factions used to have furious fights with one another. The fierce class struggle led to the failure of the regular teaching in the school, and thus students did not need to attend the classes at school, but need to take part in the public meetings where some people were strongly criticized and denounced, or to participate in production work in nearby villages under the guidance of teachers, or to be engaged in publicity activities. All the teachers felt imperiled, and a large number of private teachers were afraid of being criticized and denounced due to ill-considered wording in class and then resigned their jobs, and then engaged in the farm work in their original production team. Teachers who work in the school did not need to prepare lessons because students did not have textbooks. The teachers gave some lessons occasionally, but they completely read the newspapers. Reading newspapers and learning the Quotations from Chairman Mao Zedong became the primary teaching contents at that time. Thus, the teaching quality was seriously backward compared with that in the 1950s and 1960s.

Although a large number of junior and senior high school students were trained during this period, most of them were of poor quality. Many of the so-called senior high school students could not even write pledges, IOUs, contracts and other common forms of practical writing. There is a popular belief amongst the villagers of Tancun Village that the senior high school students during the Cultural Revolution were inferior to the higher primary school students in the 1950s.

As mentioned above, Tancun Village is a village with a tradition of people taking imperial examinations, and the villagers have always attached great importance to the education of their children. Besides, they also expect to change their social identities as farmers who have been passed on from generation to generation through education. However, in the first thirty years after the founding of the People's Republic of China, due to the specific background of the times, the local people did not pay much attention to their children's education. The children did not develop an atmosphere beneficial for learning, but just spent their schooldays in the numbing political movement. It was not until after the reform and opening up that the household contract responsibility system was implemented in the countryside and then the children's education was once again valued by the villagers.

With the recovery of the college entrance examination system, many of the junior and senior high school students who had delayed their entrance to higher schools during the Cultural Revolution went back to school and studied hard, looking forward to being admitted to universities to bring glory to their ancestors. Some parents even forced their children who were reluctant to take the college entrance examination to review their lessons at school. After all, it was the primary way out for the children in rural areas to get rid of their identities as farmers by being admitted to universities and getting a stable and lifelong job.

The traditional value orientation of the imperial examination concept and a good scholar making an official has been awakened once again. Students study to gain a stable and lifelong job and become cadres, which has also become the major basis for parents to encourage their children to study hard. It reflects that there are single channels for the rural people at that time to achieve the transformation of their social identities and ascend from a lower social class to a higher social class. The villagers often asked their children, "Which do you prefer, straw sandals or leather sandals? Do you prefer herding cattle and wearing coir raincoat or working in the office?" In the eyes of local people, the social distinctive between peasants and cadres and government staff members is the disparity in material conditions, which is the sharp contrast between leather sandals and straw sandals, between herding cattle and working in the office, as well as the structural differentiation in the aspects of social status, power network, economic conditions, social reputation and so on.

Rogers, E.M. found in his research that public education is one of the most effective means to flow upward in society (Rogers, 1988). The villagers of Tancun village also see this, and they understand that the main way to get their children out of the countryside and get rid of their social identities as farmers is to study at school. As a result, it is a big event that any student in the village is admitted to a college or a technical secondary school, and the parents of the student will serve a great feast to celebrate, while the relatives, friends and neighbors of the family in the village will congratulate to the family. The custom continued in Tancun Village until the unification of colleges was carried out, and gradually faded with the emergence of the difficulties in the employment of college students.

Corporal punishment at home is the main way adults force their children to study. The villagers of Tancun Village believe that to spare the rod is to spoil the child. It can be said that after the resumption of the college entrance examination system, any young man who was admitted to college at Tancun Village had a painful experience of being physically punished by his parents. Many people, even the adult high school students, were punished by their father for their studies by kneeling, holding water, starving, beating and scolding, and finally went out of the countryside to become so-called government staff members. In the eyes of parents, they are not trampling on the dignity of their children, but have to adopt such educational means in the process of shaping a government staff member. Here are some examples of parents punishing their children physically in the 1980s.

Case **5.1** JXW, graduating from Shaoyang Normal Training College, is now a teacher in Shaoyang County No. 11 Middle School. He failed his first college entrance exam in 1982.His mother said, "XW did well in the regular exams. His headteacher, Mr. Yang, also said that he is the most promising to be admitted to college among his classmates. As a result, six of the senior three students that year were admitted to a college that year, but XW failed. On the day the score came out, he lay in bed alone and cried all day. He was so bored that he could not even eat anything. The next day, his father came back from work. When he heard that XW failed in the exam, he was really furious. He asked XW to get up and kneel in the central room, with a bowl filled with water on the head. XW's father told him to stay on his knees and not to break the bowl. XW was on his knees, tears showering down his cheeks. He looked so pitiful. I thought he was an adult, but knelt down there, and it may damage his dignity. Then I pled with him but got slapped." After pretending the classes for a year, XW failed again in the college entrance examination, while his father punished him even more severely, and he asked XW to kneel on broken tiles. .This time, XW did not want to study anymore, and decided to engage in farm work at home. But his father beat and scolded him, forcing him to study until he was admitted to college. It was not until the third time that he was finally admitted to Shaoyang Normal Training College, and became a middle school teacher.

Case **5.2** DXG, doctor of Beijing Medical University, is now an expert in cardiovascular medicine in a hospital in Beijing. He was admitted to Beijing Medical University in 1986. His father was a math teacher in the town middle school well-known for his rigor. As the saying goes, to spare the rod is to spoil the child, which has been the fundamental experience for him to discipline his children and students. XG boarded with his father in the school. As long as he was too fond of play, or failed to finish the homework in time or fell behind in an exam, he would be beaten by his father with a bamboo root, and even he was not allowed to have meals in the canteen as a punishment. Under his father's strict discipline, he was admitted to Beijing Medical University with excellent grades. After graduating from the University with a doctor's degree, XG has a successful career and asks his parents who are retired at home to live with him in Beijing in their old age, which is envied by the villagers. XG's father's method of education has always been cited by local people as a successful example of stick parenting.

Case **5.3** JYQ, graduating from Hunan Normal University, is now a teacher of a key middle school in Guangzhou. His father was a martial artist. He has a short temper. JYQ told the author about how he was beaten when he was studying at that time, "my father had never studied at school, so he did not know how hard it was. Anyway, every time I took an exam, I could not fall behind, or I would be beaten.

Once, it was the summer vacation when I was a sophomore in high school. I wanted to have a rest for a few days. So I played cards every day with my friends in the village who were not studying. One day, before I knew why, my father came up to me, picked up a shoulder pole and hit me. I unconsciously hid for the moment, and the pole missed and fell on my head. Suddenly, my head was broken and bleeding. However, we did not have the money for treatment, so my mother smeared tung oil and some potash on my wound while crying. My father was still scolding me for failing to live up to his expectations as I slipped back to 15th in the exam. It turned out that my father was angry with me for falling behind in the exam."

According to the local people, corporal punishment is a matter of course for parents who care about their children's studies. Far from being condemned, corporal punishment is often cited as a model by villagers. Many strict fathers in the village were a little strict with their sons, but their sons were admitted to colleges. With their success, the fathers proved the creed that to spare the rod is to spoil the child, which was recognized by the villagers. In the 1980s and 1990s, school education was at its best in the history of Tancun Village. During this period, 26 students who graduated from the primary school of Tancun Village were admitted to junior colleges and technical secondary schools, including two who became PhDs. Now they are working as doctors, teachers, engineers, civil servants and so on.

In a word, from the founding of the People's Republic of China to the end of the 1990s, school education for children at Tancun Village experienced a process of tortuous development. From nothing to the existence, from existence to stagnation, from stagnation to glory, the school basically completed the historic mission of children's education at Tancun Village in the era of the planned economy. At that time, students also spent their primary school years in a difficult learning environment. Only a few students could be eventually admitted to colleges, but the formal education at school still allowed the villagers of Tancun Village to acquire the basic cultural knowledge, thereby laying an intellectual foundation for Tancun Village to become a labor-export rural community.

Current School Education at Tancun Village

Due to the implementation of the family planning system, the birth rate was gradually brought under control and the number of school-age children was declining. The original primary school at Tancun Village had to be closed in 1998 due to the shortage of students and was merged into the central primary school in the town. Thus, the village-level school education in Tancun Village came to a full stop. The children of Tancun Village were enrolled in the town kindergarten, the town primary school, and the town middle school.

The town kindergarten, also known as preschool or children's classes among the local people, is staffed by four female teachers, three of whom are substitute teachers and one is a public teacher. In terms of educational background, two of the four teachers graduate from senior high school, and the other two teachers graduate from junior high school. Among them, the public teacher surnamed Hu is more than 40 years old and she is a junior high school graduate at the end of the Cultural Revolution. The serious shortage of teachers has made the early childhood education of the children of Tancun Village extremely backward.

The teaching of the kindergarten is basically carried out according to the teaching model of the lower grades of the primary school, and the teaching organization is relatively casual. According to the school schedule, students start classes at eight forty in the morning, but the actual start time can be early or late, and teachers start classes when they think students are almost there. Each class is about thirty minutes, but it is not strictly enforced. Many times, the teachers decide the time of the class according to their mood. If they want to take a break, the class is over, and if they do not want to take a break, the class is extended. Every day, 12 o 'clock is the lunch break, while the students in the neighborhood usually go home for lunch, but those who live far away have to stay in the classroom or play on the campus. Afternoon classes start around half past one and finish around half past four. But if the parents come earlier to pick their children up, the teachers may finish school at four o'clock.

The kindergarten mainly offers five courses, language, mathematics, art, music and general knowledge, but the art classes are often changed to writing classes by teachers. The children in the bottom and middle classes mainly learn Pinyin (the standard system of Roman spelling in Chinese) and the addition and subtraction methods for one-digit figures. The children in the top class mainly learn Chinese characters and sentences, and learn the addition and subtraction of the two-digit numbers from ten to fifty. These are all taught in the first grade of primary school. Because the teachers have not been specially trained, they can not teach the children music, gymnastics, art, dance and other lessons in a practical way. The art classes are mainly about copying. Although children's songs are taught in music classes, popular songs are more popular in kindergarten.

Although this kindergarten is far from a qualified school in teaching, the villagers of Tancun Village are quite satisfied with these teachers. They would say, "My children have been much more obedient since they went to kindergarten. They used to be stubborn and naughty. But after they study in kindergarten, they become more reasonable." They may feel that the teachers in the kindergarten can teach the children well when they go to visit the school, at three to five years old, can go to kindergarten every day, and use simple addition and subtraction methods for calculation, read Pinyin and write Chinese characters. It indicates that the local people attach great importance to cultivating children's good study habits and developing the norm of conduct of observing disciplines and obeying laws, and they believe that as long as children are obedient, they will be able to do well in their studies and have a promising future.

Compared with the kindergarten, the town primary school and the town middle school provide formal education. The teachers in the town primary school are excellent, and quite a few of them graduated from normal universities, accounting for 32.6 % of the total teachers. The town middle school has more outstanding teaching conditions, and the school is equipped with computer rooms and laboratories. The composition of the teachers' educational background is also quite reasonable. Of the 67 teachers, 61 % graduated from normal colleges, and most of them are young and middle-aged teachers. Outstanding teachers and superior teaching facilities have attracted a large number of students from the surrounding Caiqiao Township and Changle Township. The children of Tancun Village have received the best education in the local area.

Now at Tancun Village, girls enjoy full equality with boys in education, which is not only due to the improvement of economic conditions, but also related to the implementation of the family planning system and the reduction of the number of children in the family. Through the interview, the author found that parents all believe that as long as their children are willing to study at school, they should try their best to support their children to go to school, both sons and daughters, or at least they will support their children to finish junior high school studies, Through their own working experience, most parents, as migrant workers, are deeply aware of the adverse impact of the low education level on their career. They told the author, "It was not until we worked outside that we learned that the less educated people would get the worst. The highly educated people can make money with ease, while poorly educated, like us, can not make much money even when we make great efforts. We hope our children will not make a living by engaging in heavy manual work like us in the future, so we expect that they can receive higher education as much as possible. "The parents, as migrant workers at Tancun Village, are most looking forward to their children not following the difficult paths as theirs.

However, it is only how the parents feel since they have been working outside for years and have been baptized by modernization, while their children who are left behind at home may not be able to realize the importance of knowledge. In recent years, the learning environment for children at Tancun Village is much worse than before, while many of them have become the worst students in the eyes of the teachers. In interviews with teachers at the town primary and middle schools, the author found that the teachers were adept at listing the children in Tancun Village who were falling in love, fighting, missing classes and skipping classes.

Tancun Village is very close to the market town. The Internet cafe and video game room in the market town become a frequent place for some of the children of Tancun Village. These children are frequently indulged in online games, chatting and romance. In Huangtingshi Town with a population of fewer than 10,000 residents, where there are three Internet cafes with more than 180 computers and two secret video game rooms. These high-tech civilizations have provided the children who are tired of learning with an extremely convenient place to kill time, so that the studies of these students are caught in a vicious circle. Online games and virtual activities, like infectious diseases out of control, spread among the children of Tancun Village, severely undermining the original cultural environment of emphasizing study and education at the Village. In the ten years since 1997, only two of the students in Tancun Village were admitted to colleges.

In the face of the seriously backward learning environment for children in Tancun Village, the villagers of Tancun Village seem calm, while they never feel worried, humiliated or blame fate and other people. The parents who work outside are treated unfairly because they fail to be highly educated, and the harsh reality forces them to realize that knowledge can change their fate. So they all declare that they will try their best to support their children to go to school. On the other hand, the difficulty of getting a job for college students and the high cost of investing in education make parents indifferent to whether their children need to go to college or not. The uncertainty of return to education has dampened the enthusiasm of some parents who support their children to go to school to some extent.

JXW's father, who was famous for punishing his children who studied at school, is now the grandfather of five children. In the past, he used tough tactics with his sons to force them to study hard, and eventually succeeded in cultivating two college students. Now he is indifferent to the study of his grandchildren who are left behind at school. He said, "now the villagers regard the study of their children as unimportant. It costs so much to support the children to study, and the children end up working outside after graduating. Some people who work after receiving higher education earn less than those who finish junior high school studies. Now there are many ways out, as long as the children are willing to endure hardship and work, so they do not need to go to college. Moreover, it does not help if they go to college but fail to get a regular job. "

According to Mr. G, a teacher in the town middle school, "Parents are indifferent to their children's learning and most of them choose to take a laissez-faire attitude. If the children can do well in their studies, the parents will get delighted, but if they do badly, they will not feel bothered. On the one hand, parents think that it is of great significance to receive an education. But on the other hand, they hold that it makes no difference whether the children are poorly or highly educated, and that it is of little use to receive higher education. Parents are more open-minded than our teachers in this respect. If students obtain poor grades, we as teachers are as anxious as if they were our children.

Sometimes when we do home visits, the parents are very warm and they will help us teach their children. But some parents do not care about their children's studies at all. When we visit their homes, the parents who are playing cards will still focus on the board and pay no attention to us. Most of the students' parents do not work in the town but work in coastal areas. If we call them and tell them about their children's studies, they just make a few casual remarks. Anyway, they said they handed over their children to us, as long as we took good care of their children. These parents earn more than us as teachers, so we feel ashamed to talk to them about how important it is to study. They mean that they just need to finish their junior or senior high school studies as long as their children do not break the law. During the summer or winter vacation, the students all rush to Guangdong Province where their parents work and will not come back until school begins, and they will not do their vacation homework. However, their parents do not care about it. Every time they go to the developed areas, they do not learn anything good, but bring back lots of bad habits."

Mr. G's words point out the difficulties for the current rural education. On the one hand, parents really want their children to do well in their academic studies, to stand out, or at least to have the necessary cultural knowledge for them to work outside in the future. On the other hand, the investment in the cost of education is not in direct proportion to the return (effect), so it is impossible for parents to predict whether their children will get a stable job by receiving higher education. Some of the students who finished senior high school studies were not able to show better earning capacity than those who finished their junior high school studies or those who even did badly in studies at school. The idea of the uselessness of study in history has quietly entered people's minds once again.

The contradictory ideas of parents have also aggravated the difficulty of school education to some extent, as teachers can hardly get positive and effective cooperation from parents. As soon as the students come to school, the parents are like kicking a ball to the teacher, but the teacher does not design an incentive to encourage the students to study hard. After all, for the people and children in rural areas, the pragmatic and utilitarian judgment of education is their fundamental value standpoint. In case that receiving higher education does not enable them to approach to a higher social status, tangible economic benefits and spiritual satisfaction, they will not make any effort to access an opportunity for higher education.

Section 3 Social Education and Cultural Discipline

Here, social education refers to the various cultural "acculturation" and personality modeling on the children by the subjects other than the family and school. The cultural holistic view of anthropology believes that a person can not separate himself from a cultural holistic in which it has lived since it was very young, and that culture is projected in various ways into the conscious or unconscious structures of each social member, so that each social member can abide by the common cultural rules. Therefore, when we study the socialization of children, we should not only observe the cultural space of the family and school where children are mostly placed in, but should also place them in a more extensive community space for interpretation.

Before the founding of the People's Republic of China, Tancun Village had a developed clan system, and the clan organization once played a role as the local authorities. The leader of the clan was the representative of the supreme authorities in the clan to deal with all matters, big or small, inside and outside the clan, based on the regulations. The clan fields and public mountains of the clans provided the necessary material basis for the clans to hold the public ceremonies to offer sacrifices to their ancestors, while the cohesion among the members in the clan and their family consciousness were constantly strengthened.

After the founding of the People's Republic of China, clan organizations gradually disintegrated, and symbols of the families, such as pedigree and ancestral temple, also began to fade from the public memories. However, the clan concept, as a deep-rooted cultural identity concept, has been firmly maintained in people's concept and culture. After the pedigree was modified in 1996, the Deng family elected a new leader, but the leader was symbolic in its actual function. Thus, there is no actual leader, but the elders still play a symbolic role in folk sacrifice and moral education. For instance, during the public ancestral worship ceremony of the Tomb Sweeping Day every two or three years, the elders in the clan, including some enthusiastic middle-aged people, would raise funds to hold the ceremony. If there are several rebellious young people in the village, the cadres of the village can do nothing about them, but when they are taught a less by the elders of the clan, they will become more docile. The prestige of the elders comes into being due to their personal charm and habits. The obstreperous young people have been taught to respect the elders since they were very young, so the early imprint of education makes them most willing to make subservient choices about their habits and traditions. It is a dominant power of culture over individuals.

The children's religious views were nurtured mainly in the rituals of ancestor worship, which is a part of the most routine form of religious life at Tancun Village. The local people believe that the death of the old man is only the end of physical life, but his soul exists in another form of life in the underworld. It is believed that ancestors who arrived in the underworld did not sever their bonds with their offspring and often came to the homes of their offspring to protect them. If a family was dogged by bad luck, its ancestors would make its presence to protect their offspring to smoothly get through the disaster. However, the spirits of ancestors depend on the filial piety of the later generations, who must offer sacrifices timely in accordance with the seasons to provide the necessities of life for the ancestors in the underworld. It is a ritual for the living to please the deceased, offering sacrifices to bribe the ancestors to achieve the emotional communication between the ancestors and the descendants. Ancestor worship is an activity that people, especially the elderly and children, must participate in. In a family, the older members are the relatives who are most familiar with their ancestors, while the children are the relatives that are most needed to be protected and blessed by their ancestors. Through the guidance of the old and the participation of the children, the sacrificial ceremony can be a good way to teach the children to worship their ancestors.

In rural China, ancestor worship is not a simple form of belief, but a variety of live cultures, including filial piety, etiquette, morality, interpersonal relationship and social consciousness. Ancestor worship is a traditional religious forum, and each ritual is a baptism of education. From the rituals, children can learn not only the history of the community, the identity of blood and the culture of filial piety, but also local cultural rules, such as religious consciousness, family ties, lifestyles and standards of behavior.

Sacrifices are divided into home sacrifice and tomb sacrifice. The home sacrifice is held in front of the shrine in the central room of the house. Local people believe that on the first and fifteenth days of each lunar month, the Ghost Festival, or the death day and birthday of the ancestors, the ancestors would return home and live in the shrine, waiting for their descendants to offer sacrifices.

At this time, old people and children are the two most religious groups. The children, led by the old man, placed the dishes and liquor in front of the shrine, and said some polite words to invite the ancestors to sit down for dinner, while the children stood at the table and bowed three times, praying for the blessing of the ancestors. Especially for the recently deceased ancestors, home sacrifice is more common. .In the first year after the death of the deceased, the family members set the table well with delicious dishes, liquor and rice, and the female elder of the family prayed "XX (the name of the recently deceased ancestor), please come back for a meal." Family members should stand aside and pray silently over a table of dishes. During ancestor worship, parents will inevitably teach their children not to be naughty, not to climb on the table when the ancestors are having the meal, and not to use chopsticks before the ancestors eat. The seriousness of honoring the dead as the living enhances the children's observance of etiquette.

Tomb sacrifice is mainly held on the Tomb Sweeping Day. On that Day, all households will hang the paper strings at the graves of their ancestors. At that time, the children, regardless of age, should be brought to the ancestral grave by adults to worship their ancestors. The Tomb Sweeping Day is the most importance place to teach the students about the history of their clans. On that day, the old man will introduce the tombs of all the ancestors of their families to his children and grandchildren one by one, and tell them which of the ancestors was the most capable and contributed to the prosperity of the family and which of the ancestors was closest to them in the kinship structure and needed to be specially worshipped. The entire cemetery hill is a community in a different pattern, where the tombs of the ancestors of the highest seniority are located on the top of the cemetery hill, representing the highest authority. The ancestors of the branches of the clan each occupy a territory of the cemetery hill, and in a specific branch, the ancestors were buried from top to bottom according to their seniority from generation to generation. Therefore, the higher the position in the cemetery hill is, the more distance the blood relationship is. The children come here once a year to familiarize themselves with their ancestors and to remember the history of the blood relationship between them and their ancestors.

The religious education of ancestor worship reflects the cultural connotation of filial piety in Confucianism. The education of filial piety for children is the vertical extension from the parents to the deceased direct ancestors, which is to try to emphasize the continuity of the blood of the clan through the sacrifice and the memorial in terms of vertical human relations. Yang Kun, a renowned anthropologist in China, believes that "offering sacrifices to ancestors is a central part of ancestor worship. Confucianism takes ancestor worship as the method of the kinship groups, which is an important foothold to achieve the planned social organization by Confucianists. The secular function of ancestor worship is to cultivate the morality of kinship groups, such as filial piety, loyalty, family continuity, etc (Li, 1996)."

It is the best way to enhance the awareness of family continuity by an extended family hanging the paper strings at the cemetery hill on the Tomb Sweeping Day. If a male parent comes to the tomb of the ancestors with a large group of children and grandchildren, he is bound to be envied by the people around him. When a father, with his sons, or a grandfather, with his grandsons, search the history of his direct family line from grave to grave, the male offspring will arouse a kind of supreme glory. The idea that having no male heir is the gravest of the three cardinal offenses against filial piety can be the most manifested in such a particular situation.

As the saying goes, filial piety is the most important of all virtues. The villagers of Tancun Village believe that a man of filial piety is a man with a conscience, while a disobedient person would be labeled unconscionable. Therefore, children learn from an early age that when they grow up, they should assume the duty of being obedient to their parents. Children are taught to be filial, and many magical stories are created to back up the truth of filial piety. Local people used to curse those who have no conscience or filial piety will be struck by lightning and burnt by fire, while parents used to say to their disobedient children, "Did you dare to scold me? Are not you scared of the Thunder God?"

The Thunder God, in the eyes of the local people, is a God who praises virtue and punishes vice. He will punish anyone who is not obedient and bullies his parents fairly. In their spare time, the elders in the village would tell the children stories about people being struck by lightning and burnt by fire. For example, a woman in a nearby village was struck by lightning and died instantly. As the muscles of those who had been struck by lightning burned and their skin shriveled into lines of various shapes, locals considered them as the writing of the Thunder God and claimed that they could only be comprehended by the people who had read ancient books. Because of the handwriting, villagers made various legends by false analogy, claiming that the writing was the verdict of the judgment of the Thunder God on the dead. People quickly collected the evidence on the crimes of the dead woman, such as her abuse of her mother-in-law and her blasphemy against her ancestors. Then, the villagers would warn their descendants not to do as the woman did so as to cultivate their filial piety.

Clan consciousness, the sacrificial ceremony, the dignity of the patriarch and the etiquette education, as well as other types of social life is interwoven to form the folk field in which individuals live. Children live in the vast ocean of this folk field from the moment they were born. They have been branded with the cultural factors of social life in various aspects, from learning language to imitating behavior, from dietary patterns to residential habits, from getting along with people to dealing with their personal affairs.

Children learn to respect their elders by mimicking the way adults address older people when the adults meet them at the entrance to the village or on the road. When entering into a marriage, the young people complete the wedding ceremony according to the procedures stipulated by the elders, such as proposing a marriage, checking whether the eight characters of the potential couple are well matched or not by the fortune-teller, becoming engaged, sending betrothal gifts and money over to the bride, fixing a date for the wedding ceremony and holding the wedding ceremony, so that the young people can develop the concept of marriage in practice. In the complicated social relationships, young people have to deal with all kinds of relationships according to the prescriptive norms of conduct that they have learned from their elders. In daily life, young people tend to seldom transgress the bounds about what they should do, how they should do it and how they should express themselves properly in the world, while they habitually conform to the behaviors passed down from generation to generation. As for how people greet each other, and how they can express their feelings and thoughts, how should they look, speak and act, it must be in line with the standardized symbol representation in a specific community environment.

As Ruth Benedict points out, "the history of an individual's life begins with his application of the patterns and norms that are traditionally handed down from generation to generation in the community where he is located. As soon as a person is born, the customs of the community begin to shape his experience and behavior. By the time he babbles, he is a creature of the culture to which he belongs. By the time he is old enough to participate in the activities of the culture, the habits of the community have become his habits, and the beliefs of the community have become him, while the discipline of the community has become his (Benedict, 1988)." On the one hand, children learn their folk knowledge by participating in a variety of social activities with their parents and relatives, such as weddings and funerals, house building, spring planting and autumn harvest, and birthday celebrations of the people of all ages. On the other hand, they learn moral concepts and values by participating in various reciprocal activities and folk etiquette activities. Through social education, individuals internalize the folk cultures into their own knowledge and experience, so that the individuals will become the cultural products of a specific society.

Social education is also achieved through the control of custom over the masses and their bodies. In daily life, every act and every smile of a child is expressed in a manner prescribed and understood by adults. Public opinion in the community, stories of the elders and the value judgment of adults have been constantly disciplining children to make choices conforming to social norms in their language, thought, behavior and value judgment. As a result, children may naturally practice social education at the early stages as they grow up. Michel Foucault proposed a theory of power microphysics (Foucault, 2003), which could well illustrate how social education intervenes and controls the physical and behavioral patterns of individuals.

Social education is the culture of daily life, the lifestyle that people turn a blind eye to, and the details of life that people take for granted as they are involved in it every day. But it is these details of life that silently discipline children's thoughts and behaviors, so that every child is transformed, molded and manipulated by social education as a type of cultural power.

The historical unity of part of the traditional cultures in Tancun Village is manifested in the education of the elders in the clan, the cultivation of family consciousness, the concept of the ancestor worship, and the formation of conscience, filial piety and other ethics and morality. The continuation of this culture takes place in daily life, shaping some cultural genes of the children that can not be cultivated through school education. But as modernization swept in, Internet technology, video games, television, the market economy and new values left children in a social mess that can not be regulated. Compared with the influence of these modernization means, the traditional educational function of the community is so fragile that the old people often complain that now it is indeed impossible to control the children. According to Margaret Mead, an eminent anthropologist, this is the era of post-figurative culture (Mead, 1987), in which children no longer care much about the expectations of their elders in the family and the community, and they have a strong impact on the educational efficacy of schools.

Television, VCD and other modern media have become very popular in Tancun Village. And the children mainly watch TV and play CDs in their spare time except for learning. At the same time, the children have spent most of their childhood days on all kinds of soap operas, martial arts films and cartoons. Happy Camp, a variety show produced by Hunan Broadcasting System, is the children's favorite entertainment program. And even the little girls, four or five years old, can name the contestants of Super Girls (a talent show of Hunan Broadcasting System) in recent years.

The preference for cartoons is common to all children. At Tancun Village, cartoons, such as Mickey Mouse, Ultraman and Inuyasha, are hardly unknown to children. They love watching cartoons and the characters in them, so much so that stickers of anime characters have become the most sought-after items for children. They may save their pocket money and the money for lunch at school to buy cartoon pictures and paste them on their textbooks and on the wall, which will make them walk on air. Children's love for animation is modeling their cultural identification with the animation creators. In their immature and vague minds, they believe that the place or country where the creator of animation lives is as beautiful and magical as the world of animation. About the question of "where would you like to work in the future" in the survey, the children at Tancun Village expressed a desire to live in the city rather than in the countryside.

Television, VCD, video and other modern media technologies transmit the spreading information about cities, modernism, consumerism and other concepts to children, so that the children all believe that the scene of debauchery with red lanterns and green wine, rich consumer goods and freeways of act in the city represent advanced and developed cultural forms. Therefore, they tend to choose to live in developed cities in the future.

It is astonishing that three of the fifteen 15 respondents made it clear that they intended to go to Japan in the future. They said, "when I was watching cartoons, I found that Japan is a developed country. I do not like China, anyway." For these children, they have not yet formed a geographical concept of where Japan is, but have made a value judgment of love for Japan just by their preference for Japanese animation. The animation culture in Japan has had a profound impact on the psychology and values of the children at Tancun Village. Television, video and other new media carry complex and deep-going cultural concepts. Among the concepts, one of the most influential is the transmission of foreign cultural patterns to the vast audience, which is a hegemonic culture. The influence of Japanese animation on the values, aesthetic tastes and interests and hobbies of the children at Tancun Village just reflects the infinite expansion of this form of cultural hegemony.

It should be said that TV, VCD and other modern media enrich children's imagination, expand their knowledge boundaries and broaden their horizons, so that they can learn a lot that they can not acquire from the textbooks while having fun and relaxing. Nonetheless, it is a space that never goes beyond the margin. Children's obsession with one TV show after another, and with increasingly sophisticated animation technologies, will inevitably affect the effectiveness of regular education they receive at school.

Many teachers said with concern, "when students come home from school, their parents have no interest in controlling them, so they just let their children watch TV as they like. Some of them do not even do their homework, but they watch TV at night and doze off when they come to school during the day." "If students watch TV without any restraint, it will certainly affect their academic performance. Students read after their teachers at school during the day and then keep watching TV after they go back home. So they do not have any time to consolidate their knowledge." "If parents do not control the time of their children watching TV properly and let them watch TV at will, the teachers in our school can not do anything about it." It is likely for teachers to take a biased view of the phenomenon from their professional standpoint, but judging by the intensity and depth of the impact of television on people's lives, it is inevitable that students will be impacted by television culture, though it is still too early to make an objective assessment of this impact.

As for the research on the social impact of television and other modern media technologies, Kirk Johnson, an American academic, achieved convincing research results through the ethnographical study of two mountain villages in Western Maharashtra, India. He believes that television has played an important role in the lives of villagers in the two mountain villages, as it has thoroughly changed the order of their daily life and thus opening up a whole new field of rural life. People who have a TV at home spend a lot of time watching it every week. Through the comparative study of the families with TV sets and those without TV sets, Kirk Johnson pointed out that the effects of television can be reflected in all aspects of family life. The villagers spend most of the week watching TV, which has changed the structure of their daily life. Moreover, the villagers are sleeping much later than they used to, but getting up at about the same moment in the morning, so they sleep for a shorter time and then they will feel less motivated to engage in farm work. The villagers complain of being too tired, but they are reluctant to turn off the TV early in the evening. What's more, the children play less but watch more TV than they used to. And they also spend less time on schoolwork than they used to (Johnson, 2005)."

As Kirk Johnson said, TV, VCD and other modern media also play an increasingly important role in Tancun Village, which has a comprehensive and profound impact on the social life of the children at Tancun Village in both depth and breadth. Compared with the traditional means of cultural discipline, the cultural discipline of TV has enhanced its discipline power due to its interesting, entertaining and liberal features and other modern technological advantages. Children are willing to accept the cultural messages conveyed by television. At the same time, the cultural factors expressed by the characters in the plots of TV shows and cartoons, such as etiquette, morality, interpersonal relationship, love bud, world outlook, and values and learning outlook, have gone far beyond the inherent rules of the traditional culture at Tancun Village.

Television and VCD have been locked in a power game with the traditional culture and even school education at Tancun Village, among various forms of cultural discipline for the social education of children. Children who indulge in TV or VCD may be criticized by the villagers as being derelict in their duties as students or failing to live up to their parents' expectations, and if students fail to finish their homework on time because of their indulgence in the TV or VCD, they will be punished by their teachers. However, no child will take his initiative to restrain his enthusiasm for cartoons and TV plays.

Chapter 6 Family Social Capital and Kinship Network for the Rearing of Left-behind Children

Child rearing is not an isolated biological behavior, but rooted in a specific social structure and constitutes a social action. The traditions and spirits of China's social structure have lasted for thousands of years, and present a unique social feature. Kang Youwei called it patriarchal society and family society, Liang Shuming called it the ethics-based society, while Fei Xiaotong called it the society of a differential pattern. The terms are diverse from each other, but they are consistent in connotation. They all emphasize that the most basic connection in China's social structure is human feelings, which is an expanding network of human relationships based on the blood relationships of the family. Child rearing is conducted within the family, while the family members, according to the intensity of blood relationship, naturally undertake the obligations that are necessary for raising children.

More than that, the family members may also resort to the social resources at their disposal to get engaged in the actions of child rearing when necessary. After all, the family is not only a dwelling unit, but also, at least sometimes, an economic unit and a legal unit. Above all, the family is a moral community from the viewpoint that the family is an organization by which members prove their identity and emotional involvement (Casey, 1989). Since the family is a moral community, ethics and the principles of action associated with ethics are bound to become the guide, by which people adjust their family relations. However, if the parents of the children fail to undertake the task of raising the children on their own, they will inevitably rely on other members of the family to partially fulfill the obligations of raising the children, which is the social obligation of the family members. The motivation for maintaining this obligation is ethics, a moral principle based on consanguinity and tradition.

When other family members are involved in the action of child rearing, it means that the parents of the child resort to their social relations. It is a web composed of various rights and obligations, responsibilities and emotions. The stronger the ability of the parents to employ their relations is, the more social resources the parents will obtain, and the abler they will be to raise their children. In this sense, social relations are a kind of resource, and a kind of social capital that boosts the formation of interest relations, and the foundation for this capital is the trust, norms and mutual benefits between people. Now that child rearing is a social action, it is a deliberate strategy adopted by the parents of the children in a specific situation by mobilizing all kinds of social capital to get involved in child rearing. Therefore, it is necessary to introduce the concept of social capital to probe into the problems in child rearing.

In general, social capital is a social network that is established based on the principle of trust, norms and reciprocity. Coleman holds that social capital is a social resource that promotes individuals to develop a sense of psychological happiness and capabilities in a group. The network of interaction among the parents, teenagers and other social members can deliver expectations, norms and information and other resources to other network members, which will increase the chance for individuals to grow up (Coleman, 1988). In Coleman's view, the study of social capital is mainly centered on the social capital within the family, which means that the family kinship network and family relationships are the foundation for the study of social capital. However, man is not a social being confined to a closed system within the family, but a social being that transcends the family into a wider open system. For this reason, social capital will not be limited to the exchange of resources between family members, but in all the social networks among the members who can provide resources or support for the realization of individual goals. Runyan believes that social capital comes from the benefits generated by the social relations between families and communities, and believes that the social capital index originates from: 1) the number of parents in the family; 2) social support from female caregivers; 3) the number of children in the family; 4) support from neighbors, and; 5) participation in religious activities (Runyan et al., 1998).

From these general concepts of social capital, it can be seen that the sources of social capital for child rearing should take into account not only the kinship network based on consanguinity identity, but also the social networks other than the blood relations, such as genetic relationship, geographical relationship, relationship with friends and classmates, and neighborhood relationship and so forth.

Since the implementation of China's reform and opening-up policy and the development of modernization, a large number of workers in rural areas have flowed to cities and coastal areas for work, which is the most significant structural and economic feature of China's rural areas, resulting in an unprecedented social problem of the left-behind children. For the parents who have been working in other cities for years, they must find a proper way to rear their children who are left behind in their hometowns and entrust reliable persons to rear their children. Since the social rearing mechanism and the related social welfare policies have not been perfected in China, it still depends on the forces of the families to rear the left-behind children, and the families should employ the kinship resources within the family and all kinds of social relation resources related to the families. It is the reality of the rearing of left-behind children in rural areas. The rearing of left-behind children, and the concepts of social capital and family social capital provide us with a right perspective of analysis to understand the special phenomenon of child rearing arising in the course of modernization in China.

Section 1 Social Capital and Family Social Capital

Pierre Bourdieu, a French sociologist, philosopher and anthropologist, conducted a systematic analysis of the modernity of social capital. Unlike previous concepts of capital, he went beyond the idea that capital is synonymous with pure economic capital, believing that, in addition to economic capital, capital also includes social capital and cultural capital. Social capital is a combination of practical or potential resources that are obtained through the possession of an institutionalized relation network. "Those resources are inseparable from the possession of a specific network, which is widely known and recognized among the public. Or in other words, the network is linked to the membership system of a group that provides each member with corresponding support from the perspective of collective capital (Bourdieu, 1997)."

For a specific actor, the amount of social capital that he possesses depends on two factors, one is the size of the social network that the actors can make effective use of, and the other is the number of various forms of capital that each member in the network possesses. Thus, it can be seen that Bourdieu defines social capital as a relation network, and a network of institutionalized relationships. A relation network refers to the social relations that an individual or a collective accumulates in a long time, which is to turn those accidental relationships, such as neighbors, working relationships, and even kinship relationships, to both essential and selective relations, and to make it necessary for the subjects involved to maintain these relations in the long term. The maintenance of these relationships is dependent on the constant construction of the social systems, such as kinship relations. In this way, social life goes beyond a simple game of chance or roulette, and thus a relatively stable social order and rules are established.

James Coleman, an American sociologist, has further explored the forms of social capital. He points out that social capital refers to the capital property of individuals, which are represented by social structure resources. They are composed of elements that constitute social structures, mainly in interpersonal and social structures, facilitating the actions of individuals within the social structure. The forms of expression of social capital mainly include obligations and expectations, information networks, norms and effective punishments, authoritative relations, multi-functional social organizations and intentionally established social organizations, and so forth (Coleman, 1999).

In the Worldly Quarterly, Francis Fukuyama mentioned that social capital plays a key role in the effective functioning of the modern economy, and that it makes up part of the culture of modern society. Social capital is different from economic policy or economic system, as the economic policy or economic system is based on the formal system, legal criteria and reason, but social capital can not be created or made simply based on the public policies. Francis Fukuyama defines social capital as an informal specification that can be illustrated by examples and can contribute to the cooperation between two or more individuals (Fukuyama, 2003).

According to Lin Nan, social capital is acquired from the resources that are embedded in the social network. Social capital is rooted in various social networks and social relationships, so it is a resource that can be positioned in a social structure and that can be ingested or mobilized in purposeful action. According to the definition, the concept of social capital consists of three components, the resources that are embedded in a social structure, the ability of individuals to ingest these social resources, and the utilization or mobilization of these social resources by individuals through purposeful actions. Such resources are not directly possessed by individuals, but are acquired through their direct or indirect personal social relations (Lin, 2003).

Since kinship is the basic feature of the social structure, and the family is the most basic and most important group in human life, the social capital of the family in the kinship network is the most readily accessible and flexible capital form for each individual, which is also known as family social capital. Family social capital refers to the mutually beneficial system that is established by each family member within the family in a community, with the help of shared emotions, values, trust and other norms. Family social capital includes both the intimate parent-child relationship and the relationship network between the child and other relatives around him. Generally speaking, the stronger the link between the parents and their children is, the abler the parents and their children will be to establish social capital in the family, and the more beneficial it will be to providing effective assistance for the personality cultivation and education of the children.

For the children who grow in the single-parent families, or those who are raised by their grandparents or those who grow in the remarried families, there may be a lack of family social capital due to the loose relationship between the parents and children, which may ultimately influence the normal growth of the children. But in the absence of parent-child relationships, the kinship network system of the children can provide effective support for their growth.

The family social capital is actually a network of interpersonal relations based on trust, norms, institutions or responsibilities in the family, which is mainly to evaluate the quality and quantity of the relationship between parents and children (Wright et al., 2004). Marjoribanks K. believes that family social capital mainly refers to the intensity of the relationship between adults and children, mainly from parents' expectations and parental involvement (Marjoribanks and Mboya, 2001).

From the longitudinal and lateral relationships of the kinship network, the family social capital can be divided into the internal social network of the family and the external social network of the family. The internal social network of the family mainly refers to the rights and obligations arising from the consanguinity identity, which takes the parent-child relationship as the core and the patriarchal family as the basic unit to carry out resource exchange between individual members. The external social network of the family means that the individual members go beyond the consanguinity identity to seek the social resources in a greater social range, such as geographical relationship, relation networks of friends and classmates and other networks.

Interpersonal relationships become the most fundamental social capital, while the realization of personal interests or goals benefits from the cohesion of some interpersonal relationships or the geographical relationship and the neighborhood relationship at a higher level of integration. As a result, the family social capital is derived from the rights and obligations that are congenitally endowed due to the blood relationship, the support of neighborhood or geographical relationship, informal social control and various social networks based on the trust of the social members.

Tancun Village is a typical labor-export community, where a large number of young parents work in the coastal areas after leaving their young children in their hometowns, leading to a large number of empty-nest families. It is so prominent that many children are left behind at home. So all parents, as migrant workers, must take the rearing of their children seriously and propose corresponding solutions. Tancun Village is located in the remote, and its basic social nature lies in its localism. All social members of the community are the most dependent on the kinship network. For this reason, it becomes of particular importance to investigate the social significance of the family social capital to the rearing and education of left-behind children in rural communities.

Section 2 Labor Mobility and Left-behind Children at Tancun Village

The status of left-behind children in a community is related to labor mobility in the community. The more people work in other cities, the more children there will be staying at home. Hunan Province is a labor exporting province, where Tancun Village is one of the thousands of labor-export rural communities. Since the mid-1990s, the number of migrant workers in Tancun Village has reached a peak. What's more, people measure the capabilities of a person mainly by checking whether he or she can go out to work for money. The family with more members working outside is more likely to be envied by the villagers. Traditionally, Tancun Village is a typical agricultural community, but there is not too much land available for villagers to cultivate. If the villagers turn to the land for survival, they can just provide for themselves. It can be regarded as a well-off family if the family members can eat their fill by living frugally and working hard at Tancun Village. The economic situation in Tancun Village has gradually improved since the workers in rural areas were able to work in coastal areas. Nowadays, except for only a few families in which a person works formally at the government department and some self-employed villagers, generally speaking, the family in which more people work outside lives a better-off life. The powerful lure of working for money has attracted almost all the young people and a majority of the middle-aged in the village, who are capable of going out to work for money.

It is not easy to make an accurate count of migrant workers, mainly because they have been changing their workplaces. Some people work away from home all year round and even come back only once every two or three years. JWD, for example, returned only once after graduating from high school in 1995 until 2006, when he came back to mourn for his dead mother, according to the author. His wife, who he married for three years, had not yet been back to his home. It is easier to make a count of such migrant workers as JWD, but some villagers just go out for work seasonally, such as building houses, harvesting sugarcane in Guangxi Province, doing odd jobs and dealing with others. People of this kind may go home many times, and they stay at home for varying periods, short or long, making it difficult to count. Therefore, before the statistics, we must make a clear definition of migrant workers.

In this book, migrant workers are defined as people who had been working outside for up to half a year, as of the time of the author's survey. The author carried on a household survey according to this scope. The statistical results showed that, in June 2006, there were 905 migrant workers at Tancun Village, whose demographic characteristics are shown in Table 6.1. Among them, there were 467 males, 438 females, 695 married persons and 210 unmarried persons. At the same time, it can be seen from the statistics that 490 migrant workers are aged between 26 and 40, accounting for 54.1 % of all migrant workers. The children of this group are mostly left-behind children. This group of people is the most productive people in the countryside. They are young and energetic. They had supposed to be the main force in the traditional villages, but now they become migrant workers, a group of farmers who are new to agricultural production.

Table 6.1 Basic information of gender, age and marriage of migrant workers at Tancun Village in 2006

Age	Male			Female			Total
	Married	Unmarried	Total	Married	Unmarried	Total	
16 - 20	0	67	67	2	56	58	125
21 - 25	62	39	101	74	11	85	186
26 - 30	67	21	88	73	5	78	166
31 - 35	68	4	72	78	0	78	150
36 - 40	93	2	95	79	0	79	174
41 - 45	34	4	38	34	0	34	72
46 and above	20	1	21	11	0	11	32

Data source: The data in this table are obtained from the author's household survey.

Farmers go out for work for many reasons. Liu Yingjie argues that there are mainly four reasons: first of all, the huge rural population and a large number of agricultural surplus labor workers in China have resulted in great pressure; second, the ability of rural township enterprises to absorb agricultural surplus labor force for employment is on the decline; third, farmers' incomes are falling, and they are not profiting from farming, the burden is rising, and more profits-driven farmers are shifting from agriculture to non-agricultural industries; fourth, there is a strong pull of the urban-rural disparity (Liu, 2000). In terms of the explanation of the local reasons for the rise of migrant workers in Tancun Village, to go out for work is to make money, and to make more money than they used to engage in farm work. In fact, it is the migrant workers who are forced by the economic poverty caused by the contradiction between the local large population and limited resources. At the same time, they go to work in developed areas to seek opportunities, which has more potential to change the poverty of their families at home than living a quiet life by working at sunrise and resting at sunset. Therefore, even if they have to abandon their parents and children for the moment, they will not give up the opportunity to earn money by going out for work.

Working is the primary source of the economic income for villagers of Tancun Village. It is fair to say that most of the expenses in the house are supported by working outside. The villagers generally have to support their children to go to school and get married, build the house, undertake the expenses for all kinds of ceremonies, and provide for the parents, by using the funds that they have accumulated for years of working in other cities. It can be seen that Tancun Village is a typical labor-export community dominated by the rural migrant economy (Zhou, 2006).

The new buildings in Tiantang Group since 1995 can well illustrate the significance of hiring out for work in the local economy. Since 1995, there have been eighteen houses newly built. Assuming that the fee for the work that the villagers themselves devote to building their houses is excluded from the expenses, thirteen houses are built completely entirely by the money they earn from hiring out for work. The other five houses are partly dependent on the income that they earn as migrant workers. One of the best new buildings cost more than 200,000 Yuan, which was built by the only boss at Tancun Village running a factory away from home, showing the glory and pride of the successful boss as a member of migrant workers.

Generally speaking, however, it takes 60,000 to 80,000 Yuan to build a new house. To accomplish the construction of a new house as one of the most important events in the life of the migrant workers, they need to spend their savings for a decade as their monthly income ranges only from several hundred Yuan to more than one thousand Yuan. Therefore, for these migrant workers at Tancun Village, they have no more financial ability to bring up their children by themselves in the place where they work, so they have to leave their children at their hometowns to reduce their daily expenses at their workplaces. Thus, the problem of left-behind children inevitably arises.

In addition, the occupations of migrant workers at Tancun Village can well explain why they have to choose to leave their children at home. According to the author's survey results in 2006, as shown in Table 6.2, most of the migrant workers in Tancun Village are engaged in the manufacturing industry, construction and other industries with low salaries, poor working conditions and intensive labor forces, in the cities where they work. In addition, most of them are ordinary employees at the bottom of the factories, with a total of 628 villagers in this aspect, accounting for 69.3 % of the total migrant workers.

The second-largest sector is the construction industry, the number of villagers in this aspect accounts for 8.3 % of the total migrant workers, among whom 64 villagers made a living by doing odd jobs, accounting for 7.1 %. In fact, in the Pearl River Delta and Jiangsu and Zhejiang Provinces at the Yangtze River Delta with high living costs, it is not an easy task for ordinary workers at the bottom of the social ladder to go back home to build a new house by living a frugal life and saving a lot of money. As a result, most of the married couples with children have no choice but to leave their children at home to be raised by their parents. The older people, who stay at home all year round, need to raise their grandchildren after bringing up their children, and then they become more valued by society correspondingly. The traditional saying that elders are treasures is only truly reflected today.

Table 6.2 Occupational distribution of migrant workers at Tancun Village in 2006 Unit: Person

Practitioner / Occupation	Male	Female
Construction	76	0
Clerk	247	381
Management	10	4
Odd jobs	62	2
Service industry	9	32
Running a factory	2	1
Doing business	17	8
Other	44	10

Data source: The data in this table are obtained from the author's household survey.

The migrant workers at Tancun Village tend to engage in low-level occupations, which is bound up with their education level and the quality of labor force, as well as the social relations developed by the first generation of migrant workers. Wang Chunguang divides the migrant workers into two generations according to the intergenerational differences. People who went out for work in the 1980s are named the first generation of migrant workers, while those who went out for work for the first time in the 1990s are named the second generation of migrant workers. Most of the second generation was born in the late 1970s and early 1980s and grew up and were educated in the 1980s. A majority of them graduated from junior or senior high schools, while a small number of them are college students who have recently graduated (Wang, 2001). In this book, according to the actual situation of Tancun Village, the author divides migrant workers into three generations, those who went out for work in the 1980s are called the first generation, those who went out in the 1990s are called the second generation, and those who went out in the 21st century are called the new generation.

The educational level of all migrant workers at Tancun Village is shown in Table 6.3. Of the 905 migrant workers, 141 had the degree of senior high school or above, including only seven college graduates. These college graduates failed to find a formal job in the inland areas after the implementation of the unification of colleges and then left home for Guangdong Province, Shanghai, Zhejiang Province and other regions for work. These people are late to the job market in the coastal areas and have not yet established solid social networks. For this reason, they can not provide reliable social capital for their relatives in their hometowns.

However, it is worth noting that those who graduated from senior high school are mainly young people under the age of 25, most of whom are the new generation of migrant workers. A few of them are technical workers and managers, but on the whole, they mostly work as ordinary staff members, service workers and small merchants. The migrant workers aged between 31 and 40 years old mainly finished their primary and junior high school education, among whom those who were primary school graduates and illiterate account for 44.4 %. This group mainly belongs to the second generation of migrant workers. Their migrant jobs are directly affected by the first generation of migrant workers, because most of them follow the first generation of migrant workers for work, and they are relatively concentrated in the places where the first generation have been working. Relatively speaking, the workers aged 41 and above have much lower cultural qualities, while most of them just finished primary school education. Quite a few of them went out to work in the middle and late 1980s, belonging to the first generation of migrant workers.

The jobs they had been engaged in as migrant workers had had the most immediate impact on the development of the migrant population of Tancun Village. As their cultural quality is generally low, they can only engage in the lowest level of occupations, and then they are unable to open up better ways out for the newcomers, such as providing information resources and building an intermediary bridge and so forth. After all, the social networks of migrant workers are mainly based on the local resources of blood relationship, affinity and geographical relationship. Under such established social capital conditions, migrant workers in Tancun Village generally do not have the ability to bring up their children in the place where they work. The migration population does not show the prominent trend to work outside with their family members, while it is only limited to the families in which the parents and their children are all workers. For most of the migrant workers at Tancun Village, it is their rational choice to leave their children at home.

Table 6.3 Education level of migrant workers at Tancun Village in 2006 Unit: Person

	Illiterate	Primary school	Junior high school	Senior high school	College	Total
16 - 20	0	0	81	44	0	125
21 - 25	0	1	144	39	2	186
26 - 30	0	10	131	21	4	166
31 - 35	2	49	87	11	1	150
36 - 40	5	88	68	13	0	174
41 - 45	7	39	21	5	0	72
46 +	3	19	9	1	0	32
Total	17	206	541	134	7	905

Data source: The data in this table are obtained from the author's household survey.

As can be seen from the above analysis, the parents who go out for work have no choice but to leave their children at home at Tancun Village, and such phenomenon has become a new tradition to some extent, which means that the young people work in the coastal and the surrounding cities to support their families mainly based on their economic income, while the elder people who have brought up these young people have to assume the responsibilities of rearing the children of these young people as grandparents in today's society. These days, young mothers routinely leave their children to their paternal or maternal grandparents when they are no more than one year old according to the convention, since the people around them all do this way. It is no wonder that the changes in the population structure in rural areas caused by population migration are referred to as the phenomenon of 386199 (38 representing women due to the International Working Women's Day, 61 representing children due to the International Children's Day, and 99 representing old people due to the Double Ninth Festival on the ninth day of the ninth month in the Chinese calendar) (Editorial Office of Population Research, 2004). However, from the actual situation of the population structure of Tancun Village, it is mainly the problem of children and the elderly, because few young women stay at home and they are the main force of migrant workers.

Before we discuss the problem of left-behind children in Tancun Village, we need to first give a clear definition of left-behind children. According to the research of relevant scholars, for instance, Luo Guofen, in the study of the scale of left=behind children, pointed out that the definition of left-behind children should be clarified in at least three aspects: first of all, it is about whether it is a left-behind child if its mother or father stays at home and lives with it; second, it is about the duration of parents working in other cities and leaving their children at their hometowns; third, it is about whether the children under the age of six and those aged between fifteen and eighteen should be counted as left-behind children (Luo, 2005).

In this book, children aged from 0 to 15 who have one or both parents continuously working outside for more than half a year are defined as left-behind children. After the age of 16, most children have finished their junior high school studies. At that time, a considerable number of them will join the ranks of migrant workers. Other children will be admitted to senior high school but they are almost able to take care of themselves. So the children over the age of 16 are no longer included in the scope of left-behind children in this book. According to this, the results of the author's survey are shown in Table 6.4. The total number of left-behind children in Tancun Village was 291, accounting for 69.4 % of the total number of children at Tancun Village. The ratio of left-behind children to non-left-behind children was 227:100. Among the left-behind children, there were 155 boys and 136 girls, and most of the left-behind children were the children at kindergartens and primary and middle school students.

Table 6.4 Comparison table of left-behind children and non-left-behind children at Tancun Village Unit: Person

Category Age	left-behind children			non-left-behind children			Sum Total
	Male	Female	total	Male	Female	Total	
0	2	2	4	4	3	7	11
1	4	6	10	5	4	9	19
2	8	8	16	6	8	14	30
3	11	6	17	1	2	3	20
4	9	10	19	2	4	6	25
5	11	11	22	4	5	9	31
6	14	12	26	6	4	10	36
7	9	8	17	2	3	5	22
8	13	11	24	5	2	7	31
9	15	13	28	2	4	6	34
10	12	9	21	4	4	8	29
11	11	7	18	3	7	10	28
12	7	6	13	2	5	7	20
13	9	10	19	5	3	8	27
14	14	7	21	5	4	9	30
15	6	10	16	7	3	10	26
Total	155	136	291	63	65	128	419

Data source: The data in this table are obtained from the author's household survey.

Section 3 Kinship Network of Rearing of Left-behind Children

In the conceptual system of anthropology, the network can be described as a social structure and a metaphor for the society, which is concerned about how people are regulated and dominated by culture in this structural system and adopt social behaviors that are in line with cultural norms. In the book Argonauts of the Western Pacific, Bronislaw Kaspar Malinowski, the master of functionalism, describes how the people of the Trobriand Islands engaged in economic behavior that could not understand as civilized people, who lavished most of the fruits of their hard work on their relatives. "Here almost all the harvest and surplus belongs not to the individual but to his relatives; for three-quarters of the food a person produces, a part goes to the chief of the tribe and a part goes to the husband and family members of his sisters or mother (Malinowski, 2002)." Such economic behavior is governed by traditional cultural practices in the local area. They take generosity to their relatives in order to maintain their status in the society and the kinship network, and play their due social roles. Only by obeying customs and traditions, and fulfilling their responsibilities as kinsmen, can community members maintain the balance of the inherent social structure. "The giving and receiving of wealth are the primary means by which society is organized, by which the power of the chief of the tribe is demonstrated, by which kinship is maintained, and by which legal relations are embodied (Malinowski, 2002)."

The economic and social behaviors of individuals, in fact, are to maintain the unique network of the region according to the traditional practices, i.e., cultural norms. Therefore, the network can be understood as a kind of binary or pluralistic relationship between man and man, and between family and family. In China, the concept of such a relationship is called a differential pattern by Fei Xiaotong (Fei, 1998), or the power game of face (Hwang et al., 2004) by Hwang, K.K. et al., scholars from Taiwan.

The family is the most basic unit for understanding and analyzing society in the field of anthropology and sociology. It is also the most basic kinship group for completing the socialization of rearing. The social network is mainly a kind of interactive relationship that extends outward with the family as the core. In China's rural areas, network relations are local, mainly manifested as blood relationships, kinship, geographical relations and so forth. The social capital of rural people is a network composed of such relations. In accordance with traditional customs, cultural norms and social capital input, people have set up a stable reciprocal system, which has complete functions. It penetrates almost every aspect of each individual and family, so that each family or individual can get due help from other families or individuals in the reciprocal system.

Current Situation of Family Structure at Tancun Village in the Context of Rural Migrant Economy

The traditional villagers of Tancun Village expect to have an extended family, so they have such an idea of an extended family of several generations living under one roof. But even before the founding of the People's Republic of China, the villagers at Tancun Village did not realize this ideal family structure model, according to the memories of the elder people and the records of the pedigree, which is because there are no high-ranking officials or millionaires at Tancun Village, leading to the absence of the economic basis for the organization of big families. In fact, there is a widespread practice of separation in the local area, while the family members tend to live apart as the children grow up. They believe that the tree will have branches when it grows up, the son will live apart when he grows up and the daughter will get married when she grows up, and that the scallions will not sprout if they are not split, and the family will not flourish if it is not divided. Generally speaking, when a son in a family gets married, the son should live in a separate house in accordance with the custom. The core of separation is to divide family property, while men usually have the right to inherit family property but women do not have such rights. The succession system reflects the cohesion of consanguinity in a patriarchal family, as it is believed that the daughter belongs to another family, which means that when daughters grow up and marry, they will become other people, not us. When the family is about to break up, the family should invite the highly respected elders n the village or the mother's brother to preside over the ceremony as a notary.

After the family breaks up, the sons of the family should share the pension expenses for their parents, mainly in the form of grain and money. In the 1980s and 1990s, it was common for the father or mother that lives alone to take turns living and dining in their sons' houses, thus constituting a meal rotation system (Gallin, 1966; Hsieh, 1986; Zhuang, 1996). But at the moment, there is no such family structure found at Tancun Village. If there are several sons in a family, the parents may live with their youngest son, but all the sons share the pension costs. If there are two sons in the family, it may be the case that one son provides for his father and the other son provides for his mother, resulting in the old couple living apart. So this way of living is not common, usually in the families where the sons are on bad terms with each other. It can be seen that separation is not equal to complete separation, but there is a combination of separation and continuity in separation (Ma, 1999).

The nuclear families after separation tend to be linked with each other by visible or invisible lines (visible lines refer to the connecting forces existing as entities, such as supporting parents and cooperating in production; invisible lines refer to the subjective emotional identity of members of the same extended family, which is manifested as the constraint of the concept of familism), thus partially achieving the effects that are exclusive to the extended or joint families. The inter-generational differentiation feature that is apparently severed but actually connected enables the nuclear families at Tancun Village to be closely united.

Due to the custom of family separation, the villagers of Tancun Village tend to live in relatively small families, with a relatively single structure. And the families are generally based on the nuclear families in the form of one couple or two generations of people. However, with the outflow of a large number of workers in droves, there have been a growing number of stem families, extended families or joint families in Tancun Village.

In the past, the newlyweds used to hold the ceremony to live apart after living with their parents for two or three months. But nowadays, young couples tend to live with their parents at home for a short time after holding the wedding ceremony at home and then go out to work together. For young people, their property is bridal furniture, often locked up in the house left to them by their parents, while the rest property is their income from working outside, which is the cash deposited in the bank. Their private property will not get confused with that of their brothers and parents. As for the fields, agricultural tools and grain in rural areas, they are nothing to the young people, and even if the young people obtain these from the family property, they have to hand over such property to their parents.

As a result, parents now have no need to hold a ceremony to ask their son and daughter-in-law that has just got married to live apart. As they put it, "now we do not need to live apart, as they are away from home all year round, and come back once every one or more years. Then, when we live with our daughter-in-law coming back, it is like receiving the guest. As long as they come back, we are not at all willing to part them out and live on their own." At the same time, even in families where a ceremony is held to part the son and daughter-in-law out of the parents' house, the new home of the young couple has to be merged with their parents' old home because the young parents themselves have been away from home throughout the year and their children are raised by their parents.

It can be seen that due to a large number of rural workers going out for work, the traditional concepts of Chinese farmers of hating to leave their native land and expecting the yield of the fields, which came into being in the era of small-peasant economy, while their family structure began to show a complex trend of diversification. Professor Zhou

Daming summarized this complex trend into four points: first of all, the families are reunited after separation; second, the children are mainly brought up by their grandparents; third, the ways of supporting the elderly have changed, while there are an increasing number of joint numbers and more families choose the meal rotation mechanism to support the elder people; fourth, the parents expect more from their children (Zhou, 1999).

These days, the meal rotation mechanism is seldom found at Tancun Village, but the other family structures are all based on child rearing. The younger generation goes out to work and has to leave their children at home for various economic and occupational reasons. In order to facilitate the raising of a child, including the cost of managing the child's life, education and medical care, the grandparents of the child have to get their grandchildren in various nuclear families who are left behind at home together and make up a joint family.

Changes in Family Relations of Tancun Village in the Context of Rural Migrant Economy

For young people who go out to work and leave only their parents and children in their hometowns, the family relationship is also undergoing some new changes. First of all, the mother may become unfamiliar with her daughter-in-law. Young daughters-in-law seldom live with their mother-in-law after they get married. So they do not have to get into a conflict over the daily necessities as the mother-in-law and daughter-in-law used to be. Moreover, they do not live face to face under one roof, while they are usually separated thousands of miles away, and rarely communicate with each other. Therefore, in recent years, it is rare for a young daughter-in-law to quarrel or fight with her mother-in-law. In view of the fact that the mother-in-law and the daughter-in-law are not familiar with each other, the discontinuity on the space increases the mutual tolerance between the two instead. The daughters-in-law come back home occasionally in one year, as if they were distinguished guests from the cities, and the mothers-in-law tend to treat them kindly and generously. After coming back home, the daughter-in-law is seldom engaged in the housework, and her mother-in-law will try her best to make some delicious dishes to entertain her during every meal as she hardly comes back. At the same time, the daughters-in-law should buy some gifts that may look strange and eccentric for the older people to their parents-in-law when they come back, and give some money to them. It is the social etiquette that young women must show to their parents-in-law when they come back from their work in other cities.

Tancun Village, by and large, is an economically backward rural community, and the old people value the economic and practical properties above anything else. As some older people put it, we are too old to carry anything on our shoulders or in our hands. So we have to live on the money given by our children and daughters-in-law. We are looking forward to our children sending some money back, and if they do not send money back, they do not need to give phone calls. Phone calls are nothing for us." Thus, the older people of Tancun Village have had high expectations for material and money, while their spiritual needs are relatively implicit. However, with the improvement of living standards and medical and health conditions, the physical quality of the elderly has been significantly improved compared with their predecessors. Most of the old people in their sixties are still able to do farm work and earn their own living.

The discontinuity of the relationship between the mother-in-law and the daughter-in-law in space also tends to normalize the tension between the two due to the reduction of face-to-face communication. Taking an old woman named Shunlian as an example, she is sixty-eight years old. The local people all consider her too capable and eccentric, so she often quarrels with her daughters-in-law. She has three daughters-in-law, but none of them is on speaking terms with her. The second daughter-in-law even used to fight with her several times. However, it is impossible for the people around to tell whether it is the fault of the mother-in-law or the daughter-in-law. As the saying goes, even an upright official finds it hard to settle a family quarrel. However, since 1998, all three of her daughters-in-law have been out for work, and she needs to take care of her six grandchildren at home, and assumed all the responsibilities of raising them. She has made great contributions to her sons and daughters-in-law feeling assured to go out for work. Thus, the mother-in-law and the daughter-in-law also begin to get along well with each other. According to the oral agreement reached in advance, the daughters-in-law should send some money back on time every month, namely, the living expenses of 150 Yuan per month for each child. She manages the monthly living expenses of 900 Yuan as a whole and tries to save money, so that she can save little living expenses as her personal expenses in daily life.

The relationship between the wives of brothers is also undergoing complex changes due to their outflow for work. First of all, many of them flow to the same area with their husbands with the affinity as the link. In the area where they flow in, they rent the houses adjacent to each other and become a supporting force for one another. Some of them even work in the same factory. During the Spring Festival, festivals and the feasts for the most important events in their lives, they all visit and present one another according to the customs of their hometowns, so that the sisters-in-law can get on better with each other because of their experience of working together. During the survey, the author met some people who went home to visit their relatives and asked about how they got along with their sisters-in-law in the place where they work, and most of them said that they were much more intimate when they went outside than when they used to stay at home. After all, the sisters-in-law are unfamiliar with the place and the people there, so they depend more on each other due to the strength of kinship.

Second, if the sisters-in-law do not work together and do not contact each other for a long time, they will become less intimate. When one family makes a feast for a wedding, birthday or other happy events, the sisters-in-law can not present red envelopes to the family since they are not at home. The traditional relationship between the wives of brothers for making a cash gift may get broken by chance because they go out to work. And they will give a gift when they stay at home, but if they are working in other cities, they will not send money back as a cash gift, unless there are major joyful events, such as the wedding of their niece or nephew. The tender and warm human relations of presenting each other has gradually weakened.

Third, the new generation of sisters-in-law after marriage tend to become friends, as they are strange to each other before marriage, and spend less time together in their hometown and have few contacts after marriage. They are only connected because of the family of their husbands. The relationship between the wives of the brother is more of an imaginary relationship. Guiying, who married in 2004 is this case. She said she had only met her sister-in-law once although she had been married for two years, and that they just stayed together for a few days. When asked about her relationship with her sister-in-law, she said that it doesn't matter whether they are close to each other, and that they are unfamiliar anyway, so they just need to be courteous to each other when they meet. The courtesy is regarded as the principle of dealing with the relationship with the sister-in-law, indicating that she regards her sister-in-law as an outsider. Hence, it can be seen that the identity of members of extended families has become weakened.

In addition, in some cases, the relationship between the married woman that stays in the hometown and her sister-in-law that works outside tends to become interest-oriented. Generally speaking, the eldest sisters-in-law stay in the hometown, as they are old or illiterate and have to give up the opportunity to make money by going out for work. However, a considerable number of eldest sisters-in-law assume the responsibility of taking care of the children of their younger sisters-in-law, which means that they are entrusted by their younger sisters-in-law to take care of their children at their homes. As a result, the younger sisters-in-law who go out for work generally feel grateful to their elder sisters-in-law staying in the hometown, and try their best to compensate them financially. The younger sisters-in-law tend to come back home every one or more years, and they are usually received by their elder sisters-in-law and seldom cooks by themselves during the short period when they stay at home. However, practically speaking, on the one hand, the elder sisters-in-law assume the responsibilities of bringing up their nephews and nieces out of the sense of responsibility of affinity and consanguinity as the aunt. On the other hand, they are driven by interests.

According to the author's survey, if the left-behind children live in their uncle's house, their parents need to pay the living expenses ranging from 150 to 200 Yuan every month. We should know that the consumption of living is generally low in rural areas, as the rural people can provide for themselves for common vegetables and grain, and they just need to pay for some meat and other pungent foods. The elder sisters-in-law who stay at home and take care of their nieces and nephews mainly depend on saving some money from the living expenses paid by their younger sisters-in-law as their service charges. If they have too little income or even pay for taking care of their nieces and nephews, or if their younger sisters-in-law do not send money back, they will relinquish the responsibility of caring for their nieces and nephews. In this sense, the relationship between them and their younger sisters-in-law tends to become interest-oriented.

Parents work outside all year round, leaving their children at home, which will inevitably lead to the absence of affection between the parents and the children. Many psychological studies have proved that the absence of affection has had serious negative effects on the development of children's moral quality, character and personality development. The general conclusion of psychological research is that the left-behind children are more introverted, scanty of words, and more emotionally stable, and persist in their old ways. Due to the lack of parents' care, children are prone to mood swings, anxiety, depression, gloom, and worry, and they have gradually become unsocial, aloof and less talkative. What's more, children's anxiety, learning pressure, interpersonal tension and sensitivity, depression, emotional instability and other psychological problems are the most prominent (Zhang, 1998; Wang, 2002).

Here, the author only briefly describes the sociological changes in the parent-child relationship caused by population mobility. The general sociological theory emphasizes the pleasant side of the family, and sociologists are willing to observe the family activities from the perspective of functionalism and describe the family as an adaptive system, which creatively responds to the pressure caused by the failure to satisfy the needs. The critical sociologists believe that the family is an anti-social unit, because the family has an internal orientation. If a society emphasizes the value of the family, it will inevitably lead people to give priority to the personal interests of the family (Barrett and Mclntosh, 1991).

Ira Reiss, an American sociologist, pointed out that the precondition of the functionality of each society is to complete the socialization of nurturing of the newborn, while the small-scale kinship group is the structural precondition to perform the function. This kinship group is based on genetic, real or fictional biological connections. As a result, the adults in the kinship group naturally gain some rights to their children in the existing family structure (Reiss, 1965). Thus, the minimum function of the family is to ensure that the child completes the socialization of nurturing. In this process, the parents gain some rights to the child, and the child also establishes a close relationship with its parents.

However, as a large number of workers go out for work, they leave their children at home for economic benefits, and then a lot of the children even lose the most direct care of their parents when they are still being breastfed. That is to say, the family does not fully perform its function of socializing the nurturing of the child, which is bound to lead a series of changes to the parent-child relationship in the family. At the same time, these changes also challenge the concept of "family" in the traditional sense, i.e., whether it is regarded as a functionalist concept of the family if the nuclear family fails to fully perform its function of nurturing. The author has no intention to dwell on the concept, but just wants to express that with a large number of rural workers going out for work, a great many children have no choice but to stay at home, and then the traditional relationship between the father, the mother and the child is undergoing dramatic changes.

The continuous contact between parents and children is separated in space, and the function of the family in the socialization of nurturing is weakened, and then the children lack the due care from their parents in their childhood memories, which is bound to affect the intimacy of the parent-child relationship. As a popular song goes to Tancun Village, mom is the worst in the world, and she gives birth to a child but never brings him up. It expresses children's strong dissatisfaction with their parents due to the absence of maternal love as they grow up.

In this book, the data on the survey of left-behind children was the results of the sampling survey, which was conducted on the 250 left-behind children in the town middle school and the central complete elementary school in the town where Tancun Village was located in October 2006. Of the respondents, there are 25 students in each grade of the elementary school, totaling 150 elementary school students; there are 33 students in grade one of the middle school, 33 students in grade two and 34 students in grade three, totaling 100 middle school students.

In the questionnaire, the author designed a question "who do you think is the most influential person in your growth", offering seven options of relatives, including the father, the mother, the paternal grandfather, the paternal grandmother, the maternal grandfather, the maternal grandmother, and another relative. According to the results, 78 respondents chose the father, accounting for 31.2 %; 72 chose the mother, accounting for 28.8 %; 62 chose the grandfather and the grandmother respectively, accounting for 24.8 %; 35 chose another relative, accounting for 13.8 %. The left-behind children still think that their parents have the most significant impact on their growth, but the influence of grandparents is obviously close to that of parents, which shows that grandparents play an essential role in the growth of left-behind children. Even 13.8 % of the left-behind children said that other of their relatives, such as the father's brother or sister, and the mother's brother, had the greatest impact on their growth.

In the investigation, the author met a woman, who was just on leave after returning from Guangdong Province, criticizing her daughter in the second grade of junior high school who did not work hard. As a result, her daughter said to her rudely, "Go to hell! I did not have a mother. Anyway, I was not raised by you, and I do not want you to care about me. It is none of your business whether I study well or not. " Even when the daughter does something wrong, she refuses the right comments from her mother. It can be seen that the relationship between the mother and the daughter tends to become less intimate but more strained.

Parents lose their rights to their children because they fail to completely accomplish their task of socializing the nurturing of their children. In the eyes of many left-behind children, parents are strange to them, or even an imaginary image, because there are few imprints about their parents in their childhood memories.

The author has a question in the questionnaire: "how old were you when your parents left you to work?" 12 % responded, "I don't know." It indicates that when parents left their children to work outside, their children were too young to remember anything. Many children do not know who their father is even when they are three or four years old, while they only know their grandparents. But they are strangers to their parents, especially their father. The absence of parent-child intimacy has weakened children's expectations of their parents since they were very young, because they believe that their grandparents or other people who bring them up are more reliable. The left-behind children in the survey, when answering the question "who do you think is most likely to provide you with satisfactory help when you are in trouble?", 66 % of the left-behind children thought that their grandmother offered the most satisfactory help. Whether this weakening of the parent-child relationship will bring challenges to traditional ethics or not is still unknown. However, in the young minds of children, there has been a hidden betrayal of the obligation to support their parents.

When asked " Do you think it is your duty to take care of your parents when they are old?" in the questionnaire survey, 22 of 250 respondents chose "No", accounting for 8.8 %. A small number of left-behind children do not think that they are obligated to take care of their elderly parents in the future, but it is sufficient to make us aware that there is a chance that the moral sense of the left-behind children to repay the love and care that they received from their parents from childhood will decline. Children can not understand their parents' going out to work from a rational point of view, and they are now not clear about their obligation to take care of their parents when they are old. Even if they choose the option "Yes" in the questionnaire, it does not mean that they will take such actions in the future. But the data show that children are increasingly alienated from their parents.

Kinship Network and the Rearing Model of Left-behind Children

As mentioned earlier, the family structure of the villagers of Tancun Village is a highly flexible concept, and there may be small or extended families, separated or joint families, all depending on the functional needs of the people in the community for the family. At present, child rearing in rural areas is basically a private matter within the family. Although the government and people from all walks of life have proposed some programs to care for the younger generation and teenagers, in fact, the children at Tancun Village surveyed by the author have not felt the existence of such care. They can access the social benefits of public education, but their socialization of their nurturing, to a large extent, is accomplished in the cultural traditions of the family and the community. Therefore, for the vast number of migrant workers, the only rational choice for them is to rely on the kinship network capital that can be utilized. The kinship network is a relational system based on consanguinity identity, emotional intimacy, the continuation of common offspring and human relationship reciprocity. In this network, the elder relatives have the responsibility and obligation (not in the sense of law, but in the sense of culture) to take care of the left-behind children on behalf of the children's parents as migrant workers. Based on the reciprocal system, the following upbringing modes of left-behind children are developed among the villagers of Tancun Village.

Rearing Model of Paternal Grandparents

In terms of the rearing of left-behind children, the first family capital that young people should mobilize is their parents, namely, the paternal grandparents of the left-behind children, who go from behind the scenes to before the scenes in their duties of rearing their grandchildren, thus becoming an important force to complete the social nurturing of the children in the current rural areas. Young people are not at home all year round, and the older people and their grandchildren make up a temporary family, which is currently known as skip-generation families in academic circles. The raising of a child in a skip-generation family is called grandparenting. Skip-generation families do not come out in recent days, but also exist in the traditional society, but at that time, they were only a special form of the concept of family structure in the field of anthropology and sociology. For example, an elderly couple had to reunite with their grandchildren as a skip-generation family because their son died when they were old and their daughter-in-law was remarried to facilitate the rearing of the minors.

However, now the skip-generation family refers to the family that the young couples, as rural surplus laborers, have to stay away from their nuclear families to work outside and ask the children's paternal grandparents to bring up the children and act as guards for their minor children on their behalf, while they do not go back home for one or more years. Such skip-generation families, which are temporarily composed of paternal grandparents and their grandchildren, are apparently a consequence of modernity (Giddens, 2002), thus resulting in the social fact that the members of the nuclear family are separated in time and space. The separation in time and space is not isolation, but the emptiness of time and space, because the family members who are separated from each other still regard themselves as one.

For children staying at home, parents' presence and absence are just a type of time-space distanciation (Giddens' definition of time-space distanciation refers to the situation that time and space are organized so that presence and absence are connected together) (Giddens, 1990).

Parents who go out for work have been always concerned about their children at home. They often keep in touch with their paternal parents who are responsible for raising their children on behalf of them in terms of economy, life, study and health. Many children said that they could understand that their parents go out to work. In the questionnaire survey, 33.8 % of the respondents said that it is good for parents to go out to work, and that only when parents go out to work can they buy something they like. As a result, 77.5 % of the children believe that they should do better at home, so as to reassure their parents who are working in other cities. In fact, most of the left-behind children do not feel that their family is incomplete, because they share a sense of identity of the family with their parents. Parents do not nurture these children face to face in space, and they also show some negative tendencies in psychology and emotion. However, they still live a separate but shared life with their parents (Cheal, 2005).

In the kinship network, the paternal grandparents, especially the paternal grandmother, are the guardians next to the biological parents of the child, and are also the most reliable persons of the child other than its parents, which has been explained in the previous Chapter 5. Even if the parents both stay at home to raise their children and give up the opportunity to go out for work, the paternal grandparents still need to help look after the child. Moreover, children spend a lot of time living with their paternal grandparents. For this reason, it is in line with the traditional cultural norms of rural areas to raise the left-behind children by the paternal grandparents. For children, they are still living in the cultural context that they are familiar with, and interact with people they are familiar with, so they do not have to undergo a painful process of cultural adaptation like those migrant children. Among the 250 left-behind children surveyed by the author, most of the children who lived with their paternal grandparents said that they were satisfied with living with their paternal grandparents, and many of them regard their paternal grandfather or paternal grandmother as one of their closest persons.

Hence, the author believes that it is more rational for the migrant workers who go out to work to leave their children at home than to bring them to the place where they work, which is not only in line with their affordability force, but can also avoid the culture shock and culture lag caused by the children's flow with their parents. In this respect, it is necessary to conduct an extensive comparative study between the migrant children and left-behind children before making the final conclusion. This book just studies the affordability force of migrant workers and the cultural adaptation capacity of children.

Rearing Model of Maternal Grandparents

In addition to the paternal grandparents, maternal parents are also important kinship resources to raise the left-behind children. In the past, a saying spread in Tancun Village that only the stupid maternal grandmother raised her maternal grandchildren, because the maternal grandchildren belong to others and they are the relatives other than the family. It used to be believed that it would be completely lost no matter how much is devoted to the children of the sister, indicating that the family of the mother's brother worries that it will be hard to get the expected return for raising the nephew. As a result, in the past, the maternal grandparents used to treat the children of their daughter only as guests, and few of them took on the responsibility of raising the grandchildren throughout the year. But now, it is more common that the maternal grandmother raises the son or daughter of her daughter. In Tancun Village, 36 children lived in their maternal grandparents' houses, accounting for 8.5 % of all the left-behind children.

Maternal grandparents raise the children of their daughter and assume the responsibilities that should be borne by the parents-in-law of their daughter, due to various reasons. First of all, it may be that the paternal grandparents have been dead or they are so old and infirm that they are unable to bear the responsibility of rearing the child. Secondly, it may be due to economic interests. In general, a child covers the living expenses of about 150 to 200 Yuan every month, so the child is arranged by his mother to go to her mother's home, which shows that the wife has a high position and greater power to make decisions in her family. Thirdly, it may be that the house of the paternal grandparents is too far away from the school where the child studies, and then it is more convenient for the child to go to school by living in the maternal grandparents' house. Finally, it is possible that the child's paternal grandparents have to engage in too heavy agricultural labor, or they have had many grandchildren to raise, so they shift the responsibility to the child's maternal grandparents.

In a word, when deciding who will raise the children staying at home, their parents tend to choose from the husband's family to the wife's family, namely, from the children's paternal grandparents to their maternal grandparents. However, with the improvement of the wife's status in the family and the modern influence of young couples who work in other cities, the familial concept is gradually changing. And it has been gradually common for the maternal grandparents to bear the responsibility of parenting the children of their daughter on behalf of their daughter.

In the author's questionnaire on 250 left-behind children, when asked the question "who do you live with now", 23 children wrote the maternal grandfather and maternal grandmother, accounting for 9.2 % of the total number of left-behind children surveyed. This figure basically coincides with the survey data of the author at Tancun Village.

Single-parent Rearing Model

As the saying goes, elders are treasures. The folk significance of this saying can be better reflected from the perspective of the rearing of left-behind children. The toughest family affair for the young people who go out to work is to arrange the rearing of their children. As mentioned earlier, migrant workers in Tancun Village are generally engaged in bottom-level jobs, and are poorly treated, so it is difficult for them to raise their children in the place where they work with sufficient economic strength.

As a result, if there are older people alive in the family, it can be very convenient and economical to solve the problem of caring for the left-behind children, and then the young couples can also rest assured to go out for work to make money. However, for some young couples whose parents are dead or whose mother is dead, they have no choice but to ask their children to live in the home of other relatives, or either the wife or the husband must stay at home to take care of their children. If one of the couple stays at home to take care of their children and the other is not at home all the year round, the rearing model will turn into the single-parent rearing model. Single-parent rearing can reduce the psychological and emotional imbalance of children due to the absence of the parent-child relationship, but because the mother is usually left at home to raise the children, the children are only tenderly loved by the mother but can not be instructed by the father. For this reason, a large number of left-behind children become naughty children out of control.

Rearing Model of Paternal Uncle

The villagers of Tancun Village have always had the idea of living with an extended family, believing that their nieces and nephews are as close as their children. For such a rural society that attaches great importance to kinship, the parents who are working outside feel assured to ask the husband's brothers to take care of their children staying at home. Emotionally, the uncles tend to make all-out efforts to bring up their nephews like their sons. What's more, such upbringing has economic returns. Generally speaking, uncles can obtain the living expenses of 150 to 200 Yuan every month for raising a child. In fact, rural people are able to support themselves in daily life, so the actual economic cost is less than 150 Yuan per month. As a result, uncles who raise the left-behind children can get kickbacks from the living expenses of the children.

An uncle of left-children told the author, "You know, the children's parents are away from at home, and my brother and sister-in-law believe me so they entrust me to raise their children. So I should be more responsible than raising my children. If the children are in bad condition, we are afraid that their parents working in Guangdong will be worried about them. If they do badly in their studies, or any other problem arises, I will be blamed for not taking good care of them as their elder uncle. They are my nephews, and I have never treated them badly in all aspects anyway. They eat the same as my children, and I have never been biased. We are uncles, so we either help them take care of their children, or try our best to look after them well if we are asked to help them. " However, the problem is that only a few uncles stay at home all year round, because they are also at the right age to go out for work. Even the uncles who stay at home may engage in heavy farm work or start a side business nearby, so they usually try not to help to raise them, but it turns to the paternal or maternal grandparents of the children to take care of them. After all, it is of a heavy responsibility to raise the children.

Rearing Model of Maternal Relatives

Besides the father's uncles, the relatives who can bear the responsibility of raising the left-behind children are the mother's brothers and sisters or the father's sisters. According to the survey, six children are raised by the mother's brother and sister or the father's sister, accounting for 2.4 % of the 250 left-behind children. It is not common that the mother's brothers and sisters or the father's sisters act as the guardians of the left-behind children, indicating that they are on the periphery of the kinship network of children. In terms of blood relationship with the left-behind children, the mother's brothers and sisters and the father's sisters are equal to the father's brothers, but the father's brothers belong to the same extended family with the left-behind children. According to the local people, the father's brothers live in the central room but the mother's brothers live in the corridor. The paternal concepts of my family and other families, insider and outsider have always been dominating people's behavior invisibly. At the same time, since the mother's brothers and sisters or the father's sisters usually live in other townships or villages, the left-behind children have to leave their villages if they live with these relatives. So, in general, the parents will not choose to ask these relatives to take care of their children when they go out to work.

However, it was found in the survey that many of the teachers in the town middle school and the cadres in the town government took on the responsibility of bringing up the children of their sisters or the children of their maternal cousins, mainly because it was more convenient for the children to go to school. However, in Tancun Village, only the children of four households were brought up by the brother or sister of the children's mother or by the sister of their father. Therefore, the kinship groups in this range do not play a significant role in the care of left-behind children.

Chapter 7 Concept, Behavior and Control of Fertility for Villagers of Tancun Village

Women's childbearing is an essential part of the reproduction of human society. Childbearing is not a simple biological behavior, but it is bound up with the culture, the environment, the ideology, and the way of production and life in a specific period. In order to analyze the phenomenon of childbearing of women in a community, it is necessary to explore the childbearing behavior, fertility concept of women and the connection between the two in the community. The fertility concept is the leading factor that influences childbearing behavior, while the changes in the fertility concept of women directly determine and influence the reproduction of the population in human society. It is generally believed that childbearing behavior is determined by the level of productivity and economic development, especially that economic poverty is the main reason for the rapid population growth in China. "Poverty tends to coexist with multiple births. The fundamental measure to transform the fertility concept of women in poverty-stricken areas is to improve the quality of the population, while requires the government to carry out scientific guarantee strategies in investment, mobility, non-agricultural development and information input and other aspects (Deng, 1993; Liu, 1993). "Generally speaking, women's concept of childbearing and its transformation involve extremely complicated factors, among which macro-social factors include ecological environment, natural resources, employment, economic development, national education, etc., while micro factors mainly include family structure, marriage mode, mode of family economy, consumer behavior, labor demand and pension mode (He, 1991).

There is no doubt that to investigate the childbearing concept and childbearing behavior of women in a community, we need to examine the following factors: first, it is economic factors, including women's employment, daily consumption, etc.; second, it is policy factors, among which the most important is to examine the only one-child policy and other relevant measures to implement the family planning policy; third, it is the social and cultural factors, including the values of traditional women, the views of marriage and family, the outlook on wealth, the outlook on filial piety culture, pension model and so on. If we regard childbearing as a cultural behavior, we must also explore the influence of various cultural phenomena, such as livelihood mode, family, clan, folk customs, rituals and symbols on the fertility concept.

Section 1 Evolution of the Traditional Fertility Concept of the Villagers at Tancun Village

The traditional Chinese ethics values filial piety, which means that, to fulfill the filial obligations is to have descendants. Therefore, the saying goes that having no male heir is the gravest of the three cardinal offenses against filial piety. It reflects that the Chinese people take their sons as their basic goal of life value. In the feudal agricultural society, the ideal families of extended families, composed of several generations of members and married brothers, came into being to care for the elderly, help each other, reproduce and raise the next generation, as well as the fight against the high mortality rate.

However, in Tancun village, no family has yet achieved the state of such an ideal family due to various reasons. First of all, in order to maintain an extended family with a considerable number of members, the family must possess substantial assets. The population of Tancun Village is dense, but natural resources such as land are relatively scarce, so the villagers do not have enough economic strength to ensure the long-term unity of the extended family without division. Second, it is not a simple matter to maintain the unity and harmony among many members of an extended family. An authoritative leader, namely, ahead with absolute prestige, is needed in the family. However, no such absolute authority has been found in an extended family in the history of Tancun Village to maintain the long-term stability of the family. On the contrary, the division is the family tradition of the villagers of Tancun Village. As the saying goes, every male should take a wife and every female should take a husband; the scallions will not sprout if they are not split, and the family will not flourish if it is not divided.

In the small-peasant society with low productivity, the tradition of family separation can better display the important social function of the structure and number of children in each small family in terms of the rearing of offspring and the support of the older people. Therefore, in order to realize these important social functions of small families, the traditional villagers of Tancun village, like most people in China, venerate the fertility concepts like early marriage and pregnancy, more children representing more blessings, and bringing up sons to support parents in their old age.

In the concept of Chinese people, marriage is the premise of childbearing; premarital pregnancy is such a matter of notorious reputation that it can not be accepted by society. Therefore, early marriage provides a logical premise for early childbirth. Among the 11 intermediate variables that influence fertility rate proposed by American sociologists Davis, K. and Blake, J. (Davis and Blake, 1956), three items are related to marriage, the age of marriage, the proportion of lifelong celibate and the childbearing period after marriage, including the interruption of marriage life caused by divorce, separation without a legal divorce or bereavement. In a relatively traditional rural community like Tancun Village, among the three intermediate variables of marriage, the age of marriage and the childbearing period after marriage should have the most significant impact on the fertility rate. The lifelong celibate is generally limited to only a few people who are physically or mentally abnormal, while separation or divorce is relatively uncommon. As for the period of childbearing after marriage, it was basically close to the natural state of childbearing before the strict implementation of the national family planning policy. It was not until the middle and late 1990s that people gradually accepted the legal provisions of late childbirth that the women at childbearing age must be older than 25 years old when giving birth to the second child, with a birth interval of 4 years (see Article 19 of the Regulations on the Population and Family Planning of Hunan Province).

In the past, the males in Tancun Village usually got married at about twenty years old and the females got married at about eighteen years old, and according to the custom, the man and the woman could get married only when the man was older than the woman. As the saying goes, in marriage, it is better for a man to be seven years older than a woman than for a woman to be one year older. For this reason, if a girl has not yet been married when she is over 22 years old, she may be ridiculed as an old maid. And when a girl is eighteen years old, more and more matchmakers will come to her house. The local people describe the scene of numerous matchmakers coming to the girl's house as breaking down the door. But when the girl reaches the age of 22, the number of matchmakers will gradually decrease, because it is difficult to match her with the right man over marriageable age. At this time, her parents will take the initiative to get her married.

After the founding of the People's Republic of China, the legal age of marriage announced was twenty years old for men and eighteen years old for women and then twenty-two for men and twenty for women. However, as far as the actual situation of Tancun Village is concerned, a considerable number of women married before they reached eighteen years old. The author interviewed 30 middle-aged women over 40 about the age of first marriage. The results showed that six of them had been married before they reached the age of 20, accounting for 20 % of the total, and that one of them was married at a minimum age of sixteen.

When asked why they got married so early, they answered "we should get married when we reach the marriageable age," "I did not think about why at that time but agreed to be engaged to him as I thought he was a right lifemate," and "If I get married early, I can have a baby early and enjoy a happy life early." Hence, it can be seen that the views of natural marriage and childbearing after physical maturity and the fertility values of early childbirth and early enjoyment are the two main driving forces for the local people to develop the concept of early marriage and early childbirth. According to demographic research, early marriage naturally prolongs the effective childbearing period of women of childbearing age, which is bound to affect the crude birth rate of the population. As a result, to control the population size, the law of marriage expressly prohibits the acts of early marriage.

However, in Tancun Village, the reason why these early married women were able to go through legal formalities was that the marriage registration was not strict at that time. As long as young couples had connections in their families, they could bluff it out in marriage registration even if they were under the legal age of marriage. Some young couples did not handle marriage registration. Instead, they first held the wedding ceremony according to the traditional customs, and started their businesses, and then applied for the marriage license after they reached the legal age of marriage. According to the local people, the legitimacy of marriage means not only that both men and women apply for a marriage certificate in the marriage registration authority of the government, but also that they must hold the wedding ceremony according to traditional customs. Moreover, they even believe that it is a personal affair for men and women to go through the marriage registration procedures, which is not well known by the public. Therefore, members of the community do not think that handling marriage registration formalities is equal to completing the wedding. On the contrary, if a young couple holds a wedding ceremony, which is considered as a civil legal marriage procedure, it is the marriage recognized by the whole society.

Nowadays, the females are better educated and the modernization is enhanced, and the females are more capable of getting involved in labor work with a large number of rural laborers flowing into cities for work. In this context, the phenomenon of early marriage has faded out. Nowadays, most of the young people get married when they are over 20 years old, generally around 22 years old. Among the 12 newly married women in 2005 and 2006, for example, one married at the age of 24, two married at 23, 3 married at 22, 4 married at 21, and 2 married at 20, indicating that none of them got married at an early age. According to the provisions of relevant laws, the marriage of the couples who marry when they are at least three years older than the legal age of marriage shall be considered as late marriage. Now, the proportion of young people who get married later in Tancun Village is 25 %, and 10 out of 12 respondents got married when they were older than the legal marriage age of 20, accounting for as high as 83.3 %. It is uncertain that nowadays, the concept of marriage and childbirth of young people in Tancun Village has shifted from early marriage and early childbirth to late marriage and late childbirth, which may be measured by a large number of demographic indicators. But we can assert that the concept of late marriage and late childbirth is beginning to take root in people's minds. A lot of young people have completed the cultural adjustment process of late marriage and late childbirth.

When they were asked "would you like to get married earlier or later?", most of them answered they would like to get married later. And they gave quite clear reasons: First of all, they do not want to take on family obligations too early, nor do they want to be restricted by family affairs too early. Secondly, they hope to make a living wandering from place to place when they are young, and then they hope to get married after they make some achievements in their careers. Thirdly, they want to get married after they have gained some economic strength, so that they can easily set up a new family on their own. Fourthly, they aspire after the freedom of personal life and do not want to be restrained by a spouse. The pursuit of the sense of well-being in personal life has become the value orientation of the young generation of the villagers of Tancun Village, which guides them to consciously and unconsciously carry out the policy of late marriage and late childbirth.

According to the local people, the family formed after the marriage of men and women can not be regarded as a complete family. They believe that to judge whether a family is complete or not, it must also have an important criterion of having children. And it is believed that the couples must give birth to a son, because for them, only in this way can they say that they have a complete family. Otherwise, the couples will be scolded as the ghost without sons. That is to say, according to the tradition, the villagers of Tancun Village attach great importance to the relationship between father and son, believing that the relationship between father and son is more important than that between husband and wife. The birth of an offspring is a necessary condition for the establishment and existence of the conjugal relationship. Only when a woman becomes a boy's mother can she have and maintain the status of a wife. As a result, some people are willing to give birth to a son at any cost. Preference for sons over daughters is an essential feature of the traditional birth culture in the local area.

DJG, 75, told the author, "It is almost the same to have sons and daughters, but we still want to have a son, and we will be happy to have a son. The daughter will get married when she grows up and then she will become a member of another family. Only by having a son, we will be able to continue our family line from generation to generation. If we have a son, our offspring will always have someone to keep the house. If there is no son, no one will guard the house after we die. " In the final analysis, the local people still pay more attention to the continuity of individual families, and they believe that only sons can carry on the family lineage, and can be regarded as the offspring. The blood lineage of male members can be passed on from generation to generation, which is the continuation of the family. Otherwise, the family will break off. In their views, daughters are excluded from the list of the offspring, to raise daughters is to do some help to other families, and to support daughters to go to school is to benefit other families. It is very embarrassing and painful for a person who has only daughters and no sons to live a life in the village.

The strong pursuit of sons is most prominent among middle-aged couples over the age of 45. When they were young, they were required not only to have sons, but also to have as many sons as possible, because they believed that they would be more blessed if they had more sons. In their view, if they do not have a son, they will never stop giving birth to children. There is no doubt that the extreme ideas of preference for sons over daughters and more sons representing more blessings have become rarely seen at present. Since the mid-1990s, new families have generally had only two children. According to the head of Tancun Village, "only a few families raise three children for the sake of having a son, and no families have four children nowadays. The implementation of family planning has been greatly improved compared with the past, and villagers can generally consciously abide by the family planning policy. "

In conversations with some young parents, the author learned that most of them think it is enough to have two children, but it is better to have a son and a daughter. A family with one son and one daughter is generally considered as an ideal family structure. On the one hand, it shows that the concept of equality between men and women has been deeply rooted in the minds of the people in such a rural community as Tancun Village, especially among the educated young people; on the other hand, it indicates that the idea of sons perpetuating the family line is still the indissoluble complex for the local people.

Due to the impact of the market economy and the general improvement of the living standards, the new generation of farmers has become aware of the fact that having many sons means heavy economic and spiritual burden, so carrying out the family planning policy has become a rational choice for them. The young people who have greatly broadened their horizons after working outside for a long time have learned that they need to make lifelong efforts to pay for the maintenance and education of a child, to manage the weddings of the adult children, to build enough houses and to purchase decent furniture. As a result, they argue that it is better to cultivate two children with all their hearts than to raise many children in a confused state. It can be seen that the traditional concepts of the villagers of Tancun Village, such as preference for sons over daughters and more children representing more blessings, are being adjusted and integrated with the modern consciousness of equality between men and women, bearing and rearing of better children. The family planning policy, mainly targeted at controlling the population, has allowed lots of local young farmers to adapt to the situation psychologically to some extent, and then they begin to change the traditional needs of childbearing from the calculation of its actual value.

However, the traditional concepts of preference for sons over daughters and carrying on the family lineage in childbirth still have deep soil. Many people don't think there are too many sons, but they still need one; they do not think it matters if the first child is a daughter, but expect that the second child is a son. Therefore, if the second child is a daughter, it is not uncommon to have an induced abortion. The head of the village said that, in the past few years (the 1990s), four couples in the village adopted the method of fake divorce to escape detection, because their second child was a daughter, but they also wanted a son, and they were afraid that if they were pregnant with a third child, they would be caught by the family planning cadres for abortion or ligation. On the surface, they went through the divorce procedures in the township government, and the woman also lived in her mother's home, but the man and the woman actually had contacts. After giving birth to a son, the man and the woman went through the remarriage procedures.

At the same time, in their cultural concept, giving birth to a child is not a private matter for a couple, but an important matter for an extended family. The parents who are still alive think that it is their great happiness to see that their family lineage can continue in their old age. For this reason, if a young woman can give birth to a son, her parents-in-law will treat her with great enthusiasm. On the contrary, if the woman gives birth to two daughters in a row, she will inevitably have a much tenser relation with her mother-in-law. The daughter-in-law of the village head, who has been married for only half a year, said to the author, "it does not matter if I have a son or a daughter, but I still hope to have a son. In that case, my mother-in-law will be delighted." It can be seen that the father-child relationship is not only the power to stabilize the relationship between husband and wife, but also the bridge to connect the ties between the father-in-law and the daughter-in-law, and between the mother-in-law and the daughter-in-law.

We can assume that the traditional fertility concepts of the villagers of Tancun Village, including the preference for sons over daughters and more children representing more blessings, are in the transition to the concept of family planning. On the one hand, due to the development of the economy, the guidance of policy and the popularization of education, the young generation has consciously or unconsciously changed the traditional fertility concepts. On the other hand, due to the pressure of traditional culture, especially the existence of old parents, young couples can not really get rid of the shackles of traditional concepts. As a result, the traditional fertility concepts, like preference for sons over daughters and carrying on the family lineage, are still deeply rooted in the minds of the local people.

Section 2 Expectations of Children and Changes in the Ideal Number of Children

As mentioned earlier, in the view of the local people, a family composed of a married couple can not be regarded as a complete family. They believe that to judge whether a family is complete or not, it must also have an important criterion of having children. When talking about the purpose of marriage with some young couples, the author found that there were mainly two purposes: first, the couple had developed profound feelings when they were dating, and love is an essential purpose for today's young people to get married; second, for childbirth, people get married to bear children. It indicates that young people have paid attention to the importance of love in the relationship between husband and wife when they set up a new family, but at the same time, they regard the birth of children as the inevitable outcome of love. They see children as an important link that maintains the relationship between husband and wife, while the children can inject new additives into the love between husband and wife, which not only conforms to the traditional concept of childbearing, but is also in line with the emotional needs of the local young couples.

Why must people give birth to children after they get married? It seems that there is no need to probe into the question. But it contains a noble value judgment of children, which means that children are highly valuable to their parents and the parents have high expectations for their future children. Children continue the lifeline of their parents, and they are the only hope for the family to carry on its family line and continue their lives. The prosperity of the family, the dependence of the older people, the source of the labor force and the spiritual comfort from the descendants all depend on the ability to have as many children as possible at a young age. It can be said that from the moment when a young couple gets married, the elders of the couple's families begin to look forward to having grandchildren. It is the greatest blessing in life for older people to have many children and grandchildren.

The older generation expects to be supported by their sons in their old age and depends on their sons to perpetuate their families. Thus, people believe that the more children they have, the more blessings they will receive. In the traditional agricultural society and in the era of planned economy, a high fertility rate tends to be accompanied by a high mortality rate due to the backwardness of medical conditions and other living conditions in rural communities. To be supported by the sons in the old age and allow the sons to perpetuate the family, the people used to give birth to as many children as possible to offset the risk that children may encounter. In Tancun Village, the older people over seventy years old used to give birth to five to eight children, at most ten children. Therefore, it was often seen that the mother-in-law and the daughter-in-law were confined in childbirth simultaneously. An example is the elder LDN in Tiantang Group. She is eighty-four years old, and she gave birth to twelve children and finally brought up ten children. Her youngest daughter is three years younger than her eldest grandson. However, the situation of the high fertility rate has been changed step by step with the improvement of economic conditions and medical technologies as well as the changes in the national population policy.

When the author talked about the value of the children with the young people, he could feel that the young people have become more indifferent to the idea of being supported by the children in their old age. Most of them believe that it is unreliable for them to rely on their children to live out their lives when they are old, and that it is better for them to accumulate more property when they are young so that they can provide for themselves in their old age. The villagers of Tancun Village hardly know anything about social welfare programs for the aged and government pension programs.

Their reason is that, first of all, in the future, the society and economy will become more modernized, and thus the children will migrate more frequently for their career after they grow up, making it difficult for the old parents to live together with their children and spend their lives in their old age. Even if children have such deep love for their parents, they do not necessarily have economic strength and time. Secondly, with the implementation of the family planning system, the number of children is now decreasing, and they will bear greater pressure to support their parents and parents-in-law after marriage in the future. For this reason, it is better not to put too much hope on relying on the children to provide for the aged. They also complain that the children are becoming more and more finicky, and they can hardly believe that now the children will be able to support the elderly with the same filial piety and a strong sense of responsibility as their elders did. Finally, from the current situation of supporting the parents by the villagers of Tancun Village, they believe that it is insignificant to provide for the aged by the children.

According to the general situation, the villagers of Tancun Village, in supporting their father or mother, should offer 300 kg of rice and five to six kg of rapeseed oil every year, pay fifteen to twenty Yuan every month and buy 7.5 kg to 10 kg of pork at the end of the year. The expenses of supporting the elderly are usually shared equally by the sons. Except for only a few wealthy children that may provide for the parents exceeding the criterion, it is not bad for the children in ordinary families to be able to bear the support expenses of parents on time and in full. As for the medical expenses and the presents for parents during the Spring Festival or other festivals, it depends on the actual situation. In fact, for most sons, after they have paid their parents the amount mentioned before and the things every year, they no longer buy presents for their parents at the Spring Festival or other festivals except for their parents' birthday. In their views, these gifts should be handled by the daughter, and it has nothing to do with the son. As a result, most of the villagers in Tancun Village believe that they can just support their lives if they are provided for by their children, and that it is impossible for the older people to obtain sufficient material satisfaction from their sons.

The expectation of young parents for their children has gradually weakened, but it does not mean that the value of children has become unimportant in the minds of the villagers of Tancun Village. It is just that, in the concept of young parents, they are not as dependent on their children as their grandparents or their parents to support them when they are old, but they have developed the awareness of supporting their old age by themselves. In fact, no matter the old or the young, they still want to have a son and a daughter, because children are still an indispensable condition to realize the traditional functions of the family under the current family-supporting model in China's rural areas.

None of the unmarried young people and the young couples who have not yet had children interviewed have indicated that they do not want to have a child, but rather that they intend to have at least two children in the future. According to Article 16 and Article 19 of the Regulations on the Population and Family Planning of Hunan Province, in the event that the husband and wife are both farmers, they can ask for having the second child four years after giving birth to a daughter. Therefore, from the perspective of the legal provisions, it seems that the control over the birth of two children is relatively loose, and then the common people can also easily accept the policy. Although the law stipulates that even if both husband and wife are farmers, they should not have the second child unless their first child is a daughter. But in fact, if a couple wants to have the second child when they already have a son, they can generally manage to have the second child smoothly as long as they pay a fine. In a word, the young couples in the local area are most looking forward to having two children. "One child is too lonely, two are the best," they said, "they can not afford to raise three children and they feel that it goes too much beyond their abilities if they have four children." For young people with ordinary economic conditions, it is obviously the result of their rational consideration to choose to have two children as the ideal number of children.

If there were no strict control by the family planning policy, would they choose to have only two children? The answer is uncertain. Some people say that even without the family planning policy, they would plan to have only two children, because they could not afford to have more children. They think it is better to have fewer children if they can not provide their children with better living conditions or fail to allow their children to receive better education, or the children do not have a promising future when they grow up. It reflects that young people now have a strong intention to bear and raise better children. However, some other people said that, they might choose to have more children if the family planning policy was not implemented. They believe that they can easily raise more children as long as they work harder. As the saying goes, they are worried about giving birth to a child rather than raising him. The villagers believe that as long as they give birth to their children, they will be able to raise them. It is evident that the traditional fertility concept regardless of cost still has an extensive influence.

In fact, in rural communities such as Tancun village where traditional culture is still very active, all kinds of cultural symbols, such as the pedigree, the Tomb Sweeping Day and family strength, etc., are encouraging the birth impulse of having as many children as possible. When opening the pedigree, the older people will get delighted in talking about the branch of their clan with a flourishing population as the ancestors make their power felt, while they feel sorry for the branch with a small population. When people go to hang the paper strings on the Tomb Sweeping Day, those ancestral tombs without offspring are in seclusion and seldom visited, while they can only accept other people's alms by putting a paper streamer into the soil to wave in the wind alone. At this time, if these people without sons were present, they would never imagine that they would face such a situation after they died as when they were alive. The author witnessed a person who had no son wanted to cry silently due to excessive emotion when the villagers went to sweep the tombs and hang the paper strings on the Tomb Sweeping Day.

Therefore, in rural communities in China, the value of children is not only reflected in the sense of being supported by the sons in the old age. To some extent, the value of children is given by culture, and the most important is the cultural significance of having a son to carry on the family name, which has been recognized by most of the scholars. In the study of birth culture in villages, Li Yinhe mentioned that the village culture has an important impact on the farmers' children being behavior. She summarized the influence of village culture on childbearing behavior in three aspects: first, great strength will arise due to a large number of people, thus encouraging the development of extended families with many children; second, because of the rule of competition, the villagers in the village tend to go all out to participate in the childbearing contest; third, due to the principle of convergence and the strong demand of people in the village for fairness, a force of mutual restriction has come into being (Li, 1994).

Therefore, if a very few young people have the intention to give up childbearing, they will be bound to be opposed by the whole family and the family members will try everything they can to force the young people to give up this terrible plan. DK, a young man in the village, is one of the special cases.

DK, 26, graduated from Zhuzhou Chemical Vocational Technology School, and he is now the sales manager of Hunan Resun Industry Co., Ltd. He has excellent conditions, as he has bought a house and an automobile. However, he once made a girlfriend with congenital heart disease, who was said to be sterile after the physical examination. DK, a well-educated man, did not care about that but was determined to get married to his beloved girlfriend. However, his family firmly opposed it when they learned about the situation. Almost all his relatives came out firmly against their marriage. In September 2006, while DK went back home to celebrate his father's birthday, his paternal grandfather, at his eighties, came forward and held a family meeting. He called all his relatives over, criticizing him for his misdeed and insisting that DK break up with his current girlfriend who was infertile. Later, the old man repeatedly instilled in DK the importance of giving birth to children and forced him to break up with his current girlfriend by writing letters, making phone calls and other ways. The letter is hereby quoted as follows:

To DK:

Hello! You are so talented and capable. You have been working since you graduated from a technical school. You have done well in your job and you are paid well. No one your age in our village can catch up with you. I am so proud of you!

However, only a few of those who are talented and capable may make mistakes. They only care about happiness for a while and never take into account how it will be when they are old. Now that you are still young, I must warn you that when you are old, you have to depend on your children's care. Your grandmother suffered gallstones in 1998 and she became seriously ill. Your father, your second eldest uncle and your youngest uncle asked your grandmother to go to Ningxia Province for medical treatment. Later, she was cured. If the three did not assume their responsibilities for your grandmother and left her ill, I am afraid she had died in 1998.

On April 4th last year, I had a heart attack. Your father rented a car and sent me to Changsha People's Hospital for medical treatment, and I was cured immediately. I am delighted that the greatest pleasure all my life is to have so many children and grandchildren. I always keep your care for me in mind. As the saying goes, a person with a son will get rid of poverty soon but the person without a son will go into poverty shortly after they become rich. We older people have a deep understanding of it. If an old man has no child, he will be a loser no matter how capable he used to be when he was in his youth.

There was an old college student in our yard, named Deng Guozhen. He had saved five thousand Yuan in the bank. When he died, he returned to this world several times but he did not give his passbook to others but waited until his sister's son came back from Ningxiang County to give the passbook to him. It is a sad ending for a person with no children when he is old. He didn't even know who to turn over his savings which were accumulated with his hard work for a long time. DK, I want to tell you with the facts around me: "those who have no children must be a poor guy when they get old. Remember to think it over!"

This time I came back from Ningxia Province and lived in your house for a few days. I told your mother that you should find the right spouse this year. Your mother sighed that she was too upset to say, as it was too embarrassing and torturous. Do you know why? It is because your current girlfriend does not have the ability to bear children at least. How can we not be annoyed as your elders?

At present, are you dreaming? Did you go the wrong way? Wake up! Someone wants to drag you into the sewage tank. I want to lift you up from the sewage pool and wash your whole body with clear water. Whether you agree or not, I am determined to grab you up from the sewage pool. Come on up, please! If you have difficulties when you come up, I will not be afraid of sacrifice. I will go down to the sewage pool and risk my life to lift you up. If you still refuse to come up at this point, I will not be afraid to hurt you, young man! In my heart, you have always been my obedient grandson. And I believe that you are and will be obedient to us. I hope you, as the eldest grandson, will soon give birth to a son as my great-grandson. It is the minimum criterion I have for you as your grandfather in his 80s.

I am looking forward to my children and grandchildren becoming prosperous in the future!

Grandpa

September 19, 2006

The letter is written with sincere words and earnest wishes of the grandfather, heavily exciting the mind. The old man talked about four points in his letter. First, a person who has no children, no matter how successful he was in his youth, is a loser; second, children have irreplaceable functions in providing for the aged parents and attending upon their funeral, while people who have children are happy, and people who have no children are pitiful; third, it is a misdeed to fall in love with an infertile woman, which must be corrected; fourth, if DK cannot correct his mistake, his grandfather will risk his life against him. It is understood that DK finally had to break up with his girlfriend due to strong opposition from his family. Although this is a special case, the fertility concept expressed by the old man in his letter is universal. During the discussion, the author discussed with other people about this incident, and they all said that if they encounter such a case, they will choose to give up, and they prefer to marry an ugly woman rather than a woman who can not bear children.

In a word, with the profound changes of economy and society, the traditional expectation of being supported by the children in the old age is beginning to weaken, the value of children to their parents is also beginning to decline, and the awareness of young people supporting their life in old age by themselves is gradually becoming prominent. However, due to the family pension model, the traditional symbols of the birth culture and the traditional expectations of the older people for childbearing, childbirth is not only of some living significance to the parents for being supported by their children in their old age, but also of profound cultural significance. Under the strong constraint of the national family planning policy, the ideal number of children of local farmers began to change from the original concept of having as many children as they can to two children as the ideal number. But if some people choose to be infertile, they will be strongly opposed by the local culture.

As a field case of a community that the villagers of Tancun Village has changed from the original concept of having as many children as they can to two children as the ideal number, to some extent, it also confirms the demographic transition theory propounded by Coale (Coale, 1973). Based on the detailed description of population change in Europe in the 19th century, the demographic transition theory puts forward that the population transition has gone through three stages: high birth rate and high mortality, high birth rate and low mortality, and low birth rate and low mortality. The main factors that promote the transformation of population or fertility are industrialization, the improvement of education level and modernization, among which industrialization has promoted the development of medical and health services, thus making the mortality tend to decline, while modernization and the change of lifestyle have gradually made the concept of small family more deeply rooted among the people. With the changes in production, consumption, culture and education in the concept of the small family, the pressure of high fertility rate has been resolved step by step, and the desire, concept and method of consciously controlling fertility have been gradually widely accepted.

Section 3 Persistence and Change of Gender Preference for Children

In patrilineal family organizations in China, sons inevitably play a crucial role. As the saying goes, having no male heir is the gravest of the three cardinal offenses against filial piety. In the traditional views, the heir is the son and only the son can carry on the family line. In the eyes of the villagers of Tancun Village, the son is the only reliable person to provide for the aged parents and attend upon their funeral and perpetuate the family.

From the actual situation of Tancun Village, the importance of the son is reflected in all aspects of daily life. When preparing for large-scale banquets for the parents at their birthdays, their sons should bear all the expenses, while the daughters seldom share the expenses. The daughters, who have been married, just need to present some clothes for their parents to show their filial respect, and buy some birthday cakes for their relatives. As for the number of birthday cakes distributed, it depends on the family's economic conditions of the daughters. The general standard is six or eight birthday cakes per household. If the parents are ill and hospitalized, the son is usually responsible for the medical expenses. Even if the daughter is required to pay, the premise must be that the daughter and the son-in-law are willing. The Spring Festival is the most ceremonious festival in the local area. Few old parents celebrate the festival with their daughters. Generally, they must stay at their sons' homes and spend the festival with their sons and grandchildren. According to the local custom, only the person who has no son spends the festival with his or her daughter, because he or she has no family to rely on. After the death of the parents, the funeral expenses must be jointly paid by the sons. A daughter is not obliged to pay for the funeral of her parents. The pedigree, which best reflects the history of the clan, generally only records the details of the sons, but seldom records anything about the daughters. Even if it is recorded, it is simply recorded under the title of the daughter's father as that "a daughter named XX was born, living in XX." It can be said that as long as the family must be inherited by the son, and the elderly parents must be provided for by the family, the importance of the son in the family and the parents' minds will not be reduced a lot, and the gender preference for sons over daughters will never change radically.

The local family planning administration department propagandizes that "the sons and the daughters are the same, and the daughter is also an heir." However, no matter the village cadres or the ordinary people, including the individual leaders of the family planning office of the local township government, all of them expect to have at least one son to continue the family line. For example, the deputy director of the town family planning office gave birth to two children, but according to the Regulations on the Population and Family Planning of Hunan Province, national public functionaries are not allowed to have two children. Before he became a father, Lao Hu, a former cadre of the family planning office, was said to be a just and stern person. He was very strict in the family planning work, and offended many people. But when he became a father, he did not hesitate to violate the family planning system to have a son as soon as he wanted because his first child was a daughter. His wife gave birth to a second child less than two years after the first. Officials even do so, let alone the ordinary people. Therefore, few people can get over the barrier of no son. It has been a permanent creed for both the old and the young to insist on having a son to carry on the family name.

Nevertheless, in recent years, the local preference for sons seems to be gradually weakening. Although slow progress is made, the change can be obviously seen.

First of all, the son is regarded as the only one to carry on the family line, but people no longer adhere to the idea of having as many sons as possible. Instead, the ideal state is to have a son and a daughter. The daughter is also wanted by everyone. As a person named DWJ said, "We always have rice and vegetables when we have a meal. it is not good if there is only rice but no vegetables. In the same way, if we have children, of course, we should have sons and daughters. It is better to have a son and a daughter. A daughter is actually better than a son and more filial to her parents. But if we have a son, we will receive a higher reputation and have a successor to perpetuate our family lineage."

Second, when giving birth to the first child, many people do not want it to be a son, but to be a daughter, which is different from the traditional concept of having a son early. According to Article 16 and Article 19 of the Regulations on the Population and Family Planning of Hunan Province, in the event that the husband and wife are both farmers, they can ask for having the second child four years after giving birth to a daughter. So if a couple's first child is a daughter, they can have a second child four years later. And the second child must be a daughter. It is forbidden to identify the sex of a fetus for non-medical purposes and terminate pregnancy artificially, but in fact, it is a simple task to identify the sex of a fetus through B-ultrasound radiography. If the couple does not want to have extra-plan births, the wife should have an abortion once they find out that the second child is a daughter, so that they can prepare to have the third child. If the third child is a son, they can give birth to him smoothly, so as to have a son and a daughter.

Finally, the new pedigree compiled by two major families in the local area no longer discriminates against the female descendants, and the female descendants are included in the pedigree as well as the male descendants, and they are treated equally as the male descendants. In the regulations of the newly revised pedigree of the Deng clan, it is clearly stated that "Family planning is the basic policy of the state. We should achieve equality between men and women. Women should have the right to inherit the family business and settle down freely. If the husband settles down at the wife's house, no one is allowed to block, discriminate or crowd out, and the surname of their children shall be chosen by the husband and the wife themselves."

Section 4 Practices of Birth Control and Family Planning Policy in Tancun Village

As mentioned above, the change of the traditional fertility concept and birth behavior of the villagers of Tancun Village is to some extent caused by the tight constraints of the family planning policy of the state, and the outcome of the mutual adjustment of the national culture and the local culture. It can be said that the family planning policy of the state and the new birth culture advocated by it can be understood and cooperated by the local people, which is a rational choice made by the local people after weighing and taking into account all aspects from the perspective of the local cultural context. Like other places in China, the villagers of Tancun Village can consciously abide by family planning and rationally implement birth control after suffering various hardships for a long time.

In the traditional small-peasant society, people aspire after the goal of more children representing more blessings, which is basically in a natural state of childbirth. Among the social norms of childbearing, there are more social norms encouraging childbearing than those restricting childbearing. For instance, the early marriage and women's status are affected by the childbirth of women, or women's infertility can be a reason for divorce or concubinage to encourage childbearing, while there are very few social norms restricting childbearing. This kind of fertility concept is suitable for the situation of backward agricultural production, medical treatment and science and technology at that time.

Fei Xiaotong made a brilliant interpretation of this: "if people want to make sure that they will not die without descendants, they must give birth to children. And because China has entered the patriarchal society for a long time, people are determined to have a son. In the past, since the medical and health conditions and facilities are less developed, children may not be able to grow up and give birth to the next generation of successors. So people have to give birth to more children to better guarantee that they can have successors (Fei, 1985)."

After the foundation of the People's Republic of China, although the social system and economic foundation have undergone fundamental changes, the fertility concept and childbearing behaviors concerning population reproduction have not been transformed significantly. Even under the encouragement of political ideology at that time, people's childbirth behavior was expanded in an unprecedented way. Data show that from 1950 to 1954, the fertility rate of total population increased from 5.81 ‰ to 6.82 ‰, and that the natural growth rate of population increased from 19.00 ‰ to 24.79 ‰, with a net increase of 51.7 million in the four years (National Bureau of Statistics, 1988).

At that time, people's unrestrained childbirth was inseparable from the political concept that a large population is good. In the initial stage after the founding of the People's Republic of China, Mao Zedong proposed that "Of all things in the world, man is the most precious. Under the leadership of the Communist Party, any miracle in the world can be created as long as there are people." Moreover, he proposed that "China has a large population, which is a great deed. And we can find proper solutions no matter how many times the population increases." "I am convinced that revolution can change everything," he said confidently, " A new China, where a large population will live a better-off life with abundant resources and prosperous cultures, will come soon (Mao, 1991)." Driven by a series of arguments that a large population is good and that there is strength in numbers, the state of natural fertility of Chinese people has not been changed in the slightest, and even the practices that control the birth behavior, such as induced abortion and contraception, have been strictly restricted (Ministry of Public Health of the Central People's Government and the Department of Public Health of the People's Revolutionary Military Committee, 1950; Subcommittee of Education and Culture of the Government Administration Council of the Central People's Government of the People's Republic of China; 1952).

The encouragement of political ideology coincides with people's traditional fertility concept, which leads to a sharp increase in the population in the 1950s and 1960s. During this period, women of childbearing age who were at the booming stage of childbirth would have four or five children, or even seven or eight children. Many people in their 70s recalled, "In the 1950s and 1960s, no one was in charge of childbirth, and people could give birth as much as they wanted. It's our own business to have children anyway. But at that time, life was so hard. When a woman gave birth to a child, she even could not eat any food with oil during her confinement." It can be seen that although the economic life was very difficult at that time, people still chose to give birth to as many children as they could because of their pursuit o more children representing more blessings and many hands making light work.

Mao Zedong clearly put forward the concept of family planning and the idea of "gradually reaching universal family planning" in 1957 and the CPC Central Committee and the State Council jointly issued the Instructions on Promoting Family Planning in December 1962. However, according to the old people, family planning started in the 1970s in Tancun Village. They said, "We also heard some programs promoting birth control on the radio before the 1970s, but it seems that no one came to implement them or held a general meeting to convey the policy of family planning. After the 1970s, the family planning policy began to be executed to the letter. At that time, the leaders used to stress it during the general meeting. At that time we all knew the policy of late marriage, the prolonged interval of childbirth and the birth of only two children. At that time, if some people had too many children, the cadres of the group would inform them to have them ligated when they gave birth to the second or third child. And mainly the man was ligated. If a person was notified but was not ligated, the village committee would deduct his grain rations."

It can be seen that in Tancun village, the practice of family planning became executed in strict rotation since the 1970s. At that time, in the era of the planned economy, the production team exercised control over the means of life and production for the members of the commune. As a result, as soon as the leaders of the production team mobilized, the parents in the families with more than one child would have to have the operation of ligation and sterilization automatically. " At that time, the economy was backward and life was hard. After people had two or three children, they did not want to give birth to any more children. If the parents had one daughter and one son, they would consciously have the operation of sterilization."

DSY, an elder man who worked as a teacher all his life in the middle school, recalled, "When I attended the meeting of all the teachers in the people's commune in the office of our people's commune, the leaders asked several teachers and me to take the lead in taking the operation of ligation with other teachers. I had two sons and one daughter, so I promised to go to the hospital without saying anything. And I did not even tell it to my wife." Judging from the conversations with the elder people, people at that time seemed to hold a calm attitude toward sterilization, and they hardly had much psychological resistance. The main reason is that at that time, the family planning system was not very strict, and people who had sterilization generally had two or three children and had at least one son. In addition, in the era of collective economy, the production team mastered the economic line of every member, and anyone who dared to violate the family planning system would be deprived of the basic grain rations. For this reason, it was relatively smooth to implement the family planning policy.

After the 1980s, the family was re-established as an independent social and cultural unit of production and life with the implementation of the household contract responsibility system, the private ownership of means of production, the domestication of production and operation, and the self-sufficiency of product distribution. As a result, the family's ability to the self-control of fertility was also strengthened. At the same time, the family planning policy of the state was tightened from late marriage, prolonged interval of childbirth and the birth of only two children to the one-child policy, and began to advocate the policy of one child for every couple and the policy of late marriage and late childbirth, fewer and better births. The idea of one child for every couple is highly diverse from the traditional fertility concept in rural areas and the cultural context and the fertility psychology faced by farmers, which is strongly resisted by farmers. In addition, government officials were too crude in implementing the family planning policy. From the 1980s to the mid-1990s, the cadres were in a strained relationship with the masses in terms of family planning. At that time, the policy and the operating methods of family planning were divorced from the reality of the countryside, and the family planning policy was not internalized into the cultural ideas of the local people, and it failed to make the local people accept and understand the family planning system from the bottom of their hearts. Therefore, extra-plan births were extremely serious at that time.

In Tancun Village, except for a few people in exile for the sake of childbearing, others dealt with the supervision of the officials from the office of family planning and the cadres of the village committee by means of hiding. They either go to their relatives' house to efface themselves, or hide in the old houses which have been vacant for half a year so as not to make them discovered by the people around and not to let her traces out. In a word, they will never give up until they give birth to a son. In this period, it is the most difficult period for rural areas to implement the family planning policy, and it is also the most painful period for farmers to change their traditional fertility concepts to adapt to the family planning system.

It was not until the late 1990s and the early 21st century that the implementation of family planning tended to truly relax in Tancun Village, and could be well understood and cooperated by the local people. Deng, director of the town family planning office, said, " on the one hand, because the leading cadres corrected the implementation methods of family planning work, so that they could avoid rude practices. On the other hand, the current regulations on family planning take into account the actual situation in rural areas and then the policy is more easily operated. If the first child of a rural couple is a daughter and they really need to have a son, they can apply for a second child only four years after thc first birth. At the same time, people now live a better-off life and become more open-minded, so they usually do not want to have too many children. There are fewer and fewer people who are truly illegal in childbearing." At Tancun Village, it has become so common that the couples have two children, while few young couples have three children. As discussed earlier, the local people are most looking forward to having two children. And the local family planning department controls the number of children for the local people within the scope of two children, and then it can undoubtedly be well cooperated by the local people.

Chapter 8 Conclusion

Child rearing is an inevitable eternal topic in the field of folklore and anthropology. Rearing is an important way to ensure the continuity of human beings, maintain culture, and complete the process of social production and reproduction. The reason why human beings are human beings is that they can take advantage of a set of cultural mechanisms to ensure that they can be passed down from generation to generation without interruption. These cultural mechanisms not only guarantee the connection of consanguinity and kinship in the family, but also guarantee the continuity of the human genes and race. To achieve this continuity, human beings first need a cultural system to acquire food, and then need a reproductive system to ensure the production of human life for generations. Reproduction itself is a biological process, but to make the smooth progress of reproduction, we must maintain the process with a set of cultural mechanisms. Hence, reproduction is a cultural system, mainly involved in cultural issues. As Bronislaw Kaspar Malinowski stated, "Reproduction has become a cultural system in human society. The continuity of race is not satisfied by pure physiological behavior and physiological function, but the outcome of a set of traditional rules and a set of related material and cultural devices and activities. This cultural system of reproductive function is organized by various institutions, such as standardized courtship, marriage, parent-child relationship and clan organization (Malinowski, 1940)."

Therefore, child rearing is not only to reproduce human lives and provide the food to maintain life, but also to include a series of cultivation methods, also known as acculturation methods of socialization methods. It should go back to the essential topic about what man is. Man is a symbolic animal, and the essential symbol of man is the symbol. As a result, mankind is always faced with the acculturation of a group of symbolic cultural symbols in the field where it lives, so that it can achieve the goal of transmitting the cultures among different regions. And then, to investigate the child rearing system of a region, we must make a comprehensive description of its local cultural phenomena, including customs, beliefs, taboos, family education, marriage practice, values and all kinds of emerging cultural events caused by social changes, and then understand the child rearing from the holistic point of view of cultural symbols.

First of all, the rearing system imparts and inherits the unique local cultural symbols. In the process of child rearing, these local cultural symbols are being remembered, recognized and reproduced.

According to Ernst Cassirer, culture is a unique symbol system. Such symbols are the accumulation of the experience of the local people in the process of survival and practice for generations, which not only integrate the universal cultural nutrition, but also summarize the experience of the local people themselves. When a person comes to the world, it is only a biological person and needs to be shaped by the culture through a group of processes before becoming a true person from a cultural perspective. Each place has a unique culture-shaping system. From the moment the baby is born, the shaping system gradually hangs the baby on the net of meaning, which is woven by the culture of the local people themselves (Geertz, 1999), such as the relationship between the birth time of a baby and the eight characters and the baby's fate, the disposal of the placenta after the birth of a baby, a series of life etiquette experienced by a newborn, and a variety of taboos and beliefs associated with the growth of a child. Moreover, it transmits the cultural standards of the local people to the children, such as respecting the elders, learning to use the traditional kinship terms to integrate themselves into the families, and telling them about profound myths to cultivate their moral sentiments, which all instill the gigantic and irresistible symbolic violence to the growth of each child (Bourdieu and Passeron, 2002). Therefore, in the process of growing up, children are constantly trained to re-recognize, understand and memorize the cultural symbols which are passed down from generation to generation, and internalize them into their own experience and knowledge.

Rearing behavior occurs in daily life, which seems to be common but almost goes deep into all levels of local culture. Through rearing, a child can not only be socialized in a cultural space, but young parents can also learn the knowledge of raising children and understand the cultural standards for them as parents. It conforms to the emotional needs of the parent-child relationship, and it is also a technique to complete the continuity of human beings from generation to generation. Through the practice of rearing behavior, the young parents can receive cultural training once again, so that the knowledge about rearing that they have inherited from their ancestors can be reconstructed. The local cultural symbols are reproduced on the young people once again in all aspects of daily life, such as the criterion for the selection of a right spouse, the taboos that a pregnant woman should abide by, the living rules that should be followed according to practices, and the knowledge on ensuring the smooth delivery of a pregnant woman, and the ways to take care of and feed the infants and to discipline children to achieve the training goals.

The rearing action embodies the interaction between children and their parents. The rearing of parents enables their child to become a cultural person, while the growth of the child itself advances the further socialization of its parents to further accept the influence of local knowledge. Some traditional folk beliefs, taboos and rituals are superstitious for those young people who are not scared of anything, and they are dismissed as bad habits. But almost everyone, as long as they get married and give birth to children, tends to cautiously abide by the taboos about pregnant women, while none of them dares to go against the taboos carelessly. Those old women may warn their young daughter-in-law or daughter with their personal experience and what they have seen and heard for years that anyone who does not abide by these taboos will eventually suffer adverse consequences when it grows old. Taboo, as a living law, has been recognized and reproduced again in the practices of women's pregnancy and childbirth.

In Tancun Village, in order to ensure the safe growth of children, people can carefully follow the taboos and rituals, such as Qi Shui and

Shu Wan ceremonies. People have developed some local experience when they treat their children's illness or prevent their children from falling ill, such as herbal practitioners, witches or Shui Shi. The diversified medical model and the living strategy of the antidote of both witchcraft and medicine have always been the rational choices for the local people. Cultural symbols of this sort have been continuously remembered, understood and practiced in daily life. Moreover, some cultural symbols are even dismissed as superstitious in feudal times. If there is no special practice to remember and identify these symbols, they are bound to get fractured forever. And rearing behavior itself is a type of cultural training for both young parents and children, which runs through the most important stage of life. In this process, cultural symbols realize their reproduction in the transmission from generation to generation.

Secondly, child rearing is the fusion of tradition and modernity.

The most popular theory of family modernization at present holds that after industrialization, the family will undergo structural changes, and that the original educational and economic functions of the family will be replaced by schools and economic organizations; that the significance of family traditions and customs will be degraded to the point of insignificant; that the concept of conjugal family promotes the personal value and well-being higher than the continuity of the bloodline and the family; that the gender egalitarianism will focus on the independence of each individual within the family; that the individuals and individual families will get rid of the control of the kinship network, because the help and services provided by the kinship groups can now be purchased from the market (Goode, 1984).

There is no denying that the development of modernization will have an impact on the inherent mode and concept of marriage and family as well as the related child-rearing pattern. Since the reform and opening up, Chinese society has entered a high-speed transformation period from the traditional agricultural society to the modern industrialized society, the economic system, social structure, social relations and patterns of social life in China have undergone dramatic changes, and there will be continuous contradictions and conflicts arising in the corresponding values. However, when we observe the substantial changes in Chinese society, we should also pay attention to the tenacious vitality of some cultural traditions related to human production and reproduction. As Yih-Yuan Li pointed out after the study and analysis of the changes of family organizations and related rituals in the highly modernized rural communities of Han people in Taiwan, regardless of the scale of the changes, he still emphasized some unchanging principles, including the principle of parent-child relationship, the principle of lineage relationship and the principle of power relationship (Li, 2002).

Marriage represents the beginning of a new generation of human life. But to get a new life, parents have to suffer a great many hardships and experience numerous anxiety and fear. Birth etiquette, childbearing taboos and faith play an irreplaceable role in balancing fear and alleviating the anxiety of parents.

In order to ensure the smooth delivery of pregnant women and the smooth growth of babies, the villagers of Tancun Village, on the one hand, believe in modern medical technology, while on the other hand, they rely on traditional etiquette and taboos. Modern medicine only solves technical problems, while traditional etiquette and taboos support pregnant women and their families from the perspective of psychology. For example, folk herbal practitioners, folk medical methods and so on have also offered practical help to the local people to some extent. Especially for newly born babies, their lives are extremely fragile. Even in modern society, people can not be absolutely sure whether the children can grow up healthily. For this reason, childbearing taboos and faith healing provide more reliable preventive means and concepts to relieve the worries about the unknown world. Hence, it can be seen that modern knowledge plays an essential rule in the special cultural domain of child rearing, but it is because of the popularity of the close relationship between child rearing and human reproduction that the traditional cultural norms are among the most tenacious in this domain. In the whole process from the wedding ceremony of the local people to the growth of the children to adulthood, religion, taboos, beliefs and a series of folk knowledge, which are bound up with the birth, rearing and education of children, can never be replaced by modern knowledge.

When it comes to the modern changes in child rearing, perhaps the most remarkable performance is that the strict implementation of the national family planning policy suppresses the traditional childbearing behavior and concept of farmers. There is no doubt that it is also inextricably linked with economic modernization and marketization. In Tancun Village, there are no prominent materials showing that the better-off a couple is, the more indifferent the husband and wife will be to the issue of childbearing. On the contrary, some couples with better economic conditions are even more driven to give birth to children. However, it is certain that the traditional concepts of bringing up sons to support parents in their old age and more children representing more blessings have been gradually fading out in the hearts of young farmers. However, nowadays, modernization is increasingly strengthened, and most farmers in Tancun Village are faced with intense conflicts between traditional and modern values in terms of an ideal number of children and gender preference for sons and daughters.

The example of Tancun Village indicates that the demand of farmers for childbearing is a cultural combination that internalizes social and cultural values, institutional norms, and the emotions and actual interests of individuals and families. It is a structural dynamic system composed of various cultural interests and real (material) interests. From the perspective of the various situations of the villagers of Tancun Village on the issue of fertility, the contradictions and conflicts of inner choice, in fact, the value and social needs arising in the reproductive motivation of the local people are not in harmony with the national public policy (the family planning system), the level of local economic development and the modernization level of the individuals.

Therefore, in terms of people's fertility concept and fertility behavior, they not only keep the inertia of traditional birth culture, but also have to deal with fertility problems rationally from the actual

reproduction of cultural capital and social capital of the previous generation can be displayed on the next generation, which is called indirect reproduction different from economic capital reproduction by Pierre Bourdieu. Non-institutional education can be divided into family education, religious education, traditional cultural habits and other means of acculturation for individuals. It can be seen that the reproduction of education is actually an outcome of socialization. Through socialization, children from diverse family backgrounds can inherit the cultural capital and social capital from the older generations, so that the gap between the members in society can be passed on from generation to generation and then the goal of the ideology of the specific ruling class can be achieved.

There are two key stages in the reproduction function of education. One stage is early socialization, which mainly depends on family education for preschool children. It contains both the conscious guidance of parents for their children and the unconscious imitation of the children from their parents, in which both the parents and the children are subtly affected. As the authorities of education, parents instill their own subjective will and the cultural criteria of communities into their children through family education and actions. In case that the children obtain the habitus of the elders, it can be said that they almost achieve the purpose of the reproduction of cultural capital at this stage. The other stage is school education. At this stage, it is mainly teachers, as substitutes of parents, who exercise disciplinary power (Foucault, 2003) against students with the help of the standardized classrooms, textbooks, rules and regulations and teachers' personal knowledge system.

However, both family education and school education take place in a certain field, while the community, the school and the family are the main fields for children to complete socialization, providing a set of complete symbolic rules for the socialization of children. It is another form of education, which is social education in a broader sense. Through family education, school education and social education, the individual obtains a set of dispositions, and internalizes external social rules, social structure schema and cultural values into his or her dispositions and habitus. In the investigation of the socialization of children, the field is an important factor. The field consists of space field and culture field. Due to the differences in the space field and culture field, various authorities of education are bound to present varied historical characteristics in the game of power relations in the course of children's education. From the perspective of the development and changes of children's education in Tancun Village, it just reflects the taste of the times in the reproduction of education in dual aspects under different social and economic backgrounds, i.e., different cultural and social fields.

The villagers of Tancun Village have attached importance to education for a long time, which is inseparable from the brilliant achievements that they made in the era of imperial examinations. In particular, in the Deng family, according to the pedigree, 52 members of the family obtained the qualifications of Linsheng (廪生, scholars who live on government grants) and higher ranks since the family first settled here, including three Jinshi and one Juren. With such remarkable achievements, many of the villagers of Tancun Village always believe in the ancient maxim that nothing is more important than learning. For this reason, before the market economy swept in, learning had been regarded by the local people as a major channel to achieve the upward flow of their social identity.

In such a community field, as non-institutional forms of education, family education and social education carry out cultural arbitrariness, which is mainly the tradition of the clan-oriented culture by glorifying and illuminating the ancestors and respecting the norms of etiquette. Moreover, the cultural arbitrariness has always been a primary content of family education and social education of the villagers of Tancun Village. However, limited by the social and economic conditions at that time, only a few children from rich families could really have access to formal education, and the vast majority of children were in the state of illiteracy and semi-illiteracy. In the process of children's growth, the concept of familism is instilled into their minds in an extremely routine way. Filial piety, conscience and various ideas condensed in kinship terms all focus on the family as the spiritual core, and they have become the fundamental acculturation force in the process of children's socialization.

After the founding of the People's Republic of China, with the fundamental change of the entire political environment, the villagers of Tancun Village established its own primary school, and the state-led institutional education began to popularize. Since then, the children at Tancun Village have gradually been engaged in the campaign to eliminate illiteracy and the school has become the primary field for children to be socialized. The school is the state inside the village, and the courses offered in the school mainly realize the life within the scope of the state regime (Li, 1999). Family education and social education also mainly point to the atmosphere of social movement and political life at that time. From the games of children fighting field battles and field hopping, we can see the influence of the ideologies in the political consciousness of the state, such as land reform, class struggle and advocating soldiers, on the children.

The host culture of the state, playing a dominant role, can be reproduced through school education. With the promotion of collectivism in community life, equalitarianism in distribution and social consciousness of equality between men and women, education equality had been realized for boys and girls in Tancun Village prior to the implementation of the reform and opening up. The sons and daughters all went to school to receive an education. However, due to the politicization of the educational content and many restrictions of the examination system at that time, most of the children left off their studies and went home to work in agriculture after finishing their primary or junior high school studies. Therefore, the education system at that time just cultivated one batch of the educated members of the production team after another.

Since the reform and opening up, with the recovery of the college entrance examination system, it has become the primary means for the children at Tancun Village to transform their social identities by being admitted to college and technical secondary school. Since all kinds of social functions of the family have been recovered and the education authority of the parents has been strengthened, the parents can effectively control their children to strive for the goals that the parents have designed. Moreover, the parents teach their children based on the creed that to spare the rod is to spoil the child. If the father physically punishes his disobedient child, he will never be criticized by the people around him. On the contrary, if many children are admitted to colleges due to the physical punishment of their children, it will be regarded as the successful experience of disciplining the children by the local people. When a child is admitted to the university, he or she can join the ranks of government staff members and consume commodity grain, so as to get rid of the social status of his or her parents as farmers, which has great attraction for rural people. The traditional cultural concept that he who excels in learning can be an official that has been reshaped in another form.

However, since the late 1990s, with the rapid increase of migrant workers in Tancun village, the rural migrant economy (Zhou, 2006) has become the primary economic pillar of the local area. Going out to work provides more opportunities for local farmers to enter the city and get jobs other than agricultural ones. In addition, the high cost of going to university is not necessarily in direct proportion to the future return (i.e. education benefit), so the local people have gradually lowered their enthusiasm for educating their children to study hard. Both adults and the children all intend to take the migrant work as their main way out. Against the background of the rural migrant economy, the changes in the community economy and family life have made the children's school education fall into an embarrassing situation. Moreover, many teachers think that it is tough to teach and manage the children now, and that they can hardly get cooperation from the parents. On the one hand, parents also want their children to receive higher education as much as they can and pay attention to their children's school education. But on the other hand, because they are out to work all year round, they fail to manage their children's learning in an effective way. As an invisible force, the lifestyle of parents' working outside leads children to such a value that making money as migrant workers instead of going to school. While TV, VCD, Internet and video games allow children to learn new knowledge, they also have a negative impact on the learning of a considerable number of children, making it more difficult to implement school education. Children's school education is also faced with severe challenges.

References

Barrett, M., and Mclntosh, M. (1991). The Anti-social Family, 2nd ed. London: Verso.

Becker, G. S. (1985). The Economic Analysis of Fertility Rate. Beijing: Peking University Press, 170.

Becker, G. S. (1987). A Treatise on the Family. Beijing: Hua Xia Publishing House, 6-127.

Benedict, R. (1987). Patterns of Culture (X.Z. He et al., Trans.). Beijing: Hua Xia Publishing House.

Benedict, R. (1988). Patterns of Culture (W. Wang, Trans.). Shanghai: SDX Joint Publishing Company, 20.

Benedict, R. (2005). The Chrysanthemum and the Sword (W. H. Lv et al., Trans.). Beijing: The Commercial Press, 2005.

Berts, M. and Schirrmann, P. (1991). Society and Childbirth (S. W. Zhang, Trans.). Tianjin: Tianjin People's Publishing House.

Blau, P.M. (1988). Exchange and Power in Social Life (F. Sun et al., Trans.). Beijing: Hua Xia Publishing House, 164.

Boas, F. (1999). Anthropology and Modern Life (S. Liu et al., Trans.). Beijing: Hua Xia Publishing House.

Bourdieu, P. (1997). Cultural Capital and Social Alchemy (Y. M. Bao, Trans.). Shanghai: Shanghai People's Publishing House, 202.

Bourdieu, P. (2003). Le sens pratique (Z.H. Jiang, Trans.). Nanjing: Yilin Press,.

Bourdieu, P. and Passeron, J. C. (2002). La reproduction. Éléments pour une théorie du système d'enseignement (K.C. Xing, Trans.). Beijing: The Commercial Press, 13-14.

Bourdieu, P and Wacquant, L.J.D. (2004). An Invitation to Reflexive Sociology (M. Li & K. Li, Trans.). Beijing: Central Compilation & Translation Press.

Bowie, F. (2004). The Anthropology of Religion: An Introduction (Z. Jin, et al., Trans.). Beijing: Beijing: China Renmin University Press, 182.

Bronman, B.L. (1982). The Early Years in Childhood Education(2nd ed). Houghton Mifflin Company, 368.

Casey, J.(1989) The History of the Family, Oxford. Burke, P. (2000). History and Social Theory (P. Yao et al., Trans.). Shanghai: Shanghai People's Publishing House, 66.

Cassirer, E. (2004). An Essay on Man (Y. Gan, Trans.). Shanghai: Shanghai Translation Publishing House.

Cheal, D. (2005). Sociology of Family Life (Y. N. Peng, Trans.). Beijing: Zhong Hua Book Company, 11-37.

Chen, Guyuan (1961). The Marriage History of China. Taiwan Commercial Press, 33.

Chen, Zhen and Chen, Junjie (1997). Cultural Marginality of Fertility of the Chinese Peasants. Population Research, Vol. 21 (6): 18-25.

Chen, Zi'ai and Li, Xinwu (2004). The Relationship between Zhang Wulang and Chiyou and Panhu. Proceedings of the Third Meishan Culture Symposium in China (Ma, Tieying, ed.). HongKong Heavenly Steed's Books Ltd., 11-23.

Clifford, J., and Marcus, G. E. (1986). Writing Culture: The Poetics and Politics of Ethnography. Berkeley: University of California Press.

Coale, A. J. (1973). The Demographic Transition. International Population Conference, Vol. 1.

Coleman, J. (1988). Social capital in the creation of human capital. American Journal of Sociology, 94 - 110.

Coleman, J. S. (1999). Foundations of Social Theory (F. Deng, Trans.). Beijing: Social Sciences Academic Press, 351-367.

Coodley, C.N.(1999). Human Nature and Social Order (F.Y. Bao & Y. Wang, Trans.). Beijing: Hua Xia Publishing House.

Crandon- Malamud, L.(1991). From the Fat of Our Souls: Social Change, Political, and Medical Pluralism in Bolivia. Berkeley: University of California Press.

Dai, Sheng (1998). The Book of Rites. Beijing: Blue Sky Press.

Damast, A.M., Tamis-LeMonda, C.S., Bomstein M.H. (1996). Mother-Child Play: Sequential Interactions and the Relation between Maternal Beliefs and Behaviors. Child Development, Vol.1996(67):1,752 - 1,766.

Darwin, C. R. (1986). The Descent of Man, and Selection in Relation to Sex. Beijing: The Commercial Press, 141.

Davis, D. and Harrell, S. (1993). Introduction:: The Impact of Post-Mao Reforms on Family Life. D. DAVIS S. HARRELL. eds. Chinese Families in The Post-Mao Era . Berkeley: University of California Press. 1-24.

Davis, K. and Blake J. (1956). Social Structure and Fertility: An Analytic Framework . Economic Development and Cultural Change , Vol. 1956 (3).

Deng, Banglin (1993). Fertility Concept and Poverty. Population Research, Vol. 1993 (2): 55-57. Liu, Changmao (1993). Research on the Transformation of Fertility Concept in Poverty-Stricken Areas in China. Population and Economics, Vol. 1993 (6): 10-16.

Deng, Qiyao (1992). Thinking Structure of Chinese Mythology. Chongqing: Chongqing Publishing House.

Deng, Xingliang and Zhong, Xiaoci (2001). Shaoyang Culture. Beijing: China Federation of Literary and Art Circles Publishing House.

Deng, Xuqing and Xiao, Jingsong. Local Annals of Huangtingshi Town, Shaoyang County (Reviewed Draft), 2-26.

Department of Population, Social, Science and Technology Statistics, National Bureau of Statistics, the People's Republic of China (2002). Main Data of the Fifth Population Census of China 2000. Beijing: China Statistics Press.

Department of Statistics of Shaoyang County (2006). Statistical Yearbook of Shaoyang County 2005. 283 - 287.

Ding, Shiliang and Zhao, Fang (1991). Section of South-Central China of the Collection of Local Chronicles and Folklore in China (Volume 1 and Volume 2). Beijing: Catalogs and Documentations Publishing House.

Dong, Xiaoping (1995). On folk belief and witchcraft. Folklore Studies, Vol. 1995 (2).

Dong, Xiaoping (2003). On Folklore Fieldwork. Journal of Beijing Normal University, Vol. 2003 (04): 43-50.

Du, Shoudong (1990). Social-Economic Analysis of the CHildbearing View in Rural and Urban Areas. Population Journal, Vol. 1990 (6): 24-27.

Duan, Chengrong, Yang, Ge and Wang, Ying (2005). A Survey of the Staying-home Children in Rural China. Academia Bimestris, Vol. 2005 (6).

Durkheim, E. (1999). Les formes élementaires de la vie religieuse (Z. J. Lin & S. Y. Peng, Trans.). Beijing: Minzu University of China Press.

Durkheim, E. (1999). Les règles de la méthode sociologique (W. Hu, Trans.). Beijing: Hua Xia Publishing House.

Editorial Committee on Shaoyang County Annals (1993). Shaoyang County Annals. Beijing: Social Sciences Academic Press, 57-625.

Editorial Committee on Shaoyang County Annals (2006). Shaoyang County Annals (Reviewed Draft), 515-516.

Editorial Office of Population Research (2004). The Phenomenon of 386199: Family Members Left Behind at Home. Population Research, Vol. 28 (4).

Education Bureau of Shaoyang County (1986). Education Records of Shaoyang County (Mimeographed Draft).

Ember, C. and Ember M. (1988). Cultural Anthropology (B. B. Du, Trans.). Liaoning: Liaoning People's Publishing House.

Emerson, R. M., Fretz, R. I., and Shaw, L. L. (1995). Writing Ethnographic Fieldnotes. Chicago: The University of Chicago Press.

Erikson, E. H. (1998). Identity: Youth and Crisis (M.Z. Sun, Trans.). Hangzhou: Zhejiang Education Publishing House.

Esterik, P .V. (2002). Contemporary Trends in Infant Feeding Research . Annual Review of Anthropology , Vol. 2002 (3).

Evans-Pritehard, E. E. (2001). Theories of Primitive Religion (S.Y. Sun, Trans.). Beijing: The Commercial Press.

Fang, Tie (1997). Traditional Culture and Reproductive Health. Beijing: China Social Sciences Press.

Fei, Xiaotong (1981). Childbirth Institution. Tianjin People's Publishing House, 29.

Fei, Xiaotong (1985). Earthbound China. Shanghai: SDX Joint Publishing Company, 65-70.

Fei, Xiaotong (1985). Traditional Ethics and Population in China (Population and Labor Research Group of Beijing Sociological Association). Sociology and Population. Tianjin: Tianjin People's Publishing House, 2.

Fei, Xiaotong (1998). Earthbound China: System of Reproduction. Beijing: Peking University Press, 24-262.

Fei, Xiaotong (2004). Peasant Life in China: A Field Study of Country Life in the Yangtze Valley. Beijing: The Commercial Press.

Fei, Xiaotong (2005). Earthbound China: System of Reproduction. Beijing: Peking University Press, 129-130.

Fong, V.L. (2002). China's One-Child Policy and The Empowerment of Urban Daughters. American Anthropologist , Vol. 2002 (12).

Foucault, M. (1997). Eyes of Power (F. Yan, Trans.). Shanghai: Shanghai: Shanghai People's Publishing House.

Foucault, M. (2003). Discipline and Punish: The Birth of the Prison (B.C. Liu et al., Trans.). Shanghai: SDX Joint Publishing Company, 153-259.

Freud, S. (1999). Vorlesungen zur einführung in die psychoanalyse (S. Peng, Trans.). Shaanxi: Shaanxi People's Publishing House.

Fu, Daobin (1990). On the Reproductive Worship Culture in China. Hubei: Hubei People's Publishing House.

Fukuyama, F. (2001). Trust: The Social Virtues and the Creation of Prosperity (Z. H. Peng, Trans.). Hainan: Hainan Publishing House, 102-103.

Fukuyama, F. (2003). Values of Trust. World Executive, Vol. 2003 (6): 16.

Gallin, B. (1966). Hsin Hsing, Taiwan: A Chinese Village in Change. Berkeley: University of California Press, 144. Hsieh, Jih-Chang (1986). Meal Rotation. Bulletin of the Institute of Ethnology, Academia Sinica, Vol. 1986 (59), 91-110. Zhuang, Kongshao (1996). The Silver Wings: The Local Society and Cultural Changes in China. Laurel Books Co., Ltd., 319-330.

Gao, Bingzhong (1994). Folk Culture and Folk Life. Beijing: China Social Sciences Press.

Gao, Bingzhong (1996). Anthropological Tendency of Chinese Folklore. Folklore Studies, Vol. 1996 (2).

Gao, Bingzhong (1996). Anthropological Tendency of Chinese Folklore. Folklore Studies, Vol.1996 (02): 6-14. Huang, Ze (2001). Origin and Tendency of Ethnology in the Anthropological Context in China. Study of Ethnics in Guangxi, Vol. 2001 (01): 6-22.

Gao, Guofan (1993). A Probe into Chinese Folklore: Dunhuang Witchcraft and Its Evolution. Henan University Press, 35.

Geertz, C. (1999). The Interpretation of Cultures (B. Nari et al., Trans.). Shanghai: Shanghai: Shanghai People's Publishing House, 5 - 5133.

Geertz, C. (1999). Thick Description: Toward an Interpretive Theory of Culture in The Interpretation of Cultures (B. Nari et al., Trans.). Shanghai: Shanghai: Shanghai People's Publishing House, 3.

Geertz, C. (2004). Local Knowledge: Further Essays in Interpretive Anthropology (H. L. Wang & X. J. Zhang, Trans.). Central Compilation & Translation Press, 97-101.

George, A. D.V. and Takao, S. (1986). Religion and the Family in East Asia . California: University of California Press.

Giddens, A. (1990). The Consequences of Modernity. Stanford, CA: Stanford University Press, 14. Cheal, D. (2005). Sociology of Family Life (Y.N.Peng, Trans.). Beijing: Zhong Hua Book Company, 37.

Giddens, A. (2002). The Consequences of Modernity (H. Tian, Trans.). Nanjing: Yilin Press.

Grant, J. P. (1994). A Letter to Physicians. Health News.

Goode, W. J. (1984). The Family (Z.L. Wei, Trans.). Beijing: Social Sciences Academic Press, 186 - 251.

Guo, Qiyong (1995). Confucian concern for life and death and its contemporary significance. Social Science Front, Vol. 1995 (4).

Halbwach, M. (2002). On Collective Memory (R. Bi & J.H. Guo, Trans.). Shanghai: Shanghai People's Publishing House.

Harris, M. (1989). Man, Culture and Context (S. M. Xu, Trans.). Taiyuan: Shanxi People's Publishing House.

He, Qinglian (1998). The Trap of Modernization: A Study of Economic and Social Problems in Contemporary China. China Today Press, 252.

He, Shaoying (2001). The History of Naxi Culture. Yunnan Nationalities Publishing House, 170.

He, Shaoying (2003). Probing Socio-Cultural Anthropology. Yunnan: Yunnan Nationalities Publishing House.

He, Yan (1991). On the microcosmic and macroscopical factors influencing the childbearing concept: On the role of family planning publicity and education. Chinese Journal of Population Science, Vol. 1991 (5): 57-58.

Hegel, G. W. F. (1999). Hegel's Lectures on the Philosophy of History (Z.S. Wang, Trans.). Shanghai: Shanghai Bookstore Publishing House.

Hegel, G. W. F. (2001). Philosophy of History (Z.S. Wang, Trans.). Shanghai Bookstore Publishing House, 126.

Henderson, V. A. and Yang, E. (2004). Researching Sexuality and Sexual Health in Southeast Asia and China. Yayasan Surviva Paski, Yogyakarta. Indonesia.

Hobsbawn, E. J. and Ranger, T. (2004). The Invention of Tradition (H. Gu & G.Q. Pang, Trans.). Nanjing: Yilin Press.

Hong, Xingzu (1983). Volume II of Supplementary Notes to the Songs of Chu: The Nine Songs. Beijing: Zhong Hua Book Company.

Hsu, F. L. K. (1989). Americans and Chinese: Two Ways Of Life (K. P. Peng & W. J. Liu et al., Trans.). Beijing: Hua Xia Publishing House, 4.

Hsu, F. L. K. (1990). Clan, Caste and Club (G. Xue, Trans.). Beijing: Hua Xia Publishing House.

Hu, Qiwang (1994). On the Yao Taoism. Social Sciences in Yunnan, Vol. 1994 (1), 61-70.

Hu, Yanming (2001). Cultural Transformation of Pingfeng Village. Beijing: Minzu University of China Press.

Huang, Runlong (1998). A Review of the Studies of the Child-bearing Culture. Population and Family Planning, Vol. 1998 (5).

Huang, Shuping (1998). Research on the Theoretical Methods of Cultural Anthropology. Guangdong: Guangdong Higher Education Press.

Huang, Ze (2001). Origin and Tendency of Ethnology in the Anthropological Context in China. Study of Ethnics in Guangxi, Vol. 2001 (1): 17-22.

Huizinga, J. (2007). Homo Ludens: A Study of the Play-Element in Culture (D. K. He, Trans.). Guangzhou: Huacheng Publishing House, 9-59.

Hwang, K.K., and Hu, X. J.et al. (2004). Favor and Face: Power Game of Chinese. Beijing: China Renmin University Press.

Issei, T. (1996). Clans and Dramas in China (H. Qian & Y.B. Ren, Trans.). Shanghai Classics Publishing House, 324.

Jiang, Youchun (2006). Subject Reactions between Folklore and Anthropology. Heilongjiang National Series, Vol. 2006 (02): 97-102.

Johnson, K. (2005). Television and social change in rural India: a study of two mountain villages in Western Maharashtra (M.H. Zhan et al., Trans.) Beijing: Beijing: China Renmin University Press, 168.

Kardinar, A. (1939). The Individual and His Society . The Psychodynamics of Primitive Social Organization. New York: Columbia University Press.

Kleinman, A. (1980). Patients and Healers in the Context of Culture: An Exploration of the Borderland between Anthropology, Medicine and Psychiatry . Berkeley, Los Angeles, London: University of California Press.

Knauft, B.M. (1996). The Genealogy for Present of Anthropology Theory. New York: Routledge.

Kulp, D.H. II Ph. D. (1925). Country Life in South China: the Sociology of Familism(Volume 1) . New York City: Columbia University.

Lemoine, J. (1987). The Religion of the Yao Nationality: Taoism (L. Feng et al., Trans.). Religious Studies, Vol. 1987 (1): 32-38.

Levi-Strauss, C. (1963). Structural Anthropology . New York: Basic Books.

Levi-Strauss, C. (1987). The Savage Mind (Y.Z. Li, Trans.). Beijing: The Commercial Press, 41.

Li, Shuilian (2001). A Preliminary Study on a New-type Childbearing Culture. Population Research, Vol. 25(1): 78-80.

Li, Shulei (1999). Inside Villages, Cultural Changes in Rural Schools. Zhejiang: Zhejiang People's Publishing House,120.

Li, Xiaoping (1992). Expected Child Transaction Price and Its Application in the Childbearing Control. Chinese Journal of Population Science, Vol. 1992 (5).

Li, Yih-Yuan (1996). Human Vision. Shanghai: Shanghai Literature and Art Publishing House, 146.

Li, Yih-Yuan (2002). On the Changes of Chinese Family System: An Anthropological Inquiry. On the Traditional and Modern Adaptation of the Chinese Family in Taiwan. Personal Anthology of Yih-Yuan Li. Shanghai: Shanghai Education Publishing House, 155.

Li, Yinhe (1994). Fertility and Village Culture . Beijing: China Social Sciences Press, 35-69.

Li, Yinhe (2004). Women, Family and Fertility. Sociological Studies, Vol. 2004 (4).

Liang, Zhiping (1996). Customary Law of the Qing Dynasty: Society and the State. Beijing: China University of Political Science and Law Press, 78.

Lin, Jiahuang (1992). Cultural Anthropology and Folklore. Chen, Guoqiang et al. Construction of the Chinese Anthropology. Shanghai: SDX Joint Publishing Company.

Lin, Nan (2003). Social Network Analysis and Status Acquisition. Getting out of the prisoner's dilemma: An analysis of social capital and institution. Shanghai: SDX Joint Publishing Company, 153.

Liu, Tieliang (1996). Village: the living space of folk custom inheritance. Journal of Beijing Normal University, Vol. 1996 (6).

Liu, Yangyang (1998). Social Changes in Modern Hunan. Hunan: Hunan People's Publishing House.

Liu, Yingjie (2000). The relationship between China's Urban and Rural Areas and China's Migrant Workers. Beijing: China Social Sciences Press, 152-153.

Lu, Yu (2003). On the Traditional Birth Culture. Dongyue Tribune, Vol. 2003 (2).

Lucien, L. B. (1995). Primitive Mentality (Y. Ding, Trans.). Beijing: The Commercial Press, 37 -248.

Lugo, J. O. (1996). Life Span Development (D. M. Cheng et al., Trans.). Shanghai: Xuelin Publishing House, 26.

Luo, Guofen (2005). A Probe into the Calculation Method of the Scale of Left-behind Children in Rural Areas. Journal of Chongqing Social Work Vocational College, Vol. 5 (1).

Ma, Guoqing (1999). Chinese Jia and Social Structure. Beijing: Cultural Relics Publishing House, 49-126.

Ma, Tieying (2004). Proceedings of the Third Meishan Culture Symposium in China. HongKong Heavenly Steed's Books Ltd.

Malinowski, B. K. (1987). Magic, Science and Religion and Myth in Primitive Psychology (A.Z. Li, Trans.). Shanghai Literature and Art Publishing House, 79-81.

Malinowski, B. K. (2002). Argonauts of the Western Pacific (Y.J. Liang et al., Trans.). Beijing: Hua Xia Publishing House, 54-184.

Malinowski, B. K. (2003). Sex and Repression in Savage Society (A.Z. Li, Trans.). Shanghai: Shanghai People's Publishing House.

Malinowski, B. K. (2003). Crime and Custom in Savage Society (R. Z. Xu, Trans.). Guangxi Normal University Press, 32.

Malinowski, B. W. (1940). The Scientific Theory of Culture (X. T. Fei, Trans.). Beijing: The Commercial Press, 26-27.

Malinowski, B. W. (2002). The Scientific Theory of Culture (X. T. Fei, Trans.). Beijing: Hua Xia Publishing House, 53.

Mao, Zedong (1991). Selected Works of Mao Zedong (Volume IV). Beijing: People's Publishing House, 1512.

Marcus, G. E., and Fischer, M. M. J. (1998). Anthropology as Cultural Critique: An Experimental Moment in the Human Sciences (M. M. Wang & D. J. Lan, Trans.). Shanghai: SDX Joint Publishing Company, 44-52.

Marjoribanks, K., and Mboya, M.(2001). Family Capital, Goal Orientations and South African Adolescents' Self-concept: A Moderation-mediation model. Educational Psychology, Vol. 2001(3):333-350.

Mead, G. H. (1999). Mind, Self and Society (G. H. Huo, Trans.). Beijing: Hua Xia Publishing House.

Mead, M. (1930). Growing up in New Guinea: A Comparative Study of Primitive Education . New York: Morrow.

Mead, M. (1987). Culture and Commitment: A Study of the Generation Gap (X. H. Zhou & Y. Zhou, Trans.). Shijiazhuang: Hebei People's Publishing House, 27.

Mead, M. (1988). Sex and Temperament in Three Primitive Societies (J. Song et al., Trans.). Zhejiang: Zhejiang People's Publishing House.

Mead, M. (1988). Coming of Age In Samoa: A Psychological Study of Primitive Youth for Western Civilization (Perennial Classics) (X. H. Zhou & Y. J. Li, Trans.). Zhejiang: Zhejiang People's Publishing House.

Ministry of Public Health of the Central People's Government and the Department of Public Health of the People's Revolutionary Military Committee (1950). Measures of Restrictions on Abortion of Women Cadres in Government Departments and Armed Forces. Subcommittee of Education and Culture of the Government Administration Council of the Central People's Government of the People's Republic of China (1952). Interim Measures for Restrictions on Birth Control and Induced Abortion.

Morita, Y. (2006). The Importance of Traditional Outdoor Games in Traditional Outdoor Cultural Education. Children's Study, Vol. 2006 (10).

Murphy, R. F. (1994). Cultural and Social Anthropology: An Overture. Beijing: The Commercial Press, 79.

National Bureau of Statistics (1988). China Statistical Yearbook 1988. Beijing: China Statistics Press.

Pan, Guiyu (2001). An Introduction to Chinese Birth Culture. China Population Publishing House, 184.

Peng, Xizhe and Dai, Xingyi (1996). Social Reputation Culture in Rural China. Shanghai: East China Normal University Press.

Piaget, J. (1982). Psychologie et pedagogie (T. X. Fu, Trans.). Beijing: Culture and Education Press.

Piaget, J. (1984). The Moral Judgment of the Child (T.X. Fu & Y. Q. Lu, Trans.). Jinan: Shandong Education Press.

Population Theory Research Office of Sun Yat-sen University (1983). Translations of Population Research (Episode 3).

Potter, J. M., Diaz, M.N. and Foster, G.M. (1967). Peasant Society : A Reader . Boston: Little, Brown and Company (INC.).

Qiu, Haixiong and Zhang, Yingxiang (1998). Journal of Sun Yat-Sen University(Social Science Edition), Vol. 1998 (1).

Qu, Yanbin (2002). On the Religions and Folk Linguistic Culture. The Volume of Folklore Theories of the Classics of Chinese Folklore in the 21st Century. Beijing: Social Sciences Academic Press, 305.

Raddiffe-Brown, A. R. (2002). Method in Social Anthropology (J.Z. Xia, Trans.). Beijing: Hua Xia Publishing House.

Reiss, I. (1965). The University of the Family: A Conceptual Analysis. Journal of Marriage and the Family, Vol. 1965 (27):443-53.

Rivers, W. J. H. (1924). Medicine, Magic and Religion. New York, Harcourt Brace, Roemer, Milton 1., ed..

Rogers, E. M. and Burdge, R. J. (1988). Social Change in Rural Societies: An Introduction to Rural Sociology (X. Y. Wang & D. N. Wang, Trans.). Zhejiang: Zhejiang People's Publishing House, 139-140.

Roseman, M. (1991). Healing Sounds from the Malaysian Rainforest: Temiar Music and Medicine. Berkeley: University of California Press.

Rubin, K.H., Fein.G.G. & Vandenberg, B. Play. InMussen, P.H. (1983). Handbook of Child Psychology (4th ed):Socialization, Personality and Social Development (Vol. IV). New York: Wiley, 715 - 716.

Runyan, K., Hunter, W., and Socolar, R.,et al. (1998). Children who prosper in unfavorable environments: The relationship to social capital. Pediatric, Vol. 1998(1):12-18.

Russell, M. (1988). Marital Revolution (J. G. Jin, Trans.). The Eastern Publishing House, 157.

Schafer, R. (1997). Variations in Traditional Marriage and Family Forms: Responses to the Changing Pattern of Family-Based Social Security Systems in Sierra Leone and Kenya . The History of the Family , Vol. 1997 (2).

Shang, Huipeng (2000). Wedding Celebrations in Bridal Chamber. Beijing: Minzu University of China Press.

Shaoyang Party History Committee of the Communist Party of China (1994). Collection of Data on Agricultural Cooperation in Shaoyang County.

Shi, Chengli (1989). The History of China's Birth Controlling. Urumqi: Xinjiang People's Publishing House.

Shi, Yilong (1996). Applied Anthropology. Xiamen University Press, 310-311.

Song, Deyin (1992). Interest of Pregnancy: A Probe into the Childbearing Customs. Beijing: China Youth Press.

Song, Zhaolin (1999). Fertility Beliefs in China. Shanghai: Shanghai Literature and Art Publishing House.

Strathern, A. J. (1999). Body Thoughts (Y. W. Wang & G. X .Zhao, Trans.). Shenyang: Chunfeng Literature and Art Publishing House, 218.

Sun, Shumin (2005). The Mate-selection Form of Farmers: The Research at Zhaocun in the Northwest. Beijing: Social Sciences Academic Press, 14.

Sun, Simiao and Gao, Wenzhu (2004). Part 3 of Fetus Nurturing of the Prescriptions for Women Ⅰ, Volume Ⅱ, Valuable Prescriptions for Emergencies. Beijing: Hua Xia Publishing House, 35.

Tang, Zhaoyun (2005). A Study of Population Policies in Contemporary China. Beijing: Intellectual Property Publishing House.

Terrell, J. and Modell, J. (1994). Anthropology and Adoption . American Anthropologist , Vol. 1994(5) .

The National Key Research Project Group of the Eighth Five-Year Plan (1994). Research on Girls' Education of Ethnic Minorities in Qinghai Province. Qinghai People's Publishing House, 2.

Tong, Xin (2006). Sociology of Population. Beijing: Peking University Press.

Tonnies, F. (1999). Gemeinschaft und Gesellschaft: Grundbegriffe der reinen Soziologie. Beijing: The Commercial Press, 61.

Turner, Victor W. (1964). An Ndembu Doctor in Practice. In magic, Faith, and Healing: Studies in Primitive Psychiatry[M. A. Krev. Ed.]. New York: The Free Press, 230-63.

Wa, Dezhong (1996). Taoist Gods (K.H. Xiao, Trans.). Chengdu: Sichuan People's Publishing House.

Wang, Chunguang (2001). Relationship between social identities of the second generation of rural migration and urban-rural integration. Sociological Study, Vol. 2001 (3).

Wang, Min'an (2004). Cultural politics of the human body. Zhengzhou: Henan University Press.

Wang, Mingming (1997). Culture and Power in Villages. Shanghai: SDX Joint Publishing Company, 267-330.

Wang, Mingming (1997). Human and social reproduction: from childbirth institution to practical theory. Social Science Front.

Wang, Ningsheng (2002). The investigation of cultural anthropology: a correct way to understand society. Beijing: Cultural Relics Publishing House.

Wang, Wenhong (1995). Breastfeeding and Infant Socialization. Population Journal, Vol. 1995 (2).

Wang, Xianming (2000). On the History of Modern Chinese Society and Culture. Beijing: People's Publishing House, 19.

Watanabe, Yoshio (1998). The folk religion of Han Nationality: a study of social anthropology (X. Zhou, Trans.). Tianjin: Tianjin People's Publishing House.

Wei, Yu (1996). Learning: The Treasure Within. Beijing: Educational Science Publishing House.

Wen, Yiduo (1954). Myths and Poems. Shanghai Classics Publishing House, 65.

Westermarck, E. A. (2002). The History of Human Marriage (B. Li, Trans.). Beijing: The Commercial Press.

Wolf, A.P. (1974). Gods, Ghosts, and Ancestors. Wolf, A. Religion and Ritual in Chinese Society. Stanford: Stanford University Press.

Wolf, M. (1972). Women and the Family in Rural Taiwan . Stanford:: Stanford University Press.

Woods, C. (1989). Culture Changes (W. D. Shi & H.S. Hu, Trans.). Yunnan: Yunnan Education Publishing House.

Wright, J., Cullen, T., and Miller, J. (2004). Family social capital and delinquent involvement. Journal of Criminal Justice, Vol. (29):1-9.

Wu, Bing'an (1985). Chinese Folklore. Liaoning University Press, 373.
Wu, Geyan (1994). Customs of praying for children in ancient China. Shijiazhuang: Huashan Literature and Art Publishing House.
Wu, Ruishu (2004). On Meishan God. Proceedings of the Third Meishan Culture Symposium in China (Ma, Tieying, ed.). HongKong Heavenly Steed's Books Ltd., 24-31.
Wu, Xinfu (1994). General History of Hunan: Section of Ancient History. Hunan Publishing House, 394.
Xiao, Zhengde (2006). Research progress on education of left-behind children in rural China. Social Science Front, Vol. 2006 (1).
Xu, Guilan (2002). The Cultural Overlap of Childbirth Customs in China. Nanning: Guangxi Nationalities Publishing House.
Xu, Jianhua (2002). Pedigrees in China. Tianjin: Baihua Literature and Art Publishing House.
Yang, Chengzhi (1989). Yang Chengzhi's Translations and Studies of Folklore . Beijing: Higher Education Press.
Yang, Kun (1997). Sociology and Folklore. Chengdu: Sichuan Ethnic Publishing House.
Yang, M. C. (2001). A Chinese Village: Taitou, Shantung Province (X. Zhang et al., Trans.). Nanjing: Jiangsu People's Publishing House.
Yang, Min and Zheng, Xinrong (2000). Women and Education. Social Gender and Women Development. Xi'an: Shaanxi People's Education Publishing House.
Yan, Yunxiang (2000). The Flow of Gifts: Reciprocity and Social Network in a Chinese Village (F.C. Li & Y. Liu, Trans.). Shanghai: Shanghai People's Publishing House.
Yang, Chengzhi (1989). Yang Chengzhi's Translations and Studies of Folklore. Higher Education Press. Lin, Huixiang (1991). Cultural Anthropology. Beijing: The Commercial Press. Yang, Kun (1997). Sociology and Folklore. Sichuan Ethnic Publishing House.
Yang, Min and Zheng, Xinrong (2000). Women and Education. Zheng, Xinrong and Du, Fangqin. Gender and Women Development. Shaanxi People's Education Publishing House, 283.

Ye, Tao and Wu, Cunhao (2002). An Introduction to Folklore. Jinan: Shandong Education Press.

Zhang, Jingsong (1988). Childbearing Customs in Ancient and Modern China. Shenyang: Liaoning University Press.

Zhang, Junliang (1999). Research on Childbearing Behavior. Chengdu: Southwest University of Finance and Economics Press.

Zhang, Kaining and Deng, Qiyao (2000). Health science in a multidisciplinary perspective. Beijing: China Social Sciences Press.

Zhang, Letian (2001). Acceptance and dissolution of state discourse -- class and class struggle in the vision of people's commune. Sociological Studies, Vol. 2001 (6).

Zhang, Qizai (2002). On Social Capital. Beijing: Social Sciences Academic Press.

Zhang, Shiya (1992). Altars and pulpits: a comparative study of religious education in Southwest China. Kunming: Yunnan Education Publishing House.

Zhang, Weiran (1995). Historical and cultural geography of Hunan Province. Shanghai: Fudan University Press.

Zhang, Xueguang (1999). Ludwig Wyttgenstein: The Cage of Language. Liaoning Publishing House, 183-184.

Zhang, Yibing (1991). Birth Culture. Harbin: North literature and Art Press.

Zhang, Yongjian (1994). Marriage and funeral customs and Chinese traditional family institution. Sociological Studies, Vol. 1994 (1).

Zhang, Youjun (1994). Comparative Study of Meishan Religious Sect of the Yao Nationality and the Ethnic Minorities in South China. Journal of Guangxi University for Nationalities (Philosophy and Social Sciences Edition), Vol. 1994 (4), 15-21.

Zhang, Zhiying (1998). Solitary Psychology of Left-behind Children. Health Psychology Journal, Vol. 1998 (1). Wang, Dongyu (2002). On the personality characteristics of the left-behind children in primary schools and the countermeasures in education. Health Psychology Journal, Vol. 2002 (5).

Zhang, Zichen (1991). A dictionary of Chinese and foreign folklore. Hangzhou: Zhejiang People's Publishing House.

Zhao, Guohua (1996). On the Culture of Fertility Worship. Beijing: China Social Sciences Press.

Zhao, Jie and Zhang, Kaining (1995). On the Child Bearing and Health Centered on Women. Beijing: China Social Sciences Press.

Zhao, Jun (2009). The Development of China's Anthropological Study Style and My Thoughts——Also on the Return of Anthropological Localization Study. Academic Journal of Zhongzhou, Vol.2009 (04).

Zheng, Fan (1996). Child-Bearing and Health Based on Communities. Beijing: China Social Sciences Press.

Zheng, Hangsheng (2004). Renmin University of China Research Report on China Social Development 2004: Moving Towards A Safer Society . Beijing: Beijing: China Renmin University Press.

Zhong, Jingwen (1998). An Introduction to Folklore. Shanghai Literature and Art Publishing House, 159-160. Yuan, Li (2003). A Course in Chinese Folklore. Guangming Daily Press, 186-187.

Zhong, Jingwen (1998). The Handbook of Folklore. Shanghai Literature and Art Publishing House, 380.

Zhong, Jingwen (1999). On the Establishment of China's Folklore Schools .Harbin: Heilongjiang Education Press.

Zhou, Daming (1999). Flow of Migrant Workers in China: A Comparative Study of the Input and Output Areas of Migrant Workers. Journal of Guangdong College of Young Cadres, Vol. 1999 (4).

Zhou, Daming (2006). Export of Labor Service in Rural Areas and Economy of Hiring out for Work --Taking Jiangxi Province as an Example. Journal of South-Central University for Nationalities (Humanities and Social Sciences), Vol. 2006 (1).

Zhou, Daming (2006). Export of Labor Service in Rural Areas and Economy of Hiring out for Work--Taking Jiangxi Province as an Example. Journal of South-Central University for Nationalities, Vol.2006 (01).

Zhou, Xiaohong (1991). Modern Social Psychology: A Comprehensive Exploration of Sociology, Psychology and Cultural Anthropology. Nanjing: Jiangsu People's Publishing House.

Zhuang, Kongshao (2002). General Introduction to Anthropology. Shanxi Education Publishing House, 273.

Zhu, Ruikai (1999). The History of Marriage and Family in China. Shanghai: Shanghai: Xuelin Publishing House.

Zhu, Zhixian (1988). The History of Child Psychology. Beijing: Beijing Normal University Publishing House.

Zhuang, Kongshao (2002). General Introduction to Anthropology. Shanxi Education Publishing House, 280-281.

Ziegler, E., Guild, I. and Lam, M. (1988). Social and Personality Development (L. Li et al., Trans.). Beijing: Beijing University of Aeronautics and Astronautics Press.

Zong, Li and Liu, Qun (1986). Folk Gods in China. Shijiazhuang: Hebei People's Publishing House.

Index

G

H

I

J

K

W

Y

Z

About the Authors

Dr. Jiang Youchun earned his Doctoriral degree in Folklore from Sun Yat-sen University. Currently, he is a professor and the Dean of College of Law and Public Administration at Huaihua University. He also serves as a post-doctoral researcher and master's supervisor at Southwest University, the distinguished expert in ethnic studies of Hunan National Religious Affairs Committee, the leader of the key discipline of ethnology of Huaihua University, the vice president of the Society for the Study of Ethnic Groups in Southwest China and the vice president of Hunan Sociological Society. In recent years, he has won one second prize of the Outstanding Achievement Award of Educational Research in Hunan Province, presided over one project supported by the National Social Science Fundation of China, participated in one project supported by the National Social Science Fundation of China, and presided over six research projects at the provincial and ministerial levels, and ten research projects at the prefectural and departmental levels. In addition, he has published one monograph, edited one book, and co-edited two books, and published more than 50 academic papers in authoritative journals domestically and internationally, some of which were reprinted by Xinhua News Digest. He has been engaged in teaching and research of social psychology, tourism anthropology, intangible cultural heritage and cultural anthropology.

Ms. Yang Yunyi has a master's degree. She is a lecturer and the deputy director of Organization Department of Huaihua University. In recent years, she has presided 4 provincial research projects, edited one textbook, co-edited two books and published 19 academic papers. She specializes in higher education and management, as well as public management.